THE SPACEMAN CHRONICLES

The Life of the Earthling Named Bill Lee

Scott Russell

The Spaceman Chronicles:
The Life of the Earthling Named Bill Lee

Visit our website at
www.StillwaterPress.com
for more information.

First Stillwater River Publications Edition

ISBN: 978-1-952521-54-6

Library of Congress Control Number: 2020919136

1 2 3 4 5 6 7 8 9 10
Written by Scott Russell
Published by Stillwater River Publications,
Pawtucket, RI, USA.

TEXT SET IN CRIMSON.

Publisher's Cataloging-In-Publication Data
(Prepared by The Donohue Group, Inc.)

Names: Russell, Scott D., 1945- author.
Title: The Spaceman chronicles : the life of the Earthling named Bill Lee / Scott Russell.
Description: First Stillwater River Publications edition. | Pawtucket, RI, USA : Stillwater River Publications, [2020]
Identifiers: ISBN 9781952521546
Subjects: LCSH: Lee, Bill, 1946---Anecdotes. | Pitchers (Baseball)--United States--Biography. | LCGFT: Anecdotes. | Autobiographies.
Classification: LCC GV865.L36 R87 2020 | DDC 796.357092--dc23

For Peg

"You're not like the others. I've seen a few:
I know when I talk, you look at me.
When I said something about the moon,
you looked at the moon."
—Ray Bradbury

For Diana

For Eugene Debs & Kurt Vonnegut

Two Hoosiers in my Daffodil Karass.

DISCLAIMERS

"All of the true things that I am about to tell you are shameless lies." *—Verse 1: from the "Book of Bokonon.*

"People need good lies. There are too many bad ones." *—Kurt Vonnegut*

"All this happened, more or less." *—Kurt Vonnegut*

"A saint is a person who behaves decently in a shockingly indecent society." *—Kurt Vonnegut*

"Sunsets are loved because they vanish." *—Ray Bradbury*

"Don't talk unless you can improve the silence." *—Jorge Luis Borges*

"The United States was founded by the brightest people in the country, and we haven't seen them since."*—Gore Vidal*

"I have no country to fight for. My country is the earth, and I am a citizen of the world." *—Eugene Debs*

"It is essential that anyone reading this book know at the outset that the author is apolitical. I was convinced in 1927 that humanity's most fundamental survival problems could never be solved by politics." *—Buckminster Fuller*

To best understand *The Spaceman Chronicles,* it is recommended by both the author and the subject of this tome that he or she read Kurt Vonnegut's *Cat's Cradle.* In fact, both the author and the subject of this book recommend that you read the entire works of Kurt Vonnegut perhaps even to begin to understand the present condition of our planet and our species.

> "The old Lakota was wise. He knew that man's heart away from nature becomes hard. He knew that lack of respect for growing living things soon led to a lack of respect for humans, too."
> —*Chief Luther Standing Bear*

> "It appears that they are anxious to pass on their religion to all races of men but keep very little of it themselves."
> —*Ohiyesa of the Santee Sioux*

CONTENTS

PREFACE

Bad Moon on the Rise

On December 31, 2019, William Francis Lee, III, aka Bill Lee, aka "The Spaceman," sat at a table in the most beautiful inn of all New England, The Hartwell House Inn in the picturesque tiny oceanside town of Ogunquit, Maine. The occasion was New Year's Eve, and the festivities heralding the New Year were just beginning.

Bill Lee's seat at the table provided him with a superb direct view of two marvelous musicians, the man and wife team of Curt Bessette and Jenn Kurtz who were about to perform. The scene to Bill's right afforded him with a serene panorama of the silent frozen streets of the quaint seaside village. Bill Lee had just removed the cap (hat?) from atop his head and placed it alongside the table. The hat resembled a cross between Ignatius J. Reilly's green hunting cap in *Confederacy of Dunces* and a knit hat that appeared for all intents and purposes like a woolen monstrosity with the floppy ears of a rabbit dangling precipitously from the sky above.

Earlier that morning, we had trudged out to Perkins Cove, a lovely inlet which rests at the edge of town. My wife, Peg, yours truly, Bill, and his lovely wife Diana were amazed at how few people were walking the beautiful streets of the tiny hamlet. Bill and Diana's dearest friends, Mike and Deirdre Mulkern, had not yet arrived to join us at the lovely inn, a magnificent place operated by two absolutely wonderful innkeepers, Eric and Charlene Taubert. I had inquired as to the derivation of Bill's hat, since I considered it an effrontery against good taste, but in typical fashion, Bill responded:

"Women love it!"

And that they did! On our trek out to the cove, where the boats of spring, summer, and fall rested peacefully in dry dock, our paths crossed with three young couples who had braved the elements. A storm was approaching, and in more ways than one. In each instance, upon seeing the hood adorning Bill's head, each female of the species exclaimed, "That's a great hat!" or, "What a terrific hat!" Of course, the fact that even at the age of seventy-three, Bill "Spaceman" Lee remains ruggedly handsome, I strongly suspect, hell, I KNOW that if it were me wearing the fleece eyesore that the trio of attractive young women would have either commented, "Jesus, what a ghastly hat!" or perhaps ignored it completely.

As the six of us sat at the table reminiscing about the past and embellishing tales of yore, some of which were actually factual, a beautiful young waitress named Natalia began to serve a spectacular six course dinner offered by Eric and Charlene, the aforementioned extraordinary innkeepers. Since I had known lovely Natalia, a breathtaking beauty from Moldova, I took it upon myself to introduce her to our gathering. With her magnetic and ebullient personality, her flashing brown eyes, and her mirthful sense of humor, Natalia, or "Miss Moldova," as I often call her, is a complete delight.

Upon their initial introduction, Bill, Diana, Mike, and Deirdre all engaged in light banter with Natalia. However—and please remember that "the Spaceman" is not what you would call a conventional sort—within moments of Natalia placing a dish in front of Bill, he suddenly exclaimed, "Oh, no! It's a curse!"

"What, pray tell, elicited such a catastrophic assertion?" I asked plaintively. Bill immediately responded as follows:

"There are two pieces of bacon that are "crossed" on my plate!"... and that there were.

"Please explain," I replied, although I then remembered that this was Bill Lee I was speaking to.

"Santeria," as I would immediately learn, is an Afro-Caribbean religion that somehow emerged in Cuba during the seventeenth century. It is apparently a fusion of Catholic practices and African folk beliefs. Obviously, as the Spaceman was attempting to educate us, it includes spells and curses.... Bill then "lapsed," for lack of a better word, into a lengthy dialogue about a former fellow major league player named Julio Gotay, who although apparently not a practitioner of the "religion," was certainly a believer in what some Hispanics refer to as "Regla de Ocha." Gotay, who played second base and shortstop for four major league teams between the years 1960 and 1969, was beyond petrified of the bewitchment and execrations of Santeria. In fact, according to Bill, if Gotay came across two batting gloves in the dugout that had suddenly become entangled and therefore, crossed, this became a major catastrophic occurrence.*

* I learned that Gotay had passed on July 4, 2008. I was afraid to ask Bill if there was any significance or if he had walked beneath an American flag that day.

So, here we were on New Year's Eve in Ogunquit, Maine and Bill Lee had become increasingly concerned about lovely Natalia crossing two pieces of bacon on his plate. Immediately seeking a resolution to this dilemma, Bill removed one of the strips of bacon, put it on Diana's plate, and completed the "transaction" by exchanging it with one of her sausages. We had somehow averted a disaster. Or at least we thought we had. We were soon to find out that Bill was apparently not a high priest of Santeria and that his preventive actions would, at least according to the Spaceman, have gone for naught.

Peg and I had spent four days in south coastal Maine with Bill and Diana. After a glorious New Year's celebration, we returned to our homes, Bill in Craftsbury, Vermont and Peg and I back in North Attleboro, Massachusetts. It was early morning January 2, 2020, when we received a telephone call from the Spaceman. Referring to me by my email address, Bill shouted, "Damn you, srussell37! Thanks to you a Moldovian princess put a curse on me!"

As I would immediately learn, Bill was running a temperature of 102 degrees. His car had fallen into a ditch. The rescue vehicle attempting to extract the vehicle had overturned and joined the other disabled automobile and Bill had somehow broken a bone in his left hand... and then there's the matter of this dastardly virus.

Listen, Natalia, the beautiful young lady from Moldova, was NOT responsible for any of the above. However, again, this is Bill "Spaceman" Lee, who has never and will never ascribe to conformity. Somewhere Julio Gotay is smiling.

In this lengthy tome, those of you who have never heard of Bill Lee will get to know him. Those of you who already know William, well, God bless you.

This much I know: Bill Lee is part Buckminster Fuller. Bill Lee is part Professor Irwin Corey. Bill Lee is part Rube Waddell with perhaps a little Woody Allen tossed in. However, Bill "Spaceman" Lee is an original. He is as unique as the Grand Canyon. You are about to read of a remarkable American life, a life that incredibly, is still evolving.

Be Well,
Scott D. Russell
North Attleboro, Massachusetts

ACKNOWLEDGMENTS

Now, I know what most of you are thinking:

"Please, dear God, I don't want to see my name among those acknowledged by these two nitwits!"

Both the author, whether that be Scott Russell or Kilgore Trout, and the subject, the earthling known as William Francis Lee, III, wish to acknowledge countless individuals, and in fact, Lee has stated that this book is a tribute to individualism. *Vive le difference!* Hey, and you guys thought we were dumb! Betcha you didn't know we were bilingual. "How did you goils know we wuz college guys?" —*The Three Stooges,* or in this case, the Two Stooges.

The first two individuals that the author would like to acknowledge are people I never met. They would be John Thorn, the official historian of major league baseball, and Ms. Jane Leavy, the greatest sports biographer in literary history. In Jane Leavy's instance, by merely reading her wonderful tomes on Sandy Koufax, Mickey Mantle, and of course, the biography of biographies, her Babe Ruth masterpiece, *The Big Fella,* Leavy's dedication, research, and nearly decade long commitment to creating the definitive work on the Bambino, provided me with an insatiable thirst to explain the Spaceman, which is the modern-day equivalent of cracking "the Code of Hammurabi." A significant amount of Grey Goose vodka may also have been involved.

Earlier, of course, we identified those designated as "assholes," "non-assholes," "good guys," (some of whom are also assholes, and it should be mentioned that some of the "assholes" are also "good guys") an actual saint, and even a few "inconsequential" entities. Life, as we know it, is subjective. If we have not offended your sensibilities, well, we just have not done our jobs.

No book is possible without a publisher, and I have the best. Steven R. Porter and his lovely wife, Dawn, are the geniuses behind Stillwater River Publications. I should also note that Steven has written the greatest novel I have ever read, a mind-bending work called *Manisses.* Steven is also the author of *The Confessions of the Meek and the Valiant,* one that truly hit home with the author. If you believe that is faint praise, please consider that my favorite authors include Kurt Vonnegut, James Kirkwood, Don DeLillo, and Philip Roth.

Without the cooperation of the subject of this book, the erstwhile (why is it referred to as "erstwhile"? Isn't he still left-handed?) southpaw of the Boston Red Sox and Montreal Expos, Bill Lee, who I have known for forty-seven years, this book would not have been possible, let alone probable. I haven't a clue as to why he chose me to write it, but I believe he mentioned something about both Dr. Hunter S. Thompson and George Kimball being deceased and the likely probability that there existed a person institutionalized in a mental health facility in northern Montana who would enjoy reading it. There may have also been a mention of termites in Bolivia, too. I do not recall specifically.

As for acknowledgements, hell, just read the book. As Billy Pilgrim was forced to do in Kurt Vonnegut's masterpiece, *Slaughterhouse Five,* the earthling known as William Francis Lee, III, by the grace of whomever (Bokonon?) has been unstuck in time. And yet, much like Billy Pilgrim, Billy Lee has kindly attempted to teach his fellow members of the human species what he has learned from his mentors, the Tralfamadorians. And as for you, dear reader, I strongly suggest you read *The Spaceman Chronicles* in random order. In this manner, you can more identify with William Francis Lee, and perhaps even empathize with his plight.

So, sincere thanks to all that were quoted, misquoted, and blasphemed in this astounding piece of American literature, but please remember the words of Bokonon:

"Live by the foma that make you brave and kind and healthy."

And so it goes,
Scott D. Russell?
Kilgore Trout?

INTRODUCTION

I've never met Bill "Spaceman" Lee. You see, that would be impossible because I am at the present time what Earthlings delineate as "dead." However, thanks to this marvelous age of science, one that includes "Artificial Intelligence Projects," I have been able to review Bill Lee's tenure here on Spaceship Earth, and I've found him to be one of the more intriguing members of our questionable species.

As I've learned, William Francis Lee III, aka "The Spaceman," is a raconteur of sorts; an author; a statesman; a championship caliber athlete; a presidential candidate; a gubernatorial candidate; a former "brother from the same hood" as his classmate O.J. Simpson, who is a human who apparently ran afoul of the law on Planet Earth; an outdoorsman; and a fan of my "creator," Kurt Vonnegut. In fact, it was Kurt Vonnegut, who is also no longer among the "living," who provided the epitaph for my tombstone, which reads as follows: LIFE IS NO WAY TO TREAT AN ANIMAL.

One of Kurt Vonnegut's wonderful characters was a gentleman named Billy Pilgrim. Billy Pilgrim appeared in Vonnegut's epic *Slaughterhouse Five,* which those living on Spaceship Earth have categorized as "fiction." Therefore, as Vonnegut was wont to exclaim, "And so it goes." In *Slaughterhouse Five,* Billy Pilgrim becomes "unstuck in time." You see, Billy Pilgrim's life is told out of order and he is forced to revisit events in his life at random times and without warning.

Well, thanks to the heretofore impossible ability to communicate with those "elsewhere," I am about to draw an analogy between Bill "Spaceman" Lee, Kurt Vonnegut, and modern-day comedian Steven Wright. I am not certain despite the three "elements" involved, if this classifies as a "dichotomy." After all, I am deceased, so cut me some slack, and kindly be mindful that I am "dead," so to speak.

Let's see, where were we? Yes, of course, while Billy Pilgrim was "forced" to relive his life in random order, Bill "Spaceman" Lee is ACTUALLY living his life in random order. Hence the quotation by Steven Wright which goes: "I'd explain it to you, but your head would explode."

Another great author named Ray Bradbury routinely rejected the notion that he was a writer of "science fiction," and was quoted as saying, "Don't try to write a novel. Write short stories and figure out how to connect them." That statement is essential when reviewing the ongoing remarkable life of Bill "Spaceman" Lee. The Spaceman is literally living his life in random order, and that is the way it is told on the pages of this volume. It is up to you, the reader, to determine its proper sequence. *THE SPACEMAN CHRONICLES* pays homage to Ray Bradbury's *THE MARTIAN CHRONICLES* in more ways than are imaginable. And as Kurt Vonnegut once declared: "ALL OF THIS HAPPENED, MORE OR LESS."

As for yours truly, I will leave you with this: IMMORTALITY IS A PAIN IN THE ASS.

KILGORE TROUT
WHEREABOUTS UNKNOWN

The Spaceman Chronicles

CHAPTER ONE

Genesis

"I tell you, we are here on Earth to fart around, and don't let anybody tell you different." —*Kurt Vonnegut*

In the beginning God created the heavens and the earth. The earth was without form and void, and darkness was upon the face of the deep—

Wait. That was a different book. This one revolves around the life of an Earthling named William Francis Lee, III, aka Bill Lee and one who would eventually be known as "The Spaceman." So that one may review the life of this improbable member of the human species, a life that is somehow still evolving, we must begin at an unlikely venue called Johnny Rosenblatt Stadium in Omaha, Nebraska. The year is 1968 and the occasion is an athletic competition commonly known as the NCAA University Division Baseball Tournament. I guess one might say this is sort of a big deal here on planet Earth.

The recipient of "The Most Outstanding Player" of the NCAA Baseball Tournament was a teammate of Bill Lee's named Bill Seinsoth, the first baseman of the University of Southern California's championship team. However, this book is not about Bill Seinsoth. Such is the price of fleeting fame in our universe.

In 1968, the world of Bill Lee revolved around the game of baseball and particularly pitching. He was good at it. Somewhat incredibly, some fifty-two years later in 2020, he is still good at it. Again, such is life in our universe. In 1968, Bill Lee, not yet "The Spaceman," that would come significantly later, pitched and won two games in the PAC-10 tournament, games that catapulted the University of Southern California into the renowned NCAA Championship Tournament in Omaha. In Omaha, the USC Trojans, "The Men of Troy," would go on to win the national championship due in large part to the efforts of Bill Lee.

The coach of this practically mythical ball club was a gentleman named Raoul Martial "Rod" Dedeaux, a legendary name in the annals of baseball history. Consider that Coach Dedeaux, who nearly invariably called his players by their uniform numbers and not by name, coached USC for 45 seasons before retiring in 1986. "Hey, #26, don't think, Tiger. You'll just hurt the team."

Dedeaux, born in New Orleans, Louisiana but raised in Los Angeles, won an absurd 28 conference titles and 11 NCAA Championships (College World Series) including five consecutive titles from 1970-74. Rod Dedeaux's teams were, for the most part, more disciplined and schooled in the fundamentals of the game than the majority of major league teams. As Bill Lee stated, "Our practices were tougher than our opponents generally were. We worked on fundamentals to the extent that once the games started, we were prepared for anything. The games were much more fun than the preparation."

Only the nation's elite collegiate baseball teams reached the finals at Johnny Rosenblatt Stadium in Omaha. The eight were powerhouse squads, and they consisted of Brigham Young University, North Carolina State, Oklahoma State, Southern Illinois, The University of Texas at Austin, St. John's University, Harvard University, and of course, USC.

Bill Lee was an All-American pitcher at the University of Southern California. His uniform number was #32. He was a "soul brother" of another great USC athlete, one who also wore #32 on his back. The other All-American #32 was none other than a youngster named Orenthal James Simpson. Most of you will recall him as "O.J. Simpson." (Lee was not a fraternity brother of O.J.'s, incidentally, as Bill refused to join a fraternity during his college days).

On June 12, 1968 in Omaha, Nebraska, Bill Lee was called upon in relief against a formidable St. John's squad in the semifinals of the tournament. The tough New York City kids on that St. John's squad had names such as Palmieri, Addonizio, Pagano, Colombo, Ciaramella, and Friechione. However, their pitcher that day was Schwartz. Said Bill Lee:

"Their lineup sounded for all intents and purposes like the names of those present at a Cosa Nostra meeting at a motel in Long Branch, New Jersey. I would imagine that Schwartz was their attorney."

It mattered little that the St. John's lineup was tough. Bill was called on to pitch in relief in a game that USC needed to win to advance to the championship game and retired every batter he faced. It remains unknown if the game was attended by members of the Organized Crime Strike Force.

On the bright sunny day of June 14, 1968, Coach Rod Dedeaux entrusted Bill Lee with the baseball despite the fact that Bill had pitched two days earlier and was no doubt still feeling the effects of his prior appearances in the PAC 10 tournament. There was a game to be won, the biggest game of the collegiate season. Bill Lee did not disappoint. The not yet to be named "Spaceman" started and pitched a strong 7 2/3 innings and allowed 2 earned runs. The University of Southern California was now NCAA baseball champions and Bill Lee was named to the All-Tournament First Team Squad.

The team that Bill Lee defeated for the NCAA World Series championship that day was an excellent University of Southern Illinois squad. To further prove that more often than not there is illogical logic in the universe, at the time of Bill Lee's athletic conquest, the University of Southern Illinois was home to a magnificent professor who would become a mentor to the impressionable athlete, despite never having met him. The professor's name was Buckminster Fuller, one of the most brilliant men of the twentieth century, and perhaps the one person Bill Lee quotes ad infinitum to this very day.

R. Buckminster Fuller was an architect, a systems theorist, an author, a designer, an inventor, and a futurist. Fuller captured the imagination of Bill Lee to the extent that in the year 2020 on Spaceship Earth, he remains an icon not only to Bill, but to countless other scholars. As Bill was in the process of retiring "Saluki" batsmen that very afternoon, Buckminster Fuller, who taught at the university from 1959 to 1970, was most likely lecturing his class back in Carbondale, Illinois.

How much of a genius was Buckminster Fuller? Please consider that Fuller authored thirty books, including *The Operation Manual for Spaceship Earth,* and he literally designed the geodesic dome at the university's religious center. The dome itself, a magnificent piece of architecture, has been described as "a daylight planetarium." It is breathtaking. Perhaps even more amazing is the fact that the original center link for the geodesic dome hangs from a maple tree in Bill Lee's garden in Craftsbury, Vermont!

Buckminster Fuller was an assistant professor at Southern Illinois from 1959 to 1967 but was awarded full professorship in the School of Art and Design in 1968, the year, of course, that Bill "Spaceman" Lee was winning a national championship. Again, there is order in our universe.

To truly make events even more intriguing, as a student, Buckminster Fuller had been expelled from Harvard University for "irresponsibility and lack of interest." Buckminster Fuller proved that the esteemed Ivy

League university does not always get it right, especially upon considering that Fuller served as the second "World President of Mensa" from 1974 to 1983.

Oh, I had mentioned the tournament MVP, Bill's teammate Bill Seinsoth, a slugging first baseman. Bill Lee and Bill Seinsoth were both twenty-one years old and NCAA champions. Seinsoth, in fact, was drafted by the Los Angeles Dodgers and his future seemed infinite. He was truly gifted.

On September 7, 1969, a year later, Bill Seinsoth, a truly promising Los Angeles Dodgers prospect, was tragically killed in a traffic collision in Bakersfield, California. Implausibly, Bill Seinsoth was on his way to watch the professional football debut of his friend, O.J. Simpson. He later died at Harbor General Hospital in Torrance, California. He was twenty-two years old.

One of the letters received at Bill Seinsoth's funeral was from California governor Ronald Reagan, who wrote:

"One thing you know more than anyone is how much better the world is because your son passed this way. You have every reason to be proud of him."

As an athlete, Bill Seinsoth's coach, the late, great Rod Dedeaux, stated: "If Bill Seinsoth had lived, there's a good chance no one would have heard of Steve Garvey."

As for Bill Lee, he was on his way to his next stop in the universe: Waterloo, Iowa. Bill Lee was about to meet his own "Wicked Witch of the West," and this one was a man named "Rachel." The cornfields of Iowa lie in wait for the twenty-one year-old pitcher. William Francis Lee, III was about to learn that there were few if any Rod Dedeaux's coaching in minor league baseball. Young Bill Lee was about to, much like Galinda and Elphaba in "Wicked," learn how to defy gravity.

CHAPTER TWO

Rude Awakenings

"In insanity there is strength." —*Kurt Vonnegut*

"Hey, Mister, can you tell me
Where I can find a bed?
He just grinned and shook my hand
'No,' was all he said."
—*"The Weight," by The Band—written by Robbie Robertson*

In Kurt Vonnegut's epic novel *Breakfast of Champions,* the crazed author who wrote the introduction to this book, Kilgore Trout, is a widely published, but mostly ignored writer. Trout travels to a distant town called Midland City, much like young Bill Lee was about to travel to Waterloo, Iowa to begin his professional baseball career.

In Midland City, a chief character in *Breakfast of Champions* is a wealthy businessman named Dwayne Hoover who owns practically everything in the town. Kilgore Trout's arrival as a keynote speaker in Midland City at a local arts festival piques the interest of Dwayne Hoover, who considered anyone arriving in "his" territory his business. Hoover, an aggressive sort, demands a message from Trout, and the eccentric author hands him a copy of a novel he brought with him.

A confused but impressionable Dwayne Hoover reads the novel, which purports to be a message from the Creator of the Universe that the reader, in this case Dwayne Hoover, is the only individual in the universe with free will and that everyone else is a machine. Hoover was already experiencing some substantial mental health issues, and the "knowledge" attained from reading Kilgore Trout's novel deeply affects him. It pushed him over the edge. Dwayne Hoover goes on a violent rampage, one in which he severely beats his son, his lover, and nine other people before finally being taken into custody.

In the preface of *Breakfast of Champions,* Kurt Vonnegut states that he tends to think of human beings as huge, rubbery test tubes, with chemical reactions seething inside. The fledgling earthling pitcher, Bill Lee, was traveling unaware that he was about to enter his own "Midland City."

In his brief heretofore unchartered travels on Planet Earth, the young Bill Lee, barely removed from his formative teenage years, derived pleasure by competing in sports. With his humble beginnings in Canoga Park, California and then in Marin County in northern California, Bill Lee was considered a terrific athlete, one with major league aspirations, albeit one with a "below average" fastball, at least velocity wise. Because of his less than overpowering hard stuff, Bill learned how to "pitch," and not to merely "throw," as those blessed with so-called million-dollar arms did. Bill was a master at changing eye levels and altering speeds with movement and location.

Bill Lee's mentors were his father, William Francis Lee, Jr., a former semi-pro ballplayer as well as a lifelong hardworking employee of Pacific Bell, a major telephone company. However, Bill Lee's aunt, Annabelle, was the one who literally taught Bill how to pitch. You see, Annabelle was a legendary "girls'" baseball pitcher in the famed All-American Girls Professional Baseball League, an association that inspired the great motion picture *A League of Their Own*, starring Geena Davis and Lori Petty.

Annabelle, a 5′ 2″ beauty, was a left-handed pitcher like her nephew, Bill, and a switch-hitter. Annabelle hurled a perfect game for the Minneapolis Millerettes in 1944 and followed that up with another no-hitter for the Fort Wayne Daisies in 1945. The fact that Annabelle described herself as a "junk-baller" no doubt had a significant impact on Bill Lee's pitching style and acumen. Bill's mom, Paula Theresa (Hunt) Lee was a hardworking housewife.

Up to the point of his relatively brief life on planet Earth, and his attaining notoriety as a major league prospect, despite being more than perhaps slightly eccentric, Bill Lee was a coach's dream. He worked hard at his craft, eagerly listened to instruction, and for the most part, was the essential teammate... and then he arrived in Waterloo.

Unlike Napoleon Bonaparte, who suffered his final defeat at The Battle of Waterloo, Bill Lee was about to suffer his initial "defeat" in Waterloo, Iowa, and ironically to a 5′ 8″ 160 lb. baseball manager with a Napoleonic complex. And get this: This incident took place nearly 153 years to the day (June 18, 1815) of The Battle of Waterloo! This would be, as Bill Lee would eventually find out, just the initial "battle" he would have with "vertically challenged" authority during his illustrious career.

Bill Lee, an iconoclast and hero to the counter-culture movement, for the initial time in his life was about to be branded a malcontent, albeit undeservedly so. Having just won the College World Series on June 14, 1968, and celebrating with his teammates, Bill, anxious to begin his professional baseball career, took a red-eye flight from Omaha, Nebraska, arrived in Waterloo with a zero amount of sleep, and in an attempt to impress his new bosses, arrived at Riverfront Stadium, the home of the Waterloo Hawks of the Midwest League.

It should be noted here that Bill had signed his major league contract illegally. You see, even as he was in the process of pitching the USC Trojans to the NCAA baseball championship, Bill had already inked a modest contract to play minor league baseball for the Boston Red Sox... except that act, in itself, was prohibited by major league baseball. Nevertheless...

The manager of the Waterloo Hawks was the aforementioned diminutive Rachel Wayne "Rac" Slider, a retired minor league infielder with, yes, a Napoleon complex. "Rac" as he was known, was renowned for being a frustrated hard-assed Marine drill instructor wannabe, but these were baseball players and Rac was not a Marine. A sleepless exhausted Bill Lee arrived at the ballpark that morning, and rather than be congratulated for his exhausting efforts in attaining college baseball immortality, Rac Slider, who clearly was not even aware of Bill's accomplishments the past several days, and quite frankly wouldn't have given a rat's ass if he were, immediately instructed Bill to put on his uniform and run several laps around the field.

The young southpaw Bill Lee peered at the thirty-five year-old little man from Simms, Texas and responded truthfully and plaintively, "I can't."

What Bill had hoped was that his new coach would have a modicum of knowledge as to who his new arrival was and therefore reply, "Son, why don't you check into the hotel and get some sleep?" Ah, but reality is seldom compassionate, or intelligent for that matter.

It would be just five years later on April 30, 1973, that Red Sox Hall of Fame catcher, Carlton "Pudge" Fisk, who, of course, would become Bill's battery mate in Boston, sat in front of his locker and as the late journalist George Kimball described, was reading Kurt Vonnegut's *Breakfast of Champions*. Manager Eddie Kasko approached and asked Fisk what he was reading. Upon being informed of the author and title of the book, the bespectacled Kasko then asked, "What is the moral of the book?"

Carlton Fisk, and the fact that Pudge was even reading a book no doubt, would surprise Bill, who looked up and replied, "In insanity there is strength."

Eddie Kasko nodded his head approvingly, but as he turned to walk away, he suddenly spun around and informed his catcher, "Oh, speaking of insanity, tell Bill (Lee) he's starting tomorrow." Bill had been a reliever up until that point, but the next day, May 1, 1973 versus the Washington Senators, Bill Lee started and defeated the Washington Senators. Before the year was over, Bill Lee would be selected to the American League squad for the All-Star Game.

There would be many more Rac Sliders to follow.

CHAPTER THREE

Goodness Prevails

DEAR READER: It should be noted at this point that there exists some confusion as to the actual author of this biography. There are those that claim that the writer is an aging nitwit named Scott Russell, whose name appears on the cover of the book. However, several renowned literary scholars claim that the actual author is none other than Kilgore Trout, who of course, penned the introduction to this book. Regardless of the identity of the writer, perhaps the book's subject, Bill "Spaceman" Lee, offered some illumination upon stating:

> "No matter the true identity of the author, I can assure you that this tome is the result of the predestined semi-coherent logical chronological disorder of the universe." *—Bill "Spaceman" Lee*

> "I don't try to describe the future, I try to prevent it."*—Ray Bradbury*

Bill Lee's tenure among the cornfields of Iowa was short-lived, and not because of the speed bump named Rachel Slider. The earthling Bill Lee's inexorable but unlikely ascension to major league baseball was unpreventable, even to "minds" such as Rac Slider. Bill Lee was simply too far advanced athletically and mentally to remain tethered by mere mortals.

The competition provided in the Midwest League proved no match for the twenty-one year-old Californian. The opposition in major college baseball was light years ahead of what Bill briefly faced as a member of the Waterloo Hawks. In a mere eight appearances, young Lee had an astoundingly efficient ERA of 1.33. The sub-novice hitters Bill faced were no match for the left-hander whose ability belied his tender age. There were other places on the planet to visit. It is not known if Rac Slider drove Bill Lee to the airport, and it is also quite likely he had no idea he was gone. For Rac Slider, there were more games to lose, more young minds to impede.

It is conceivable that the most intriguing aspect of spending a few weeks in Waterloo, Iowa, was Bill having teammates with names such as Porfirio Cacerez and Jesus Llamozas. Another of Lee's teammates in

Waterloo was a Puerto Rican youngster named Rogelio Moret. Like many characters in Kurt Vonnegut's books, he too, will reappear. I wonder if they understood Rac Slider.

The earthling William Francis Lee, III, the subject of this volume, is not your typical protagonist. Despite his being a 6′ 3″ rather imposing athlete on the field of play, he was/is also wont to know the wherefores and the whys. It is highly likely that his crucibles began long before Rac Slider stepped out from behind the cornstalks in Iowa. When you're the type of youngster who figures out how to throw a baseball properly, one that spins in a manner which confuses those attempting to strike the round object with a rounded wooden stick and therefore, hit it squarely, the average youth gives zero thought to the dynamics of such an unusual competition. However, Bill Lee's thoughts extended far beyond the field of play.

Every hero protagonist, of course, "requires" an antagonist or a nemesis, as it were. For some unknown reason, obstructionists abounded in significant numbers throughout Bill Lee's life on planet Earth. It is possible that Bill Lee was, like many of the characters in Kurt Vonnegut's novels, perhaps placed on the wrong planet, or maybe even in the wrong cosmos. Unlike Dwayne Hoover in *Breakfast of Champions*, however, "Spaceman" Lee was not about to be pushed over the edge, so to speak, into a world of ruthless and unforgiving insanity. He would merely continue to abide, but not under the same rules and regulations created by those in charge of the celestial body on which he resided... Quite frankly, Bill Lee learned early on that in actuality he was not questioning authority, but rather authority was questioning him.

Unrelated (?) to the life of Bill Lee, it should be noted that on planet Earth on Tuesday, September 19, 1961, the year that another earthling named Roger Maris broke the immortal Babe Ruth's home run record, an incident involving a UFO allegedly occurred in rural northern New Hampshire, when a man and wife team were returning to their home in Portsmouth, New Hampshire after a brief vacation in Montreal, Quebec, Canada, an eventual "landing" place of Bill Lee. The couples' name was Barney and Betty Hill.

Barney and Betty Hill claimed they were abducted by extraterrestrials on that date and were forced to board a "flying saucer." This event marked the first publicized report of an alien abduction in the United States of America. However, what made this story somewhat believable is that at a "National UFO Conference" in New York City in 1980, Betty Hill produced some of the UFO photos she had allegedly taken while aboard the spaceship.

Regarding photos, there are numerous photographs interspersed throughout this volume. One of these snapshots, and it has been authenticated, is a photograph of Bill "Spaceman" Lee wearing a spacesuit while standing on the pitching mound at Milwaukee's County Stadium. However, what makes this spacesuit different from those seen in *Star Wars* motion pictures is Bill is wearing the spacesuit of American astronaut Alan Shepard and the photo actually appeared on the cover of *Sports Illustrated*.

In addition to the alleged alien abduction of Barney and Betty Hill on September 19, 1961, that exact date also coincided with the death of a woman named Helen Kimble, the fictional wife of Dr. Richard Kimble in an incident that triggered the lengthy saga of the television series, *The Fugitive*, starring actor David Janssen.

According to the tale, Dr. Richard Kimble, a prominent Chicago vascular surgeon, arrives home to find his wife, Helen, fatally wounded by a one-armed man. Kimble struggles with the killer, who escapes. Exactly why this is relevant would escape the minds of most sentient people on planet Earth, but please remember that this book is about the life of earthling, Bill Lee.

CHAPTER FOUR

A Lesson in Caste

"You don't organize metaphors... you explode them. In our time the search for extraterrestrial life will eventually change our laws, our religions, our philosophies, our arts, our recreations, as well as our sciences. Space, the mirror, waits for life to come look for itself there." *—Ray Bradbury*

Bill Lee had little choice other than to attend the University of Southern California. As Bill has stated on numerous occasions, everything in time and space is predestined. Bill's legendary coach at USC was, as you have learned, Rod Dedeaux, who was "assigned" and therefore, "ensnared," thereby becoming a "trustee" concerning the life of his impressionable southpaw, Bill Lee.

Rod Dedeaux, however, was literally and figuratively prepared for such a convergence, because of his association with another #37 and this despite of the fact that Bill wore #32 at USC and would not be allotted #37 until reaching the major leagues. Again, Bill's theory of "pre-destination" applies.

Rod Dedeaux, you see, also played baseball at USC many years before Bill Lee arrived. Dedeaux was a shortstop, one in fact who was good enough to be scouted and signed by none other than Brooklyn Dodgers manager, the zany and unpredictable Charles Dillon "Casey" Stengel, a previous #37. Casey inked Rod Dedeaux to a modest contract and immediately promoted the recent USC graduate to the major leagues. Incredibly, Rod Dedeaux played exactly two games with the Dodgers in 1935, went 1-4 and instantly broke his back.... Rod never played another major league game and the rest is history.

Bill Lee had little choice but to attend USC. Again, the predestination factor prevailed. Rockwell Dennis Hunt, Bill's maternal great grandfather, a noted California historian and prolific author, had been the Dean of the graduate school at the university.... Legacies are nearly impossible to avoid.

As the coach of Bill Lee, Dedeaux was quoted, "My hours spent with Casey Stengel prepared me for Billy Lee."

Bill Lee became aware of the inequities of life at a relatively early age. Bill's hardworking dad, William F. Lee, Jr., the telephone company employee of Pacific Bell, had been relocated from Canoga Park in southern California to San Rafael, a suburb of San Francisco in northern California. At Terra Linda High School in San Rafael, Bill busied himself by playing football, basketball, and of course, his first love which was baseball. Bill, a happy and fun-loving youth, was quick to pick up on the disproportionate "lifestyles," for lack of a better description, regarding the lives of his neighbors.

One of Bill's "fellow" students at Terra Linda High School was an attractive young girl. I suppose she was what one would refer to as Bill's girlfriend. One of the other students was a teenager named Alan Ladd, Jr. Yes, the son of "that" Alan Ladd, the star of the silver screen, Alan Ladd, renowned for motion pictures including the notable award-winning *Shane*.

To briefly sum up what occurred, Bill stated: "I drove a '59 Chevy. Alan Ladd, Jr. drove a Ferrari. End of relationship." These types of disparities in life would have a huge influence on Bill's psyche and how he viewed the world. Many years later, upon being unceremoniously traded by the Boston Red Sox to the Montreal Expos, the management in Montreal offered Bill a lengthy four-year contract. Bill reacted by replying:

"Large incomes are one of the symptoms of the final debauchery of the industrial age. It will all soon reach the saturation point because it is putting so much strain on the owners, the players and the fans."

Please keep in mind that Bill issued the above comment some forty years ago! It was prophetic. The game is now ruled by agents such as Scott Boras and other acolytes of the religion of more and nearly only major corporations can purchase season tickets. For the record, Bill Lee played his entire major league career by representing himself. Not once did Bill ever hire an agent or an attorney… or buy a Ferrari.

Sad note: Alan Ladd, the movie star, succumbed to an acute overdose of alcohol and sedatives. He was fifty years old. $$$ is not the end-all, apparently.

CHAPTER FIVE

The Female of the Species

"Sometimes I think I understand everything. Then I regain consciousness." —*Ray Bradbury*

"A woman drove me to drink and I didn't even have the decency to thank her." —*W.C. Fields*

The women in the life of the earthling named Bill Lee have all been beautiful. The first of Bill's wives was Mary Lou Helfrich, the Miss Universe representing the state of Alaska. Honest. And Mary Lou was not just a contestant, she WAS Miss Alaska.

Bill met Mary Lou in Fairbanks, Alaska in 1967. The blonde beauty was part of a military family and Bill joked that her competition in the beauty pageant was two malamute dogs and a polar bear. That, of course, was far from the truth. Mary Lou was/is drop dead gorgeous. Bill and the former Miss Alaska were married "in a fever" as the song says, in Jackson, Mississippi and they honeymooned, where else, but in New Orleans, Louisiana during the Mardi Gras.

Mary Lou, who Bill frequently referred to as "Dutch," is of Indonesian and Dutch descent and at the time she met her future green-eyed USC pitching husband, she was living in the Tlingit Indian Village called "Klukwan" which is in the Indian Village of Yakutat, Alaska. Therefore, it was logical (remember what Bill said in regard to his life which was, "I can assure you that this tome is the result of the predestined semi-coherent logical chronological disorder of the universe.") that Bill and Mary Lou Helfrich would meet up. Sort of like *Star Wars* on steroids.

Now one might think that Mary Lou was completely sane, and perhaps she is, but also consider that she considered "buying a giraffe for the backyard," at one time during her marriage to the Spaceman. Our universe is rife with such empirical tales.

Consider that on Saturday evening August 24, 1974, Mary Lou Lee's half-crazed husband, Bill, was standing on the pitcher's mound at Fenway Park and he was locked in an epic battle with the great Oakland A's Hall of

Fame pitcher, Jim "Catfish" Hunter. The fact that Bill had downed seven beers before the game even began is irrelevant, based on one's point of view.

The circumstances surrounding the game itself were significant because two enormously gifted pitchers had their best "stuff" going and the two men each hurled eight brilliant innings and were tied 1-1. For a fan of this greatest of games, it was nirvana. 34,693 were present at the old ball yard that night, and one of them was the former Miss Alaska wife of Bill Lee. What was truly significant, however, was that Mary Lou, who was seated directly behind home plate was pregnant... very pregnant.

On this warm starlit evening, Mary Lou Lee was seated next to Bonnie Harper, the lovely wife of Red Sox left-fielder Tommy Harper. Bonnie Harper, in fact, was signaling the length of Mary Lou's contractions to Bill as he pitched against the likes of Reggie Jackson, Sal Bando, and Joe Rudi, as if the Spaceman had nothing more to worry about. Therefore, Bill stared into his catcher for the sign, nodded his head in approval, and then peered beyond Carlton Fisk to receive the additional "signs" from Bonnie Harper.

Now those who were fortunate enough to watch Bill Lee perform are aware that he normally worked rapidly, but on this occasion his cadence was more indicative of a man who had his car illegally parked in a tow zone. The two great competitors, Bill Lee and Catfish Hunter, battled each other and were still deadlocked 1-1 heading to the ninth inning. Upon Bill retiring the side in the top of the eighth inning, Bonnie Harper's last signal indicated that a new member of the Lee family was imminent.

Upon seeing Bonnie Harper's last motion which apparently called for a FAST ball, Bill rushed off the mound, hurried off the field, and while in full uniform, rushed Mary Lou to Beth Israel Hospital where she gave birth to the couple's second son, Andrew. Andy Lee, who also became a pitcher, and in fact pitched in the Cape Cod League, came perilously close to being born at Fenway Park.

It is little wonder then, that Bill's current and final wife, Diana Donovan Lee, a beautiful woman who hails from Vancouver, British Columbia, has become a good friend of Mary Lou. One of the chapters in this thick biography describes the courtship by Bill of Diana, one that borders on zaniness and stalking, at least on Bill's part.

It speaks volumes that Bill Lee's first major league win came on the evening of September 20, 1969 at Detroit, a mere two days after Tiny Tim and Miss Vicky got engaged. The universe surrounding Bill "Spaceman" Lee is an infinite and often preposterous site of unimaginable wonder. For a man who was often photographed wearing a gas mask, a Daniel Boone cap, and a beanie with a propeller atop it, the world of Bill Lee is one that even Kilgore Trout, the greatest of all science fiction writers, could not have imagined.

CHAPTER SIX

Origins

> "I have never listened to anyone who criticized my taste in space travel, sideshows or gorillas. When this occurs, I pack up my dinosaurs and leave the room." —*Ray Bradbury*

It was John Kennedy who bestowed Bill Lee with the nickname "Spaceman." No, not the president, although this John Kennedy also had reddish hair. John Edward Kennedy was a light-hitting, good defensive infielder who was a Red Sox teammate of Bill's between the years 1970 and '74. The actual date of the sobriquet "The Spaceman" being given to Bill Lee remains unclear, although it apparently took place during the 1970 season, but the name fit.

Somewhat surprisingly, at first Bill did not necessarily approve of his newly assigned moniker, but it was not as if it offended him. He was just ambivalent to its implication, pro or con. In time he not only grew to accept it, but it eventually reached the point that he wholly embraced it. Today, "The Spaceman" is a most worthy accoutrement, an accessory, as it were, to Bill Lee's very existence. Even the most casual baseball fan who hears Bill's nom de plume will exclaim, "Bill Lee, the Spaceman!" Even non-sports fans, particularly those not old enough to recall Bill as a professional athlete will express, "Hey, that's the Spaceman! He's a cool dude. He ran for governor of Vermont!"

Obviously, Bill, with his eccentricities and his quick-witted lack of tolerating bigoted fools and highly partisan blowhard politicians, has not only lived up to the name, but made it as much his as "The Babe" did for George Herman Ruth or "Joltin' Joe" did for Joe DiMaggio.

Eccentricities aside, it is still impossible to determine even an approximate date to place on the calendar for Bill Lee becoming "The Spaceman." However, it appears as if John Kennedy, the aforementioned infielder who played for five teams during the years 1962-74, was "responsible" for Bill Lee's now permanent adjunct.

There was one theory advanced that "The Spaceman" was affixed upon Bill winning his first major league game in Detroit, and being asked by a reporter as to how it felt. Bill allegedly replied, "We just landed on the moon, and you're asking me about something as mundane as a baseball game?" Although that's a possibility, it just doesn't fit the timeframe, since John Kennedy, the ballplayer that is, did not join the Red Sox until 1970 and our initial manned moon landing had already occurred in November of 1969. Of course, Bill indeed won his first major league game on September 20, 1969, but knowing Bill, perhaps he was having a vision of the future.

Regardless of how, when, or where William Francis Lee, III, officially became "The Spaceman," it is now firmly implanted in his DNA. Sadly, John Kennedy passed on August 9, 2018, so we cannot consult with him.

John Kennedy, a slick-fielding shortstop and third baseman was a character in his own right.

The universe of Bill Lee, Space Traveler, included some of the more intriguing and outrageous characters known to the annals of mankind and beyond. One of these gentlemen was an iconic giant of a man named George Edward Kimball, III, or simply "George" to his many friends and colleagues. George, who wrote eight books and numerous essays, was a sports columnist for *The Boston Herald* after serving several years as both a music critic and then the sports editor of the renowned Boston counter-culture newspapers *Boston after Dark* and *The Boston Phoenix*.

Since George was considered a bit of a "rabble rouser" to the conservative establishment, it was inevitable that he and "Spaceman" Lee would become good friends. It should be noted that George had one eye, having "lost" an eye when a stranger approached him from behind and clobbered him over the head with a bottle in Kansas City. There was no provocation of any sort, just a deranged lunatic wielding a glass weapon, which resulted in George having one eye, the other now being a glass eye, one that George frequently popped in and out of his skull.

It should also be noted that Bill "Spaceman" Lee was renowned for jumping out of hotel windows into swimming pools. It is logical then, that his friend, George Kimball, was also wont to dive into swimming pools, however, invariably from an actual diving board. Well, during a Red Sox road trip to Kansas City, George decided to indeed, plunge into the pool below from a diving board at the team's hotel. Unfortunately, he had forgotten to remove his glass orb before his leap.

George's plummet into the pool below was successful if inartistic, but as expected, his glass eye did not complete the entire journey. The pool at the hotel, one which I suspect contained as much chlorine as existed in the entirety of the Midwest, was a greenish blue haze and therefore, quite difficult for anyone attempting to locate a rather small object resting at its bottom. One by one, Red Sox players and officials dived into the bottom of the pool as guests of the hotel and various other onlookers looked on in astonishment. It resembled one of those scenes from a motion picture filmed off the coast of Greece or Cypress in the Mediterranean as nearly drowning baseball playing Mark Spitzes of the world re-emerged from the depths, albeit empty-handed.

After several anxious moments, John Kennedy, infielder, arose from the water, holding the precious pearl aloft.... Hey, "J.K." always did have "good hands." Within moments, George Kimball and his wayward eye were reunited.

Next, we will tell improbable but true tales of George Kimball and the Spaceman, two of the greatest counter-culture figures of our lifetime(s).

The earthling known as William Francis Lee would eventually be featured in a full-page *Sports Illustrated* photograph wearing the actual spacesuit worn by U.S. astronaut Allen Shepherd on one of his space missions.

CHAPTER SEVEN

Comrades

"The past is never where you think you left it."
—*Katherine Anne Porter*

As unlikely as it may seem, George Kimball was perhaps even a more improbable character than Bill "Spaceman" Lee. Therefore, in the logical irrational order of the universe, the two were destined to meet and become great friends.

George Kimball was seemingly omnipresent. George appeared to know everyone on planet Earth and conversely, everyone seemed to know George. The author of this book, either Scott Russell or Kilgore Trout, and perhaps they are the same person, once spent an entire rainy day at a Winter Haven, Florida Holiday Inn lounge with George. The year was 1977 and Winter Haven was the spring training site of the Boston Red Sox and therefore, Bill "Spaceman" Lee. As the author stated:

"Since the game was rained out, it was decided by our 'committee' that we'd basically spend the entire day enjoying libations. Everyone who entered the establishment immediately gravitated towards George. These people included the great author Doris Kearns Goodwin and her renowned *New York Times* journalist husband, the great, late Richard Goodwin. The crème de la crème of society pulled up chairs next to us and engaged in lengthy conversations and joined in downing various beverages. There were ballplayers, writers, and yes, even a few women of questionable repute. All knew George and basked in his enormous presence."

On the day in question, George had already run afoul of whatever the conservative Red Sox management believed proper protocol consisted of. In their infinite stupidity, the Red Sox front office issued a directive to its players that associating with George, who was often critical, and rightfully so, of the fools who ran the ancient organization, would be considered treasonous and looked upon with scorn. In short, players were told they would be punished, and heavy fines would be part of their wrath. George Kimball was clearly persona non grata.

Bill "Spaceman" Lee, however, never believed in conscription or adhered to the archaic rules of established nitwits, and therefore, of course, was perhaps the lone player on the Red Sox who pretty much ignored the edict. Bill Lee invariably gave his all on the field of play but would not even consider bowing to the idiotic whims of misguided imbeciles. It was the great, late Warren Zevon who composed and sang and recorded "The Ballad of Bill Lee," which explained an awful lot. Zevon followed up with another song about Bill, titled, "Bad Luck Streak in Dancing School." The Spaceman danced to his own drummer. He still does.

Steve Dillard was a rail-thin utility infielder attempting to stick with the Red Sox in the spring of 1977. Dillard was born in Memphis, but spent considerable time in Tupelo, Mississippi. Dillard, Bill's teammate, a good kid, was Elvis Presley's cousin.... No, really.

As George Kimball's "entourage" sat around the big lug and thrilled to his many wonderful tales (hell, the man was a close personal friend of the incomparable journalist and author, Dr. Hunter S. Thompson!), in walked young Steve Dillard. George beckoned him by calling out:

"Hey, 'Goober,' c'mon over and meet my friends!"

Steve Dillard's facial expression seemed to convey, "Hey, man, I'd love to, but...." As it was, Steve Dillard's spot on the roster and his chances of going north to Boston were questionable at best. George explained to all present that the poor kid was just "avoiding" likely retribution by the powers that be. Steve Dillard would find another locale in which to enjoy a meal.

It is little wonder why the Spaceman and George Kimball enjoyed each other's company. Both men are/were intelligent, well-read, and opinionated individualists. Oh, and get this: Additional proof of the natural logical order of the cosmos. Bill's classmate at USC was, of course, O.J. Simpson. George Kimball's fraternity brother at the University of Kansas was none other than the great Gale Sayers, who was Barry Sanders even before Barry Sanders was Barry Sanders.

George Kimball, a great writer who was nominated for a Pulitzer Prize in journalism for his essay, "Only Skin Deep," was a piece of work. George attended college on a Naval ROTC scholarship, but his participation in the antiwar movement led to several arrests. George penned eight books including a renowned classic, *Four Kings*, a book about legendary fighters "Sugar Ray" Leonard, Marvin Hagler, Thomas "Hitman" Hearns, and Roberto Duran. The book included a foreword by perhaps the greatest columnist/author of the twentieth century, Pete Hamill, who was a close personal friend of George. In fact, as George was literally in the final stages of throat cancer, the disease that would claim his life in 2011 at the age of sixty-seven, Pete Hamill would speak for George as they promoted the book, since George's fatal condition precluded him from speaking. Much more on Kimball later along.

In 1980, the Red Sox ownership crawled into an even lower hole in their attempt to banish George Kimball from the press box at Fenway Park. It was a contemptible undertaking that failed miserably, thanks to the efforts of noble men such as Joe Fitzgerald, the Executive Sports Editor of *The Boston Herald*, and George's colleague, the late columnist and the then president of the Boston chapter of the Baseball Writers Association of America, Larry Whiteside of *The Boston Globe*. Bill had been "banished" to Montreal by then, in a trade that proved disastrous for the Red Sox.

The "effort" to banish George Kimball from the press box at Fenway Park was a joint and classless collaboration by Red Sox lackey Bill Crowley and the then hapless Commissioner of Baseball, Bowie Kuhn. Bill "Spaceman" Lee chose his own friends then as he still does today. One of them was the great, late George Kimball.

My arrival in Winter Haven on March 6, 1977, was hilarious and spoke volumes in regard to the state of Florida, or is that Floriduh. My ex and I had flown from Logan Airport to Orlando with a brief stopover in Atlanta. Upon dropping our bags off at the Ramada Inn, we took a short walk to Chain O' Lakes Park to pick up the tickets to several home games that the Spaceman had dropped off at the ticket office. The Boston papers did not indicate what Red Sox pitcher was scheduled to appear that afternoon, but there was a distinct possibility it was Lee. What ensued should have served as a precursor to yours truly that both my honeymoon and immediate future were relegated to something better than doom, but not exactly good fortune.

After picking up the envelope containing the tickets at the Red Sox box office, I spied an elderly man leaning on a brick wall outside of the stadium. He appeared to be approximately seventy-five to eighty years old, he was smoking a cigarette, and to be entirely forthright, had the countenance of an old redneck. He was. His leathery skin had looked as if he had spent the entirety of his considerable life out in the Florida sunshine. Since I had not yet contacted the Spaceman, I asked the codger the following:

"Sir, did you see the game today?"

"Yup," the man replied with a pronounced southern drawl.

"I was wondering if Bill Lee pitched today."

The man took a long drag on his unfiltered cigarette before replying slowly, "Yup... it was Lee.... Ah (sic) think it was Lee."

"Well, sir, was he left-handed?"

"Yup.... Ah (sic) think he was left-handed."

"Sir, can you tell me how he did?"

The elderly man responded, but slowly, "Ah (sic) think he did okay... but I don't remember."

At this point I ascertained our conversation would not avail anything meaningful, so I asked him in jest and a failed attempt at humor, "Sir, you did catch the game today, right?"

As God is my judge, the octogenarian took another deep drag on his cigarette, exhaled, tossed the butt on the ground in front of him, and extinguished it with his foot before drawling thoughtfully, "No... Fisk caught it."

CHAPTER EIGHT

The Artist

"If you wish to glimpse inside a human soul and get to know a man, just watch him laugh. If he laughs well, he's a good man."
—Fyodor Dostoevsky

Bill Lee was not being prepared properly to make him a major league pitcher. The Red Sox, in truth, did not consider their eccentric free-thinking southpaw to have what is referred to as "sustainable ability," ergo his modest signing bonus. Bill Lee was just one of those youngsters inked to fill minor league rosters assigned to "test" legitimate prospects. Thanks for trying to make it: Good luck with your postal career.

In "major league" parlance, Bill Lee just did not throw hard enough. Oh, he was successful against college athletes because they couldn't hit his off-speed pitches. However, Rod Dedeaux, Bill's coach at USC, was a lot smarter than the geniuses who make the decisions at the "higher levels" of professional baseball. In fact, Rod Dedeaux was once quoted as stating that Bill Lee was a better "pitcher" than the great George Thomas Seaver as a collegian. Tom Seaver could throw a ball through a brick wall, but Bill Lee changed speeds, had total command of his pitches, and could size up a hitter by merely watching how he set up at the plate.

Oh, and get this: Bill Lee's best pitch, despite having a devastating changeup, was his fastball! Or should I say fastballs? Bill threw two-seam fastballs that sunk down and away from powerful right-handed hitters, an occasional four-seam fastball to keep hitters off-balanced, a nasty "cut" fastball that bore into right-handed batsmen, and an occasional over-the-top curve. Again, it is called "pitching" and the art form is intended to keep a hitter off-balance. As Bill is wont to say, "I never had a heater, unless it was the one that exploded in my home in Vermont."

But the Red Sox "brain trust" (don't you love that term?) merely figured that Bill Lee was a stopgap hurler whose arm and body were expendable. Therefore, Bill's quick rise through their farm system must have confused the "experts."

After dominating "professional" hitters in Waterloo (1.33) and a brief stop at Winston-Salem shortly thereafter (1.72), Bill was promoted to Pittsfield in the Eastern League in 1969. It was there that the recent USC alum had a magnificent 2.06 ERA, so the Red Sox front office brass figured what the hell, just get it over with. Therefore, they promoted Bill to the major leagues to close out the 1969 season. It is believed that they felt that major league hitters would simply batter the erudite lefty and he would be sent packing to his family in San Rafael. Bill Lee, despite his collegiate success, was not drafted by the Red Sox until the 22nd round of the 1968 major league draft. He was simply not being taken seriously. As in most instances during William Francis Lee, III's life, he was once more going to prove people wrong.

Bill Lee made his major league debut on June 25, 1969 at Fenway Park versus the Cleveland Indians. However, he nearly failed to make it to the old ballpark. Bill drove from Pittsfield, Massachusetts to Boston, and despite his seeing the light standards of Fenway Park from the Massachusetts Turnpike, he continued to get off at the wrong exit. Remember now, this is "The Spaceman." When he finally arrived at what would be his home until 1979, he explained his geographical failure.

Legend has it that upon hearing the left-hander describe his predicament, they looked at each other and decided to dust off uniform #37, worn for several years by Jimmy Piersall, whose battles were nothing less than insanity, and whose travails were transitioned into the major motion picture, *Fear Strikes Out* starring Anthony Perkins as Jimmy Piersall.

Note: The author, whoever he might be, toyed with the idea of titling this book, "Fear Doubles to Left Scoring Two Runs."

Several years later, Bill Lee met his predecessor Piersall, who was doing color on White Sox games, at a game in Chicago. The Red Sox were in town, and the two #37's shook hands and stared into each other's eyes. Bill described the meeting as follows:

"No words were spoken. It was sort of like the scene in *Annie Hall* when Woody Allen and Diane Keaton first meet. They didn't speak, but they were kindred spirits who just read each other's minds. Jimmy and I just grinned at each other."

Jimmy Piersall's days as the White Sox color analyst were short-lived. Working with the legendary broadcaster Harry Caray, Piersall once read off the underachieving White Sox starting lineup and included each player's salary. "Batting first, batting .235, making $75,000, is..." and he would announce the player's name. The players were livid and demanded Piersall be fired. Cooler heads prevailed and Piersall was merely given a warning.

However, it wasn't until Harry Caray announced that the White Sox were holding a "charity bake sale," and that the players' wives would be stationed at various gates outside the ballpark before a Saturday afternoon game, that Piersall remarked, "Ah, they're just a bunch of horny broads anyhow." End of Piersall's broadcasting career.

It did not take that long to get Bill acclimated to the major leagues. Bill pitched four innings in relief on that June 25, 1969, merely a bit more than a year after winning the College World Series. Bill allowed two hits and one run that evening in a stellar performance. Although he wasn't an immediate star, Lee displayed enough ability to assure that his days playing minor league baseball were over.

As we documented earlier in *The Spaceman Chronicles,* Bill would earn his initial major league victory on September 20, 1969. During that 1969 season, Bill made one unmemorable start and appeared in 19 other games as a reliever. He finished 1-3 with a 4.50 ERA. The following season, Bill made five starts, relieved in six other games, and ended 1970 with a 4.62 ERA. It was in 1971 that Bill Lee began to show his full potential. Bill only started three games, but relieved in 44 others and posted a stellar 9-2 won-lost record with a terrific 2.74 ERA.

Not only did Bill make a lasting impression as a somewhat zany southpaw (redundant?), but as he entered Fenway Park for the initial time in his life, he peered out at the imposing left-field wall, a wall whose distance measurements were found out to be false (they were even closer than marked!) and remarked, "Do they take that thing down when they begin the game?!" He was most likely serious. The lack of symmetry in some ballparks is astounding, and the "Green Monster" in Fenway Park has served as an executioner for Red Sox left-handed pitchers, as well as opposing southpaws throughout history. However, Bill Lee has never been anything but atypical.

CHAPTER NINE

Chapter Nine has been retired to honor Ted Williams, an unlikely but good friend of the Spaceman.

"Ted Williams was the greatest 'hitter' of all time. In fact, he 'hit' on all three of my wives." *—Bill "Spaceman" Lee*

CHAPTER TEN

Primordial Servants

"Do not waste your time looking for an obstacle.... Maybe there is none." *—Franz Kafka*

"Once, during Prohibition, I was forced to live for days on nothing but food and water." *—W.C. Fields*

The life of Bill "Spaceman" Lee would most likely be turned down by most Hollywood film producers. Even before his off-the-field improbabilities which would eventually actually result in his being literally blacklisted from the game he so loved, the characters within the game he embraced or fought with, and the characters within the game who embraced him even AFTER fighting with him, were/are all extraordinary.

Bill Lee would eventually become one of two pitchers in major league history to win EXACTLY 17 games for three consecutive seasons. Bill attempted to explain this phenomenon by stating:

"Seventeen games for three consecutive seasons. Do the math. 17 X 3 = 51. The Spaceman = Area 51."

One of Bill's teammates in Boston was still another eccentric southpaw reliever named Albert "Sparky" Lyle, who routinely would plop down butt naked on any birthday cake delivered to the Red Sox clubhouse. It was just a "hobby." The two screwball lefties, of course, became good friends, although Bill was the one who actually threw a "screwball," as Sparky's out pitch was a devastating slider, one which would eventually garner him a Cy Young Award as a member of the Yankees in 1977.... Oh, and just as Bill Lee's trade to the Montreal Expos for a hapless utility infielder named Stan Papi for what was obviously "disciplinary" reasons proved disastrous for Boston, Sparky's trade from Boston to the Yankees for a journeyman infielder named Danny (Why Me?) Cater would also be heralded as one of the dumbest trades in the annals of baseball history. The Red Sox never learned by their absurdly ignorant transaction, one that sent another left-handed pitcher, some guy named "Babe" Ruth, to the Yankees decades earlier.

One day during the 1971 season, both Bill Lee and Sparky Lyle decided to indoctrinate a young right-handed pitcher, a big burly youngster named Mike Garman, to the joys of road travel. The Red Sox had arrived in New York to face their bitter rivals, the Yankees, and Bill and Sparky, who by the way were two characters in Kurt Vonnegut's *Breakfast of Champions*, were about to introduce Mike Garman to a "game" they often played while on road trips.

This "competition," for lack of a better word, consisted of all involved getting off the bus or team plane and stopping for ONE drink at every bar and lounge they encountered on the way to the team's hotel headquarters, which on this evening was the Statler Hilton in Manhattan. Off the three young hurlers went, downing their beverages and moving on to the next watering hole. After approximately twelve stops, the semi-novice inebriate hopeful, Mike Garman, decided he had gulped down enough alcohol for the evening.... "Piker!" Bill and Sparky, of course, soldiered on.

Incredibly, after approximately fifteen stops, Bill, accurately assessing that his turn in the bullpen rotation may be imminent the following evening, informed Sparky that he was going to the hotel to get some shuteye. Sparky, knowing that Bill had always proved to be a standup, straightforward guy, accepted Bill's decision as wise.

Approximately three hours later, Sparky Lyle collapsed outside of the last bar in which he had enjoyed an alcoholic beverage. He literally was lying on the pavement, his head resting against the huge brick New York City building. Sparky squinted and he became aware that a mere fifty feet from where he had collapsed, there were numerous taxi cabs parked at the curb. However, Sparky was four sheets to the wind and basically paralyzed from the brain down. It was nearly 5:00 a.m. when Sparky Lyle eventually managed to struggle to his feet, and he staggered over to one of the cabs lined up at the curb. The sun was coming up. The inebriated southpaw climbed into the backseat of the cab, and slurred:

"Please take me to the Statler Hilton."

The cab driver pointed to the spot from which Sparky had finally arisen, and humanely proceeded to softly inform his prospective passenger:

"You were leaning on it."

Sparky Lyle, unknown to him, had somehow downed his last drink at the bar and lounge of the team hotel.

During Lee's rookie season in 1969, a veteran right-handed relief pitcher named Ron Kline joined the Red Sox. At that stage of his career, Kline was merely attempting to hang on to a major league roster. Bill, of course, was also competing for a spot on the roster... Ron Kline's spot.

At first, Bill did not think it suspicious during the frequent times that Ron Kline would take him carousing. Kline, Bill thought, was a great guy. After all, the veteran pitcher bought all the drinks... then it dawned on Bill:

"Here I was, battling for a spot on a major league roster, and Kline is buying me drink after drink. Then I noticed that Kline was 'nursing' his drink while I was downing them at a tremendous pace. Yeah, Ron Kline taught me a lot. He taught me how to hold a cut-fastball and a shot glass."

CHAPTER ELEVEN

The Forbidden City

"God does not know whether a skin is black or white. He sees only souls." *—Katherine Anne Porter*

"I waited at the counter of a white restaurant for eleven years. When they finally integrated, they didn't have what I wanted." *—Dick Gregory*

China has its "Forbidden City," the Gugong Palace Complex in Central Beijing, where the proletariat seldom set foot. Major league baseball has its "Ghetto." The "Ghetto" is nearly invariably reserved for non-Caucasians. It is where blacks and Hispanics congregate on "the back of the bus." It is generally a place inhabited by African American and Hispanic ballplayers.

It is not that often a white player seating himself in that non-designated area would be entirely unwelcome, but one where if he plopped himself down, that silence would be the norm. The vicinity is "by invitation only," but the "invite" is never spoken or written. There are no general formalities. It is that area of either a bus or team plane that Bill "Spaceman" Lee would not only be welcomed, but where he would feel more comfortable.

There are no admission procedures for a Caucasian player to receive such privileges, but merely daily examinations, as it were. Trust is earned, there are no tryouts. It is a natural process, and Bill "Spaceman" Lee is "natural."

One of the most common phrases heard in such locales is the expression "nigger, please." You will note that there is no exclamation point following the idiom, "nigger, please." When it is spoken the intent is to placate and not to anger. It is invariably said by one member of a minority to another. It is off-limits to Caucasians, no malevolence intended. It is in such a world that Bill "Spaceman" Lee was provided with a membership which was neither written nor spoken, but implied.

The intonation of a minority athlete proceeding a comment to another minority athlete with a "nigger, please," normally has the underlying and understood connotation, "Who the hell are you kidding?" It is into that universe that Bill "Spaceman" Lee was accepted, a rarity among white athletes.

Oh, it is not that Bill did not have occasional spats with black or Hispanic players, it's just that everyone was treated equally. Black or white, an asshole is an asshole. Bill did not and does not discriminate. Bill's official designation among "people of color" is that he is "color blind." It is perhaps the highest compliment a Caucasian player can receive from a minority athlete.

Bill Lee developed closer on and off the field relationships with minority athletes. There is much less pretense among those who have been and are being discriminated against. They are more hardened to the harshness and realities of life than those whose rites of passage did not include unspoken, but actual roadblocks. While it may seem patronizing or perhaps contain misunderstood implications, Bill's sensitivity to injustice has fomented his outlook on life.

Ironically, the compassion and humanity instilled in Bill Lee's thought process, literally and figuratively eventually would be his "downfall," at least upon considering his strong public defense of two of his teammates, Bernardo Carbo, a Hispanic, and Rodney Scott, an African American; as Bill was, and REMAINS to this day, blacklisted from baseball. Bill Lee simply saw two teammates being treated unjustly and rather than ignore the unjust inequities involved, as sadly most would, he became enraged at what was clearly unacceptable and issued what is commonly known as truth.

Later we will expound on those two events. As the old adage states, "No good deed goes unpunished."

CHAPTER TWELVE

For Everyman

"The inhabitants will always see both sides of an argument so long as it can result in a fight." *—J.P. Donleavy*

Bill Lee's "politics" can perhaps be best expressed in the quote by J.P. Donleavy that appears above. James Patrick Donleavy, a remarkable Irish-American novelist, was the son of Irish immigrants and much like the great novelist Pete Hamill, was born in Brooklyn, New York, but in Donleavy's case, he eventually moved to Ireland where he died on September 11, 2017 at the age of ninety-one, in Mullingar, County Westmeath.

Among other works of genius, Donleavy penned the critically acclaimed *The Ginger Man,* and his writings, much like Bill "Spaceman" Lee's musings, were rife with a coarse sense of humor.

Donleavy's statement, "The inhabitants will always see both sides of an argument so long as it can result in a fight," is especially apropos today in this age of bitter diatribe, invective, and finger-pointing that too often occurs on "social" media. There exists little civil discourse these days as the overwhelming specter of partisan politics precludes most sentient thought. The mere fact that anyone belonging to a specific political party is subject to its doctrines and is rendered incapable of individual thought, like moths to a flame, with the same end results. In the words of Franz Kafka, "It's only because of their stupidity that they're able to be sure of themselves."

Bill "Spaceman" Lee claims, on occasion, to be a "Marxist." However, it more likely that Bill is merely a citizen of the world, one who believes in free will, free thought, and individual interpretation. Bill Lee's father, William F. Lee, Jr. was once described by Bill as a "Goldwater Republican." Regardless of his political affiliation(s), Bill's dad loved his son and the feeling was mutual.

One must only look at the people in Bill Lee's life in order to ascertain that he is more open-minded than the majority of the sheep on "social" media.... Actually, the mere fact that the Spaceman does not participate on social media speaks volumes.

Bill Lee's dearest and closest friend for years has been, and is, Michael Mulkern. Mike and his beautiful wife, Deirdre, whose background is both fascinating and improbable, but factual, are staunch conservatives. We will be discussing Mike Mulkern in greater detail as the tale of *The Spaceman Chronicles* unfolds. Yet both Bill and his stunning bride, Diana, are avowed liberals. Bill and Diana's friends include countless liberals, conservatives, Christians, lapsed Christians, Jews, Muslims, Hindus, atheists, and perhaps even a handful of former New York Yankees players. Bill Lee does not cover his ears (or his mouth) upon hearing conflicting views. He is a throwback to the days of civility, albeit a highly opinionated one.

Bill "Spaceman" Lee has challenged conventional thought since he reached the age of reason. It is possible however, that the Spaceman is still evolving. Franz Kafka once stated, "I am in a cage, in search of a bird."

Bill "Spaceman" Lee has always refused to be caged, or in any case, stereotyped.

It was Fyodor Dostoevsky who wrote: "The best way to keep a prisoner from escaping is to make sure he never knows he's in prison."

There are no enclosures surrouning the earthling known as Bill "Spaceman" Lee.

CHAPTER THIRTEEN

The Essential Southpaw

"Don Hoak never understood you, Spaceman
It wasn't in the stars
Don's nose was just too hard, I reckon
He couldn't conceive of people like you and Hans Arp
who hurl the truth into the bourgeois face of language

People like Reggie Smith and Pudge Fisk
will never understand you either
because you tell it like you see it

You told it like you saw it that time with Ellie Rodriguez
and lost a few teeth for it
but what are a few teeth in the face of the truth?

You tell it like you see it in Spaceman Language like your
spiritual grandfather Picabia
even when you get into hot water" —*poet Tom Clark*

Baseball in the year 1971 on planet Earth was a significant entity. It was then that a space traveler named Bill "Spaceman" Lee became an excellent, if not elite, major league pitcher. In 1971 Bill was merely twenty-four in "Earth years." During that timeframe the inhabitants of planet Earth paid homage to legendary ball clubs such as the New York Yankees, whose power-laden lineups throughout the decades included fearsome stalwarts such as icons "Babe" Ruth, Lou Gehrig, Joe DiMaggio, Mickey Mantle, Yogi Berra, Roger Maris, Reggie Jackson, and Thurman Munson. These were household names, and their mere mention would send shivers down the spines of those unfortunate pitchers who were assigned to throw baseballs in anger at them.

Bill Lee was not yet officially a starting pitcher since he was only permitted to start three games that season, but appeared in a total of 47 games, compiling an impressive record of 9-2 (.818) with an excellent 2.74

ERA. For some reason unknown to most "experts," the earthling Lee was not at all intimidated by the superior aura of the Yankees or their history of routinely winning championships.

Not only was Bill Lee effective versus the mighty New York Yankees, he fairly dominated them. Consider that during his career, Bill compiled a 12-5 record in 38 appearances versus the "Bronx Bombers," and that mark included 21 starts. Bill, in fact, had the third highest winning percentage versus the Yankees in history. One of the two hurlers who managed a higher winning percentage was another left-handed Red Sox pitcher, and he too, was foolishly traded by Boston. His name was George Herman "Babe" Ruth, who compiled a 17-5 (.773) mark against the Yankees in a mere 23 appearances. Records on planet Earth indicate that Mr. Ruth then switched positions and became a fair to good batsmen. It is likely you have heard of him.

It should be also noted that Bill "Spaceman" Lee tallied 119 victories during his major league career, more than any Rastafarian pitcher in baseball history, a record which will most likely never be equaled.

Historians, including the more than slightly deranged author of this book, Scott Russell (or was it Kilgore Trout?) have also discovered that Bill Lee finished his career with a 95-69 record on grass, and a lesser 24-21 mark on artificial turf, to which when informed of that fact, Bill Lee exclaimed, "I always pitched better on weed."

During Bill Lee's pitching days, he remarked to the author:

"I always preferred pitching to Bob Montgomery and Tim Blackwell, rather than (HOF catcher) Carlton Fisk. Fisk was a great catcher, don't get me wrong, but he had a tendency to slow me down and I was a rhythm pitcher, much like Jim Kaat. I liked to get the ball and throw it."*

> * The author once advised Bob Montgomery, an affable man, of that reality upon meeting him at a memorabilia show years ago, and "Monty" replied, "Well, your friend, Bill, is not playing with a full deck of cards, as you are aware."

Ah, but that is why they keep records of such happenings. Consider that during Bill Lee's career, the following numbers exist as truth:

EARNED RUN AVERAGE BY CATCHERS WHEN BILL LEE IS PITCHING

Tim Blackwell	3.30
Bob Montgomery	3.39
Gary Carter	3.34
Carlton Fisk	3.75

It should be noted that Bill Lee lost his first decision in 1971, when he came on in relief versus the Cleveland Indians on April 19. After that, Bill compiled a record of 9-1 over the balance of the season, mostly as a reliever. However, perhaps his signature moment of the campaign came on the evening of August 2 at Memorial Stadium in Baltimore. The Red Sox starting pitcher that day was the inimitable great Luis Tiant, but El Tiante, who belongs in the Hall of Fame, was ineffectual on that occasion and departed in the first inning after allowing four runs and falling behind a great Orioles squad who included several Hall of Famers.

Bill Lee "inherited" that 4-0 deficit and pitched a masterpiece, hurling shutout ball for 8 & 1/3 innings and allowing only two hits in a 7-4 victory. It would not be until 1973, however, that the Spaceman became a starting pitcher on Earth. It was then that our planet began spinning on a more coherent axis.

CHAPTER FOURTEEN

"Reality is not always probable, or likely." —*Jose Luis Borges*

"It ain't over 'till it's over." —*Lawrence Peter "Yogi" Berra*

If there was one game that fully explained Bill "Spaceman" Lee's baseball career, it no doubt occurred on the afternoon of Saturday, September 21, 1974... and on the evening of Saturday, September 21, 1974. I suppose we can subtitle this chapter "Midgets Don't Win Tractor Pulls Either."

On a dreary overcast morning in late September, the Fenway faithful who inhabit the old ball yard in the Fenway section of Boston, Massachusetts on planet Earth, made their usual trek via foot, subway, and automobile in order to witness still another baseball game at the historic venue. Little did they know they were about to witness history, at least those that remained through an ordeal that would have tried the patience of the victims of the Spanish Inquisition.

Those arriving at the stadium near Kenmore Square were anticipating seeing their hero, Bill "Spaceman" Lee take on the Baltimore Orioles legendary Hall of Fame hurler, Jim Palmer, a character in his own right. The match was not an unusual occurrence since the two men faced each other frequently and Bill more than held his own against his alleged superior. The author of this tome, Scott Russell, attended this game, one to which I walked from my apartment at 83 Marlborough Street located in Boston's Back Bay, and why that site has not been listed as a National Monument, I haven't a clue, but I digress. Much like the most in attendance, I was there to see the ubiquitous Spaceman, who had already become legend to the true fans of Boston.

What began as an unexceptional contest would change, but not quickly, into a remarkable event, but it appeared as if Bill Lee would not be around for too long. That should have been the first sign, since everything the Spaceman is involved in, well, can get weird. Bill allowed two runs in the top of the first inning to the Orioles, who boasted a formidable lineup that included the likes of Hall of Famers Eddie Murray and Brooks Robinson, along with an array of other superstars who comprised Paul Blair, Doug DeCinces, Tommy Davis, Don Baylor, and Mark Belanger. The O's manager was another Hall of Famer, a rather portly and oft-obnoxious little person (let's face it, he was a midget!) named Earl Weaver, who cursed, drank, and who smoked cigarettes in insane quantity. Also, the fact that the Red Sox had fallen behind 2-0 to the great Jim Palmer did not portend good things were about to occur. The overcast drizzly day cast a darkening shroud over the playing field.

As the rain increased, so did the inexorable gloom accompanying the soft sound it made as it fell softly atop the 21,655 spectators, many of whom had departed by the end of the sixth inning. The Spaceman had fallen behind 4-1 to the Orioles and bulk of the unhappy rain-soaked crowd decided there were better and drier things to do with their lives.

Jim Palmer, the O's great, was removed from the game after the sixth inning concluded. Implausibly (then again, nothing really serves as an impediment to the Spaceman) Bill Lee remained on the mound. There was a game to be played, and by God, the Spaceman was and is, a "gamer." The eighth inning had ended with the Red Sox still behind 4-1. Then the rains came pelting down... heavily. It amounted to a deluge. Even I, the penultimate fan, headed home. The field had been covered. There was no reason whatsoever to resume it.

The original crowd of 21,655 had dwindled to a few hundred diehards, who presumably had no lives elsewhere. Huge puddles formed atop the glistening tarpaulin covering the infield, and the outfield had been reduced to a massive lake. In those days if a rain delay lasted upwards of an hour, the powers that be, in this case the umpiring crew, would postpone the game, especially when considering it was 4-1 entering the ninth inning. After all, the field for all intents and purposes was rendered unplayable since the sport was not water polo.

Upon trudging back to my apartment on Marlborough Street, I removed my soaked clothing, jumped into the shower, and then turned on the T.V. I soon became aware of the magnificent events unfolding at Fenway Park. The game had been delayed for close to three hours. It was unheard of for a game to be resumed after a lengthy delay of that nature, but remember that "Spaceman" Lee was involved and nothing ordinary occurs when the erstwhile southpaw is part of the equation.

Incredibly, at the ballpark a mere few blocks from the Charles River, home plate umpire Armando Rodriguez, along with Bill Kunkel, Merle Anthony, and crew chief Bill Haller, had emerged from the clubhouse to examine the field. Earl Weaver, the aforementioned volatile midget manager of the Baltimore Orioles, popped out of the visitor's dugout and despite not being formally invited to the conference, concluded that the field was unplayable and demanded the game be postponed, therefore ending "The Longest Day," thereby insuring his team a 4-1 victory.

It was then that Bill Lee, God bless him, not about to be upstaged by an angry egotistical midget, came charging out onto the field. The Spaceman had changed into a drier uniform and was completely prepared to proceed with the baseball game despite trailing 4-1, midgets be damned.

As the umpires instructed the ground crew to peel back the tarp in order to further examine the conditions beneath it, Earl Weaver and Bill Lee, and I cannot make this up, engaged in a tug of war over the tarpaulin!

Here was 6' 3" athlete Bill Lee practically dragging the now enraged midget across the infield surface as the two contended for possession of the rain-soaked field covering. Monty Python enters the national pastime!

Crew chief Bill Haller, obviously impressed by the Spaceman's determination to continue playing the game of baseball on an absolutely miserable rainy overcast afternoon (actually by this point it was early evening), instructed the ground crew to remove the tarpaulin from the infield in preparation to finish what would be a six hour and twenty-seven minute telethon of sorts, albeit with an additional three hours added on due to rain delays and field reparations, not to mention an epic tug of war between an enraged midget and a professional athlete.

Once the tarpaulin was removed, the field of play was tended to by the ground crew with the addition of turf and drying agents.

Meanwhile Bill Lee was getting himself ready for the resumption of hostilities, crazed pint-sized managers be damned. Red Sox manager Darrell Johnson, seeing Bill Lee's determination to resume pitching, allowed his eccentric hurler to warm up.

Once play resumed in front of what resembled a gathering of revelers in Salt Lake City, Utah on New Year's Eve, Bill retired the Orioles in the top of the ninth inning, but it would require a miracle to achieve a seventeenth win for the left-hander.

In the bottom of the ninth inning, Carl Yastrzemski led off by reaching first base on a single. Juan Beniquez then walked and a glimmer of hope had appeared. However, the midget emerged from the Baltimore dugout to summon his estimable closer, Grant Jackson, from the bullpen. Jackson immediately retired Deron Johnson on a fly ball and then legendary Red

Sox right-fielder Dwight "Dewey" Evans stepped up to the plate. Incredibly, on what was already an extraordinary day and night, Evans delighted the tiny assemblage with a three-run blast into the screen atop the left-field wall (Yes, there was a wonderful screen in those bygone years of the twentieth century). Tie game!!!

Darrell Johnson, the Red Sox manager, had instructed Diego Segui to warm up in case a miracle would occur in the bottom of the ninth inning. It had. Therefore, as Diego Segui came trotting in from the Red Sox bullpen to pitch the tenth inning, he suddenly stopped in his tracks.

Bill "Spaceman" Lee was not and is not, a normal accommodating athlete. Bill had invested a lot of time and effort into the afternoon and evening's proceedings and was not about to allow someone else to finish what he had started. Hell, do you think it's easy to drag a heavy rain-soaked tarpaulin halfway across the infield with an invective-spewing stocky midget attached to it?

Darrell Johnson merely shrugged his shoulders. This was Bill Lee's game. He had earned it. Therefore, Darrell Johnson in his infinite wisdom, something he was not often accused of possessing, acquiesced. Oh, but the plans of Spacemen often go awry. Unfortunately, upon Bill hanging a pitch to Orioles catcher Andy Etchebarren, the long afternoon and evening got uglier (pun intended for those recalling Etch's less than attractive countenance). Etchebarren deposited Lee's hanging something or other into the net in left. Home run and a 5-4 Orioles lead.

In the Baltimore dugout, the midget smiled. Bill retired the next two batsmen. And then the bottom of the tenth inning happened.

Deron Johnson capped a two-run inning with a game-winning (thankfully, there were no "walk-offs" in those days) single and Bill "Spaceman" Lee had captured his seventeenth victory of the season... the hard way, while the midget invented new curse words in the dugout. Bill Lee never accomplished things the easy way.

In the process, Bill Lee had pitched the lengthiest complete game, timewise, in major league history, some 6 hours and 27 minutes including rain delays and other added "attractions." The elements on planet Earth have never been a hindrance to the space traveler named William Francis Lee, III.

It should be noted that former Red Sox manager Joe Morgan was in attendance during this marathon and had stated it was the second greatest game he had ever seen pitched, the other being Harvey Haddix's legendary twelve-inning no-hitter.

CHAPTER FIFTEEN

Stranger in a Strange Land

"Now there is one outstandingly important fact regarding Spaceship Earth, and that is that no instruction book came with it."
—R. Buckminster Fuller

Anyone tagged with the sobriquet "Spaceman" would of course, attract other unique individuals here on planet Earth. It is the law of nature that "unstrung" beings somehow find each other intentionally or by chance. Aberrant behavior has been a staple of William Francis Lee's existence, whether by choice or happenstance. It is written.

As a firmly established star pitcher at USC, Bill obviously dreamed of the day that he would be playing baseball for a major league team in front of large crowds. One evening at the renowned Los Angeles watering hole The Hollywood Bowl, the precocious hopeful southpaw spotted Los Angeles Dodgers vice president in charge of player personnel, Al Campanis. This occasion would not mark the initial time in his life that Bill would encounter ignorance, but it certainly heralded the beginning of an entirely new level of dealing with those members of the human species entirely incapable of sentient thought.

On the evening in question, upon noticing Al Campanis seated at a table at the popular establishment, USC senior All-American Bill Lee figured it would be worth an attempt to see if the high-ranking member of the Los Angeles Dodgers hierarchy could perhaps shed some light as to whether or not the Dodgers considered him a prospect in the upcoming major league draft to be held later that summer. At the time that Bill and Al Campanis' paths had crossed in the cosmos, the Los Angeles Dodgers had perhaps the most potent and powerful pitching staff in all of major league baseball. The Dodgers had superstar hurlers such as Hall of Famers Don Drysdale and Don Sutton, as well as Bill Singer. However, their ace was perhaps the greatest pitcher of our times, a young Jewish southpaw from Brooklyn, New York named Sandy Koufax.

To fully understand Sandy's powerful arsenal, which improbably merely included an overpowering four-seam fastball which seemed to accelerate and explode as it approached the plate, and an absurd, over-the-top "Bugs Bunny" type curve ball, you simply would have had to see it. Hitters were left virtually helpless when attempting to make contact versus the tall, rangy Koufax. Therefore, upon his approaching Al Campanis at the Hollywood Bowl, young Bill Lee was not even remotely expecting the inane babblings of a complete imbecile. Thus the random and unexpectedly brief meeting with the Dodger front office "guru," would serve as a precursor to the fledgling USC southpaw, that there were truly nonsensical and overwhelmingly ignorant people residing in our universe, and that many of them had been foolishly promoted to positions of authority.

"Mr. Campanis," Bill Lee asked politely, "I'm Bill Lee of the USC Trojans, and I was wondering what you thought my chances are of being drafted by your organization in the upcoming major league draft."

Al Campanis, the brilliant sage and overseer of the vast Los Angeles Dodgers farm system, peered at his young inquisitor and responded as follows:

"I've seen you pitch, Bill. You don't have Sandy Koufax's fastball, you don't have his curveball, you don't have Sandy's command, you don't have Sandy's poise and you don't have..."

It was at this point the aspiring Spaceman interrupted Al Campanis and replied, "And I'm not Jewish, either."

Bill Lee then turned around and walked away from one of the keepers of the keys, a renowned scholar of the famed Los Angeles Dodgers members of government.

This conjured up thoughts about a prospective twenty-year-old applicant at The New England Conservatory of Music, asking the school's admissions director, "Hi, what are my chances of attending your fine school, sir?"

"Well, to be truthful, you don't play the piano like Stravinsky, you don't sing like Caruso, you don't compose like Mozart and you don't produce stage plays like Andrew Lloyd Webber."

Postscript: Several years later, an older and "wiser" Al Campanis, then seventy years old in human years, was a guest on ABC Television's *Nightline*. It was there that Campanis shocked viewers and amazed them with the enormous depth of his ingrained and unimaginable stupidity. As the host, the renowned journalist Ted Koppel looked on, his mouth agape in wonder, the Dodgers vice president in charge of player personnel opined that "blacks lacked the necessities to be a field manager or general manager in baseball," and somewhat incredibly voiced doubts if they even desired to be.

In his travels through the universe, Bill "Spaceman" Lee, would of course, meet countless other homo sapiens, many of them as dimwitted, but many others worthy of praise and admiration. All, however, just as the "Spaceman is/was, were flawed to a certain degree. As Bill still understands, it is the inherent and intrinsic nature of the species.

CHAPTER SIXTEEN

The Spruce Goose

"Some people never go crazy. What truly horrible lives they must lead." —*Charles Bukowski*

"Not only is there no God, but try finding a plumber on Sunday." —*Woody Allen*

As the earthling William Francis Lee, III, approached adulthood, in addition to his honing his skills as an athlete, it was decided that during the summer months during those times that schools were closed, he would be provided with an opportunity to "learn a trade," as the vast majority of human civilization endeavor to. Since Bill's uncle, a man with the estimable name Grover Cleveland Souder, owned and operated a locksmith shop in the affluent community of Malibu, California, it was determined that the young southpaw would study the locksmith trade. Just as one of Bill's eccentric baseball predecessors, and one who also wore #37 on the back of his uniform, Casey Stengel, who was a bank manager in Glendale, California when not managing in the major leagues, Bill Lee would be trained at a useful occupation.

"Grover's Key Service" was often put to use by the numerous Hollywood residents who resided in the posh section of Beverly Hills in those days, but none more than by a gentleman named Howard Hughes, perhaps the most noted eccentric and mysterious mogul in U.S. history.

Throughout his life, Howard Hughes was always considered strange, to say the least, but in the final ten years of his life, he became perhaps the weirdest human being on the planet. Born in Humble, Texas on December 24, 1905, and he was far from humble, Hughes was a business magnate, a billionaire investor, a record setting pilot, a film director, a noted philanthropist, a pioneer of aviation history, but above all, bat shit crazy. There were rumors, in fact, that Hughes had connections to President Richard Nixon and was directly involved in "Watergate." Some even claimed that Hughes was perhaps involved in the death of President John F. Kennedy, but none of that was ever substantiated. What is known, however, is that the already paranoid, schizophrenic Howard Hughes became even more of a deranged recluse between the years 1966 and1976, which comprised the final years of his already improbable existence on planet Earth.

Howard Hughes, for lack of a better term, was a renowned "lady's man." He dated countless Hollywood starlets, and their identities sounds like a who's who of the silver screen. There were Ava Gardner, Olivia de Havilland, Katherine Hepburn, Hedy Lamarr, Ginger Rogers, Janet Leigh, Rita Hayworth, and Mamie Van Doren to name just a handful, no pun intended.

It was widely speculated that Howard Hughes was deeply engaged in the clandestine activities of the United States Central Intelligence Agency, and that involvement led to his being more secretive and paranoid, especially after Watergate. To fully explore the possibilities of the true depths of Hughes' psychosis, he would often use aliases, such as his frequent usage of the name "John T. Conover." The man was clearly nuts!

No matter Howard Hughes' neurosis, and he was indeed, a madman, he was also a genius, and those two designations often are synonymous. To more fully comprehend his abject paranoia, consider that between those years of 1966 and1976, Hughes would live in hotels in many cities, constantly altering his location. Oh, and he would literally purchase most of these hotels! Howard Hughes would alternate between Beverly Hills, Boston, Las Vegas, Nassau, and Freeport in the Bahamas and Vancouver, always taking up residence on the top floor!

One could only imagine what the young aspiring pitcher, Bill Lee, thought when considering what his uncle, the locksmith told him in regard to his receiving telephone calls in the middle of the night from Howard Hughes, telling him to come to his home in Malibu to change the locks on his doors at 3:00 a.m.! Grover Cleveland Souder, on occasion would also "assist" Mr. Hughes in "breaking into" other homes, as well. It was not known if those homes belonged to Howard Hughes or others.

One of the actresses who refused Howard Hughes was the beautiful star of numerous motion pictures, Joan Fontaine. In fact, according to Ms. Fontaine, Hughes proposed marriage to her on numerous occasions, only to be rejected each time. Joan Fontaine detailed that fact in her autobiography *No Bed of Roses*. Perhaps even more interesting is that Joan Fontaine's sister, Olivia de Havilland, indeed, dated Howard Hughes. Oh, and get this: This will most likely come as a huge surprise to most film aficionados, but Joan Fontaine, in her role in Alfred Hitchcock's *Suspicion,* is the ONLY actor or actress in motion picture history to win an Academy Award in any of Hitchcock's films! Secondly, Joan Fontaine's sister, the aforementioned Olivia de Havilland, and Joan are the lone siblings to ever win Academy Awards!

One thing we do know and that is Joan Fontaine was no doubt "suspicious" of Howard Hughes. It was one conquest Hughes failed to accomplish. Bill "Spaceman" Lee's paths crossed with many intriguing characters during his lifetime as a space traveler, but none as truly odd as the one known as Howard Hughes.

CHAPTER SEVENTEEN

Ascendant "Liabilities"

"All forms of specialization breed extinction."
—R. Buckminster Fuller

"Organized crime in America takes in over forty billion dollars a year but spends very little on office supplies." *—Woody Allen*

Weirdness begets weirdness, and the world of the young space traveler William Francis Lee, III, confirmed that long established fact. All one must do to at least partially understand the world surrounding the formative "Spaceman" Lee was to examine, but not too closely, those people and elements around him.

In the spring of 1968, Bill Lee was being "followed," for lack of a better word, by major league baseball scouts. After all, the youngster was in the process of compiling an impressive 38-8 won-lost record (.826) versus formidable collegiate competition. One day at the unlikely venue of a San Diego naval base, Bill was among those competing in a Pac-10 tournament and his opponent on that day was a powerful University of Utah squad.

It should be noted that even Andrea Bocelli must on occasion, hit an "off-note," and that Igor Stravinsky most likely had struck the wrong key on his piano during his lifetime. It happens. However, on that sunlit day (is there any other kind in San Diego?) young Bill Lee, in the parlance of baseball, "had nothing." His fastballs had no life, his curve balls hung, and his changeups did not "change." He was getting hammered, and mercilessly.

Unfortunately, the pounding he was experiencing came at the most inopportune time. The seats directly behind home plate were occupied by several major league scouts, many of whom were present to evaluate the young eccentric hurler. One by one, hitters stepped up to the plate and crushed each offering by the now besieged southpaw. To make matters worse, Bill's dad, William F. Lee, Jr. sat among the scouts and winced each time a batsman made solid contact versus his beleaguered son.

In attendance that day was the legendary future Los Angeles Dodgers Hall of Fame manager, Tommy Lasorda. Lasorda was renowned as a tough, brawling, take-no-prisoners foul-mouthed and often sarcastic baseball "lifer." Lasorda's often profane rants to the media, which are now forever available on YouTube, are both hilarious and acrid. Therefore, when Bill's dad was approached by Lasorda, who unexpectedly draped his arm around the father who was in the process of seeing his major league prospect son being humiliated, William Francis Lee, Jr. was surprised, no make that shocked, upon hearing Lasorda's soothing and heartfelt words: "Tell your son to not hang his head. He's got the stuff and the makeup and he WILL be a major league pitcher!" Tommy Lasorda, of course, would be proven correct, despite the idiotic comments to the contrary by Al Campanis.

Earlier, we had reported that during Bill Lee's major league career that he would throw the longest game (time wise) in major league history, and that Lee would wind up as one of only two pitchers in major league history to win EXACTLY seventeen games for three consecutive seasons. However, on this date at a naval base in San Diego, Bill Lee would set another record, albeit a dubious one by allowing up two home runs on two successive pitches... with the SAME baseball!

No, really. Upon one University of Utah hitter taking the shell-shocked Spaceman deep, a United States Marine stationed at the base retrieved the baseball, flung it back onto the field of play, and yes, Lee wound up with that very same baseball, and on the next pitch, watched in wonder as the following hitter blasted it over the far reaches of the outfield fence. At the precise moment Bill Lee was pitching against the University of Utah at the naval base in San Diego, U.S. Marines were conducting "Physical Fitness Tests" beyond the outfield fences. They were participating in a "training event." You cannot make this up. Apparently, part of their exercises on that afternoon was the recovery and return of Bill Lee's errant pitches! Incredibly, after the second blast, still another Marine threw the second ball back onto the field. Bill peered at the ball as if it were a live hand grenade and flung it as far as he could. There would not be an addendum added to Bill's already dubious distinction.

The second hitter to take Bill deep on that particular afternoon was a rather strange character in his own right, a young slugger named George "The Stork" Theodore, a gangly 6′ 4″ 190 lb. outfielder who hailed from Salt Lake City. Theodore was nicknamed "The Stork" because of his unusual appearance, a countenance that consisted of a thin body and a neck which appeared to be the length of Hollywood starlet's Cyd Charisse's long shapely legs. That and his glasses, which may very well have been the forerunner to today's "geek look," made him appear to look like an alien from an intelligent universe.

In addition to the Stork's physiognomy, he was also an unusual character, to say the least. The Pac 10 apparently seemed to comprise a breeding ground for bizarre individuals. With his offbeat personality and idiosyncratic interviews, the Stork never failed to provide juicy tidbits for the writers covering the league. Once George Theodore exclaimed, "I've been trying transcendental meditation and that helps me be passive and wait on the curveball, but I've got to find something else in order to hit the slider."

One of Bill's USC Trojan teammates in 1968 was a "walk-on" youngster from Pendleton, Oregon named Dave Kingman, a 6′ 6″ equally eccentric earthling. At least he was believed to be from planet Earth, although Kingman would eventually earn the nickname "Sky King." Between the Spaceman and Sky King or "King Kong" as the Oregonian would also be named, legendary coach Rod Dedeaux had his hands full with two highly strung and outlandish athletes.

The author of this book, either Scott Russell or Kilgore Trout—and no one, as we have stated, has ever seen them in the same room together—was once regaled by the Spaceman in regard to Dave Kingman's "tryout" at USC. Said Lee:

"Dave Kingman was a virtual unknown coming out of high school. One day, Coach Dedeaux held an open tryout for the team. Seldom did 'walk-ons' make the team. Well, on this afternoon, this huge 6′ 6″ kid walked out to the mound. Kingman fancied himself as a pitcher. None of us knew anything about him. The way Rod Dedeaux held 'auditions' for aspiring high school pitchers was by seeing how they would fare against the top hitters on our team. Each of the kids trying out were given 'temporary' USC shirts to wear.

Within a span of three minutes, Kingman had struck three of our best hitters in the ribs with fastballs. Coach Dedeaux was livid. He yelled at Kingman, 'Hey, kid, get off the mound and take off that shirt! I never want to see you around here again!'"

Bill Lee continued, "About ten minutes later, Coach Dedeaux was speaking with some writers behind the batting cage. He was oblivious to the fact that Kingman had snuck back on the field and was now taking cuts against some of our best pitchers. Crack. Crack. Crack. Dedeaux heard the unmistakable sound of baseballs being absolutely crushed. He turned to face the field. He immediately saw the same youngster he had chased off the mound clobbering these 450 feet blasts over the outfield walls, one after another. Each shot was majestic. These were not common 'home runs,' but towering shots. Coach Dedeaux was astonished. After watching about a dozen of these shots disappear over the far reaches of the outfield barriers, Dedeaux yelled out to Kingman, 'You can stay, kid, but I never want to see you on the pitching mound again!'"

Many years later, the author attended a spring training game at Scottsdale Stadium in Arizona during spring training. Upon spotting Dave Kingman, I introduced myself as a friend of Kingman's former collegiate teammate, Bill Lee. I recounted the tale told to me by Bill. Kingman, surprisingly affable, replied:

"You know, your friend Bill has an overactive imagination." The huge Kingman then hesitated before continuing, "But in this case, his memory is pretty much accurate."

Dave Kingman would go on to a highly controversial major league career, one in which he continued to hit majestic home runs, and frequently, 442 of them in fact, including one that measured at least 530 feet. Kingman, who played on several major league teams, was once described by a New York Mets teammate as "having the personality of a tree trunk." Apparently, he did not ingratiate himself to a large majority of folks. However, keep in mind that the author of the comment was none other than Mets catcher John Stearns, who himself was, to put it bluntly, according to Bill Lee, "a bit of an asshole."

Consider the following: The Atlanta Braves had a mascot, a Native American named "Chief Noc-a-Homa," whose actual name was Levi Walker. Chief Noc-a-Homa would rest atop a teepee over the center field fence at the ballpark in Atlanta, but when a Braves hitter would "knock" a home run, he would slide down a lengthy ramp as the home town fans would rejoice. Chief Noc-a-Homa was a harmless and admired, if not beloved mascot of the Braves. Then one day a Braves batter blasted a home run and as was his wont, the Native American performed his downward spiral... into the waiting arms of the asshole catcher of the New York Mets, John Stearns, who tackled him and proceeded to beat the crap out of him, thereby sending the poor man to the hospital. Stearns had leaped over the

Mets bullpen fence to "welcome" the unsuspecting "good luck charm" of the Braves. The kids in the stands were horrified. Many most likely still experience nightmares and flashbacks.

Once in 1980, one of his teams, the Chicago Cubs, held a "Dave Kingman Tee-Shirt Day" promotion at Wrigley Field in Chicago. At the time, Kingman was injured and on the disabled list. Rather than show up for the festivities, Kingman spent the day at Navy Pier, promoting Kawasaki Jet Skis at ChicagoFest. On still another occasion, Kingman sent a live rat in a pink box to Sue Fornoff, a sportswriter for the *Sacramento Bee*. Attached to the rat was a tag that read, "My name is Sue." Dave Kingman called it a "harmless practical joke." Kingman's team the Oakland A's, however, found little humor in it and fined their eccentric slugger.

In 1980, Dave Kingman drew the ire of his Chicago Cubs manager, Joey Amalfitano. In a tight and crucial game, "King Kong" came to bat with a runner on second base and no one out. A "team player," that is, one who is properly schooled in the nuances of the game, would at least attempt to hit the ball behind the runner, in this case to the second baseman, in order to set up a potential run, one whose probability was much greater if the runner were advanced to third base with less than two out. But this was Dave Kingman, who was, well, all about Dave Kingman. Upon making absolutely no attempt to advance the runner, manager Amalfitano was rightfully pissed off. It was how Kingman reacted to his own obstinacy that further infuriated his manager. For the next several games, regardless of the situation, Kingman, and unfortunately successfully, began a "streak" of hitting weak grounders to the second baseman.

If you thought Dave Kingman was a bit warped in those days, think again. Today's Dave Kingman is perhaps even more debased. The former major league slugger now resides in Tahoe where he often lives within the confines of a converted bus, one that Kingman built with impenetrable armored plating, "protection" that would prevent fifty caliber weapons from penetrating its walls. Exactly who or what Dave Kingman is attempting to dissuade from "threatening" his very existence is not known, and those who truly know the man are most likely hesitant to ask.

Bill Lee still plays professional baseball in "Senior Leagues," and we will touch on some amazing tales regarding those organizations. Some of the truly bizarre characters playing in these associations are household names to even casual baseball fans. One, in fact, was the great Mike Cuellar, a superb left-hander and one that the Spaceman styled his pitching after. Another was a journeyman hurler named Darrell "Bucky" Brandon. The two men, and again, these are facts, once purchased a Cadillac convertible from a junkyard for $150, and converted it into the recipient of golf balls the two retired players would plop into the vehicle with nine irons.

One thing remains certain: Those earthlings encompassing the world of Bill "Spaceman" Lee could not exactly be described as "The boy next door." That is, not unless you lived in a very strange neighborhood.

CHAPTER EIGHTEEN

Pink Palm Trees and a Society Gone Berserk

"Expect the worst and that's what you'll get. Only it will be much worse." *—J.P. Donleavy*

The period known as 1974 on Spaceship Earth proved to be a consequential year in the life of Bill "Spaceman" Lee. The now twenty-seven year-old athlete was both coming into his own as a baseball player and a citizen of his spring and summer home, Boston, Massachusetts. Perhaps it should have served as a premonition of sorts that while attending spring training in an outpost called Winter Haven, an outpost in central Florida renowned for its oppressive heat, black flies, and an occasional appearance of the Klu Klux Klan marching down its main street, that the Spaceman got into an incident with a UFO. In that time during our nation's somewhat sordid past, the city of Boston was also not exactly the epicenter of racial equality or conscious thought.

Therefore, when the Spaceman's rental car was struck by a "pink palm tree* that fell out of the sky," surely it should have portended that the year would not go entirely smoothly.

> * It should be noted that the falling palm tree that had descended atop of the Spaceman's vehicle may have done so (it most definitely was) because he had backed his car into it. Also, as for the hue of the tree being "pink," that may very well have to do with the fact that Bill was wearing pink sunglasses at the time of impact.

The prior year of 1973 was the first of his historic three consecutive seventeen-win seasons and his now permanent placement into the Red Sox starting rotation, but 1974 was about to get a bit rocky for the left-handed space traveler. Boston, despite its national reputation as a "liberal" city, due in large part to the Kennedys, was far from it. In fact, the city of Boston was in truth a racially polarized city and one in which strict ethnic boundaries existed, and they were not to be challenged, either literally or figuratively. Shortly there arrived a monumental and honorable decision by a gentleman named Judge W. Arthur Garrity, Jr.

For the record, not only was Judge Garrity a competent federal judge for the United States District Court of Boston, he was a graduate of the School of the Holy Cross in Worcester, Massachusetts, had served as a sergeant during World War II in 1944-45, and then went on to receive his Bachelor of Laws degree from prestigious Harvard University.

Accurately assessing the inexcusable inequities existent in the Boston public school system, Judge Garrity courageously issued a 1974 order which mandated that Boston schools be desegregated by means of busing. This bold and proper decision, and one that forever changed the landscape of what was then a horrific and inequitable complex, literally turned violent. The long-established racists of Boston, and there were far too many, became enraged to the extent that they hurled rocks at black school children, in what was both a sickening and beyond despicable display.

Most Boston athletes, other than the great retired civil rights activist, Bill Russell, the most dominant team sport athlete of the twentieth century, remained basically silent. Russell, who moved out of the area because of his disdain for what he knew was a racist city, issued his criticism from afar at his home in Washington State. Despite winning eleven NBA championships in thirteen professional seasons in Boston, William Felton Russell was looked upon as a "militant" rabble-rouser by far too many improper Bostonians.

So, as many of Boston's athletes remained "sidelined" during these bitter demonstrations and physical confrontations, Bill "Spaceman" Lee, now an established major league star, albeit on a team with a questionable, actually, an awful history in equality, issued his criticism of those bigots that desired to maintain the "status quo," while endangering poor innocent minority school children.

During this sad period in Boston's past, there existed a rather egotistical, bigoted, homophobic, mean-spirited misogynist and staunch opponent of desegregation. His name was Congressman Albert Leo "Dapper" O'Neil. In short, he was a prick. Even consider how "Dapper" O'Neil handed out a compliment. When speaking of the First Lady, Nancy Reagan, O'Neil remarked for everyone to hear, "You know, Nancy doesn't have a bad tush for an old broad." "Dapper" O'Neil also steadfastly opposed the building of a statue to honor the slain American civil rights leader, Dr. Martin Luther King, Jr.

Someone apparently must have told Congressman "Dapper" O'Neil that Bill "Spaceman" Lee had come out in strong support of the noble effort to integrate the Boston school system, since it's doubtful that he read it himself, since the Spaceman's comments did not appear in a coloring book. The nasty officious congressman then obviously dictated a seething, angry letter to Bill Lee c/o Fenway Park. The missive consisted of two pages, each sentence containing more invective and verbal abuse and vitriol than the prior one. On and on the congressman went. The letter, of course, was issued with the heading which read, "Congressman Albert L. O'Neil, Boston, Massachusetts." Incredibly, O'Neil also "wrote," although it's highly doubtful he could've spelled cat if they spotted him the "c" and the "a," that Bill should just keep his mouth shut and concentrate more on his pitching. As part of his illiterate and likely alcohol induced missive, Congressman O'Neil emphasized, "I could pitch better than you on most daze (sic)." O'Neil actually added, "You don't have the guts to respond." Bill, of course, had actually been selected to the American League All-Star team.

During an additional part of Congressman O'Neil's ill-advised rant, he scolded the southpaw with, "The City of Boston is in the midst of a serolous (sic) situation." Bill, of course, although a geography major at USC, paused to research the word "serolous," which some forty-six years later, he has yet to find in any English dictionary.

Bill Lee assessed the official dispatch from the elected official and removed a piece of paper from a drawer and penned the following response to Congressman O'Neil:

Dear Congressman O'Neil,

I believe you should be advised that some imbecile is using your stationery.

Sincerely,
Bill Lee

CHAPTER NINETEEN

Some Libraries Have Books, Others Merely Bottles, Benefactors, and Silent Beneficiaries

"I don't think many New York bars ever had such a glorious mixture of newspapermen, painters, musicians, seamen, ex-communists, priests and nuns, athletes, stockbrokers, politicians and folksingers, bound together in the leveling democracy of drink."
—Pete Hamill of his times spent at The Lion's Head, a renowned Greenwich Village hangout of some of the giants of literature.

It was at The Lion's Head in Greenwich Village in New York City, that the young major league star, William Francis Lee, III, would rub elbows and engage in conversation with some of the more remarkable journalists of the twentieth century. Make no mistake, while the Spaceman enjoyed the company of his fellow athletes, he was not the quintessential baseball player. Bill's philosophy and outlook on life was nurtured by his insatiable thirst for knowledge, ergo his fascination with the likes of Buckminster Fuller and numerous other geniuses of our time.

Even while perfecting the art of pitching at the University of Southern California, Bill not only busied himself in learning how to throw a curveball, but also in the dynamics of why the ball curved. Therefore, even upon reaching the pinnacle of his profession, the "major leagues," although he would "hang" at various watering holes with his peers, many of whom were looking to hook up with lovely ladies, Bill would also spend considerable time with some of the most brilliant sages in American journalistic history… and perhaps indeed, "hook up" with a lovely lass or two.

While still in college, Bill Lee would spend hours at places such as Edward L. Doheny, Jr. Memorial Library reading the prose of Buckminster Fuller and other literary heavyweights. Of course, if a cute librarian were around to assist him, all the better. The aforementioned Doheny Library, incidentally, was used as a film location for Mike Nichols' iconic motion picture *The Graduate* in 1967, starring Dustin Hoffman and Anne Bancroft.

In the 1970s, and now a legitimate major league star, the Spaceman would be a regular at such watering holes as Daisy Buchanan's on

Newbury Street in Boston's Back Bay and at the famed Eliot Lounge on Massachusetts Avenue, places where extraordinary characters of all sorts would hang out.

With the amount of cultivation the young Spaceman attained by his inquisitiveness and his penchant for learning about the world around him, whether it was via the books he read or those established minds he was privileged to mingle with, the young man Bill Lee developed a strong sense of sensitivity to injustice and both an admiration and yet a condemnation for the human condition. It became clear that Bill was a typical professional athlete neither in thought nor action. Although one would hardly classify the Spaceman as a "highbrow," he was certainly more cerebral and polished than most of his peers.

There would come a time, one which would prematurely end Bill's major league career and preclude any opportunity of the Spaceman ever acquiring a position in the game he so loved, and you'll read of those circumstances as we continue with *The Spaceman Chronicles*. However, it is doubtless that Bill Lee's proclivity for sentient thought did not flourish to the extent that it "contaminated" the minds of his fellow players and the front office executives who remain at the controls to this very day. Unlike the deadly virus that brought planet Earth to its knees in the year 2020, intelligent or unbiased thinking did not endanger those bastions of "integrity," and in order to "protect" the game of baseball, and the world in general from a "mutinous revolutionary" such as the Spaceman, baseball, in its infinite wisdom would cut the umbilical cord which connected William Francis Lee, III to "America's Pastime."

Sadly, since no good deed goes unpunished, even those who Bill nobly defended did not come to Bill's defense upon his literally being blacklisted from the sport. Some forty years later, Bill Lee remains twisting in the wind and the sport of baseball not only remains in the Stone Age, but somehow implausibly continues to destroy itself from within.

CHAPTER TWENTY

Commonplace Inhabitants Need Not Apply

"Insanity is relative. It depends on who has who locked in what cage." —*Ray Bradbury*

"Always carry a flagon of whiskey in case of snakebite, and furthermore always carry a small snake." —*W.C. Fields*

The spring of 1973 found this author exploring new haunts in his newly adopted Boston. I have always felt that the best way to effectively delve into new and unfamiliar surroundings is to "hoof it," so to speak. Therefore, one of my initial stops was coincidentally one that Bill "Spaceman" Lee often frequented, "Daisy Buchanan's" on Newbury Street. I was also attracted by the fact that the entrance was below street level. Since I was thirsty, I ventured inside.

It was a Thursday afternoon and very few patrons were present. There were two men at the far end of the bar and another "gentleman" who had literally face-planted on the bar, seemingly deeply into the throes of the healing grape. Although he seemed to be wearing an expensive leather jacket, he was motionless, far from clean-shaven, and he had the countenance of, well, a bum.

I took a seat on a stool approximately twenty feet from the poor soul, and the bartender, a man I would come to know as "Chip," poured me a drink. Within minutes, the inebriated stranger began to regain consciousness, albeit a tenuous awareness. He lifted his head slightly at a forty-five-degree angle, peered at me through what were surely clouded eyes, and spewed:

"Hey, Johnny! Hey, Johnny! Why don't we get something to eat?"

It appears as if I looked like a "Johnny." His head immediately came crashing down atop the leather bar and he resumed his prior senselessness. I paid him no heed as I was quite accustomed to seeing numerous of my New York friends under the influence of something stronger than Ovaltine. Moments later, the semiconscious male of the species once more showed signs of life:

"Hey, Johnny, hey, Johnny! Why don't we blow this joint and grab some food?"

Immediately, the inebriated stranger once more drifted into a state of unconsciousness. It was at this point I finally asked Chip the bartender, "Why don't you eighty-six this guy? Bounce him or call a cab?"

Chip laughed and asked, "You're new around here, right?"

"Yes," I replied.

Chip, an affable young man then responded:

"I can't bounce him."

"Why not?" I replied.

"Well, for one thing," Chip offered, "he owns the joint!"

And "own the joint" he indeed, did. And that is how I met legendary Boston Bruins hockey star Derek Sanderson, a Stanley Cup winner who was one of the seven owners of Daisy Buchanan's.

These days, Derek Sanderson, God bless him, is a financial advisor for athletes, and yes, a great person.

A few blocks away from Daisy's was another great establishment called "The Eliot Lounge," whose bartender was the great Tommy Leonard, the man who founded the Falmouth Road Race. The Eliot Lounge was often home to Bill "Spaceman" Lee, George Kimball, and countless other eccentric characters.

One of the other owners of Daisy Buchanan's was a gregarious individual named Armand, a powerfully built but genial middle-aged Armenian gentleman. One busy evening at Daisy's, Armand was pouring drinks from behind the bar and noticed that a rather large man had entered through the door above. Remember now, that Daisy's was situated beneath street level. For some reason, the owners of the establishment had placed a rather comfortable good-sized sofa at the entrance for those patrons that decided to briefly sit as they either entered or exited the lounge. Armand, a good judge of character, took one look at the huge man's face, a face he did not recognize, and immediately became suspicious of the stranger.

Armand watched as the imposing outsider stopped and peered around the lounge. According to Armand, "He seemed to be casing the joint." Suddenly, the man reached down, picked up the huge sofa, hurled it atop his shoulders, and took off with the heavy couch perched on his shoulders and began running down Newbury Street towards the Public Garden!

Armand, as I stated, was a broad-shouldered powerful man and one not to be trifled with. Armand surmised the situation and instantly sprang into action. He leaped over the bar, exited the door, and began to chase the furniture thief down Newbury Street. The huge burglar, the sofa established firmly atop his broad shoulders, ran with the angry bartender in close pursuit. They ran past Gloucester Street, Fairfield Street, Exeter Street, and then Dartmouth Street towards the Public Garden and Boston Common.

It was upon nearing Clarendon Street that Armand finally began to gain ground on the purloiner, but also experienced an Epiphany.

Now it should be noted that the male of the species is not the most intelligent being on the planet, but Armand experienced a moment of clarity. Coming to his senses, Armand reasoned, "If this crazy bastard outran me for four blocks while carrying a heavy piece of furniture, if I catch him, the beast is going to kill me!" Armand, of course, ended his pursuit.

On another evening at Daisy's, the Spaceman's closest friend, an equally brilliant, albeit eccentric character named Mike Mulkern, was stopped at the door.

"I'm sorry, but we have a dress code," Mike was informed by a rather sizeable bouncer. Mike had arrived wearing blue jeans. At that moment, two extremely attractive young women, also donning blue jeans, were allowed admittance.

"Hey," Mike protested while pointing to the pretty ladies, "what about them?"

Once more, the officious "guard" spewed:

"Sorry, but no men are allowed in with blue jeans."

Mike Mulkern, as I stated, has been Bill's sidekick for decades, did what any "normal" person would do. Without hesitating, Mike Mulkern dropped his pants and walked into Daisy Buchanan's.

This was Bill "Spaceman" Lee's Boston in the 1970s. As you will soon learn, other road cities were equally insane. Detroit is our next stop on the Spaceman's travels through our green planet.

I wonder if the thief placed the furniture in his living room or family room.

Leigh Montville was arguably the greatest of all the sportswriters at the *Boston Globe* in the 1970s, and that is saying an awful lot. *The Boston Globe* in those days featured the likes of Peter Gammons, Bob Ryan, Kevin Paul Dupont, and various other legends of journalism. It was the host of the popular Boston sports talk show *Sportscope*, Eli Schleifer, who originally made me aware of Leigh's superb and often witty prose; however, what he said set Montville apart is that other than many of the writers of that era, on those occasions he was critical, he wrote in a manner which was sympathetic.

In recalling his days of covering the Spaceman, Montville found Bill to be always capable of infusing humor into his responses. As Leigh recalls:

"Bill once asked me if I knew how Carl Yastrzemski managed to maintain his level of excellence deep into his career. I replied, 'No.' Lee then explained that Yaz wore his uniform to bed and when he laid down, his #8 turned sideways and became the symbol for infinity."

Leigh continued:

"One of the most hilarious lines I heard Lee utter occurred right after 'Pudge' Fisk had a tough day at the office. Fisk was sitting at his locker, grumpy and looking down when Lee approached and offered, 'C'mon, Pudge, even gynecologists have bad days sometimes!'"

Leigh Montville had the honor and privilege of being seated next to the Spaceman's parents on a flight from Cincinnati to Boston during the 1975 World Series. Bill's mom, Paula, confessed to Leigh and said, "You know, it would've been better if all of this happened to Paul (Bill's brother)." Bill Lee was very aware of how his mom felt, since the Spaceman was nearly invariably involved in controversy, and Bill's thoughts were, "Yeah, I would've been a fucking drunk or just another insurance salesman."

However, the most hilarious tale Leigh Montville recalled involved Lee's teammate in Montreal, Ron LeFlore, another eccentric character, and perhaps the funniest and most unique comic of the twentieth century, the late Andy Kaufman (Man on the Moon), and not surprisingly, the incident took place at Daisy Buchanan's! I mean, where else?

Eli Schleifer recounted this delicious tidbit:

"Ron LeFlore and Andy Kaufman were drinking at Daisy's one night and they wound up staying after the bar closed. They were snorting cocaine and still drinking in the back room. They were still there as the sun was coming up. When they went out to Newbury Street, Kaufman was on all fours and barking at Taxi Cabs! Oh, and LeFlore went out to Fenway Park and went 3-4!"

Perhaps even more outrageously, Leigh recalled being in Houston at a Super Bowl, and his fellow drinking partners that evening were George

Kimball, Dr. Hunter S. Thompson, and another terrific journalist, the late Clark Booth.

Not surprisingly, a brawl broke out at the crowded establishment and Kimball, who had already lost an eye to a beer bottle, immediately reached for a cocktail waitress. Glass was flying everywhere. As I recall, Kimball had written, "I was wielding her around like an American League chest protector."

During the melee, Clark Booth had somehow wended his way towards the door and gotten out. Leigh Montville, in an excellent career move, also made it out the door to safety. Upon Clark Booth's escape, an impressed Dr. Hunter S. Thompson, remarked, "That Booth Clark fellow (he had somehow gotten Booth's name backwards) has a remarkable instinct for survival."

Regarding Dr. Hunter S. Thompson, Leigh Montville remarked, "He was an interesting fellow, but certainly was capable of making you nervous. He was escorting us around town and his driving was really fucking weird. At the bar he was dropping blotter acid (LSD) into his drink."

CHAPTER TWENTY-ONE

Motor City

The following statement can be corroborated by any number of actuaries in the universe:

"In the year 2307 in a scientific experiment gone terribly awry that was conducted by a hermaphrodite named Dr. Scott Russell Wilbur Swain Daffodil IV, the former 'King of Detroit,' planet Earth flew off its axis and hurtled towards the sun where it entirely disintegrated.

"Tens of millions of baseball cards were destroyed, and the human race was completely obliterated. However, only one card survived. It was a 1978 Topps card of an earthling named Bill 'Spaceman' Lee.

"The card, one that depicts Bill Lee throwing a baseball while wearing a Boston Red Sox uniform, floated gently through space until it landed softly on a picnic blanket of a family enjoying lunch on the planet Tralfamadore in the year 2389.

"The card was in mint condition." —*Kilgore Trout*

Suggestion: The following chapter is best accompanied by the soothing sounds of Martha and the Vandellas "Dancing in the Streets" playing in the background and perhaps a bottle of Chianti.

"Other people's interruptions of your work are relatively insignificant compared with the countless times you interrupt yourself.
—*Brendan Behan*

Bill "Spaceman" Lee's endeavors in what earthlings often refer to as "gainful employment" would often take him to a godforsaken location in the universe, one named Detroit, Michigan. It was there that Lee and other members of athletic teams would gravitate towards a drinking emporium known as the "Lindell AC," the "AC" representing "Athletic Club" although virtually no games were played there other than perhaps a nightly physical altercation or three.

The visitors to the Lindell AC included some of the more prominent names on planet Earth. They contained legends from all walks of life: Athletes, entertainers, motion picture stars, mobsters, "normal" white collar workers and frequent visitations by the local police to either prevent mayhem or to prevent additional destruction and violence.

Among those celebrities who frequented the Lindell AC were Mickey Mantle, Milton Berle, Jayne Mansfield, Muhammad Ali, and countless other notables. The Lindell AC was first opened in 1949 by a Greek immigrant named Meleti Butsicaris. He and his two sons, Johnny and Jimmy, purchased the land on which a seedy hotel stood and converted it to perhaps what would become other than the renowned "Toots Shor's" in New York City, the most famous or perhaps infamous sports bar in American history.

In 1963 one of the part owners of the Lindell AC was one of the most beloved athletes in American history, and he would go on to become one of the zaniest actors in Hollywood annals. His name was Alex Karras, an overpowering NFL lineman whose role as Mongo in Mel Brooks' 1974 classic motion picture *Blazing Saddles* remains as an indelible reminder and proof as to when non-politically correct and hilarious comedy were acceptable.

Alex Karras was also one of two major subjects in the great, late George Plimpton's epic tome *Mad Ducks and Bears*, Karras being the "mad duck" and his Lions offensive lineman teammate John Gordy, "the bear." The book describes the daily lives of the members of the NFL Detroit Lions and comprises as much hilarity in any sports volume ever written.

Alex Karras, in fact, had been suspended along with another NFL superstar, the Notre Dame and Green Bay Packers legend, Paul Hornung. Their crimes against society consisted of their allegedly gambling on the outcomes of NFL games, and apparently ones they had participated in. Therefore, the two athletes were banished from the league for a full season. Karras was also ordered to divest his part ownership in the Lindell AC, since it was a renowned hangout for various unsavory characters. This edict, however, did not preclude Mongo from patronizing his former place of ownership.

In an attempt to offset much of the lost income he would incur during his one-year layoff from the Detroit Lions, since the behemoth Karras was already accustomed to clobbering his opponents, Karras decided to try his hand at professional wrestling. What better way to earn a considerable amount of revenue than by continuing to pummel other human beings, something he was not only accustomed to, but had developed a proficiency at?

During Karras' eventful year as a professional wrestler, he appeared one evening at The Olympia in Detroit. His opponent was a fellow wrestler named "Dick the Bruiser." The two fought each other and although there are few on the planet who can recall the outcome of the match, the two huge combatants decided to cap their evening with a few libations at the Lindell AC.

What began as a minor disagreement between the two mammoth athletes (and who says professional wrestling is false?) soon deteriorated into angry words, which of course, eventually dissolved into a physical confrontation between the two now inebriated and massive giants. A brawl ensued, one which once more necessitated a visit from the local police department and ended with a significant amount of damage to the bar itself. In the melee, it should be mentioned that several of the police who arrived at the scene had to be taken to a nearby hospital to be patched up. Mongo not only liked candy, but absolutely loved to fight, God rest his soul.

Alex Karras, one of the spontaneously funniest big fellas on planet earth, often was a guest on late night television. On one of his appearances on *The Tonight Show*, Karras described his senior year in high school to Johnny Carson. To begin with, just having been raised in Gary, Indiana, Karras no doubt not only learned survival skills, but also intrinsically acquired a terrific sense of humor.

Karras' parents had promised their football star son a graduation present upon his receiving his diploma, but it included strict stipulations. If he fulfilled each ordinance, he would receive his first car. Number one, he would have to ask their neighbor's daughter to the prom. The girl was a heavyset Polish girl, and Karras, the star athlete at the school, was adamantly opposed to this strictly required conscription.

"No, Mom! Please, anyone but her!"

Alex Karras' rebuttal fell on deaf ears. No date, no car.

Secondly, he would have to dance with the said young lady at the Senior Prom.

"Why, Mom? Can't I just take her there?"

Sorry, no dance, no car.

Thirdly, he would have to compliment the girl upon the dance being concluded.

"Are you kidding me, Mom? This is too much!"

Sorry, do it or no car.

Alex Karras really wanted the automobile... desperately. Therefore, he indeed asked the rotund Polish girl to the prom. She anxiously accepted since she was about to experience a rite of passage, being asked to the prestigious event by the star athlete of the high school. Alex Karras even admitted that, "You know, she really wasn't that bad looking."

Secondly, Alex asked her to dance, a major step for the unrefined lout.

At the conclusion of the dance, however, Alex Karras was now faced with a significant dilemma. The final obstacle in obtaining his cherished car was being obligated to offer a compliment to the young girl as quickly as the dance concluded. Alex Karras, certainly not incapable of intelligent conversation, thought hard in regard as to what to say to the attractive stocky member of the female species who was now no more than an arm's length away. Karras' mind searched for the proper words, but his mind just went blank. Then he thought of the prospect of losing the opportunity to drive his very own automobile and all at once, he found the proper words.

"Gee," remarked the courteous and thoughtful defensive lineman, "you don't sweat much for a fat girl."

We are about to discuss other planetary events at the Lindell AC, a venue that is now no more than a precious memory, having closed its doors in 2002.

Postscript: It should be noted that upon the 1978 baseball card of Bill "Spaceman" Lee silently landing atop the picnic blanket on the planet Tralfamadore in the year 2389, the family's dog, a Rottweiler-Don Zimmer mix named Bernardo, immediately devoured it, thus forever removing any trace or evidence of the possibility that human civilization ever existed on planet Earth.

In the year 2537, theologians on Tralfamadore would still debate if they themselves were the only inhabitants of the universe.

CHAPTER TWENTY-TWO

Last Calls and Close Calls

"Render unto Caesar the things that are Caesar's, and unto God the things that are God's.

"Retort to biblical advice:

"Pay no attention to Caesar. Caesar doesn't have the slightest idea of what's really going on." —*From the Holy Scripture of Bokonon**

* Bokonon, for those not properly educated, was a black British Episcopalian from the Island of Tobago whose actual name was Lionel Boyd Johnson.

The tales emanating from Detroit's Lindell AC are worthy of their own book, reality indeed, being much stranger than what most perceive as truth. In fact, I suspect that on each of the 365 days of the year, there was at least one incident surrounding the establishment often frequented by Bill "Spaceman" Lee and his contemporaries. Not only did "local" Detroit athletes make the Lindell their home, but those visitors to town seemed to gravitate towards the illustrious, if not infamous lounge.

One of the regular patrons in those days was the brash eccentric and beloved first baseman of the Detroit Tigers, a colorful hard-hitting and perhaps harder drinking Texan named Norm Cash, an accomplished batsman. "Stormin' Norman" as was his popular sobriquet, was a great friend of the owners at the Lindell AC, Jimmy and John Butsicaris.

One late summer evening in the 1970s, neither of the Butsicaris brothers for one reason or another was present at the lounge. However, the invariably loquacious and hospitable Norm Cash was in the process of entertaining some out-of-town visitors to the bar, and they were unaware of the fact that Norm knew that Jimmy Butsicaris kept a cigarette lighter in a desk drawer in his room above the facility. Therefore, at closing time, Norm Cash, renowned for being as playful as his pal, the great Mickey Mantle on occasion, invited his guests to join him upstairs.

What I neglected to mention was that the "cigarette lighter" that Jimmy

Butsicaris kept in his desk drawer looked exactly like a pearl-handled Colt .45 pistol. Norm Cash, whose 1961 season was nearly the equal of Mantle's and Roger Maris' in its statistical splendor, decided to frighten the daylights out of his unsuspecting friends. Therefore, he reached into the desk drawer and removed the "cigarette lighter" and commenced to wave it around the room, pointing it and basically acting like the overgrown child he was, as the others ducked and ran for cover.

It was then that Cash decided to smoke a cigarette. Placing it in his mouth, he pointed the lighter at the Marlboro dangling loosely from his lips... and proceeded to come within an eighth of an inch of blowing his brains out! Unknown to Norm Cash, himself, Jimmy Butsicaris also kept an ACTUAL revolver in his desk.

According to Boston journalist George Kimball, the Spaceman, and former Tigers catcher Bill Freehan, Norm Cash stood transfixed in that spot, his hands trembling, and literally proving that it is indeed possible to turn completely white. According to those present, the gun had to be pried out of Cash's hands, slowly and carefully.

Athletes are often even a more improbable species than their counterparts. Bill "Spaceman" Lee recalls Boston Bruins hockey legend Wayne Cashman running three red lights upon leaving Daisy Buchanan's in Boston and being pulled over by the police. Upon being arrested and brought down to police headquarters, Cashman was informed he was allowed one phone call. Therefore, he immediately telephoned a Chinese restaurant and had meals delivered for himself and his captors.

On another occasion, and this is a recent admission, the Spaceman had been out carousing on the town with the popular New England Patriots quarterback, Jim Plunkett, a Stanford graduate and a classy kid. It was on that occasion that there was an "incident" of sorts, one in which Jim Plunkett tore up his knee. The Patriots, however, did not display great patience with their young star and proceeded to jettison Plunkett to the Oakland Raiders... where he won a Super Bowl. No Chinese food was involved, however.

Speaking of questionable locations in our universe, Bill "Spaceman" Lee and his Red Sox teammates often found themselves somehow ensconced in a foreign outpost called Cuyahoga County and in particular Cleveland, Ohio, a place of which no one of any intelligence has ever explained the reason for its existence. In the year 1978 on planet Earth,

Lee and his teammate, fellow pitcher Bill Campbell, upon completing their baseball responsibilities, decided to repair to a local gin mill. Participating at America's pastime can lead to substantial dryness. Even while in what former Cleveland Indian Cliff "Heathcliff" Johnson described as "The Mistake by the Lake," a man must quench his thirst.

The two "Bills" therefore, left the ballpark in search for perhaps a beer or ten. Within minutes Lee and Campbell entered a debatable facility with the name "The Theatrical Restaurant" emblazoned on its door and windows. However, Bill and Bill failed to see any "theatrics" within its confines and after a few drinks decided to explore other haunts, so across the street they went... that is, after hearing a gunshot or three.

As Lee and Campbell walked the short distance from one bar to the other, they witnessed a multitude of police cars outside the Triangle Grill. There was also a body lying in the street, having been gunned down. Bill Campbell recalled having to step over the deceased gent. Lee and Campbell then entered the Triangle Grill where another body lay prostrate on the floor of the establishment. An attempted holdup had taken place and the bartender, although he had also been shot in the leg, was apparently a much more accomplished "shooter" than the two would-be robbers.

"What better place," thought the Spaceman and his companion, Bill Campbell, "to have a few beers than the Triangle Grill?" It is not known, however, if Randy Newman frequented the liquor emporium. What the Spaceman did recall though, was the night that legendary Boston Celtics 6′ 8″ center Dave "Red" Cowens, a Kentuckian, was refused a drink at the Triangle, and reacted by wiping the top of the bar with the bartender's face. Cowens was renowned as being one of the more congenial and truly respected individuals in the NBA, so it is highly suspected that the reluctant bartender was simply an asshole.

CHAPTER TWENTY-THREE

Bernardo

"Thinking is the enemy of creativity." —*Ray Bradbury*

On the evening of October 21, 1975—actually it was during the early morning hours of October 22, 1975 because moments before the clock had struck midnight—one of the most iconic scenes in baseball history was viewed by millions of people throughout the world. In what remains the most memorable image of perhaps the greatest World Series ever played, an NBC cameraman named Lou Gerard captured Boston Red Sox Hall of Fame catcher Carlton "Pudge" Fisk waving the baseball he had just crushed off of Cincinnati Reds pitcher, Pat Darcy, shouting "fair." "Fair ball! Home run!" was the cry of young broadcaster Dick Stockton. Except that image of Fisk jumping up and down and willing the ball fair appeared on millions of television screens because of a rat. No, really.

Legendary NBC director Harry Coyle shook up the world of baseball by placing a camera in the outfield in order for viewers to watch games from behind the pitcher, rather than from behind the plate, a practice that had gone on for generations. He believed that angle would be preferable since it would enable the viewer to "track" the pitches. However, once the ball was struck, the cameramen were instructed to switch to another angle that followed the flight of the batted ball. At the Fenway Park venue, it should be noted that the outfield camera was situated inside of the ancient left field wall.

Just seconds before Carlton Fisk's memorable game-winning blast atop Fenway Park's famous left field wall, cameraman Lou Gerard had alerted his director that there were rats scurrying around… Director Coyle had instructed Gerard to switch to the flight of the ball if a batter made contact.

In the bottom of the twelfth inning of the now legendary sixth game of the 1975 World Series, with the score knotted at 6-6, Carlton Fisk, indeed, struck the ball. Only as cameraman Lou Gerard initiated his attempt to switch to an infield camera in order to track the majestic blast, a large rat draped itself over his foot!

Gerard described the rat as "being the size of a cat." Therefore, by pure luck, the camera angle was never switched and NBC and millions of fans watching were treated to Fisk's choreography, which is now immediately recognizable to all baseball fans some forty-five years hence. And all of this occurred because of an appearance by an uninvited furry guest.

What far too many baseball historians fail to recall, however, is that Carlton Fisk's historic home run never would have happened if not for the exploits of Bill "Spaceman" Lee's teammate and close friend, Bernie Carbo. With the Red Sox trailing in the World Series three games to two, and in game six in the bottom of the eighth inning 6-3, the Fall Classic was ostensibly over. Even the great Luis Tiant who had completely shut down the "Big Red Machine" in game one, had been hammered for six runs.

When Bernie Carbo came to bat in the bottom of the eighth inning against Reds reliever Rawly Eastwick, there were two men out and two on and things looked bleak for the hometown club. Bernie had been sent up as a pinch-hitter for Red Sox reliever Rogelio Moret. On a two-two pitch, Bernie remained alive by barely making contact with a pitch in on his hands. Bernie took a half-hearted half-swing and looked pathetic in doing so. The slightest "tick" saw the ball spin out of Hall of Fame catcher Johnny Bench's mitt.

The next pitch, however, was hard stuff away. The crack of the bat was unmistakable and when the ball disappeared into the far away bleachers in center field, the game was tied 6-6! "Spaceman" Lee was quoted as follows:

"With one swing of his magic wand, Bernie Carbo turned fall into summer!" And that he did. Upon Fisk's now historic game winning shot in the twelfth inning, Bill Lee would then get the opportunity to start game seven of the World Series. Bill had started game two and pitched splendidly, but the bullpen could not hold the lead in the ninth inning and the Reds would win. Unfortunately, that same fate awaited the Spaceman in game seven as well. Bill Lee would wind up pitching 14 & 1/3 innings allowing merely five runs, but two of those scored when his relievers failed to prevent the inherited runners from scoring.

As for Bernie Carbo, his pinch-hitting acumen would win many a game for the Red Sox, until a fool named Don Zimmer decided he didn't want Bernie around any longer and sold him to the Cleveland Indians for two pieces of gum and a jockstrap. Later we will definitively statistically prove how Zimmer's mismanagement of the Red Sox cost the great 1978 Boston club a chance not only for a World Series victory but prevented the club from even reaching the Fall Classic.

CHAPTER TWENTY-FOUR

Bernardo Part Two: A Tale of Two Rats?

"It's lack that gives us inspirations. It is not fullness."
—*Ray Bradbury*

Everything Keith Hernandez told the United States District Court concerning Bernie Carbo was true. As harmful and as pointed as the words were, they were clear, concise, and as hurtful to Bernie Carbo as any words ever directed to him or about him. The occasion occurred in a federal courthouse and Keith Hernandez was "informing" prosecutors of his participation in his usage of illegal substances, and his days as a cocaine user. Mr. Hernandez, a star first baseman, was also naming names. One of those names was a fellow player and his former teammate, a young man named Bernie Carbo.

By 1978 Bernie Carbo's days with the Red Sox were numbered thanks in large part to Bernie's "association" with the free-thinking free-spirited Bill "Spaceman" Lee, whose days with the ball club he had been a part of for a decade were also approaching their expiration date. The manager of the Red Sox was a combative, inarticulate, tobacco-chewing, uneducated and obstinate inveterate dog-track gambler named Don Zimmer, a former major league shortstop who was once heralded as the great "Pee Wee" Reese's heir apparent in Brooklyn, but simply never fulfilled his promise.

As a minor leaguer and as a major league player, Don Zimmer had been struck in the head on two occasions by pitchers. In fact, in one of those instances, Zimmer lay in a coma for a significant period. His injury necessitated holes being drilled in his skull in order to relieve pressure, something that Zimmer was hesitant to discuss or even acknowledge because there are those that made light of the less than eloquent manner in which he spoke. It was falsely reported that Zimmer had a metal plate inserted in his skull and that it would set off alarms at airport security, and because of these reports, Zimmer would react with embarrassment upon learning that he was the brunt of jokes.

** Note: the author's wife has had both knee and hip replacements and she carries a card explaining her "sound effects." She considers it amusing.

Don Zimmer, therefore, was not necessarily partial to pitchers, since they comprised the "species" that nearly killed him. "Zip," as was his nickname (there was a popular chimpanzee named "Zippy" in the 1950s) was particularly not fond of pitchers, or reporters for that matter, with college backgrounds. Zimmer, to be truthful, struck many as intimidated by the "King's English." Put it this way: Bill "Spaceman" Lee's often glib tongue no doubt confused and angered his manager, whose Rhodes scholarship opportunities had no doubt vanished by grade school.

Manager Don Zimmer was once described by the Spaceman as "not being able to identify a pitcher even if one bit him on his ass." Later you will see statistics which unfortunately for Zimmer, seem to validate Bill Lee's assessment. This was never more evident than in 1978 when Zimmer incorporated changes to his pitching rotation that were equally baffling and ineffectual. In truth, Zimmer had begun the destruction of his pitching staff in 1977, but the full effect of his lame-brained "plan" entirely imploded the following season, a sanction that would result in perhaps the biggest collapse in baseball history.

During that infamous 1978 campaign, Bernie Carbo apparently enraged Zimmer by "joining," as it were, a group of Red Sox liberated thinkers led by, of course, "Spaceman" Lee. The name of this illustrious group was "The Buffalo Head Gang," and their mere mention causes delight among true Red Sox fans that have always enjoyed their more eccentric athletes, going back to the days of "Babe" Ruth, Jimmy Foxx, Ellis Kinder, and Jimmy Piersall. The Buffalo Head Gang, for which of course, the Spaceman bore the blame, was actually given its name by Hall of Fame pitcher, Ferguson Jenkins, and not because of Zimmer's less than attractive appearance, but because as Fergie stated, "The buffalo is the dumbest member of the animal kingdom." Despite that it was the great Ferguson Jenkins who provided the group with the name "Buffalo Head," Zimmer's hatred of Lee "allowed" him to blame Bill for its inception. As the Spaceman joked, "If this were Ringling Brothers, Fergie would've been P.T. Barnum."

This group of social outcasts included "Spaceman" Lee, Rick Wise,

Jenkins, Jim Willoughby and the lone non-hurler, Bernie Carbo, who actually traveled with a stuffed gorilla aptly named "Mighty Joe Young." "Mighty Joe" often had his own seat on team flights and Red Sox Hall of Famer Carl Yastrzemski wanted the gorilla to be placed on the bat rack in the dugout.

The great Luis Tiant, perhaps the greatest pitcher ever to not be enshrined in the Hall of Fame, was also one of the greatest characters in the annals of baseball history. The Spaceman recalls that Luis absolutely hated flying, but he was especially neurotic during takeoffs and landings. As the plane taxied down the runway in preparation for takeoffs, El Tiante would commence shrieking, "Ay Maria! Ay Dios! Ay! Ay! Ay!" Bill would then pop in a recording of "The William Tell Overture" and play it at full blast to drown out the nervous and delightful Cuban.

The exploits of the Buffalo Head Gang were often told by the outrageously witty journalist George Kimball in the *Boston Phoenix*. The author always considered it a fortuitous bounce that some of the wives of the players during those times were not in the habit of reading the counter-culture weekly periodical. Bernie Carbo in so many ways, was as big a hero to Boston sports fans as his pal, the Spaceman. However, there were bad days ahead for both gentlemen, especially for poor Bernardo, who for all intents and purposes was about to be offered as a sacrificial lamb.

Earlier we had described the rat in the scoreboard at Fenway Park, the one whose peculiar timing had resulted in perhaps the most iconic video imagery in baseball history. The beloved Bernie Carbo, who had few if any enemies on or off the field, was about to be the victim of a superstar first baseman named Keith Hernandez, albeit perhaps a blameworthy victim. As Bernardo would admit, there is a much higher judge, and Carbo is neither a bitter nor a vindictive person.

Even at the time of Bernie Carbo's heroic efforts in the 1975 World Series, he was a junkie of sorts. Bernie's downward spiral began as early as his playing days with the St. Louis Cardinals where he was a teammate of Keith Hernandez's. By 1985 there was a full-fledged federal investigation into drug usage in major league baseball, one in which Keith Hernandez, who had earlier denied cocaine usage, was deeply involved.

As reported by Harold Friend in the *Los Angeles Times* on February 17, 2012, a Philadelphia Phillies clubhouse caterer named Curtis Strong was on trial for distributing cocaine to athletes. Here is where it got sticky for some household names. The players involved were granted immunity for their testimony. According to Murray Chass of *the New York Times* on September 7, 1985, twenty-four hours after both Hernandez's St. Louis teammates Lonnie Smith and Joaquin Andujar had testified that they had used cocaine, Keith Hernandez stated that there were perhaps as many as eleven Cardinals players involved, but could not recall their names! However, Keith, who would go on to a be a World Series hero for the New York Mets and then their broadcaster, for some reason vividly recalled that the 1975 Red Sox World Series hero, Bernie Carbo, had turned him onto the drug. Hernandez's somewhat foggy memory did not preclude him from naming former hurler Lary Sorensen, either. Immunity from prosecution can also be a strong "narcotic."

The impact of Keith Hernandez's "admissions" had a devastating effect on the life of Bernie Carbo, whose life was already a mess. Bernie's major league playing career ended in 1980 after a brief period with the Pittsburgh Pirates. Bernie had studied cosmetology and had opened a hair salon, but upon the news that he was the one "responsible" for the downfall of Keith Hernandez, Bernie had lost both his house and his salon because of the bad publicity. Again, Keith Hernandez, at least regarding Bernie Carbo, was telling the truth, but as Alex Cora would learn many years later, one "scapegoat" will often suffice.

A downtrodden Bernie Carbo's life would spin entirely out of control afterwards. By 1989-90, Bernie hit rock bottom while playing in a senior league. Bernie's mom had committed suicide and his father died two months later. Bernie's family had entirely disintegrated. Bernie Carbo, the fun-loving smiling beloved goofball, needed significant intervention, and he received it from an unlikely source.

Bernie was so despondent by 1992 that he contemplated suicide. In his book *Saving Bernie Carbo*, the distraught Carbo gave credit to Bill Lee for saving his life. One day, Bernie suffered such loss of hope that he telephoned the Spaceman to inform him that he was about to blow his brains out with a gun. The telephone call was merely to say farewell to his old friend. The Spaceman's reaction was priceless. Bill responded:

"What type of ammunition do you have? What caliber gun?"

Bernie Carbo began laughing through his tears. Before their conversation was over, Bill made Bernie promise to call their fellow Buffalo Head Gang member, the great Hall of Famer Ferguson Jenkins, not only an extraordinary pitcher, but a human being that had also suffered devastating tragedies throughout his lifetime. With the assistance of Bill Lee, Ferguson Jenkins, and "Sudden Sam" McDowell, who had major experience with his own substance abuse, life-saving help was initiated, and much of it through the wonderful "Baseball Assistance Team" (BAT).

While in the clutches of cocaine, which at that point saw Bernie spending $32,000 a month for the drug, a former Red Sox player named Dalton Jones reached out to Bernie. Dalton, who was part of the Red Sox 1967 "Impossible Dream" team, simply told Bernie, "You need Jesus." The rest is history.

It should be noted that the lawyer for the accused cocaine dealer, Curtis Strong, a defense attorney named Adam Renfroe, insisted, and perhaps accurately so, that "major league baseball was on trial" and that the players were "nothing but junkies." Adam Renfroe, Esq. had referred to the players as "hero criminals who are still selling drugs around the league." Some of the other players, in addition to the players whose names Keith Hernandez "could not recall," were major stars such as Dave Parker, Gary Mathews, Enos Cabell, Al Holland, Jeff Leonard, and J.R. Richard.

Make of it what you will, but Dalton Jones' "recommendation" that Bernie Carbo explore the possibility of his requiring Jesus to make him whole, certainly worked out in Bernie Carbo's case. Today Bernie Carbo is an evangelist, a minister, and in fact, the head of Diamond Ministries, a church that has come to the aid of various others who have fallen on hard times... and Reverend Carbo holds no ill feelings for those who may or may not have wronged him. He believes in "a higher judge."

CHAPTER TWENTY-FIVE

A Funny Thing Happened on the Way to the World Series

> "The first thing in life you learn is you're a fool. The last thing you learn in life is you're the same fool."
> *—Ray Bradbury*

A funny thing happened on the way to the 1978 World Series and his name was Don Zimmer, the highly disputed "venerable" manager of the Boston Red Sox. Well, at the very least he was funny looking. But Bruce Bochy of the San Francisco Giants was not exactly mistaken for a matinee idol either, but Bochy is considered one of the greatest managers in baseball history. Don Zimmer? Not so much, although in 1978 "Zip" had the reins of perhaps one of the greatest teams that failed to reach the post-season.

Despite Zimmer having dispatched both Rick Wise and Hall of Famer Ferguson Jenkins after the 1977 season, the Sox skipper certainly had a solid starting pitching rotation at his disposal, one that included three time 17 game-winner, Bill "Spaceman" Lee, the great Luis Tiant, Hall of Famer Dennis Eckersley, and Mike Torrez. Zimmer was also fortunate to have a solid everyday lineup which included Hall of Famers Carl Yastrzemski, Carlton Fisk, Jim Rice, and other oft-time All-Stars such as George Scott, Fred Lynn, and Dwight Evans; and in Bernie Carbo, he had perhaps the preeminent pinch-hitter in baseball. Solid veterans such as the feisty middle infield of Jerry Remy and Rick Burleson rounded out a formidable lineup. Heck, Butch Hobson, the third baseman, generally batted ninth in that powerful lineup, and Hobson had clubbed 30 home runs in 1977!

Hobson, as the Spaceman recalls, had an errant throwing arm, but had a decent excuse. Said Lee:

"Butch was a triple option quarterback for Bear Bryant at Alabama. His elbows were completely shot from landing on the artificial turf. He had difficulty throwing across the infield. Every time he came charging in on a slow roller, I would hit the ground. I didn't know where the fuck the ball would end up. Hell, neither did Butch. He could only throw around corners. Each time he came charging in on a ground ball, my first words were, 'Oh, fuck!' The fans behind the Red Sox dugout used to ask the front office if they could relocate to a safer section."

The Red Sox had already jettisoned Rick Wise and Hall of Famer Ferguson Jenkins after the 1977 season, Zimmer and team president Haywood Sullivan apparently arriving at an absurd conclusion that neither man had much left in the tank. Therefore, Rick Wise, a veteran starting pitcher, was shipped off to Cleveland where the "washed up" hurler would win 15 games in 1979. As for the great Fergie Jenkins who had compiled a 10-10 record in 1977 (please remember that mark, it would repeat itself) was sent to Texas where the "over-the-hill" legendary hurler would immediately turn in a typical Jenkins season (18-8, 3.04) in 1978. Of course, both Wise and Jenkins were "members" of the Buffalo Head Gang, the bane of Zimmer's existence, at least in the manager's mind.

Don Zimmer was in the process of ridding himself of all elements of the group he believed was ridiculing him, and the Spaceman and Bernie Carbo's days in Boston were coming to an end. Therefore, what greater place for Zimmer, another authority figure with a Napoleonic complex, in which to exile Bernie Carbo to than Elba, or in this instance, Cleveland, Ohio? It is written that on June 15, 1978, the Red Sox sold their best (only?) proficient pinch-hitter to the Cleveland Indians. There would be no more magical late inning come-from-behind victories due to an accomplished substitute batsman coming in cold from off the bench... literally. You see, after Bernie's banishment to "the mistake by the lake," not a single Red Sox pinch-hitter would knock in a run for the balance of the entire season.... As Casey Stengel would say, "You can look it up."

In 41 (that's a lot, incidentally) plate appearances after June 15 through October 2, the inglorious day that the Red Sox ship sank, not one Red Sox pinch-hitter knocked in a run. Knocking in runs after sitting throughout a ballgame was Bernie Carbo's specialty. I suppose Don Zimmer, bless his heart, was not a strong believer in the skill of specialization. (The Spaceman laughed, "Bernie, though, was not a specialist. He never met a drug he didn't like.")

In Peter Golenbock's book *Red Sox Nation,* Bill Lee recalled an occasion during a meaningless "Hall of Fame Game" in Cooperstown that Bernie went out behind a fence to catch up on his sleep. The Spaceman was quoted as follows: "Bernie was getting some shut-eye during the game because since it was an exhibition game it didn't mean anything. Zimmer found him and woke him up. He sent Bernie up to bat to embarrass him, figuring that Bernie would look bad. Bernie walked to the plate, hit a home run, and went back to sleep."

Upon learning that Bernie had been sold to the Indians, Bill Lee staged a one-day walkout. Upon the Spaceman's return the following day, Bill was fined $500 by general manager Haywood Sullivan. Bill responded by telling Sullivan, "Fine me $1,500 and give me the weekend off."

Immediately after Bernie was sold, Don Zimmer was quoted as saying regarding his deposed outfielder, "Bernie was like a son to me." This further infuriated the Spaceman who knew the truth, that Zimmer wanted Bernie gone at all costs. Bill Lee was the head player representative of the American League in those days, and therefore often communicated with front office executives of other teams. Bill had a brief conversation with Phil Seghi, the general manager of the Indians, Bernie's new place of employment, and Seghi admitted, "Zimmer wanted Bernie gone. He said he didn't even want anything in return, 'not even a bucket of baseballs.' Just get him out of here!"

The Spaceman also made this point, something most missed:

"Cleveland acquired Bernie for half the waiver price. I believe to this day that it was to make payroll because Buddy LeRoux and Haywood Sullivan were paying 17 ¾ percent to the American Finance Corporation of Cincinnati."

Note: The author recalls hearing several people remark in regard to the Spaceman's one-day strike that it was nothing more than an "act," and that Bill was merely attempting to draw attention to himself, but I know for a fact that this is entirely untrue.

The day of the Spaceman's walkout, I was at work in West Roxbury, Massachusetts when I received a phone call from Bill's then wife, Mary Lou. She asked if I could possibly do a favor. Said Mary Lou:

"Can you call Bill? Perhaps you can calm him down. I've never seen him like this. Bill is trembling, he's practically in tears and he's actually ripped the phone off of the wall a while ago. I finally put it back."

Obviously, I promised to call my enraged friend. I did not want him to do irreparable damage to his career. The conversation went something like this. Oh, and there was no caller ID in those days:

Bill: Hello!!! (Angrily)

Scott: Was it something I said?

Bill: Sorry, Scotty. I thought it was Haywood again. We've called each other a half-dozen times and each time we took turns slamming the phone down and hanging up.

Scott: Listen, I just want you to know that no matter what you decide to do, I'm in your corner one hundred percent. But just think of Mary Lou no matter what you decide.

Bill: I really appreciate that. In fact, you're only the second person to say that to me. The first was Bernie.

Scott: Have you called your dad?

Bill: No, I'm just too upset right now. But I will as soon as I calm down.

Scott: I can't even imagine what your dad is thinking.

Bill: That's why I haven't called him yet!

I got Bill to laugh. So, there was that, and no, Bill's reaction to Bernie being sold was NOT an act.

Don Zimmer, who merely wanted to hurt Bernie and Bill Lee, was in the process of hurting his own ball club. He would soon destroy it from within.

CHAPTER TWENTY-SIX

A Farewell to Arms

"One day in retrospect, the years of struggle will strike you as the most beautiful." —*Sigmund Freud*

After "ridding" the Red Sox of both Rick Wise and Ferguson Jenkins after the 1977 season, Haywood Sullivan and his crackerjack manager and loyal sidekick Don Zimmer went to work on the demise of the 1978 Boston Red Sox. It wasn't easy. With the aforementioned Hall of Famers Carl Yastrzemski, Jim Rice, and Carlton Fisk in the lineup, and with "near" Hall of Famers such as Dwight Evans, it would not be that easy to prevent success. But this was the law firm of "Sullivan & Zimmer," no disastrous collapse out of reach.

Jim Rice, the Red Sox left-fielder had one of the greatest seasons of our times in '78, as the strongman put up "Ruthian" numbers. The big man with the beautiful short stroke batted .315 and compiled 25 doubles, an astounding 15 triples, 46 home runs, scored 121 runs and knocked in 139! His slugging percentage was .600 and his OPS a magnificent .970. The Red Sox could flat out hit!

Despite "losing" both Fergie Jenkins and Rick Wise, because, well, they were card-carrying members of the Buffalo Head Gang, the Red Sox rotation was still solid. There was Hall of Famer Dennis Eckersley, SHOULD be Hall of Famer Luis Tiant, three-time 17 game winner Bill "Spaceman" Lee, and veteran strong-armed Mike Torrez. And then Don Zimmer happened. Not leaving bad enough alone in the dispatching of his ONLY accomplished pinch-hitter in Bernie, his dismantling of what was an excellent starting pitching rotation continued.

Remember our mentioning of Ferguson Jenkins 10-10 record in his final Red Sox season? Well, Bill Lee also posted a 10-10 mark due to some poor run support which was accompanied by the Spaceman's excellent 3.46 ERA. Not good enough for Zimmer, though. When the chips were down, Zimmer's disdain for Bill Lee overcame what little common sense the manager had, and Bill, a proud member of the Buffalo Head Gang was eventually exiled to the bullpen for reasons beyond comprehension. It was clearly personal. The great Luis Tiant, who finished at 13-8, 3.31, was also subject to missing a few starts and not because of injury... but it wasn't easy. Don Zimmer's self-destruction and the demise of his powerful ball club would require some significant ingenuity.

The 1978 Red Sox got off to an enormously great start. Consider that after baseball action was completed on July 17, the Red Sox sat atop the AL East with a remarkable record of 61-28. They owned an 8 & ½ game lead over the Milwaukee Brewers and a 14-game lead over the New York Yankees. However, Don Zimmer was capable of "inventiveness."

I want you to consider that Bill Lee was replaced in the rotation by pitchers named Jim Wright, who albeit won eight games that season, and a young lefthander named Bobby Sprowl, among others. I would also like you to consider that the Spaceman had already won 10 games in 1978... and that would total one more game than Wright and Sprowl would win in their entire careers COMBINED!

In the two-year period in which the Red Sox "brain trust" removed four outstanding veteran pitchers from the rotation and shipped them elsewhere, where Luis Tiant would win 25 more major league games, Bill Lee also 25 more, Ferguson Jenkins an additional 71, and Rick Wise another 34, none of Zimmer's "replacements" would accomplish anything other than put their names in the record books, albeit dubiously.

In this universe of ours, the one in which "Spaceman" Lee still exists, there exists great irony. With Zimmer's proclivities for self-imploding, on the final day of the 1978 season, a one-game extension of the season, a year in which the Red Sox had squandered a 14 game lead over the Yankees, it came down to a final match at Fenway Park. The Red Sox led 2-0 entering the seventh inning behind Mike Torrez, who had outpitched Yankee legend Ron Guidry up to that point. But Torrez had dug himself a hole.

With two men on base and weak-hitting Yankee shortstop Russell Earl "Bucky" Dent up at the plate, the Spaceman had begun to warm up in the bullpen. Bill Lee OWNED the Yankees (12-5 career) and irony of ironies, the banished southpaw had taken upon himself to be the unlikely savior for the rotund Don Zimmer, the manager who so despised him. Bill described how his "stuff" was in the bullpen that day:

"I could feel the hair on my arms tingling. Everything was perfect. I had full command and all my pitches were sinking."

Don Zimmer, however, still had one more nail to pound into his own coffin. He spotted the Spaceman warming up, picked up the dugout phone, and called the bullpen and spewed:

"Who the hell told Lee to warm up? Tell him to sit down!"

According to *Boston Phoenix* writer George Kimball, "As soon as she saw Bill sit back down, Mary Lou Lee began to cry from her seat behind home plate. She knew their days in Boston, a city she had grown to love, had ended."

Within seconds, Bucky "Fucking" Dent, as he would be forever known in Boston, hit a home run into the left field screen to give the Yankees a 3-2 lead, one they would not relinquish. Don Zimmer had completed the impossible by orchestrating the greatest collapse in MLB history. Again, as Casey Stengel would say, "You can look it up."

A pitcher often knows how he will fare in a ballgame upon what his warm-up indicates in the bullpen. In 1978, as a rookie catcher named Gary Allenson walked through the clubhouse one day, he came across a copy of *The Sirens of Titan,* one of the many Kurt Vonnegut novels the Spaceman had been reading. Out of curiosity, Allenson picked up the novel and quickly picked up on the fact that Bill was using a rolled-up joint as his bookmark.

Another day during a road trip to Detroit, Allenson was warming the Spaceman up in the bullpen Lee described as a "pillbox," when the young catcher remarked, "I'm amazed at how you hit my target on every pitch." Lee replied, "Welcome to the big leagues, kid."

Somewhat implausibly, decades later, Don Zimmer wrote in his autobiography that he was proud of leading the Red Sox to one of their most thrilling seasons.

Not surprisingly, on December 7, 1978, a date renowned for the original "Day of Infamy," Bill Lee, much like his buddy, Bernie Carbo, was traded for virtually nothing, the "nothing" in this case, a hapless utility infielder named Stan Papi, a man Bill would actually out homer. Punitive or not, Bill "Spaceman" Lee, earth traveler, was on his way to still more adventures, this time in another country, Montreal, Quebec, Canada.... Don Zimmer, on the other hand, was on his way to infamy and virtual oblivion, and presumably, the dog track.

CHAPTER TWENTY-SEVEN

White Men Can't Jump, but Their Fathers Can Shoot

"If we try to deny the darkness in our souls, then we'll become completely dark." —*Ray Bradbury*

"Anyone who can rejoice at a time like this is a fool. Political systems and not men are the enemies." —*Fidel Castro, 1963*

It is highly likely that the father of one of the Spaceman's friends assassinated President John F. Kennedy. As we have already stated, the universe in which the earthling named William Francis Lee, III resides can be a strange place.

On November 22, 1963, of course, President John F. Kennedy was assassinated as his motorcade drove by Dealey Plaza in Dallas, Texas, and the face of American history was forever changed. Initially as it is still mostly accepted, Kennedy was the victim of a lone crazed left-wing assassin named Lee Harvey Oswald. However, even as an eighteen-year-old youth, the author thought it quite odd that within moments of the horrific event, the F.B.I. issued a nearly complete dossier of the alleged assassin. Please consider that in those days information of that nature was not necessarily disseminated that quickly.

A short while afterwards, the alleged "shooter," Lee Harvey Oswald, was reported to have gunned down a police officer in front of a Dallas movie theater. The policeman's name was J.D. Tippit. Oswald, it appeared, was a madman, a crazed killer... or was he?

It should be noted that Lee Harvey Oswald was portrayed as a "Marxist communist" by the "authors" of the Warren Commission Report. However, it should also be noted that Lee Harvey Oswald had ENLISTED in the Marine Corps and apparently was a high-ranking member who had access to the Frances Gary Powers highly classified U-2 documents during the "Cold War" with the Soviet Union, hardly a typical M.O. for an alleged communist.

Some fifty-seven years later, conspiracy theories abound, and unfortunately the majority of them seem more believable than the nonsense provided to the media and therefore, the American public, that afternoon and the years that followed. As is unfortunately also true, false conspiracy theories detract from the few that are reliably researched. Too many people are influenced by those seeking to sensationalize historic incidents and these bogus tales render "factual" reports as nearly worthless.

Books have been written, motion pictures produced, and new theories still evolve, but the fact remains that the majority of sentient Americans are certain that although we may never fully learn what really occurred, we certainly are aware that the "investigation" referred to as the "Warren Commission Report" was one huge obfuscating cloud of unadulterated bullshit. Many decades later, our government would finally admit that "a conspiracy existed," but that the files were now "closed." In other words, we lied. Get used to it.

Two of the more intriguing books written regarding the subject were *A Heritage of Stone* by former New Orleans District Attorney Jim Garrison, and American attorney Mark Lane's tome titled *Rush to Judgment*. Those efforts were both critically appraised and discredited by "experts," dependent upon their predetermined opinions, much like the divide between partisan political pundits during these contentious times. A third book written by a great American novelist named James Kirkwood,* called *American Grotesque*, was heralded, much because of the identity of the author, but may have very well been the most biased.

> * For the record, the author of *The Spaceman Chronicles* lists James Kirkwood as one of his favorite authors but considers *American Grotesque* to be highly prejudicial regarding the events surrounding the Kennedy assassination.

New Orleans District Attorney James Carothers Garrison, born Earling Carothers Garrison, was a giant of a man, standing 6′ 6″. As a Democrat and the D.A. of the Orleans Parish Louisiana from 1962 to 1973, Garrison was convinced that members of the New Orleans underground that included high-ranking members of government agencies had conspired to have President Kennedy killed. Garrison claimed that a man named Clay Shaw, a renowned New Orleans businessman, was the mastermind behind the plot.

Garrison, a brilliant man, quietly opened an investigation regarding the assassination. Soon, Clay Shaw was arrested and charged with attempting to assassinate the president. Garrison made startling assertions regarding both the assassination and the cover-up. Garrison remains the ONLY person to hold a trial in relation to the murder. Garrison, despite presenting some significantly powerful and seemingly strong evidence, was ridiculed by many, of course, as merely a conspiracy theorist. However, the brilliant political commentator and satirist, Mort Sahl, a great friend of the Kennedy family, believed what Garrison had presented as fact. Others in the New Orleans community, in several educated opinions, also believed that several potential witnesses had been intimidated to the extent they were not forthcoming with their knowledge.

The aforementioned lawyer Mark Lane's book *Rush to Judgment* was also condemned by highly partisan "defenders" of our government as nothing more than hearsay. Clay Shaw, the accused, was acquitted of the alleged crimes in 1968.

The third book I had mentioned was written by one of the true geniuses of the twentieth century, an astoundingly great novelist and playwright named James Kirkwood, a man who grew up in a theatrical family. Kirkwood's parents were Lila Lee and James Kirkwood, Sr., two stars of the silent screen. Kirkwood, Jr. wrote "Chorus Line" which at the time, became the longest running musical in Broadway history, and it was not exceeded until 1997 when Andrew Lloyd Webber's "Cats" set the new record for longevity. "Chorus Line" garnered Kirkwood a Tony Award and a Pulitzer Prize. James Kirkwood also penned what I consider to be the most hilarious novel ever written, *P.S. Your Cat Is Dead.*

P.S. Your Cat Is Dead also became a long-running stage play. The premise of the book was that it was New Year's Eve, your best friend just died, you just lost your job, your girlfriend just left you and your apartment had been robbed three times in recent months and the only one you had left to talk to is the gay burglar you have tied up in your kitchen. Oh, and P.S., your cat is dead.

James Kirkwood was commissioned by *Playboy Magazine* to cover the trial of Clay Shaw, accused of murdering the president of the United States. Therefore, Kirkwood attended every minute of the trial from start to finish. Kirkwood's book *American Grotesque,* based on his trial coverage, sprung forth. The account of the entire trial was penned by Kirkwood shortly after Clay Shaw's acquittal.

Make of this what you will, but "after" the fact, Kirkwood apparently arrived at the conclusion that Clay Shaw was innocent as the jury had also decided. But let us take a quick glance at what the highly respected "Kirkus Reviews" had to say about Kirkwood's *American Grotesque*.

In the review we learn that James Kirkwood admitted to becoming a great friend of the defendant, Clay Shaw, in what "forthrightly colors this long, exuberantly pictorial of his Playboy trial coverage, but only scratches the surface of New Orleans' politics." Kirkus Reviews also accurately states that "Shaw's homosexuality is delicately avoided." My bookshelves are filled with the works of James Kirkwood, who also happened to be gay, as was the defendant, Clay Shaw. I, myself, have no intent of insinuating anything other than the fact that I found the "friendship" Kirkwood admittedly developed with the defendant over the course of the trial to be somewhat intriguing. Conflicts of interest often present themselves.

As for the numerous claims that those representing our military industrial complex may not have been enamored with President John F. Kennedy and therefore were seeking to "remove" him from office by any means possible, as we read in Jim Garrison's non-fiction offering, JFK had fired Alan Dulles from his position as the head of the Central Intelligence Agency. Also, as Garrison accurately pointed out, when Chief Justice Earl Warren decided to "investigate" the murder of the President of the United States, he appointed none other than the deposed Allen Dulles to head the Warren Commission! Seriously, if that isn't a conflict of interest, then what is?

To the minds of conspiracy theorists, the "Warren Commission" was NOT created to investigate IF Lee Harvey Oswald killed JFK, but rather WHY? To this day, Oswald certainly appears to have been set up as a "patsy."

We began this chapter with the words, "It is highly likely that the father of one of the Spaceman's friends assassinated President John F. Kennedy." Now we will delve into why we have arrived at that conclusion, one that holds much more water than the complete B.S. spewed forth by the Warren Commission.

What you are about to read are FACTS, ones that can be corroborated by those still alive and in addition by checking photographs, documents, and testimony of those whose relatives may or may not have been involved in the assassination of a beloved president of the United States.

Fact: Charles Voyde Harrelson was a murderer. It was his occupation. He was a "hitman." As for whom he worked, well, that we do not know for certain. He was also a sharpshooter, something Lee Harvey Oswald was most definitely not. As a professional hitman, Charles Harrelson had already served fifteen years in a federal penitentiary for a murder other than the one(s) we are alluding to. Once released from prison, Charles Harrelson, a Texan, was charged with and convicted of killing a federal judge named John H. Wood, Jr. Thus, the victim became the first federal judge to have been killed in the twentieth century. Harrelson was sentenced to two life-terms for the murder and died in a federal prison on March 15, 2007, a place he spent most of his adult life. However, it was the murder Charles Harrison ADMITTED to, one that occurred at Dealey Plaza in Dallas, Texas on November 22, 1963 that was even more startling.

The bull spewed forth that the fatal shots on that fateful day had been fired by Oswald from the Book Depository were suspect at best. A vast majority of people in the vicinity claimed, and some testified to law enforcement, that the shots derived from the grassy knoll on the other side of the street. Several claimed they saw men running from that scene and disappearing behind the knoll. Then there were other cogent facts....

Uniformed police did NOT run towards the Book Depository, but rather towards the grassy knoll, and even more telling is that three men were ARRESTED! The three men—and they can be seen in official photographs—were named Charles Rogers, Chauncey Holt, and yes, Charles Harrelson, sharpshooter. The men, who were dressed like hoboes and branded, "The Three Tramps," were handcuffed and taken into custody where they were interrogated by the F.B.I... and RELEASED!

When the Dallas Police ran towards the grassy knoll, they tracked the trio of "suspects" to the Union Pacific Railroad Yards behind the knoll. They were found hiding in a boxcar. They were arrested and escorted through Dealey Plaza. The F.B.I., however, as I stated, released them.

Bill "Spaceman" Lee has many friends in this world. One of them, in fact, is the famous and gifted actor Woody Harrelson, a former star of *Cheers* where his character "Woody" Boyd was a popular figure on the NBC sitcom. Woody Harrelson is also a star of motion pictures as well as a successful producer and director. His classic role in *White Men Can't Jump* is a Hollywood classic. Woody Harrelson's father was Charles Harrelson... hitman... and a man who ADMITTED killing John F. Kennedy. His son, Woody Harrelson does NOT deny what he considers the likely truth, that his father was responsible for the murder of JFK.

According to the elder, and now deceased assassin, he and Charles Rogers, two of the "Three Tramps," did the shooting, while the third, Chauncey Holt, assisted.

Woody Harrelson described his father as follows:

"My father wasn't always the greatest husband or father, but my father is one of the most articulate, well-read, charming people I've ever known." Woody Harrelson issued that statement in a 1988 interview.

While we are confronting demons of the past, William Francis Lee, III, aka the Spaceman, is a descendant of another rather famous person. Bill Lee's great-grandfather was none other than Rockwell Dennis Hunt, one of the actual founders of the University of Southern California, where his great-grandson, the Spaceman would achieve collegiate baseball immortality in 1968. From 1900-1937, Rockwell Dennis Hunt was the Dean of the graduate school at USC.

Mr. Hunt was also an eminent Californian historian, a professor at USC and at the University of the Pacific, and a prolific author who penned 16 books and numerous other articles dealing with the state's history. Rockwell Dennis Hunt was named "Mr. California" by Governor Goodwin Knight in 1954. To this date in 2020, the "Rockwell Dennis Hunt Scholastic Award and Trophy" honors USC graduate students whose undergraduate degree is from USC.

The Spaceman believes there are no coincidences in the cosmos, and therefore, finds it interesting that Dennis Rockwell Hunt's father, Dennis Rockwell Hunt, Sr. was born in Vermont where the Spaceman now resides. Hunt, Sr. married a woman named Nancy Zumwalt Cotton, who was born in Indiana, birthplace of Kurt Vonnegut. Nancy came to California in a covered wagon!

The 1960s were a much different time than these days of the twenty-first century, and even learned men such as Dennis Rockwell Hunt, the Dean of the graduate school of the University of Southern California as well as the great-grandfather of "Spaceman" Lee were not quite "ready" for modern times. As Bill "Spaceman" Lee recalls: "Rockwell, then ninety-seven years of age, was seated on a sofa watching his alma mater playing football. It was 1965 and the star halfback of the USC Trojans was a great player named Mike Garrett, a slightly built blur who was on his way to winning the coveted Heisman Award that season as the best player in the nation. Garrett, an African American kid from Los Angeles, had already scored a touchdown and was in the process of running for another one, when Rockwell Hunt shouted, 'Look at that little nigger run! He's going to score again!'"

Bill Lee stated that the term "little nigger" seemed to be uttered almost endearingly.... The sons and daughters, thankfully, and hopefully, should never be judged by the sins of their fathers, or their great-grandfathers for that matter. I believe that both Woody Harrelson, actor and producer, and Bill "Spaceman" Lee are certainly proof of that. Past demons should never be denied or disregarded, no matter how awkward and indecent they were. It is only then that we can prevent their depravity from repeating.

The planetary pilgrimages of William F. Lee, III, noted space traveler, have resulted in his knowing some incredible and improbable people... and some of them had or have interesting backgrounds. One thing is certain: Confronting demons of the past is often uncomfortable, but necessary to our survival as a species.

It should also be noted that Michael Lockett Garrett, that enormously great 5′ 9″ 180 lb. running-back who won the Heisman Award, would eventually be appointed as the athletic director at the University of Southern California, and in a bold move which at the time was controversial and unpopular, hired Pete Carroll as his head coach. Carroll's hiring would herald the most successful run of Pac10 and National Championships for the football squads at USC.

CHAPTER TWENTY-EIGHT

Gravity

> "Every normal person, in fact, is only normal on the average. His ego approximates to that of the psychotic in some part or other and to a greater or lesser extent." —*Sigmund Freud*

There is a scene in the now iconic motion picture about the life of Jimmy Piersall, *Fear Strikes Out*, in which Piersall, whose #37 predated Bill Lee's, in a moment of, well, craziness, climbs the screen behind home plate at the alleged precise moment that he suffers a nervous breakdown.... It made for intense drama... except it never happened. Hey, a good producer embellishes some, right? However, an earthling named Bill "Spaceman" Lee really did climb the backstop immediately following a major league game.

Unlike Jimmy Piersall, Bill Lee, at least to my knowledge, has never undergone shock treatments or been fitted for one of those "continental sports coats," you know, the ones without sleeves. Bill Lee did, however, climb the screen behind home plate. The incident occurred, where else, but Detroit, and it happened on the afternoon of April 26, 1975.

Even Bill Lee's detractors refer to the Spaceman in baseball parlance as a "competitor." In other words, he hates losing. In fact, he despises losing. Bill has never for a moment given less than complete effort while on the ball field. It is just not in his DNA.

The afternoon of April 26, 1975 began ominously for the Spaceman. He had allowed the powerful Detroit Tigers lineup runs in both the first and third inning, the third inning run abetted by an error by terrific defensive third baseman Rico Petrocelli which led to an unearned run. However, Bill Lee pitched magnificently for the balance of the afternoon as he hurled shutout ball from the fourth inning through the ninth. Some of you old enough may recall that in the days of what was REAL baseball, pitchers roamed the earth, ones whose ability and intent was to go the distance.

To settle down after an inauspicious beginning requires determination, a strong will and a competitive spirit, and Bill Lee was fortified with all of the above, and if it necessitated even more, as in hurling extra innings, the Spaceman was all in.

It should have served as an ominous sign upon seeing the Red Sox leaving the bases loaded in the top of the tenth inning. As what was left of the sparse crowd of 9,594 at Tiger Stadium looked on, both Jim Rice and Juan Beniquez struck out with the bases loaded. Then Bill Lee, gamer, took the ball and went out to once more finish what he had started. In 1975 there were few "middle relievers," "short relievers," or an overabundance of legitimate "closers." Back then men were men and the sheep were very afraid.

In the bottom of the tenth inning Tom Veryzer led off with a single against Bill and Aurelio Rodriguez sacrificed him to second. No problem as Ron LeFlore, who would become a teammate of Bill's in Montreal, hit a soft fly ball to right field for the second out. Bill then faced Gary Sutherland with the winning run perched at second base with two out.

Unfortunately for Bill and the Red Sox, standing perhaps sixty feet over his left shoulder was Red Sox Doug "Dude" Griffin, a rail-thin second baseman who had this annoying habit of playing ground balls off to his side, rather than getting "in front" of them. In other words, block them with his body. His style of "defense" was reminiscent of a matador avoiding the charging bull with his cape. Ole! However, the game being played was called "baseball" and there were no charging bulls, but rather baseballs, or in this case, a baseball heading towards him.

Bill had performed his job that day and was about to conclude the tenth inning until Doug Griffin got in the way... actually Griffin did not get in the way, and that was the problem. The Spaceman induced Sutherland to hit a bouncing ball towards him. As was his wont, Griffin played the ball off to his side. The ball took a weird hop and "Dude" failed to block it, an act that required thinking. After all, even if Sutherland reached base, the runner at second would have merely advanced to third base.... *Olé!* Obviously, the ball bounced softly beyond the sieve known as Doug Griffin and Tom Veryzer happily raced from second base to home plate with the winning run, or in this case, the "losing" run for the Spaceman.

Only a professional athlete who has put in extreme effort under daunting conditions knows what it's like to lose, but "losing" such a contest because of circumstances that were based on a lack of fundamentals, irked the "gamer" known as Bill Lee.

Bill Lee, apparently imitating an enraged bull, one who had been gored by the sword of Doug Griffin, charged off of the field and headed towards the screen behind home plate.... Yes, the Spaceman did what Jimmy

Piersall had been purported to do in the motion picture *Fear Strikes Out*. Bill leaped atop the backstop and proceeded to climb the screen.

Shortly after alighting from his perch behind home plate, Bill was approached by the Detroit Tigers legendary broadcaster, the great Ernie Harwell, who congratulated the Spaceman for his noble effort—in the game, that is, and not for his ascent atop the backstop. A two-minute live interview ensued, one of which only a great reporter of Harwell's stature could have conducted.

The Spaceman eventually made his way into the clubhouse where he went on a tirade that would have impressed Tommy Lasorda. Bill's diatribe was accentuated by his literally ripping off his uniform. Most players merely remove their livery after the game is concluded, but Bill Lee is nothing if not unconventional.

Rod Dedeaux, Bill's legendary coach at USC would no doubt be proud of Bill's "protest" against the lack of proper fundamentals in baseball.

It should be noted that although Jimmy Piersall had never actually climbed the screen behind home plate, that at one time during his minor league career, he had been ejected from the game and simply relocated himself to the roof of the stadium and commenced to squirt the home plate umpire with a water gun from his perch behind the netting.

Many years ago, the author met Jimmy Piersall, who I consider one of the greatest defensive center fielders I have ever seen. I vividly recall seeing Jimmy taking these short mincing steps as he patrolled center field, ones in which he appeared to be some sort of predator sneaking up on his prey, in his case, a baseball. I remarked to Mr. Piersall that I considered him to be at least the equal of Willie Mays defensively. Jimmy Piersall, and he was dead serious, responded, "Willie made more errors in one season than I did in five years!"

I peered at the Spaceman's predecessor and must have appeared incredulous at his statement. Jimmy smiled and said, "Don't get me wrong, Willie was the best, but he took more chances than I did."

I laughed at Piersall's remark all the way home. Then I pulled out the record book. During the 1954 season, perhaps Willie Mays' most iconic year, "The Say-Hey Kid" committed a total of nine errors while playing center field superbly for the New York Giants. In the years 1960 through 1967, while playing center field, Jimmy Piersall made a total of eight errors, combined... but Jimmy Piersall climbed a total of zero screens to "Spaceman" Lee's one.

CHAPTER TWENTY-NINE

Positive Negatives

"Love, hatred and respect do not unite people as much as a common hatred for something." —*Anton Chekhov*

Haywood Sullivan and Don Zimmer were two former, mediocre at best, major league ballplayers, but they were in solidarity in regard for their common disdain for the earthling known as Bill "Spaceman" Lee. Lee represented some sort of mystifying refinement and neither gentleman saw a need for any amount of enlightenment that this space traveler could offer. Much better than to ship Bill Lee to a foreign country as a punitive measure, regardless that in their haste to discipline their star hurler, they would choke up a huge hairball and a 14-game lead to the Yankees.

Stan Papi was the name of the "athlete" the Red Sox acquired for Bill "Spaceman" Lee, erstwhile winner of seventeen games for three consecutive seasons (1973-1975). The thought was likely, ship the bastard to a "foreign" country, in this case, Canada, and to a place where the "Spaceman" would become a member of a poor ball club. Obviously, as they overlooked most things "baseball," as the sport confused them, they never reasoned that they were jettisoning Lee to a young team coming into its own.

Stan Papi was at the utmost, a marginal major leaguer. Although he could not hit, to be brutally honest, he could not field either, those two requirements generally considered prerequisites for major league players other than pitchers. And since Stan Papi was not a pitcher either, well, he was mostly useless to his new bosses, the Red Sox. The Fenway Faithful also let Red Sox ownership know about their displeasure regarding the absurdly one-sided deal. Fortunately for Stan Papi, he received little abuse from the Boston fans since he was so pathetic he seldom appeared on the field of play. Oh, but on local sports talk radio, the hierarchy of the Red Sox were described in extremely unflattering terms by both sportscasters and angry fans who had thrilled to the exploits of the "Spaceman," who entertained them both on and off the field.

For the record, and it was not a good one, Stan Papi batted .188 with one home run and six RBI's in 1979. To make matters worse, at least for the hapless shortstop, Papi's lifetime fielding percentage was a lowly .931. Bill Lee, in fact, would resurrect his career in Montreal, where he would be named National League Left-Handed Pitcher of the Year, posting an outstanding 16-10 record with a great 3.04 ERA. Not only that, but Bill would outhit Papi by batting .216 in 1979, .220 in 1980 and a team-LEADING .364 in his final full-season for the Expos in 1981, a campaign in which he also compiled a .500 Slugging Percentage and an OPS of .864. As for Stan Papi, he was gone from the Red Sox after that unremarkable 1979 season. But there was more to Stan Papi than meets the eye... or the pancreas for that matter.

It was widely acknowledged, after it became public, of course, that Stan Papi had been diagnosed with hypoglycemia, a serious health condition, albeit not one categorized as a "disease."

Note: For full disclosure, the author Scott Russell, or perhaps Kilgore Trout—that remains up for conjecture—is a bit of an expert regarding hypoglycemia. You see, his long-suffering bride, Peg, was diagnosed with hypoglycemia in late 2006. The lone reason the author is an "expert" is simply because after his wife Peg's diagnosis, he was given a rather vast education regarding the disorder by some of the most learned doctors in the world. Upon Peg's primary care physician, an award-winning Massachusetts General Hospital doctor named Dr. Michael Bierer stating that "true" hypoglycemia was rare and often misdiagnosed because of confusion in regard to certain types of medications used to combat diabetes, such as insulin and sulfonylureas, two drugs commonly administered, the presence of low blood sugar dropping below normal levels was often mistaken for "actual" hypoglycemia. The fact that Peg did not and does not have diabetes was the first clue. Therefore, Dr. Bierer sent her to a brilliant endocrinologist, Dr. Juan Carlos Pallais, then of MGH and now at Brigham & Women's Hospital in Boston.

Dr. Pallais, as affable and charming as any doctor we have ever met and the pride of Nicaragua, confirmed the rarity of Peg's condition! Despite not having diabetes, as Peg learned from Dr. Pallais, INVARIABLY "actual" hypoglycemia is caused by a tumor in the pancreas. Voila! An ultrasound, X-rays as well as other examinations indeed, located the tumor! Peg indeed, had "actual" hypoglycemia!

It should also be noted that symptoms of hypoglycemia include clumsiness, difficulty in speaking, confusion, loss of consciousness, and even seizures. Hypoglycemia was renowned as a condition in those days, as one in which the affected patient often acted strangely. This, as some of the author's caustic acquaintances have said, is no doubt the reason Peg agreed to marry him in the first place! The girl had to be confused.

The next step for Dr. Pallais was to summon a superb surgeon named Dr. Juan Fernandez del-Castillo to examine Peg, and then to schedule delicate surgery to remove the tumor. The surgery was performed at Massachusetts General Hospital in January of 2007. Peg was on the operating table for nearly four hours and the surgery was eminently successful, although she was still stuck with her nitwit husband afterwards. He could not be surgically removed.

At the time Dr. Fernandez del-Castillo performed his magic, he was only one of a handful of doctors in one of only three hospitals in the United States capable of such wizardry. Despite having graduated from the large University in Mexico City, where he hailed from, Dr. Fernandez del-Castillo had earned additional medical degrees from perhaps the most prestigious university in the U.S., namely Johns Hopkins University. Because of the positioning of the tumor which lay near vital organs, the surgery was quite tricky, but again, Peg had a wizard for a surgeon, and a young one at that.

Back to Stan Papi who had been diagnosed with hypoglycemia. To this moment I am not aware if the man traded for Bill Lee had "actual" hypoglycemia. However, it had been reported that Stan Papi had often exhibited what was described as "somewhat bizarre behavior."

Upon Papi's trade to the Red Sox, legendary *Boston Globe* and *Sports Illustrated* columnist, Peter Gammons wrote an article regarding Papi's arrival in Boston and the fact that he had battled the illness. You see, while Papi battled the condition, it was explained that several folks in Papi's life had mistaken his illness for, well, a touch of insanity. (Peg is painfully aware of that since she married a madman while she was in its throes).

Within days following Gammons' thoughtful and educational article, Peter Gammons began receiving phone calls at his desk. A large quantity of the calls Peter was receiving were from people pleading for his help. Many of these callers were calling from the confines of mental institutions! "Please, Mr. Gammons. Tell them that I'm not crazy! Tell them I have hypoglycemia!"

Peter Gammons, as I recall, felt horribly. While he fully realized that the vast majority of the calls were either crank calls and many even perhaps from legitimately crazy people, what if, he thought, that five percent of them were actually from those misdiagnosed because of hypoglycemia?! As I also recall, Peter Gammons placed a sign above his desk in the office that read, "Hypoglycemia Hotline."

It certainly appeared upon reading Peter Gammons' outstanding article that Stan Papi had mistakenly been identified as some sort of loony until his condition had been diagnosed properly. It was then evident to the reader that Stan Papi had been a "victim" of his disorder. We should point out, however, a poignant and hilarious and yet true tale regarding the now "remedied" middle infielder.

One of Bill Lee's good friends is a lovely young lady who worked for a cable television company in western Massachusetts. Her name is Lynne "Line Drive" Nelson, and she was tagged with the sobriquet by legendary Red Sox broadcaster, the late Ned Martin, since there was a major league player in the 1940s named "Line Drive" Nelson. Lynne conducted numerous television interviews with Boston athletes at her company's studio in Westfield, Massachusetts.

Despite the fact that Lynne was a bit downtrodden over the trade of her good friend, the Spaceman being a hospitable person, she decided to invite the newly acquired Stan Papi to the studio in order to introduce him to the fans of Boston. Lynne arrived at the studio from her home in Wilbraham, but was merely five minutes late.

I should preface the following by saying that Lynne has a delightful sense of humor and a quick wit. Before she could even apologize for being five minutes late, upon arriving at the lobby of the studio, she found Stan Papi pacing back and forth like a caged tiger. The new Red Sox player appeared quite perturbed as he scolded, "Where have you been?! Everyone is staring at me!" I should now note that other than Stan Papi there were only three other people in the lobby. One was the receptionist and the other two were a middle-aged couple deeply in conversation with each other. Stan Papi was virtually alone, except apparently in his own mind.

Lynne Nelson peered incredulously at the newcomer to the Red Sox and responded, "Staring at you? No one is even looking at you, that is, until now. No one even knows who the hell you are!" It was then that Lynne thought to herself, "Yes, and I suspect that no one ever will!"

Well, Lynne was nearly correct, since no one in New England would ever be capable of picking Stan Papi out of a police lineup, but he is now legend in Boston. To this day, upon being asked, knowledgeable Red Sox fans or historians respond regarding Papi's claim to fame some forty-one years later, "Say, isn't he the bum the Red Sox acquired for Bill Lee?"

The next stop for the earthling known as William Francis Lee, III was the wonderful city of Montreal, Quebec, Canada. The Spaceman achieved his craziness naturally. He did not require hypoglycemia.

CHAPTER THIRTY

A Bad Rapp?

Tranquility

"Critics are like eunuchs in a harem: they know how it's done, they've seen it done every day, but they're unable to do it themselves." —*Brendan Behan*

"I like long walks, especially when they are taken by people who annoy me." —*Fred Allen*

The Earthling named Bill Lee's spacecraft splashed down in Daytona Beach, Florida in the springtime of 1979. The now former Boston Red Sox hurler was now a member of a National League baseball team named the Montreal Expos and the occasion was to endure the rigorous annual preparation for the season by participating in what is commonly known as "Spring Training" which is held each year in order to get professional athletes physically and mentally prepared for the interminably long summer months of the "regular season."

Bill, despite his undeserved reputation as a malcontent and an outspoken rebel, aka a person having the audacity and unmitigated gall to question authority, had already been warmly welcomed by the brass of the Montreal Expos front office. Also, his "new" manager was one he was quite familiar with, Dick Williams, Bill's former skipper with the Red Sox at the very beginning of his big league career. Williams, who was unceremoniously fired by the Red Sox despite having turned the long-time defeatist mentality of the organization into one of a prideful confidence by leading a storied group of athletes to an American League pennant in 1967. That team will forever be known as "The Impossible Dream Team." Therefore, as he told Bill Lee, "Forget what happened in Boston. I hate them more than you do!"

It was upon donning his Montreal Expos uniform for the first time on the very first day of spring training that Bill was approached by a veteran of minor and major league baseball, a venerable baseball "lifer" named Vernon Fred "Vern" Rapp. Vern Rapp, fifty-one years of age at the time of his initial meeting with the Spaceman, was the first base coach of the Expos. Vern Rapp, a conservative gentleman, much like Bill's dad, was signed as a catcher upon his graduation from high school in 1945 in his native St. Louis. Vern Rapp—and you've got to love baseball to have had his will—wound up playing 16 minor league seasons, campaigns that were only interrupted for two years of military service during the Korean War. Minor league players, especially during those times, were not paid very well, so Rapp's love of the game was genuine.

Vern Rapp played in 1,016 games in the minor leagues during those 16 seasons and never made it to the big leagues. However, he became a coach and a manager. His commitment to the game was never questioned. Rapp at one time, albeit briefly, managed the St. Louis Cardinals in 1977-78 and the Cincinnati Reds in 1984. However, as Vern Rapp approached Bill Lee on that warm spring day in Daytona Beach, Florida, the Spaceman wasn't exactly expecting the "hello" he received from the baseball "warhorse."

"I just want you to know that I don't like the way you look, I don't like the way you act, I don't like the way you dress, I don't like your beard, I don't like the way you think, and I don't like your politics."

Although momentarily stunned, Bill Lee composed himself and replied, "It's nice to meet you, too, sir." Vern Rapp turned and walked away. Somewhat implausibly, the two men never again spoke during the entirety of spring training, that is, until the day the Expos were breaking camp and flying north to begin the 1979 season.

On the very last day of spring camp with the bags packed and flights scheduled, Vern Rapp suddenly approached the surprised Spaceman, who turned upon hearing Vern Rapp calling his name.

"Bill, I just want you to know that I've been in professional baseball for thirty-four years and I've never seen anyone more dedicated to the game. I've never seen anyone put in the effort or the time that you do, and I've never seen anyone do more running or working on the fundamentals of the game than you do. It's been an honor to watch you work at your craft throughout this spring."

Vern Rapp then turned on his heels and began walking away, but he suddenly wheeled around and concluded with, "But I still don't like your politics."

Bill Lee, to this moment, does not treasure any compliment paid to him more than the one he received by his coach on that day. Vern Rapp and Bill Lee are both throwbacks to the days when civil discourse was possible and respect, albeit grudgingly, was given to those deserving of it. Those that engage in today's highly partisan politics could learn a lot from those two men. Two generations collided that spring and neither gave an inch, nor did they have to. It is somewhat refreshing to peer back at a time when an "adversary" was judged by his deeds and merits and not partisanship.

CHAPTER THIRTY-ONE

Le Homme de L'Espace

"Truth never penetrates an unwilling mind." —*Jose Luis Borges*

After our brother, the Spaceman, was traded to the Montreal Expos for a hypoglycemic utility infielder named Stan Papi on December 7, 1978, a group of us, the author included, convened at the Eliot Lounge in order to discuss a surprise going-away party for our mutual friend. Included in our gang of misfits, incorrigibles, and Bulgarian midget worshippers, were a who's who of Boston notables. These people comprised a notable group of accomplished professionals, yours truly notwithstanding. There was a noble gentleman named Dick Waterman, a remarkable writer, concert promoter, and the agent for many of the most legendary Mississippi Delta blues artists ever recorded. Dick Waterman's biography, in fact, is told eloquently in a book titled *Dick Waterman: A Life in Blues* by Tammy L. Turner, a marvelous writer. I should add that Dick Waterman was also Bonnie Raitt's "road manager," but as I learned later, he was much more than just that.

Other "sponsors" of the Spaceman's going-away bash were the great, late George Kimball; Eliot Lounge proprietor Don Akin; Andy Anderson, a Rhode Island golf companion; Cambridge author Jane Appleton; the *Boston Globe's* Peter Gammons; fellow writer Michael Gee; Bill's closest friend, Mike Mulkern; and the zany WBCN radio personality, Charles Laquidara.

Each of us invited ten guests and we enlisted several Boston University hockey players to keep the peace (imagine hockey players insuring peace). We had rented the Harvard Boat Club in Cambridge on the Charles River on a snowy night in February. As for it being a "surprise party," Bill called the author earlier that week to inform him that he was aware of the planned "ambush" because his soon-to-be-former teammate Dwight Evans had telephoned him and the conversation went something like this:

Evans: Hey, Bill, I'm afraid I cannot make it to your party this week.
Bill: What party?
Evans: The party at the Cambridge Boat Club.

Upon calling me, the Spaceman said, "Don't worry, Scotty, I'll act surprised."

We had written our invitations in French!

The legendary Boston based band, "The James Montgomery Blues Band," graciously supplied their talent free of charge, and Celtics great Dave "Red" Cowens arrived to pay his respects. Bonnie Raitt, who was performing elsewhere, forwarded a gracious message.

We had arranged a modest bar and a small buffet for our guests, but upon arrival we noticed that the entire affair had been catered! There was a sumptuous offering of raw oysters, clams, roast beef and ham, and enough liquor to sink the *Titanic*. We soon learned that it was all due to the quiet generosity and graciousness of the aforementioned Dick Waterman! We thanked the humble man of blues profusely.

To make the evening even more poignant and hilarious, we had all pitched in and presented Bill with a sterling silver bowl, but it was what was inscribed inside of the bowl that elicited a side-splitting reaction from the Spaceman. Don Zimmer, Bill's nemesis in Boston, had scolded Bill with, "Someday you won't even have a pot to piss in!" Therefore, we had etched into the bowl, "Here's your pot, now go piss in it!"

During their contentious relationship as manager and pitcher, Zimmer, not a particularly tolerant man, especially when he felt humor directed at him, was, well—not funny!—was extremely upset by Bill apparently calling him a "gerbil." However, the nickname derived from a compliment! In what was intended as a harmless reference, any respect Don Zimmer retained for Bill Lee was gone upon the manager hearing that the Spaceman had referred to him as a "gerbil." Regardless that its aim was merely to make a comparison to a much less "admired" animal, Zimmer was infuriated.

During a rather pointless question posed to the Spaceman by an out-of-town journalist, Bill was asked the following question: "If Billy Martin (Yankees manager at the time) were a member of the animal kingdom, what would he be?"

Note: Bill Lee and Billy Martin were avowed foes. Martin, a combative manager, often got into physical altercations with opposing players, and tellingly, with his own teammates. Martin's often violent behavior was often fueled by his reputation as a heavy drinker.

Bill's response regarding Billy Martin, who admittedly despised the

Spaceman, was "If Billy Martin were a member of the animal kingdom, he'd be a no-good dirty rat. His eyes are always darting around like a rat and he's got the demeanor of a rat."

Bill was then asked about his own manager, Don Zimmer. The Spaceman replied, "Zim would be a gerbil. Zim's fat and he's puffy and he's got big cheeks. Kids like him. If they were casting for a remake of *Damn Yankees*, he should get the role. On top of that I really like his wife (Soot). She's really nice."

Unfortunately, all Don Zimmer heard was the word "gerbil," or at least that is the only word he acknowledged. As Lee explained, "It was basically a compliment, but he took it the wrong way."

The oversensitive manager had no love lost for pitchers and particularly those who spoke their mind. To make matters worse, the Boston press, already not enamored with what most of them felt were Zimmer's failures as the skipper, absolutely loved the sobriquet supplied by Bill Lee, "The Gerbil." Zimmer was already being reviled in the press and this provided the media with additional fuel to ridicule him. And all of this happened because of what Lee believed to be an innocuous offhanded remark.

It mattered little: Bill Lee was on his way to Montreal, Quebec, Canada, and he had his pot to piss in.

CHAPTER THIRTY-TWO

Popeye and "Popeye's"

"The problem with the world is that the intelligent people are full of doubt, while the stupid ones are full of confidence."
—*Charles Bukowski*

Question: Do you hate people?
"I don't hate them.... I just feel better when they're not around."
—*Charles Bukowski*

Despite his having many detractors in Boston, to be fair, Don Zimmer also had a decent amount of people that admired him. Make no mistake, Zimmer, with his butchering of the English language and its nuances which he never bothered to even consider investigating, could be charming. Zimmer would often hold court with reporters in the dugout and he'd regale them with tales of his days with the Brooklyn Dodgers and the writers would feast in regard to learning of the days of Jackie Robinson, Duke Snider, Roy Campanella, Carl Furillo, Gil Hodges, and the many other legends he had played with.

To be clear, however, Zimmer did not appreciate "free-thinkers" and never considered that each of the men's lives he was describing in detail were indeed, individualists, and several of them iconic because of their varying backgrounds and vastly differing traits.

What Don Zimmer failed to master was that each individual player had to be treated differently and that the majority of successful managers and coaches in professional sports did not treat their players equally, and that is precisely the reason they were successful. The adage "Twenty-five cabs for twenty-five players" often applied to championship teams. Players did not have to socialize or even like each other to win games, but rather to come together on the field of play. Competition amongst teammates, in fact, often resulted in greater cohesion between teammates. Consider the 1970's championship teams of the Oakland Athletics, who would literally battle each other off the field, and the Oakland Raiders (what's up with Oakland?) who were a zany bunch of misfits, but championship ones at that.

Eccentric and high-strung athletes have also marched to their own drummers. Consider "Babe" Ruth, Mickey Mantle, Ken Stabler, Pete Rose, and Ty Cobb, to name a few. Oh, and of course, Bill "Spaceman" Lee. The idea is not to inhibit distinctive athletes by restricting them, but to fortify them by treating each differently. Don Zimmer never understood this concept.

I recall the great Hall of Fame New York Yankees manager Casey Stengel being asked by a reporter a question regarding several of his star players being involved in a brawl at the Copa Cabana one booze-filled early morning in New York City. "Casey," he was asked, "what are you planning to discipline the players involved in the fracas?" The players included Mickey Mantle, Hank Bauer, Billy Martin, and "Whitey" Ford, who comprised much of the strength of the ball club.

Casey Stengel immediately responded, "Discipline them? What for? I'm going to send my milk-drinkers out to join them next time, 'cause none of them are hittin' worth a damn!"

Casey Stengel was also once quoted as saying, "The idea of successful managing is to keep the five players who hate you away from the other twenty players that are undecided."

Several readers are most likely thinking that perhaps I was too harsh in describing Zimmer's faults, especially in when considering how I poked fun at his less than articulate speech. Lest you believe that, I will now draw an analogy to another less than articulate manager, a wonderful man named Charles Fuqua Manuel, the former manager of the Cleveland Indians and the World Champion Philadelphia Phillies. "Ol' Charlie," and he'll never have to buy a drink in Philadelphia for the remainder of his lifetime, has a thick Appalachian accent and he's never been accused of sounding like William Shakespeare, and was perhaps one of the greatest managers in MLB history. Manuel treated each of his players as individuals, and in the nine seasons he was allowed to complete, his teams never finished lower than second place, and he won five consecutive Division titles and a World Series. Charlie was also a great hitting coach.

Then there was the great Jack McKeon (John McKeown) who won a World Series with perhaps the lowest payroll in baseball. The year was 1993 and he won with a young talented hard-throwing right-handed youngster named Josh Beckett, who for lack of a better term is, well, a complete asshole. He won by handling Beckett sternly, but also by allowing him to flourish.

Beckett, who would continue to earn his stripes as a complete asshole later, was a brash flamethrower, but one who did not display the same dedication to the game as the Spaceman. Jack McKeon, an auxiliary police officer in his hometown in New Jersey during the off-season, had an eye for troublemakers, for lack of a better description.

Josh Beckett would often disappear from the dugout during games and re-emerge after a lengthy absence. It did not take too long before McKeon, a man with vast experience in the field, detected the empty beer cups that Beckett had deposited near his locker.

The following day, Beckett attempted to enter the locker room during the game, but found the door locked.

"Hey, Skip, the door is locked."

"I know," said the worldly McKeon.

Josh Beckett responded, "Well, I've gotta go to the bathroom."

With that, the venerable manager handed his twenty-two year-old hurler a "bathroom pass," the ones that were once handed to grade school children back in the day. McKeon then unlocked the door.

"You've got five minutes to return or I'm coming to get you." McKeon warned.

"Why?" the startled Beckett replied.

Jack McKeon, bless his heart, and he is still around to confirm the story, replied, "If you're going to act like school children, you'll be treated like school children."

Several years earlier, as a minor league manager, Jack McKeon, the auxiliary policeman during the off-season, was also licensed to carry a gun. McKeon, who also served as the third base coach, managed a rather over-aggressive outfielder who had this annoying habit of foolishly running past McKeon's stop signs and getting thrown out at home plate. The time came that McKeon had seen enough of his over-exuberant base runner. Therefore, he informed his belligerent player, "The next time you run past my stop sign I'm going to shoot you." The player smiled.

Within days, that very same player was at first base with none out as the hitter lined a ball in the gap. As the ball was retrieved and thrown to the cut-off man, here came Jack McKeon's obstinate runner. The player once more failed to recognize McKeon, who held both hands aloft signaling for him to stop at third base. With total disregard, the athlete continued to run towards McKeon, who was now backpedaling towards home plate. As the runner approached, Jack McKeon, and again, he would confirm this, removed the pistol from his back pocket and shot his runaway base runner in the chest from point-blank range.

The "wounded" athlete collapsed in a heap, perhaps forty feet from home plate. He peered down at his chest and rubbed his fingers over the injury, fully expecting to see blood on his fingertips. Hey, even "blanks" hurt like hell, and this poor bastard really thought he had been shot with an actual bullet!

Jack McKeon stood over his fallen outfielder and remarked calmly, "I told you if you ever ran through a stop sign again that I'd shoot you."

By now, the catcher stood approximately thirty feet away from the downed player. The young catcher was frozen in place as he held the baseball in his hands. He stared incredulously at the smiling Jack McKeon. The catcher was literally afraid of getting any closer to the scene of the "crime." McKeon looked at the shocked catcher as he replaced the revolver back in his pocket and said softly, "It's all right, son. You can tag him out now." Oh, that player never again ran through another stop sign.

Several years later, Josh Beckett, Jon Lester, and another complete asshole named John Lackey, managed to get their GREAT manager Terry Francona, fired, by their continually drinking beer, eating "Popeye's Chicken," and playing video games DURING ballgames. As the *Boston Globe's* Bob Hohler also reported, they cut back on their exercise regimens, despite appeals from the team's strength and conditioning coach, Dave Page. This resulted in the Red Sox blowing a substantial lead in their division and thus getting their manager canned. Rules don't apply to some.... In fairness to Jon Lester, a good guy, he owned up to his role in the fiasco.

It should also be noted that by 2012, Popeye's Chicken in Kenmore Square placed a huge and hilarious banner outside of their establishment which read, "FOUR OUT OF EVERY FIVE PITCHERS PREFER OUR CHICKEN BEST."

Don "Popeye" Zimmer, nicknamed "Popeye" because of his resemblance to the cartoon character, managed for 13 years, but never took his team to the World Series or won a pennant (he did win one division) and never adapted to individuals. The Spaceman was on his way to resurrecting his career in Montreal, but there were also considerable roadblocks ahead in that city, as well.

CHAPTER THIRTY-THREE

Splashdown in Montreal

"The future is inevitable and precise, but it may not occur. God lurks in the gaps." —*Jose Luis Borges*

"I am a compassionate misanthrope." —*Bill "Spaceman" Lee*

In 1979 while the earthling William Francis Lee, III was in the process of resurrecting his outstanding baseball career, the combination of Don Zimmer and Haywood Sullivan were proceeding, albeit unintentionally, the demise of both their careers and therefore, the Red Sox. The baseball team left in the wake of the departures of Ferguson Jenkins, Rick Wise, Luis Tiant, and Bill Lee continued its inexorable slide into oblivion and ignominy. While the quartet of former Red Sox pitchers succeeded elsewhere, the Red Sox rotation now featured the likes of Steve Renko, Chuck Rainey, and Joel Finch.... Who...? Exactly.

Back in Beantown, the Fenway faithful saw their team slip to third place in 1979 and to fifth place in 1980. Of course, Don Zimmer was out of a job, but not for too long. There were more games to lose elsewhere. Once more, the theory that people are promoted to their level of incompetence would be validated. We are all employable in one manner or another.

Bill Lee's new ball club, the Montreal Expos, was a young team first coming into its own. The first two players to introduce themselves to the Spaceman in Daytona Beach were left-fielder Warren "Cro" Cromartie and Hall of Fame first baseman Tony Perez. Tony Perez, in fact, had been the backbone of the great Cincinnati Reds powerhouse team, "The Big Red Machine." Tony was in the twilight of his Hall of Fame career by 1979, but he could still flat out hit. Tony had blasted a mammoth two-run home run off Bill in game seven of the 1975 World Series, a shot which cut Boston's 3-0 lead to 3-2. Bill would leave the game in the seventh inning and the Boston bullpen would relinquish the lead, the game, and of course, the World Series.

Ironically, Bill and his former wife Mary Lou would become great friends with Tony and his wife Pituka, two of the genuinely nicest people on the planet. The '79 Expos also featured a future Hall of Fame centerfielder named Andre Dawson, whose knees would be ravaged by the artificial turf of Stade Olympique, the home base for the ball club. The right-fielder, a great person named Ellis Valentine, was a power-hitting, rifle-armed, terrific all-round ballplayer. That young African American outfield of Cromartie, a line-drive hitter, Dawson and Valentine had no peer in major league baseball. Bill's catcher was another Hall of Famer, Gary Carter, who was not only popular, but "worked" on his image, and that is not a criticism. He enjoyed being a role-model.

The Expos had another young African American named Rodney Scott, a rail-thin slightly built second basemen who hailed from Indianapolis. Bill and Rodney, whose moniker was "Cool Breeze," became good friends and often shared some weed together. I can assure you they were not alone in that regard. Rodney and Bill are still good friends in the year 2020.

Breeze, although not a great hitter, was one of the more fundamentally sound and intelligent players in the game. He hit enough, but what he accomplished on the base paths and in the field was astonishing. Rodney Scott stole 39 bases, a lost art, in 1979. He followed that up with 63 steals in 1980 and another 30 stolen bases in 1981, but it was what he did defensively which set him apart. Breeze had incredible range and great hands and the pitchers appreciated the fact that he took away countless opposing runs with his stellar defense.

Bill Lee's National League debut; and he was thrilled because he once more had an opportunity to play actual "baseball," and not the crap instituted by weak minds in 1973 that invoked the "designated hitter rule," which according to the Spaceman, heralded "the end of civilization as we know it." Bill Lee would once more be able to bat, and he was a much better hitter than Stan Papi, the half-crazed hypoglycemic utility infielder he was traded for.

The Spaceman's N.L. debut came at the seedy, but historic venue of Shea Stadium in Long Island, Queens, N.Y. Bill pitched a solid eight innings allowing just seven hits and two runs, but left tied 2-2. The Expos would go on to win the game 3-2.

Bill's second start was memorable for lots of reasons. First of all, it was his initial start at his new home field, Olympic Stadium in Montreal, and it also marked his introduction to the young fans of Montreal, many of whom had already "adopted" Bill as their hero, much like the Fenway

Faithful did back home in the U.S. You see, Bill had already displayed his enormous wit while in spring training at Daytona Beach, and his remarks once more would find him in hot water with the conservative hierarchy of major league baseball.

Back in Daytona Beach, under the palm trees, the Spaceman was holding court one day with the Montreal press, many of whom had not yet been privileged to hear Bill's somewhat outrageous sense of humor. However, it was a question posed by a visiting Boston writer (they were scheduled to play the Red Sox in an exhibition game) that fueled what would once more be "controversy." According to Dick Lally in his outstanding book, *The Wrong Stuff*, the Boston scribe asked, "There's one question we've been dying to ask you for a long time. Was there any sort of drug problem on the Red Sox?" Bill responded, tongue firmly planted in cheek, "There sure was. I think the entire team abused nicotine, caffeine, and alcohol far too much."

As stated in Lally's book, "I explained that coffee and amphetamines were not being used for kicks, they were being used to sober up. A player did not gulp down greenies with the expectation that it would enhance his performance. He did it to get his pulse going on the morning after the night before. The reporter wasn't satisfied that his question had been answered, so he said, 'No, I don't mean coffee or greenies. I was wondering if the club had a problem with marijuana?'

"I said, 'Hell, no. How could they? I've been using that stuff since 1968, and I've never had a problem with it.'" Twenty pencils hit the floor simultaneously.

The following day, of course, the headlines in Canada and elsewhere read, "Lee Admits to Smoking Marijuana!"

Bowie Kuhn, the extremely conservative Commissioner of Major League Baseball immediately sprung into "action." Bill was soon visited by some lame-brained pencil and notepad carrying geek named Art Fuss, who informed the Spaceman that he was sent by the commissioner to in order to "clarify" Bill's comments.

Art Fuss, and he was writing everything down in his small notepad (he was one helluva secretary) asked, "We'd like to hear more about your smoking marijuana."

Bill, a ball-buster extraordinaire, responded, "I never said I smoked marijuana. I only said that I had 'used' it." Art Fuss had a job to do, and he was going to get to the bottom of this, come hell or high water, or in this case, some hilarious bullshit. Therefore, he asked Bill, "How do you use marijuana without smoking it?"

The Spaceman, eager to set the record straight, explained, "Each morning I run five miles to the ballpark. After waking up, I prepare myself for this arduous task by making a huge batch of organic buckwheat pancakes. I sprinkle the marijuana on the pancakes while they are cooking. The THC absorbed by the pancakes makes me impervious to all the bus fumes and other forms of air pollution I may encounter while running."

Art Fuss, God bless him, bought it lock, stock and barrel. Bill considered asking him if he wanted to buy a bridge, too, but then reasoned that the poor man had already destroyed more than enough brain cells during their brief conversation.

Bill eventually heard from the Commissioner's office, who told him that his comments were "not in the best interests of baseball." He was fined, of course, and advised to refrain from future such statements. Meanwhile, unknown to the Spaceman, thanks to the media, as he had previously in Boston, he had already become a counter-culture hero to the fans of Montreal.

It was at Olympic Stadium in Montreal that Bill would make his first start in front of his new fans. Pitching versus the Chicago Cubs, the Spaceman hurled a masterpiece, going the full nine innings and allowing only two hits in a 2-0 victory. Bill's mound opponent was an excellent right-hander named Mike "The Polish Prince" Krukow, who would go on to become one of the wittiest broadcasters in baseball history. Teaming with Duane Kuiper, "Kruk & Kuip" would become legend in San Francisco. But it was what occurred on the pitching mound that day which made the game even more memorable for Bill Lee.

As Bill Lee hurled shutout ball against a formidable Chicago Cubs lineup, he noticed that small objects seemed to be landing around him on the pitching mound. They seemed to be small spheres of some sort. Bill thought to himself, "These fans are fucking crazy. What the hell are they doing?" Then one of the tiny objects hit him in the chest and fell at his feet. "Ow! That hurt!" The Spaceman peered down at the piece of tinfoil that had struck him and then landed harmlessly on the mound. Bill bent over to pick it up. Bill placed the tinfoil in his pocket and between innings, he investigated its contents. He then realized that the objects were hashish and marijuana wrapped tightly in tinfoil! After returning to the mound in the following inning, Bill made sure to retrieve the other pieces of tinfoil that lay scattered around the mound. He placed them all in his pocket. Bill received a bonus of thirteen grams of hash that day!

From that moment on, the Spaceman, now a firmly established hero, especially in the beautiful cobblestone streets of old Montreal, a place where both the young French and English of the city gathered, would always tip his cap upon receiving another "flying gift" from his adoring fans.

There would be many more great games hurled by Bill Lee in that remarkable season of 1979. They would include a 2-0 six-hit shutout victory over the Phillies on May 30, an eight-inning one-run gem (unearned run) at Atlanta on June 4, another complete game seven-hit shutout versus the Los Angeles Dodgers on July 9, and a combined 2-0 shutout on August 24 at Atlanta. The Spaceman, who was "washed up" according to Don Zimmer and Haywood Sullivan, had compiled a 16-10, 3.04 mark in Montreal, and was named "The National League Left-Handed Pitcher of the Year," by both wire services.... But the conservative establishment of major league baseball simply didn't like the Spaceman or what they believed he represented.

CHAPTER THIRTY-FOUR

A Confederacy of Dunces

> "When a true genius appears in the world, you may know him by this sign, that the dunces are all in confederacy against him."
> *—Jonathan Swift, borrowed from* A Confederacy of Dunces *by John Kennedy Toole*

> "Wise men speak because they have something to say, fools because they have to say something." *—Plato*

The four elements that have always been present within the heart and mind of the earthling named William Francis Lee, III, have been friendship, truth, loyalty, and honor. In the early 1980s, an astoundingly great journalist named George M. Plasketes wrote an essay regarding the man known as the Spaceman. The name of the work apropos of Bill Lee emanated in a publication called *The Journal of Popular Culture* and it appeared in Volume 21, Issue 1 of the periodical.

The author, George M. Plasketes, at the time was an assistant professor of mass communications at Auburn University in Auburn, Alabama. Of all of the articles ever recorded in regard to Bill Lee, I feel confident that Professor Plasketes truly captured the very essence of the man known as "Spaceman."

The article is titled, "The Rebel Hero in Baseball: Bill 'Spaceman' Lee in an Orbit All his Own."

Note: The quotes attributed to Bill Lee in this chapter appeared in this article.

In the piece written by George Plasketes, he describes Lee as "intelligent, stubborn and articulate, the free-spirited lefthander has been baseball's Yossarian*, a sole voice of sanity in a game run by 'planet-polluting owners' and played by 'blood-thirsty carnivores.'"

> * Yossarian was a delightful character in Joseph Heller's epic novel, *Catch-22.*

As Plasketes wrote in regard to the Rebel Hero, "The rebel hero, although gifted, is mainly characterized by a great vitality for life. The rebel hero also opposes the dominant culture. It is often the establishment, and the corruption of it, that provokes their heroism. In Lee's case, this rebellion occurs at two levels: society in general, particularly the corporate mind set and structures that violate human rights, the environment, and mother earth; and baseball's structure as a microcosm of the larger culture."

Bill Lee, on the perfect pitcher:

"Tibetan priests can sit naked in the snow at 18,000 feet and they have such powers of mental discipline, that if they put their minds to it, they can generate enough heat to melt snow for 20 feet around. Now you put that Tibetan priest on the mound, naked or not, with a baseball in his palm, and he'll take that power of concentration and make the ball disappear and then materialize down the line in the catcher's mitt."

George Plasketes also wrote:

"Lee's vitality for life is deeper than mere antics. Probably the greatest majority of his heroism is transmitted through the perspectives he offers verbally. Although an iconoclast, Lee's values and vitality for life are rooted in rather traditional values: simplicity, conservation, and loyalty to friends, among other things. In between attempts to straighten out the universe, Lee talks to animals, appreciates trees, does yoga, eats health foods, ponders Einstein, Vonnegut, and Chief Joseph, quotes from Mao, seeks psychological guidance from mystics like Ouspensky and rock musicians like Warren Zevon. In short, Lee is very aware that another world exists outside of baseball."

One need only to examine a quote issued by the Spaceman back in May of 1977 in order to fully appreciate his fears in regard to the future, many of which have already adversely affected our planet and the game of baseball, two allegedly separate subjects he doesn't feel are necessarily incongruous:

"It's just a game and not a long-term thing. The weather's gonna change before long and we'll slip back into another glacial age or we'll be sucked back in by some black hole or something due to the fact that we've polluted our planet beyond repair. Like the dinosaur became extinct, baseball will become extinct because it's become overly specialized. They went to the designated hitter... astro-turf... stadiums with no quaintness made of concrete… it's just the nature of the system's view of baseball, within the structure of the earth as a spinning spheroid with a type G star many billion times from anywhere else."

Bill Lee has actually been accused of being a "purist" or a "naturalist," as if those are less than admirable traits.

In addition to a myriad of worthy praise heaped upon the Spaceman by George Plasketes was the following:

"Another factor that perhaps contributed to Lee's values and awareness was his education, which surpassed the level of most baseball players who sign contracts out of high school and head for the minors rather than college campuses. Lee graduated from Southern Cal, where perhaps many of his social conscious attitudes and values were shaped during the 1960s. He also has a Master's degree in geography from Southern Mississippi."

Said Plasketes: "The old-guard sportswriters, like *New York Daily News* columnist Dick Young, had no use for free-thinkers like Lee, because they believed them to be dangerous to the game."

In George Plasketes' terrific essay, he quotes Bill's former Southern Cal teammate and longtime major league relief pitcher Tom House, who stated: "Deep down inside—where nobody has ever gotten to him—Bill is a great human being. It's just that in baseball the Peter Principle reaches its highest level, and the absolute worst people run the show. Bill realized very early the ludicrousness of being in a position where so many intellectual vegetables have so much authority and influence over the way he runs his life. I always thought Bill was an accident looking for a place to happen. But he's too intelligent to be self-destructive. He knows marginal players have to play by the rules. Any deviation from the norm is a ticket out. But he's a master of walking the tightrope. Bill never let anyone diminish his character. And he never will."

Later in Professor Plasketes' essay, he quotes Bill as saying, "I went to a psychiatrist at Harvard once. He said I was the greatest con artist he had ever met. He said don't dare stop."

Delving even more into George Plasketes' "The Rebel Hero in Baseball," we read, "Lee's existence and self-perception is at times filled with contradictions. Lee is a Spaceman, but he is entrenched in Mother Earth. He seeks harmony, but his protests cause disharmony. Baseball brings him peace and it brings him turmoil. Perhaps contradictions are a part of the nature and existence of the rebel hero. 'I walk the tightrope between two worlds. Between the oral and the doing, which I think are contradictory worlds,' said Lee. 'And the only way to solve contradictions is to do them both.'"

Plasketes continues, "It is not surprising then, that Lee sees himself more as more philosophical than political, because political 'just hides what's beneath.' Lee believes in a bumper sticker he once saw: 'Don't vote. It only encourages them.' He doesn't believe in political systems the way they stand, but in 'interrelation, like Chief Joseph and the Nez Perce Indians.' Lee is more concerned with irreconcilable contradictions:

"'Christians believe in God, in helping one another, and do unto others. On the other hand, atheists don't believe in God, they say we're only here for the moment, nothing else matters. Now capitalism says every man for himself, do whatever you want to better yourself, while communism has everyone sharing and working together. Logically, communists should be Christians and capitalists should be atheists, but it's just the opposite.'

"Lee even describes himself in somewhat contradictory terms, 'a radical conservative with a liberal heart.'"

CHAPTER THIRTY-FIVE

First Impressions

> "The aim of psychoanalysis is to relieve people of their neurotic unhappiness so that they can be normally unhappy."
> —*Sigmund Freud*

> "I really didn't say everything I said." —*Lawrence Peter "Yogi" Berra*

> "If you don't know where you're going, you might not get there."
> —*Lawrence Peter "Yogi" Berra*

Soon after the earthling known as Bill "Spaceman" Lee arrived in Montreal, he didn't immediately ingratiate himself to the English speaking fans of the great city, a metropolis that Jackie Robinson claimed to his dying day, provided him with the will to persevere. In particular, the wonderful French fans of Montreal had embraced Jackie and his beautiful wife, Rachel from their very arrival.

Upon observing the inhabitants of the city for merely a few weeks, the Spaceman was asked regarding his initial impressions of Montreal. Without hesitation, and keep in mind that this brief "interview" was being conducted by an English-speaking station, Bill responded, "I can tell the French fans from the English fans without even hearing them speak."

"How so?" Bill was asked.

In typical fashion, the Spaceman immediately replied, "The French fans are the ones having fun."

And that they were. Bill—and we have photographic evidence—would literally sneak out of Olympic Stadium and join various French revelers at the Montreal Beer Gardens next door to the ballpark during the game! Oh, and in full uniform!

The interviewer, as most newcomers to Lee's planet generally were, had no retort and most likely had been shocked into silence. Of course, both the young natives of the great city, as well as older open-minded folks, had already grown quite fond of their outspoken social outcast. In truth and in general, many of the French speaking people had the more menial jobs in the city, a larger percentage of the English-speaking citizens, holding more "powerful positions." In 1979, there were often contentious confrontations between the two "factions," but fortunately, these days things have indeed, changed for the better.

The author, (Scott Russell or Kilgore Trout?) recalls visiting Bill at his rented home on ironically, Landsdowne Street in the Westmount section of the city, and having Bill and Mary Lou taking him to dinner in "Old Montreal," where it was obvious that the younger generation, both English and French, enjoyed good camaraderie.

After Bill's being blackballed from MLB baseball, a disgraceful fact which implausibly continues even into the year 2020, I visited Bill as he was appearing with an All-Star group of former Red Sox, Bruins, Patriots, and Celtics players. Bill was playing and coaching this legendary group against teams of firefighters, police, and other first responders, the beneficiaries being local charities. I approached Bill's "shortstop" that afternoon, a former great New England Patriots quarterback named Steve Grogan, a great and humble person. I introduced myself and informed #14 that I was a friend of the Spaceman. Grogan, a gracious man with a dry wit, shook my hand and replied, "I'm sorry to hear that." I liked him immediately.

I then invited Grogan to a "Jimmy Fund" (Dana-Farber Children's Cancer Institute) event at Harvard University and he and his beautiful wife, Robbie, graciously and anxiously agreed to attend. Bill Lee would also join us at those functions. Bill, Bob Montgomery, and Rico Petrocelli in particular, seldom turned down such invitations.

One of the more memorable moments of Bill's playing career in Boston occurred outside of one of his favorite watering holes, the Eliot Lounge on Massachusetts Avenue. As the 1973 baseball season wound down to its close, the Spaceman, George Kimball, and a few other patrons of the historic bar were downing a few drinks as the legendary bartender, the inimitable Tommy Leonard, was holding court. In walked a man named Upton Bell.

If the name Upton Bell rings a bell, pun intended, it is because at the time, Upton was the youngest general manager in the National Football League. Upton, who at the time was the New England Patriots GM, was the son of the great Bert Bell, the former commissioner of the league, and the man credited for saving the NFL from financial ruin after World War II. The elder Bell, in fact, was the man who coined the phrase, "Any given Sunday."

The younger Bell knew a thing or two about the game of football. He had worked for the Baltimore Colts and served for two of the more legendary men in coaching history, namely Weeb Eubank and the recently deceased Don Shula. During Upton Bell's tenure, the Colts won two NFL championships during the time he was the personnel director for the scouting department. Again, Upton Bell had an eye for talent.

On that sunny early fall September day at the Eliot Lounge, Upton Bell joined Bill and George Kimball at the bar. Quickly, the conversation turned to the sad state of the Patriots punting situation and the fact that Coach Chuck Fairbanks was not exactly enamored with his current punter. The Spaceman, and alcohol may have been involved, suddenly suggested that he audition for the team. Again, Bill is a great athlete and he was at the very least half-serious.

Truth being stranger than fiction, as it has been for the majority of Bill Lee's life, bartender Tommy Leonard, God rest his soul, produced a football from behind the bar.... No, really. Hey, don't all good bartenders keep footballs behind the bar?

Out into the street they went. A star pitcher of the Red Sox, a one-eyed half-crazed journalist, the GM of the New England Patriots and an assorted group of other inebriates. Bill "Spaceman" Lee's "tryout" for the New England Patriots went rather well. Upton Bell, perhaps the only reasonably sober gentleman inside or more accurately now outside the establishment, watched in awe as Bill "Spaceman" Lee booted majestic kicks above the buildings on Massachusetts Avenue! Time and time again, the football soared high atop the rooftops and descended in the street as cars honked their horns, and a vast group of spectators had gathered to watch the spectacle. Not only did Bill kick the football with great "hang-time," but it never went askew, and therefore, no one had to climb stairs to a rooftop to retrieve it.

Bill Lee had impressed the GM of the New England Patriots to the extent that Upton Bell officially invited him to come out to Foxboro to officially try out for the team. Why not? After all, there have been other two-sport athletes in the past. The plans of mice and punters, unfortunately, often go awry. The Red Sox Vice President and General Manager, Dick O'Connell, forbade his southpaw pitcher from even attempting to try out for the New England Patriots.

After winning the American league pennant and starring in the World Series in 1967, legendary Red Sox hurler turned dentist, Jim Lonborg, decided to go skiing in the off-season.... He tore up his knee and was never again quite the same dominant pitcher. Dick O'Connell invoked "the Lonborg Clause" in all subsequent contracts. Play baseball and nothing else.

We will never know what would have transpired, but at least we know what did happen. Coach Chuck Fairbanks was still stuck with a horseshit punter.

CHAPTER THIRTY-SIX

Nobility

"The mountains are calling and I must go." —*John Muir*

"Because I'm a civil rights activist, I am also an animal rights activist. Animals and humans suffer and die alike. Violence causes the same pain, the same spilling of blood, the same stench of death, the same arrogant, cruel and vicious taking of life. We shouldn't be a part of it." —*Dick Gregory*

One of Bill Lee's heroes was a man named Guy Waterman. Waterman was a naturalist and he wrote several books about hiking in the mountains of New England and the preservation of the purity of the wild. Waterman and his wife, Laura, lived in East Corinth, Vermont not far from where Bill and Diana Lee reside in Craftsbury, Vermont.

Guy Waterman climbed every peak in the northeast high county in winter and from all the cardinal directions. One of Waterman's most noted books was *Wilderness Ethics*. Guy and Laura Waterman voluntarily maintained a famous open trail for many years, an open treeless trail on Franconia Ridge in New Hampshire. Guy and Laura Waterman's cabin in East Corinth had no electricity, plumbing, or telephone. The Watermans genuinely loved the solace of the mountain. Their home was at least a mile from the nearest road.

Guy Waterman was also a renowned jazz pianist, a speechwriter for three presidents, and he taught physics at Yale University in New Haven until he was appointed the first director of the National Science Foundation.

Guy Waterman was greatly influenced by researching that nomadic tribes throughout history had been known to leave their elderly behind in the wild when their times seemed over. However, Guy Waterman was determined to do the reverse.

On February 6, 2000, Waterman left home and drove east and climbed to the summit of his beloved Lafayette Mountain, where he and Laura maintained their trail. In the dead of winter, Guy Waterman calmly sat down atop the mountain and froze to death. He was sixty-seven years old. He had apparently planned his suicide for months.

On February 10, four days later, alerted by letters Guy Waterman had written to them, five of his friends ascended the 5,260 foot peak in order to recover his body. They carried him down on a litter.

By the time you read this, Bill Lee will have cut down a tree on Waterman's property at the behest of his widow, Laura, enabling him to carve commemorative baseball bats out of it.

CHAPTER THIRTY-SEVEN

Dancing with the Stars

"No matter what, nobody can take away the dances you've already had." —*Gabriel Garcia Marquez*

Annabelle Lee Harmon, or Annabelle Lee as she was known to most, was, of course, the Spaceman's beautiful and gifted aunt. Although Bill's dad, William F. Lee, Jr. had indeed instructed his son on the fine art of pitching, it was his sister who was his greatest mentor in that regard. The Spaceman's dad was an outstanding semi-pro hurler, but military service got in the way. However, Annabelle was legend in the AGPBL, a blonde beauty who pitched two no-hitters, including a perfect game, in successive seasons.

Not only did Annabelle tutor her nephew in the fine art of pitching, she perhaps had an even greater impact on his personality. Annabelle, a left-hander herself, was also a bit eccentric and as ebullient and yes, a bit "flaky" as many southpaws are. Even "maturity" does not get in the way of eccentricity and Annabelle Lee was as delightful as any woman even half her age on planet Earth.

In 2004, eighty-two year-old Annabelle was visiting Bill Lee and his beautiful wife, Diana in New England. Therefore, they gravitated towards the storied Eliot Lounge on Massachusetts Avenue in Boston for a drink or three. Unknown to the Lees, they had "crashed" a bachelor party being thrown by some wild Charlestown Irishmen. No problem, the more the merrier. There were three men and their father, who were in the middle of engaging in a "chugging contest." Bill Lee stated, "There was one guy who was amazing. I had never seen anyone down a beer as quickly as he did." Annabelle, and that would surprise absolutely no one who has ever met her, quickly became the life of the already raucous party. Again, Bill's aunt was eighty-two!

There is video footage of what transpired during this celebration, which eventually evolved into Annabelle literally dancing atop the bar! The video—and it is documented—can be viewed on a short feature titled, "High and Outside."

On July 3, 2008, while Bill and Diana were visiting her in Costa Mesa, California, Annabelle Lee, eighty-six years of age, passed while Diana was holding her in her arms. With her passing, the world got a whole lot duller.

The Spaceman recently wrote an amazingly poignant poem about his dad and Aunt Annabelle. Here it is in its entirety:

"Just the other day
I looked into my father's eyes
I hope you're not mad that your sister had better control
Before you hurt your arm from coming back too soon
from Okinawa
You could've been Tom Seaver
But your aspirations were only to be as good as your father."

CHAPTER THIRTY-EIGHT

Harsh Realities

> "I believe that God's decision to allow the human species to have free will was an error in judgment. Hey, nobody's perfect."
> —*Scott Russell (or perhaps Kilgore Trout).*

Bill Lee's former teammate George "Boomer" Scott was a slick fielding first baseman and power hitter. Boomer, however, was never noted for his attractive appearance, especially during the latter stages of his career, a time in which he developed quite a girth. Recently, Denny McLain, the last thirty-game winner in baseball, described George Scott as having "a Kardashian ass with the softest hands," according to Bill Lee. The affable Scott who hailed from Greenville, Mississippi was both colorful and outspoken and his humor would not, for the most part, be acceptable today under the current guidelines of "political correctness."

Bill Lee and George Scott were tight. Each time the Red Sox visited Detroit, both Boomer and Lee would visit an African American store called Harry's Haberdashery, where both men would purchase bell-bottom pants, since it was apparently the only place the two friends could find them.

Boomer was one of the most beloved of the 1967 Red Sox "Impossible Dream Team," and the large African American's sharp tongue often provided both his teammates and opponents with great mirth. Upon the Red Sox reacquiring "Boomer" from the Milwaukee Brewers in 1978, he would still bust the chops of his former teammates during those occasions when the two ball clubs met. Such a gathering occurred at Fenway Park during the season.

One of Boomer's former teammates in Milwaukee was a powerful slugger named Gorman Thomas. To be kind, Gorman was not a matinee idol. In truth, Gorman Thomas was one ugly son of a bitch. In fact, George Scott would often tell Gorman Thomas (remember, these were the days when Mel Brooks could produce motion pictures) that he was the ugliest white man on the planet. For the record, few who ever saw Gorman Thomas would disagree with that sentiment. Those were the days that a typical conversation between friends consisted of, "If I had a face like yours, I would pull down my pants, shave my ass, bend over and walk backwards!"

Just before the reunion of Boomer and the equally "colorful" Gorman Thomas, Thomas had just completed a successful week of play. In fact, "Mullion Man," as Boomer nicknamed his friend, and, despite the fact that no one knew what the name meant, were all aware it wasn't complimentary, and no doubt in Mississippi slang, most likely translated as "ugly white motherfucker," George Scott approached his friend behind the batting cage during batting practice. "Hey Mullion Man, I understand you had one helluva week."

Gorman Thomas, fully expecting a compliment, puffed out his chest and responded, "Yeah, I did. I hit seven home runs last week!"

Boomer immediately replied, "Yeah, and you scared six of them out of the park!"

On another occasion during spring training, Red Sox oddball Danny Cater had been struck on the batting helmet by a fastball during an exhibition game. Cater hit the dirt and was writhing on the ground while holding his head. It was then that his opponent, the loquacious Boomer approached. Cater cried out, "I'm blind, I'm blind! I can't see!"

"Boomer" Scott peered down at his fallen fellow first baseman and shouted, "Well, man, open yo' eyes!" Cater after being struck had apparently clenched his eyes shut!

As the Spaceman stated, he witnessed a lot of strange shit during his playing days.

Another highly politically incorrect but hilarious moment occurred at a low point in George Scott's career, and it arrived because of perhaps the funniest man to ever wear a major league uniform, perhaps the most beloved figure in Red Sox history, the inimitably great Cuban pitcher Luis Tiant, whose exclusion from the Hall of Fame in Cooperstown remains an egregious injustice.

Luis Tiant was not only a great pitcher and teammate, but his playfulness and comedic timing kept the entire ball club loose. "El Tiante" would relieve all pressure during tense moments during games, even those in which he played. His comedy was both timely and side-splitting and his high-pitched voice made that precise timing even funnier.

The cries of "Boomer" would often rain down upon the playing field, especially during George Scott's earlier playing days, a time in which the now rotund first sacker was a much more proficient player. However, now that the Red Sox had reacquired the virtually over-the-hill version of the once svelte batsman, the shouts of "Boomer" were shortened to the first three letters of the word.

On a Thursday afternoon, however, one in which the Red Sox trailed in the late innings, George Scott stepped into the batters' box and was greeted with some loud significant verbal abuse. The Fenway Faithful were letting their formerly admired player know that they preferred Cecil Cooper, the terrific young first baseman the Red Sox had traded to Milwaukee for their overweight slumping hitter. George Scott had been 0-3 on that afternoon and he was in the throes of a horrific batting slump. As for Cecil Cooper, the Spaceman's neighbor at the Knollsbrook Condominiums in Stoughton, Massachusetts, the young African American natural hitter had become one of the finest batsmen in major league baseball.

As luck would have it, George Scott connected on a fastball and it disappeared into the camera well in dead center field. The late inning grand slam home run had erased a two-run deficit and put the Sox up by two runs! All was forgiven.... Well, at least by the fans.

"Boomer! Boomer! Boomer!" Thirty thousand people rose as one to cheer George Scott, and they were not going to sit down until Boomer came out of the dugout to acknowledge them... however, George Scott was not about to acknowledge the sudden reappearance of his worshipping fans. While the throng repeatedly sang "Boomer," the large Mississippian sat solemnly on his dugout seat and refused to budge an inch. It was then that the great Luis Tiant intervened. In his typical shrill voice, Luis exclaimed:

"You got to tip your cap. They love you!"

"They can kiss my black ass!" replied George Scott.

Luis answered, "No, man, listen to them, "They (sic) yelling 'Boomer, Boomer.' They love you!"

A defiant George Scott could not care less as he repeated:

"They (sic) been ridin' my ass for weeks. They can kiss my black ass!"

At one point, Luis Tiant actually attempted to shove the huge man out of the dugout to tip his cap to the crowd, to no avail. Finally, Luis Tiant, in an act that is still indelible in the author's mind, shouted:

"All right, you don't do it? I do it!"

Luis Tiant, as God is my judge, climbed the steps of the dugout and doffed his cap to the crowd. Immediately, 30,000 satiated fans sat back down in their seats.

Moments later I saw six Red Sox players literally fall off the bench clutching their stomachs while laughing hysterically. It was not until I met the Spaceman at the Eliot Lounge following the game that I knew what had transpired. Immediately after tipping his cap to the crowd and silencing the large gathering, Tiant returned and shouted in his treble voice:

"You see that? You see that? They see one fat nigger and they don't know the difference!"

As reported, Bill, George Scott, and Tommy Harper were all good friends. Tommy, another terrific African American player mishandled by the Red Sox, like Cecil Cooper was a neighbor of Lee's in Stoughton and the three would often drive to Fenway Park together. Once while in spring training in Winter Haven, Florida, not exactly the center for racial equality in the U.S., Spaceman joked to both Tommy Harper and Boomer, "The only way you'll get into the Elks Club down here is if you're on the menu."

That line was reminiscent to one uttered in the 1950s by the Puerto Rican black superstar first baseman Vic Power, who had entered an "all-white" diner for breakfast. Power mistakenly was not entirely aware of the Jim Crow laws of the state and sat down at a table, but was immediately approached by an employee of the restaurant who informed him, "I'm sorry, but we don't serve Negroes." Vic Power, bless his heart, immediately responded, "That's all right, I don't eat Negroes, I eat rice and beans."

CHAPTER THIRTY-NINE

Normal People Need Not Apply

"Always remember that you are absolutely unique. Just like everyone else." —*Margaret Mead*

"The lion and the calf shall lie down together, but the calf won't get much sleep." —*Woody Allen*

The Earthling known as Bill "Spaceman" Lee is not like the rest of us. Men such as Bill Lee—and they are few and far between—seem to be a powerful lure for peculiar individuals. Even in the year 2020 there is no scientific explanation for such magnetism. Consider Bill's second stop in professional baseball after being signed out of the University of Southern California. That relatively brief layover occurred at Winston Salem in the Carolina League in the year 1968.

As you walked into the clubhouse for the initial time, imagine what most would think if a young man reached out and offered his hand in welcome and exclaimed, "Hi, I'm Pia DeSalvo, the nephew of the Boston Strangler!" However, remember that this is Bill Lee who was offered the friendly greeting. Therefore, in typical Lee fashion Bill smiled and extended his right hand to young DeSalvo.

Bill, who of course was not yet "Spaceman" in those days, was impressed with the overt friendliness of Pia DeSalvo, who he would immediately learn was the team trainer for the ball club. Not surprisingly, Bill was not aware that Pia's uncle, Albert DeSalvo, was one of the most infamous murderers of the twentieth century. In fact, upon hearing the friendly youngster introduce himself as the nephew of "the Boston Strangler," Bill Lee thought the young man's uncle may have been a professional wrestler! Hey, "The Boston Strangler" is certainly a great name for a wrestler.

I will say this for Pia DeSalvo: he certainly managed to immediately get the notorious facts about his family history out of the way. It sure beat the hell out of someone whispering to you, "Psst, I think you should know that your trainer's uncle is the Boston Strangler." It should also be noted that Pia DeSalvo and Bill became good friends during the short time they spent together.

Pia's uncle, Albert DeSalvo, had murdered thirteen women in Boston by knocking on doors in Boston's Back Bay. He would introduce himself as a "handyman." Once being allowed entrance to their apartments, DeSalvo would strangle the unsuspecting women. The great actor Tony Curtis, who starred with Marilyn Monroe and Jack Lemmon in the comedy classic *Some Like it Hot,* portrayed DeSalvo in the motion picture *The Boston Strangler*. Curtis, whose real name was Bernard Schwartz, hailed from Intervale Avenue in the South Bronx, the same neighborhood as the author (Scott Russell or Kilgore Trout), and was nominated for a Golden Globe for his performance. Henry Fonda played chief detective John S. Bottomly, who solved the case.

What surprised many in the aftermath of the DeSalvo case being solved was the question as to why so many women, being aware there was a strangler running amok in Boston, would permit a stranger to enter their apartment? After all, there were no signs of forced entry in any of the murders. That, of course, indicated that the women either knew DeSalvo or allowed him access to their apartments. After viewing the motion picture, a common funny response by women was, "Wouldn't you let Tony Curtis into your house?"

Upon being asked about Pia DeSalvo, the killer's nephew and team trainer, the Spaceman replied, "You didn't want to fall asleep on his table. Pia had very strong fingers."

CHAPTER FORTY

Spaceman, U.S. Army, Ret. REMF

"You can make yourself happy or miserable. It's the same amount of effort." —*Ray Bradbury*

Bill Lee's dad, the aforementioned William Francis Lee, Jr. was a staff sergeant and a veteran of World War II who had fought at Okinawa. In the illogical logical world of Bill Lee, it would stand to reason that he would also become a sergeant in the Army Reserve, where the eccentric southpaw served his nation between the years 1970 and1976.

While the rest of America slept cozily in their comfy beds, the Spaceman was in the process of taking aptitude tests in order for the U.S. Army to further decide in exactly what capacity he should serve in order to best protect us. Don't you feel safer now? One of these "aptitude" tests given to the Earthling known as William Francis Lee, III (and everyone else, for that matter) was an exam based on a fictional language.... No, really. The questions were based on that fictitious language, and based on the responses given those who showed an ability to decipher the alleged language in a coherent manner would be given promotions of some sort. It should serve as a frightening reminder to all of us that there are people in upper echelons of government that take these tests seriously. It should also be of no small concern that the Spaceman scored one hundred percent on the quiz.

Said Bill Lee, "They said they'd give me a commission to first lieutenant and ship me off to Fort Huachuca to be a 'spook' for the NSA. Another aptitude test indicated I would be a great undertaker."

Upon being asked what his classification "REMF" stood for, the Spaceman proudly replied, "Rear Echelon Mother Fucker."

So much for "amusement"; as "punishment," Lee was assigned to a MTST computer. The Spaceman described his responsibility as follows: "I had joined as an MP, but I was immediately sent to a general's office to work on a computer. I had to process all the dead bodies that came home from 'Nam. 'Would you like to claim two-thirds of your son and a bronze medal?'"

Putting humor aside, in 1973 Bill's dad, the veteran of Okinawa, reacted harshly to his son being offered the initial dealership of Honda that was to be located on Brookline Avenue near Fenway Park. "I was supposed to be on the first ad for Honda; my dad said, 'If you bring back a rice-burning car, I'll run you through with a bayonet I took off a dead Jap.'" Somewhat incredibly, the first ad was to feature Bill Lee and... Buckminster Fuller! Oh, and Fuller indeed, appeared in the ad!

CHAPTER FORTY-ONE

An Idiot Wind Blows in and Crashes upon the Love on the Rocks

"Now the beach is deserted except for some kelp
And a piece of an old ship that lies on the shore
You always responded when I needed your help
You gimme a map and a key to your door." —*Bob Dylan from his song "Sara."*

The Earthling known as Bill "Spaceman" Lee locked Bob Dylan out of his home in Malibu... no, really.... Actually, the home, at least legally, was no longer Bob Dylan's according to the magistrate. By the late 1970s, rock 'n roll Hall of Famer Bob Dylan's oft-time contentious and publicized marriage to former Playboy Bunny Sara Lee Lowndes was ostensibly over. The media on occasion reported a possible reconciliation, but the relationships of the rich and famous often get complicated.

During happier times, Bob Dylan and his wife had a beautiful home up on the bluff just north of Malibu and just south of Trancas Beach (Zuma Beach) towards the Ventura County Line. During the winter months after the baseball season ended, "Spaceman" Lee still helped his uncle Grover Souder out at his "Malibu Lock and Key" shop in Malibu. I believe you see where this is going.

According to Bill Lee, Sara "caught" her husband one evening and that "investigation" was the final straw for the beautiful, but scorned woman. Sara, in her mighty wrath, made a quick and decisive decision. Bill "Spaceman" Lee whose other occupation was shutting hitters out, was summoned to change the locks on the doors of what was now legally Sara's home, and she had the documents to prove it. Bob Dylan, just as the likes of other Hall of Famers Reggie Jackson and Harmon Killebrew, were also "shut out" by the locksmith known as Spaceman.

The impressive vista of the Pacific Ocean could no longer be viewed by Bob Dylan... well, at least from that location.

At other times during Bill Lee's career as a locksmith, he also managed to bar both Neil Diamond and James Arness from their former homes by the installation of new locks. It takes balls and some seriously strong bolts to prevent Marshal Dillon from busting through "security."

Speaking of being "locked out," thanks to his being blackballed, and I mean that literally, from major league baseball since 1982, Bill Lee has persevered and somehow implausibly respected and honored the game despite his permanent disbarment. Much like the great Negro Leaguer Buck O'Neil who notwithstanding his never being permitted to play what was erroneously referred to as "major league baseball," Bill Lee has no regrets. The Spaceman has honored the game for these last thirty-eight years by barnstorming in senior leagues, charity events, and yes, even professional baseball at a lower level. You can take a boy away from his game, but you can never take the game away from the boy.

Again, while there are those that found Don Zimmer charming, that is, as charming as an inarticulate underachieving nitwit of a manager as he was, he was most definitely one of several major league figures that conspired—and that is NOT conjecture—to place a spoken, however, unwritten, "document" barring the Spaceman for life. This "non-formal" agreement, for lack of a better term, most surely exists and cannot be broken. That much, as we will discuss later, has been admitted by many in the game, and some of the names will astound you.

On May 10, 2020 on a podcast emanating from Detroit, the Spaceman was interviewed by former Detroit Tigers ace, Denny McLain, who has admittedly run afoul of the law on several occasions and served several years in federal penitentiaries for serious white collar crimes, many of which were despicable, but to McLain's credit, he has owned up to them. McLain has not only admittedly hurt others, but he has also done permanent damage to himself, as well.

Denny McLain, who at one time was on top of world, questioned the Spaceman regarding his contentious relationship with his former manager Don Zimmer. McLain queried, "How come he hated you so much?"

Lee responded, "He despised all pitchers. He was nearly killed by pitchers on at least two occasions. They're the reason he had holes drilled into his skull."

McLain then recalled Don Zimmer as a utility infielder with the lowly Washington Senators. Zimmer, who never reached his potential as a major league player for a myriad of reasons, was playing in his final season in the majors in 1994. As McLain remembered:

"Zimmer came up as a pinch-hitter late in the game in Detroit. We had Mickey Lolich on the mound. The count went to 3-2 and rather than challenge Zimmer with a fastball, Mickey threw a 3-2 back-door breaking ball and got Zimmer looking. It was the final at bat of Zimmer's career."

What Denny McLain did not mention, however, was that as Zimmer stepped up to the plate, his batting average stood at exactly .200. Therefore, he finished the year at .199. In so many ways that at bat, according to Bill Lee, "represented a microcosm of Zimmer's entire playing career, one in which he underachieved. Here he was no doubt thinking that Lolich would be challenging him with a fastball, but instead, threw him an unhittable back-door slider and Zimmer ended his inglorious playing career standing there with the bat on his shoulders."

Bill Lee continued, "It was deep in his subconscious that lefthanders were tricky and conniving and didn't challenge anybody. That is the duality between pitchers and hitters. He took it to his grave because he never figured out it was all about pitching and defense, the poor little fucking asshole."

CHAPTER FORTY-TWO

"Sundown" Arrived Too Early

"Sometimes I think it's a shame
When I get feeling better when I'm feeling no pain
Sundown, you better take care
If I find you creeping 'round my back stairs
Sometimes I think it's a sin
When I feel like I'm winning when I'm losing again."
—Gordon Lightfoot, "Sundown"

The earthman known as Bill "Spaceman" Lee would no longer be called out to change the locks on the doors of the bungalow which had become a home away from home for John Belushi. During the time Bill worked at his Uncle Grover's locksmith shop in 1976, Bill had indeed, changed the locks on those very doors. However, now in 1982, John Belushi, the star of *Saturday Night Live*, would not be using the bungalow any longer. You see, John Belushi was dead.

On Friday, March 5, 1982, the beloved megastar of *Saturday Night Live* fame was found dead alone in a room at "Chateau Marmot" in Los Angeles. He was merely thirty-three years old. He had overdosed on a concoction of cocaine and heroin administered to him by a woman named Cathy Smith, a woman who would be "immortalized" in Gordon Lightfoot's powerful song, "Sundown."

Catherine Evelyn Smith, a native of Hamilton, Ontario, was an occasional backup singer, rock "groupie," drug dealer, and legal secretary. How is that for a lethal combination? Cathy was a "groupie," and her initial famous acquaintance was the great, late Levon Helm of "The Band." For the record, Levon Helm was a wonderful human being.

As reported earlier, Bill Lee's uncle, Grover Souder, owned a locksmith shop on Santa Monica Boulevard in Hollywood before opening another in Malibu. The Spaceman's uncle also owned and operated a shoe repair store and a bar on the corner. Grover's home on Genesee Avenue was used as the backdrop in the motion picture *Nightmare on Elm Street*. Yes, the world of "Spaceman" Lee is a wondrous one. Bill and his uncle would also service Hollywood greats such as William Holden and Lee Marvin, and, of course, the strange Howard Hughes.

Long before the shocking death of John Belushi, Bill Lee had been called out to change the locks on the doors at the Chateau Marmot in Hollywood for other Hollywood icons such as William Holden and Lee Marvin. Bill described himself as "a master at key-tumbler replacement."

Bill Lee stated, "I changed so many locks under the pins at that hotel that anyone who had an illicit relationship at that hotel could've given me COVID-19."

Gordon Lightfoot, who wrote the above song "Sundown," was not in denial that the song was written about Cathy Smith, who the Canadian balladeer admitted was his former girlfriend and that he was aware of her nefarious connections. Lightfoot had admitted that fact in a 2008 interview. It has been written that "The Band" member Rick Manuel had once offered to marry Cathy Smith but was refused. Rick Manuel, it should be reported, later committed suicide. He was a renowned alcoholic.

In Bob Woodward's book *Wired*, Cathy Smith appears a drug dealer to Ron Wood and Keith Richards of the Rolling Stones. Cathy was "bad news." Cathy Smith had apparently originally met John Belushi on the set of *Saturday Night Live* in 1976. She later met Belushi again through Wood and Richards, and Belushi contacted her to purchase the drugs that eventually killed him. The lethal combination of cocaine and heroin contained eleven "speedballs," enough to kill a horse.

The Chateau Marmot was renowned for its discretion among Hollywood stars, that is, until Belushi's death blew the doors off the place. This was Hollywood's quintessential "no-tell-motel"... and "Spaceman" Lee became a part of its history by merely changing the locks. One of the regulars at the Chateau Marmot was superstar actor Robert DiNiro, who only hours before Belushi's death was said to have stopped by to snort cocaine with the comedic icon. To his credit, DiNiro shied away from Cathy Smith, who he considered dangerous. Gordon Lightfoot's lyrics were certainly indicative of that reality.

Both Belushi's wife Judy and Belushi's brilliant comedic sidekick Dan Aykroyd were painfully aware that Belushi's life had spun out of control and they had been attempting to convince him to return to New York City to resume work on the enormously popular show.

At 8:00 a.m. on the morning of Belushi's death, Cathy Smith had ordered room service for the bungalow and a waiter delivered wheat toast and jam and a pot of coffee. According to the woman's testimony, Cathy ate her breakfast, cleaned up the room, especially the drug paraphernalia, and "checked in" on Belushi who was "snoring loudly in bed." Cathy Smith then left.

Cathy Smith served a mere fifteen months in the California prison system for fatally injecting John Belushi. Perhaps she got time off for being a junkie, herself. "Good behavior" would be a stretch.

On Saturday mornings at Grover's locksmith shop, the Spaceman and Grover Souder's son, Buddy, would work until noontime, but then return to the shop to close. During one of those Saturdays, Bill and Buddy decided to light up a huge "fatty" to celebrate the end of another work week. However, just as they were enjoying their toke, the phone rang. Two women had somehow managed to lock themselves out of their car with the motor running.

Being "responsible" and caring individuals, Bill and Buddy headed to the scene where they found two elderly women stranded outside of their Volvo on Malibu Pier. The two women had just concluded lunch at Alice's Restaurant (yes there is one there, too). Their motor was indeed, running and the keys locked inside the car. It should be noted that both Bill and Buddy were "stoned out of their gourd," on the "fatty" they had smoked, but the Spaceman picked the lock within ten seconds! A crowd of perhaps thirty people had gathered to witness the unusual occurrence of seeing a major league star pitcher rescue two elderly women. Once opening the door and handing the ladies the keys to the ignition, Lee announced to the grateful women, "There'll be no charge." The crowd immediately reacted by giving Bill and Buddy Souder a rousing standing ovation.

Buddy had turned to Bill and complained, "Hey, we should've been paid!" Lee replied, "Anytime you get a standing ovation for ten seconds of work, you just walk away!"

The world of the earthling named William Francis Lee, III, is nothing if not often bizarre.

CHAPTER FORTY-THREE

The Root of the Problem

"One of the things I keep learning is that the secret of being happy is doing things for other people." — *Dick Gregory*

"The free man is the man with no fear." —*Dick Gregory*

Richard Claxton "Dick" Gregory was a groundbreaking comedian, a renowned civil rights activist, a social critic, an actor, and the first black standup comic to perform "no-holds-barred" comedy attacking bigotry and racism in the early 1960s. Gregory's hilarious, poignant, laidback humor was both sophisticated and powerful, and he set the stage for the likes of Richard Pryor, Eddie Murphy, and other great African American comedians to follow. Dick Gregory was also a close personal friend of both Dr. Martin Luther King, Jr. and Medgar Evers, who literally paid for their courage with their lives.... Dick Gregory was also a great friend of Bill "Spaceman" Lee.

After winning 17 games for three consecutive seasons from 1973-1975, Bill Lee was locked in a tight 1-0 game at Yankee Stadium versus the Yankees in the sixth inning on May 20, 1976. The intense rivalry became even more heated when the fiery competitor Lou Piniella was thrown out at home plate and became entangled with Lee's battery mate, the equally competitive Carlton "Pudge" Fisk. A major brawl ensued, one in which the Spaceman suffered a severely separated shoulder. There would be no fourth consecutive seventeen victory season for Lee. In fact, the Spaceman's injury was so severe that he would not rejoin the rotation until September, but there was no longer "life" on his fastball. His injury was not healing quickly or properly. Bill had lost at least 10 mph off his pitches.

During the off-season, the Spaceman peered out of the window from his home in Belmont, Massachusetts and saw a brown Rolls Royce pulling into his driveway. Out of the driver's side emerged the legendary Dick Gregory. Upon entering Bill and Mary Lou's home, the brilliant and loquacious Gregory advised Lee, "You've got too much lactic acid buildup in your shoulder, like too much soap suds in a washing machine." Lee laughed as the comedic genius resumed his lecture:

"You've got to get bone, man! You've got to get comfrey root. Have you ever seen two hambones boiling in a pot of comfrey root?"

Bill Lee, of course, responded, "No."

As Dick Gregory explained, comfrey root was an herbal remedy (that fact "hooked" Bill instantly, since the Spaceman was/and is fond of herbal "remedies.") that relieved pain from blunt injuries, promoted healing of broken bones, reduced swelling and edema, and assisted with the healthy regrowth of skin and tissue cells.

By the time dinner was complete, Bill "Spaceman" Lee was completely sold on Dick Gregory's Bahamian diet. Incredibly, Bill's shoulder began to feel stronger immediately after instituting Gregory's diet! To this moment, the Spaceman credits the great Dick Gregory for resurrecting his pitching career.

Before departing, Dick Gregory, an icon of the civil rights movement, offered a passionate plea to one of his favorite athletes, "You've got to get healthy. You've got to come back. You've got a lot of generations out there that are pulling for you!"

Improbable as it may seem, Dick Gregory was the one most responsible for restoring the career of the Earthling known as William Francis Lee, III.

Author's Note: In the late 1960s, I sat at the Village Vanguard in New York City's Greenwich Village. The featured performer that evening was none other than Dick Gregory. There were no "rows" at the Vanguard, but rather tables, and I along with my date, a blonde (the only blonde I ever dated!) from Des Moines, Iowa had a table directly in front of the stage! I never laughed so hard in my life. Dick Gregory's sharp and biting wit was mesmerizing. Incredibly, Gregory was so exceptional that he was the prominent act following jazz legends Arthur Prysock and Jimmy Smith, and to think he became a close friend of my friend, Bill Lee!

CHAPTER FORTY-FOUR

Picked Off and Ticked Off

"Another flaw in the human character is that everyone wants to build, but nobody wants to do maintenance." —*Kurt Vonnegut*

The two legendary Hall of Fame ballplayers wanted to talk, but Bill "Spaceman" Lee wanted to play baseball. After all, it was a baseball game. The earthman known as William Francis Lee, III felt strongly that both his first baseman, Carl Yastrzemski, and the Cleveland Indians player-manager, Frank Robinson, should have considered the venue before entering into what Lee certainly believed to be a worthy discussion, but one which should have been held at a different locale.

The date was May 1, 1975 and the place was Fenway Park in Boston. Bill "Spaceman" Lee, and he never once in his lifetime considered the game of baseball to be mundane, except perhaps during those times he was not in the process of competing at it, was locked in a pitching matchup and his mound opponent was Jim Perry, an accomplished right-hander, and the brother of another Hall of Famer, Gaylord Perry. Runs, Bill reasoned, would be at a premium and therefore, Bill thought, he should prevent as many of them as he possibly could while on the mound.

The Cleveland Indians had made major league history that off-season by hiring one of the greatest players in the annals of the game to be their manager. It was not that anyone had not appointed great players as managers, but this one in particular, Frank Robinson, was black. Being the first African American manager in history was not only long overdue, but a huge step for the alleged "national pastime."

It was in the top of the second inning that the Spaceman, and discretion being the wisest part of valor, walked the icon, Frank Robinson, to lead off the inning. Although Robinson was long in the tooth, Bill deducted, and accurately so, that he was still a dangerous man with a bat in his hands. It was best to go after the other Indians hitters. After retiring Charlie Spikes on a fly ball to left field, Bill towed the rubber as John Ellis came to bat.

It should be noted that Bill Lee, proving once more that pitchers, especially left-handed members of the species, were tricky and conniving, and no one was more deceptive while out on the mound, decided to at least make an effort at removing the base runner. It should also be noted that the Spaceman had developed one of the better pickoff moves in the lengthy annals of the game. Bill, in fact, had picked off an incredible total of 16 men in a season, at the time a major league record. That is a lot of deception.

The Spaceman had various signals he contrived to alert his first basemen that he was about to attempt to pick off another unsuspecting base runner. These gestures would nearly invariably be acknowledged by Lee's first sackers, the only exception often being Yastrzemski, who was currently holding Frank Robinson on the bag and apparently engaged in deep conversation with the Indians player manager. Therefore, upon receiving Lee's advance alert of a pickoff attempt, Yaz merely wiggled his glove, a sign which indicated, "Listen, I'm busy, don't bother me." The Spaceman, never having experienced this resistance from his other first basemen, figured what the hell, give it a try anyway. Those of us that know Bill are aware that he is willing to attempt anything at least twice.

Frank Robinson was standing no more than one foot off the base and neither of the two men was even remotely aware that the crazed iconoclastic hurler had thrown a baseball in their direction. Upon releasing the clandestine sphere, the Spaceman shouted, "Heads up!" Yastrzemski, startled, looked up just in time to see a baseball arriving within an inch of the equally unsuspecting Frank Robinson's ear and shoulder. Being a great athlete, Yastrzemski reacted instinctively, snared the baseball in his glove, and inadvertently tagged Frank Robinson out. In effect, Frank Robinson, albeit embarrassed, had tagged himself out.

Bill "Spaceman" Lee, in his exuberance to win a baseball game, had somehow managed, with one toss of a baseball, to infuriate both his opponent and his legendary teammate, Yastrzemski. Robinson, the first black manager of all time, had been humiliated, and in full view of his players. Yastrzemski was equally livid. I mean, hell, what are you trying to do, win a ballgame?

There's an old joke about a game warden down in Louisiana, who once had been warned about a local fisherman who rather than catch fish conventionally, had been throwing sticks of dynamite into the water in order to "acquire" his haul. Therefore, the undercover warden decided to manage to receive an invitation from the alleged offender and went out to the lake on the man's small rowboat.

Within minutes, the fisherman lit the fuse on a stick of dynamite and threw it into the water, and within seconds it exploded. Fish flew high up into the air and landed at the bottom of the tiny boat. The game warden pulled out his badge and informed the scofflaw that he was placing him under arrest for fishing illegally. The fisherman, however, reacted by immediately igniting another stick of dynamite, but this time rather than toss it into the lake he held it in his hand as the stick's fuse grew closer to exploding. Undaunted, the fisherman then turned to the game warden and asked calmly, "Do you want to fish, or do you want to talk?" That's a lesson that Frank Robinson and Carl Yastrzemski should have perhaps considered on May 1, 1975.... Oh, and Bill Lee won that game that day by ONE RUN... the run represented by the great Frank Robinson. The Spaceman always "fished" for victories.

CHAPTER FORTY-FIVE

What to Do When It's Raining in Minneapolis

"Drugs may lead to nowhere, but at least it's the scenic route."
—*Steven Wright*

The earthling known as William Francis Lee, III found himself in the clubhouse inside of Metropolitan Stadium in Bloomington circa 1974. The Red Sox were in town to play the Minnesota Twins, but the game had been rained out. As the majority of Spaceman's" teammates had left to go back to the hotel or to perhaps visit a drinking emporium or two, Bill's old buddy Bernardo Carbo informed the southpaw that he had just crushed two lines of mescaline in the bathroom.

As Lee recalled, "I was all wired out and since we weren't going to play, I snorted these two lines of mescaline. I returned to my locker, my shirt is off and I'm in my running clothes. There was a thunderstorm brewing, there's thunder and lightning out there and suddenly Gammons (Peter) comes by my locker and asks what we're planning to do and stuff, and he asked if I was upset about the rainout. I looked at Gammons and he's got this pinstriped shirt on with a pink line in it, so I said, 'Peter, you've got to take that shirt off before I can talk to you.'"

Note: the author, either Scott Russell or Kilgore Trout, take your pick, denies any knowledge concerning the effects of mescaline. However, for a thorough "description" of the drug's "capabilities," I suggest reading the late Richard Fariña's masterpiece, *Been Down So Long, it Looks Like up to Me.*

As Bill Lee recounted, "I went out and ran all the way back to the hotel which was like seven miles from Bloomington and it was the greatest damned run of my life! I was dodging raindrops and lightning bolts and it was like my feet never touched the pavement. I probably ran the 10K in record time. I hope Gammons donated that shirt to the Andy Warhol Museum in Pittsburgh."

Note: The author strongly recommends Richard Fariña's aforementioned book. However, for those not inclined to "research" the wonders of mescaline, I will fill you in on Fariña, who I found to be one of the true geniuses of the twentieth century.

Richard Fariña received a full academic scholarship to the prestigious Cornell University. He entered the Ivy League school majoring in engineering but switched to English. Fariña was born in Brooklyn to an Irish mother and a Cuban father. Fariña's closest friends at Cornell were people such as the great novelist Thomas Pynchon.

Fariña dropped out of Cornell shortly before achieving his degree. He then traveled to Europe, where in Paris in 1962, he would meet his future wife, Mimi.... In Paris, Fariña was a "blind street singer" who somehow miraculously regained his sight in the evening. Fariña, not blind of course, was a cunning and great looking curly-haired youngster. It was on the streets of Paris where Richard would "see" Mimi, who the author still believes was the most beautiful girl he has ever seen. And yes, she was a "girl."

The somewhat devious Fariña, passing himself off as a blind street performer, hit on Mimi as he sized her up behind his dark glasses. A bright young lady, Mimi quickly caught on to his act, but she fell in love with him anyhow. Richard and Mimi Baez were married in 1963. Yes, "Baez," the younger sister of Joan Baez! At the time of the wedding, Mimi Baez was seventeen years old!

A gifted couple, Mimi could sing and play guitar like her sister, and Richard Fariña was a simply amazing songwriter and had mastered the difficult art of playing an Appalachian dulcimer, a rare feat. They soon inked a recording contract with the famed folk artist company, Vanguard Records, and produced some of the most superb folk songs of the era, rich in controversy and beauty. Richard Fariña wrote Joan Baez's legendary classic "Birmingham Sunday" for Mimi's sister, a song about the cowardly church bombing which took the lives of young black school children in Alabama. The song, sung hauntingly by Joan Baez, remains as a sad reminder of what the south was in 1960s America.

Two days after the publication of his novel, Richard Fariña left a book signing at a Carmel Valley Village bookstore, The Thunderbird. He accepted a ride on a motorcycle which was said to be traveling in speeds exceeding 90 mph. Although the driver of the vehicle survived, Richard Fariña was killed instantly. The date was April 30, 1966. Richard Fariña was twenty-nine years old.

As for mescaline: It is a hallucinogenic psychedelic drug which derives from a small spineless cactus known as "Peyote." It is comparable to LSD.

CHAPTER FORTY-SIX

What to Do in Cleveland When You're Bored

"Short people got no reason to live." —*Randy Newman*

"Burn on, Cuyahoga, burn on."—*Randy Newman*

The earthling known as William Francis Lee, III found himself in Cleveland, Ohio, the "mistake by the lake" on Saturday, April 21, 1973. Lee and his Red Sox teammates had arrived there a day early to play the Indians. Since boys must be boys, upon arrival in a road city, players generally seek out places of "entertainment" or perhaps places of interest such as historical landmarks, but remember now, this is Cleveland. It was seventy-seven degrees and sunny, but sunshine gleaming down on the city of Cleveland still does not exactly magically transform the place to Xanadu.

Since the initial game of the series was on a Friday night, Bill decided to call the Chamber of Commerce before deciding his itinerary for Friday morning and afternoon. The line was busy for six hours. By then it was time to travel to the ballpark.

The Spaceman would not join the starting pitching rotation until May 1, so Lee went out to the bullpen with his other fellow relievers at the start of the 6:05 p.m. game on Saturday. Lynn McGlothen was the starting hurler for the Red Sox that afternoon and he was the lucky recipient of two home run blasts by newly acquired Hall of Fame immortal Orlando Cepeda, aka "Wounded Knee," or "knees" in his case. Before the advent of arthroscopic surgery all Cepeda could still do was hit, but damn, could he hit!

McGlothen ran into trouble in the sixth inning, so the Spaceman was summoned from the bullpen to enter the fray. Hell, he was in Cleveland and had nothing better to do. In the bottom of the eighth inning the Tribe had their designated hitter due up at the plate, but since he was Oscar Gamble, owner of the largest and most impressive 'fro in baseball history, and how in hell he got that under his helmet remains a mystery of the ages, they decided to send up a pinch-hitter named Walt Williams.

It should be noted that Walt Williams' nickname was "No-Neck." The reason Walt Williams became renowned as Walt "No-Neck" Williams was because, well, he had no neck. Also please keep in mind that these were the days before political correctness, and come to think of it, baseball players even in 2020 are not what you would describe as practitioners of "political correctness."

No-Neck's physical appearance, which included a compact torso, was due to a typhus injection he had received as a baby. Because of Williams' hustle, his determination, and the fact that he was a darned good hitter, he became a darling of his home fans, and there was no shortage of "home fans" because during Williams' ten year major league career, he toiled for the Houston Colt 45s, Cleveland, the Yankees, and the White Sox.

Not only was Williams sans a neck, he was listed at 5′ 6″ inches tall, and that was perhaps a generous elevation listing. No-Neck appeared to be closer to 5′ 4″ and his muscular build also made him to appear as if he was the model for a popular children's toy or action figure hero.

Bill Lee described the scene as follows:

"As Walt Williams came up to the batters' box, you could hear the pitter patter of his little feet. I'm telling you, he looked like a little hard-on. He looked like the little black guy in "Behind the Green Door."

Spaceman watched as No-Neck Williams stepped into the batters' box. "What the heck," thought Lee, "I'm in Cleveland, I might as well enjoy myself." As Walt Williams, the pride of Brownwood, Texas dug in, Bill peered in for the sign from his catcher, Carlton "Pudge" Fisk, who at 6′ 4″ tall even while crouching behind the plate, appeared to be as tall as No-Neck. As the Spaceman went into his windup, he turtled his neck, scrunching it down into his shoulders in order to "level the playing field." No-Neck was not amused and after the count reached 2-1, the slightly perturbed outfielder turned to the home plate umpire, George Maloney, pointed to Lee and protested, "He can't do that, make him stop!"

George Maloney, a fine umpire fully aware of the rules of the sport, informed the offended batsman, "Sorry, but there's no rule prohibiting a pitcher from mimicking a hitter."

"Just shut the fuck up and hit," offered "Pudge" Fisk. When the count reached 2-1, once more, the impersonator Bill Lee fired a pitch which crossed directly over the center of the plate.

"Ball three," shouted umpire George Maloney.

Now it suddenly appeared that Carlton Fisk had become the latest "offended" player. Fisk asked the umpire, "Where the hell was that?!"

Home plate umpire George Maloney replied, "The pitch was low."

"What?" countered Fisk, "How the fuck can a pitch be low to a midget?!"

Said Lee, "Walt was pissed!"

Once more, a fuming No-Neck Williams dug into the batters' box. He vowed to get even with both Lee and Fisk by roping a line drive for a hit. However, on the 3-1 pitch, No-Neck merely hit a soft pop fly to right field for the second out. He was not happy.

In recalling the incident, Lee described the 3-1 pitch. "It was ball four. I jammed him with a high fastball, but he was a midget and he loved high fastballs. Maloney was a good ump."

It should also be noted that while No-Neck played for the White Sox, the outfield consisted of him, Carlos May, and Pat Kelly. May had lost his thumb in a military training exercise. Pat Kelly, the other outfielder, was renowned for having a weak throwing arm. Therefore, the White Sox colorful Hall of Fame broadcaster, Harry Caray described the Chicago outfield as "No neck, no thumb, and no arm."

What amused many folks is that in Walt Williams' 1959 Topps baseball card, he was photographed wearing a turtleneck shirt beneath his powder blue White Sox uniform. That provided additional hilarious irony for true baseball aficionados.

After the ballgame, one in which the Spaceman hurled 3 & 2/3 hitless and scoreless innings to pick up a save, he returned to the hotel. He once more dialed the Cleveland Chamber of Commerce "hotline." Once more, all he got was a busy signal.

CHAPTER FORTY-SEVEN

L.A. Freeway

"Tania's" Hideout(s)

"*Adios* to all this concrete
Gonna get me some dirt road back street
If I can just get off of this LA Freeway
Without getting killed or caught
I'd be down that road in a cloud of smoke
To some land that I ain't bought bought bought."
—Guy Clark—song by Jerry Jeff Walker

"In waking a tiger, use a long stick." *—Mao Zedong*

"We shall use only peaceful means and we shall not permit any other kind of method." *—Zhou Enlai*

"If you don't go to other people's funerals, they won't go to yours."
—Lawrence Peter "Yogi" Berra

The earthling known as William Francis Lee, III attended Zhou Enlai's funeral in China, who served as the first Premier of the People's Republic of China from 1898 until his death on January 8, 1976. Zhou Enlai served under Chairman Mao Zedong and was instrumental in the communists' rise to power.

Bill "Spaceman" Lee had traveled to China in the winter of 1975-76 with a group of remarkable American individuals. This group included attorney Alan Silber, the brilliant former NFL star George Starke, and a brilliant professor of economics at Rutgers University who coincidentally was also a world class athlete named Phil Shinnick. Shinnick, in fact, had at one time held the world record for the long-jump and twice represented the United States at the Olympic Games. But it was what Shinnick accomplished off the athletic field that was most noteworthy.

Phil Shinnick, who became a good friend of the Spaceman, is a peaceful political activist and the founder of Athletes United for Peace and the Moscow Peace Marathon. Shinnick was enshrined at the University of Washington's Sports Hall of Fame in 1992. He's also written for the *New York Times, Sovietski Sport, New China, Runner's World,* and has also been published in many scientific journals. In 1972, Phil Shinnick became the athletic director at Livingston College of Rutgers University. In other words, the man was a rare combination of extreme intelligence and athleticism. But it was what he was "involved" with in 1974 that gave the Spaceman's friend even more notoriety.

In a shocking incident that captured the attention of people worldwide, on February 4, 1974, nineteen-year-old millionaire heiress Patricia "Patty" Hearst was kidnapped from her apartment in Berkeley, California, an event that began a spellbinding nearly two-year drama. Patty Hearst was the granddaughter of American publishing magnate William Randolph Hearst, the renowned head of a family with immense political influence, one with a strong position of anti-communism since the conclusion of World War II. William Randolph Hearst had created the largest newspaper and magazine business in the world.

The kidnappers of the heiress were a "left-wing terrorist group" known as the "Symbionese Liberation Army." It was during young Patty Hearst's captivity by the group that she was either forced to follow its doctrines or perhaps literally became an avowed member of the group! Although that is still up for conjecture, it appears likely that the latter is a greater likelihood. Consider the following:

With Patty Hearst in tow, the group initiated a string of bank robberies. Patty Hearst participated in those holdups, but there are still debates as to whether her partaking in those crimes was voluntary or involuntary. What we do know is that at one of the holdups recorded on surveillance tapes, Patty Hearst wielded an M1 Carbine while robbing the Sunset Branch of the Hibernian Bank at 1450 Noriega Street in San Francisco. During the robbery, Patty seemed to proudly use her pseudonym "Tania." Not only that, but as the other accomplices looked on, and some looked shocked, Ms. Hearst sprayed the ceiling with bullets! In the incredulous manner with which the other robbers' heads turned, it almost appeared as if they were saying, "Yo, Patty, chill! Don't kill anyone!"

So, how was "Spaceman" Lee's friend and fellow China travel partner Phil Shinnick involved? It is likely that Shinnick assisted his friends (who also happened to be Bill Lee's friends!) in avoiding her capture! On top of that, Shinnick also may have been involved in driving Patty Hearst to an "undisclosed location" which happened to be a farmhouse in South Canaan, Pennsylvania!

All right, where to begin? The FBI believed that Jack Scott, a "radical sports figure," and his wife, Micki, had rented a farmhouse in South Canaan, Pennsylvania, a location at which Patty Hearst managed to avoid capture. This was during the summer of 1974. Oh, and the feds believed that Jack Shinnick may have also abetted her possible capture in participating in this venture by driving her there.

As for the Spaceman, well, there is this. The couple who rented the farmhouse in Pennsylvania, Jack and Micki Scott, were frequent visitors to Bill Lee's home in Montreal.... No, really. As Bill stated, "Jack and Micki would come over often and cook for me. The people who helped Patty Hearst elude capture were regulars at my home in Montreal." Bill Lee described his own home in Montreal as a "safe-house." Read into that what you will.

Before Patty Hearst's capture, Phil Shinnick, the Spaceman's other friend, refused to testify and stated that the inquiry violated his rights to privacy and the Fifth Amendment. Despite never being charged for a crime, he was imprisoned at the Allenwood Federal Penitentiary in Pennsylvania for "civil contempt" in front of a grand jury in Scranton on August 13, 1975. Shinnick had refused to give the FBI his fingerprints, a sample of his handwriting, and clippings of his hair. The handwriting issue seemed strange, because they were available through Air Force documents he had written while in the service. Shinnick represented himself and never hired an attorney.

Incredibly, there is more. Basketball superstar Bill Walton also offered his support for Phil Shinnick. And if that is not weird enough, the FBI had records of telephone calls between the farmhouse and Walton's home in Portland, Oregon!

On September 18, 1975, Patty Hearst, or "Tania," was finally arrested in a San Francisco apartment along with another SLA member, Wendy Yoshimura, nineteen months after she had been abducted, by which time she was officially classified as a fugitive. The great majority of the American public now believed Patty to be a willing member of the terrorist group. At the trial, in fact, Patty Hearst listed her occupation as "an urban guerrilla." Patty also asked her attorney to relay a message that read, "Tell everybody that I'm smiling, that I feel free and strong and I send my greetings and love to all the sisters and brothers out there."

There is this thing about people with wealth and power, and the American public felt strongly that her family's enormous resources would enable Ms. Hearst to avoid significant jail time. The federal prosecutors, however, wanted Patty Hearst to be held responsible for her actions and had an extremely strong case against the heiress. At one of the robberies, in fact, a witness reported Patty was the last one seen leaving the bank while running towards the getaway car. She could have easily escaped her "captors" on that occasion. Upon adding Patty's defiant statements after being captured, it all certainly indicated she had been radicalized.

The grand jury certainly thought so, as they found Patty guilty of numerous counts and she was sentenced to thirty-five years in prison. Of course, upon testifying and realizing that she would be locked away for her entire youth, she claimed she had been raped and threatened with death. The jury, once more, did not buy her accusations.

The life of the rich and famous is often quite forgiving, however. Upon testifying against other members of the group, Patty Hearst's thirty-five-year sentence was reduced to a mere seven years. Money talks, somebody walks. And then it even got better for the heiress. Proving that money can even buy freedom, President Jimmy Carter commuted Patty Hearst's sentence and she was eventually pardoned by President Bill Clinton. Oh, to be white and rich.

Well, once more, "Spaceman" Lee has had some interesting friends and acquaintances. Phil Shinnick and Jack and Micki Scott certainly fit in that category. Speaking of Jack and Micki Scott having cooked for the Spaceman at his home in Montreal, Bill Lee stated, "Jack and Micki Scott were responsible for ruining Bill Walton's basketball career. During his time at UCLA and for two years with the Portland Trail Blazers, Walton was perhaps the most dominant center of all time, but the Scotts' recommended diet weakened the bones in Walton's feet, and he never fully recovered."

It should also be noted that upon Patty Hearst's arrest, she was examined by Dr. Margaret Singer in October 1975. Dr. Singer described Patty Hearst as a "Low IQ, low affect zombie."

Bill "Spaceman" Lee's trip to China was eventful and he's still friendly with the brilliant Phil Shinnick, who he describes as "a great guy." Hey, can you imagine being part of a group traveling to China and attending Zhou

Enlai's funeral? However, Bill nearly did not make it to China. There was a scary moment during takeoff from New York City. As the Spaceman described the ordeal:

"We took off in an L10-11 and we hit a flock of geese and almost went down. We had about four or five geese that got sucked up in the engines. The starboard engine (leave it to a southpaw to identify the correct engine) stalled and we 'blew out' about fourteen or fifteen pillowcases, but we managed to regain altitude. I really thought we were going down."

Apparently, the flight back home was also daunting, as Lee reported: "On the flight back home when I got kicked out of Shanghai from the group, I went from Shanghai to Osaka, from Osaka to Anchorage, from Anchorage to Chicago, and from Chicago to Boston. I saw the sun come up and go down three times. I was sick as a dog by the time I got home. As for China, with the fucking coal dust in the sky, it was the most polluted place I've ever been to outside of Los Angeles."

The Spaceman, a psychologist pitcher in his own right, had some interesting takes regarding the "victim" Patty Hearst:

"The amazing thing about the psychology of suppression is that when you get a girl like Patty Hearst who is pampered, it's like the formation of a mountain. When you suppress layers of sediment and it gets down to the 'Mohorovicic Discontinuity*,' it sags and pushes on the mantle, and as the mantle gets under it, it forces this uplift of emotion and that is how mountain ranges are built. When someone is raised like Patty Hearst, they become so indoctrinated. It's like 'the Freedom of Information Act' as applied to Patty Hearst, the line between the crust and the mantle. It's the process of the building of erogenous stimulation. It reminds me of getting laid."

In summation concerning Patty Hearst, the Spaceman may have uttered the best comment in regard to the heiress upon exclaiming, "There's nothing worse than giving a white chick a semi-automatic weapon."

* Mohorovocic Discontinuity (Croatian), as I have learned is usually referred to as "Moho." It is the boundary between Earth's crust and the mantle. It is defined by the distinct change in velocity of seismological waves as they pass through changing densities of rock... or perhaps in this case, through Patty Hearst's thick skull.

CHAPTER FORTY-EIGHT

Bounced from the People's Republic

"I love being a schizophrenic because I'm never alone."
—Bill "Spaceman" Lee

"The first thing that strikes a visitor to Paris is a taxi." *—Fred Allen*

"Some guy hit my fender, and I told him, 'be fruitful and multiply,' but not in those words." *—Woody Allen*

"The master class has always declared the wars. The subject class has always fought the battles. The master class had all to gain and nothing to lose while the subject class had nothing to gain and all to lose, especially their lives." *—Eugene Debs*

The earthling named William Francis Lee, III never completed his full planned itinerary in China. Bill was sent packing by a combination of being ill and one of the leaders of the American tour group, a self-righteous man named Dr. Harry Edwards, a sociologist, a civil rights activist, and the architect of the Olympic protest for human rights which led to the black power salute by Tommie Smith and John Carlos at the 1968 Summer Olympics in Mexico City.

Dr. Edwards was the professor of sociology at the University of California in Berkeley, California. In truth, the Spaceman had eagerly anticipated meeting Dr. Edwards, a man he considered a hero, but upon meeting him, said Lee, "I had idolized Harry Edwards until having to travel with him for fourteen days. What a prick!"

Dr. Harry Edwards would often argue with Bill concerning numerous topics and Edwards was wont to anoint himself as the world's greatest authority on whatever subject was being discussed. He accused Bill of becoming ill on the trip because he was a member of the "bourgeois." At the time he condemned Bill for being a member of the "bourgeoisie," the feminine of bourgeois, or perhaps a person with the characteristic traits or viewpoint of the bourgeoisie, Bill, a learned scholar for an athlete, recognized the insult for what it was and responded in kind, "Me, a member of the bourgeoisie? I drive a friggin' Volkswagen and you're tooling around in a Cadillac, and I'm bourgeois? You don't have to go to Chattanooga to see Rock City!" Immediately upon hearing that, both Phil Shinnick and David Silber "spit bird's nest soup all over the table. They were laughing their asses off."

"Imagine," said Lee, "being tossed out of Communist China by an officious asshole who decided to 'vote' me out of the group, proving conclusively that the man is an avowed capitalist."

Dr. Harry Edwards' questionable integrity came into question when in 1989 he scheduled midterm exams on Yom Kippur, a major Jewish holiday, for one of his classes. It certainly appeared as if Dr. Edwards was not devoid of bigotry.

Lee noted that during the iconic black power salute at the 1968 Olympics, that Tommie Smith and John Carlos wore their gloves on different hands. Apparently, they only had one pair of gloves. As the Spaceman joked, but of course, was NOT criticizing the action, "That is not solidarity, that is ambidexterity."

Other than Dr. Harry Edwards, the Spaceman enjoyed his trip to China immensely. One of the highlights of the trip was becoming the first American to down twenty-two ounce Tsingtao Beers and to smoke Chinese filter-less "Phoenix" Cigarettes, the brand of cigarette that eventually claimed the life of Zhou Enlai, whose funeral the Spaceman attended during the trip. During that period in the life of the earthling Bill Lee, he would smoke up to a pack a day.

Two of the more delightful people Bill Lee met on the trip were "two gay women from Oberlin College in Ohio. They were funny as hell. They would talk to everyone and then raise up three fingers."

As for Bill Lee being possibly branded as a "communist sympathizer" because of his oft controversial comments and his trip to China, Lee remarked, "Do you know the 'Freedom of Information Act'? If I got that I could be standing in the White House on my dossier and be able to change the light bulbs without having to use a ladder."

On the trip to China, the plane landed in Hong Kong. As the Spaceman explained, "We took a bus to the border and then had to walk about four hundred yards to cross into China. We then hopped on a train to Canton before they renamed it 'Hangzhou.' That's a long way to travel for Cantonese food."

Perhaps the most unexpected part of the trip occurred in Shanghai. As the Spaceman explained:

"Merely a few months earlier in October, I had given up a home run to Tony Perez in the seventh game of that World Series. After the game I told the writers that there were three billion Chinese who weren't aware I had hung a curve ball to Perez and couldn't have cared less. In one of those *New York Times* east coast editions the following day, there was a front-page photograph showing me on the mound hanging that curve before he had hit it.

"The most amazing thing that happened on the trip to China was walking into a library in Shanghai two months later and seeing a copy of that *New York Times* sitting on a table out in the open! They had a Chinese version of the *New York Times* just resting on that table showing me throwing the hanging soft pitch! What are the odds?!"

I never questioned Bill Lee in perhaps drawing an analogy between Dr. Harry Edwards and geniuses such as Dick Gregory and Phil Shinnick, but it appears to me that pseudo-intellectuals such as Edwards learn to toss around fancy words such as "bourgeoisie" in order to impress people. It must be somewhat frustrating in communicating with such self-righteous self-indulgent pompous people.

Just as with everything else in the life of the earthling known as William Francis Lee, III, expect the unexpected.

Note: The author, in this case Scott Russell, has observed Bill Lee from both up close and afar for nearly fifty years. The Spaceman may disagree, but I believe that Lee is more of an anti-establishment activist than a pure socialist, not quite in the vein of an Abbie Hoffman, because Abbie was more of an anarchist. Although the Spaceman's humor often borders on anarchy, it is both hilarious and serious as well.

Bill Lee questions authority on both sides of the aisle. Bill Lee, in my opinion, seeks truth and the brotherhood of man. Upon seeing hypocrisy, whether it be on the left, right, or even in the "middle" for that matter, self-righteous people will not escape the Spaceman's wrath. In short, Bill Lee does not tolerate intolerance....

I believe the Spaceman is perhaps more a disciple of Rodney Dangerfield than he is any sort of political pundit. A favorite quote by Dangerfield is as follows:

"There are only two things worth fighting for. Number one: to protect your wife and kids. Number two: for a good piece of ass."

CHAPTER FORTY-NINE

The Vortex

"Nobody ever went broke underestimating the intelligence of the American public." —*H.L. Mencken*

Virginia Lee, the wife of Bill Lee's Uncle Grover the locksmith, had a cabin near Slide Rock State Park in scenic Sedona, Arizona, a place where Bill would often take his kids to slide down the slippery rocks into a natural pool. The algae on the rocks provides for a slippery ride. The popular park stretches for one half-mile in Oak Creek Canyon and it is open for swimming and for wading and sliding. Within Oak Creek Canyon is sacred Kachina Park and the Sedona red rocks and the area comprises one of the most beautiful sites in the United States. The town of Sedona is built atop a sacred Indian burial ground.

In Kachina Park, the Native Americans set up tables where they sell beautiful hand-crafted jewelry which includes turquoise bracelets and earrings and numerous other wonderful trinkets. Recently, the former Red Sox and Montreal Expo ace, Bill Lee, revisited the area with his beautiful wife, Diana. He was having a conversation with Diana when a voice called out from behind them, "Hey, it's the Spaceman!"

Bill and Diana turned to see an eight or nine year-old boy pointing excitedly at his discovery. Here was a child who had recognized Bill Lee from merely his voice! Diana peered at her half-crazed husband and queried, "How in hell does a small child in the middle of nowhere recognize you by just hearing you voice?!" She was incredulous. The Spaceman just smiled.

The town of Sedona, however, is renowned for its magical and mystical aura. There are "Pink Jeep Tours" that take visitors up into the cliffs above the town to see the beauty and shading of the red rocks which change spectacularly dependent upon the light of day. It is said that the Native Americans state unequivocally that the area is spiritual and that power can be derived from beneath the ground, where a "vortex" has strong gravitational pull.... I, for one, believe it.

The author and his wife, as well as the Lees, have traveled to the spot of the vortex. On the warmest of afternoons—and it gets awfully warm in that area—if one sits peacefully in silence, you can feel a soft cooling breeze despite temperatures approaching one hundred degrees Fahrenheit.

The vortex, which is beneath the ground, consists of water moving rapidly in a circle with a hollow in the center akin to a whirlpool. It is a maelstrom, and the Spaceman is quite familiar with being involved in maelstroms, his entire life being one.

In *The Odyssey*, Ulysses is trapped between the six-headed monster, Scylla, and Charybdis, a deadly whirlpool that threatens to suck his ship down. The Spaceman has encountered many such close calls as well as a few sirens on the rocks beckoning him to God knows where.

Upon having a conversation with the Spaceman about the vortex, the author, and it still remains unclear if he is Scott Russell or Kilgore Trout, or perhaps both, had a rather vivid dream recently, and despite also learning that Daryl Dragon's sister, Antoinette (the late Daryl Dragon and Toni Tennille of "The Captain and Tennille" fame) was into psychedelics and 'shrooms, had this bizarre dream despite going to bed entirely "sober."

In the dream, the Spaceman is the ceremonial "puck dropper" at a celebrity hockey game. After the national anthem is sung by Colin Kaepernick, the players gather at center ice as Bill Lee prepares to drop the puck to begin the evening's festivities. As legendary Boston sportscasters Bob Lobel and Clark Booth look on, the Spaceman suddenly gets into a conversation with Don Zimmer. During this lively discourse, Bill Lee is attempting to explain the vortex to Zimmer, who has a vacuous look on his face.... Of course, it should be noted that Don Zimmer invariably had a vacuous look on his face. The crowd anticipating a hockey game grows restless. Suddenly, the great Boston Bruins hockey star Bobby Orr arrives at center ice and shouts at the flustered Bill Lee, "Just drop the fucking puck!"

...I'm afraid at that point I awakened because one of my cats walked across my face. I am hopeful that the balance of the dream will provide me with hope that intelligent beings once roamed our planet.

CHAPTER FIFTY

The Ties that Bind

> "There is no reason why good cannot triumph as often as evil. The triumph of anything is a matter of organization. If there are such things as angels, I hope they are organized along the lines of the mafia." —*Kurt Vonnegut*

As the Cessna Turbo was approaching what passed for an airport in Sedona, Arizona, the earthling known as William Francis Lee, III was not at all nervous despite his being aware that the landing strip consisted of a rather short stretch of what appeared to be flat top table rock. As Lee stated, "There's no room for error. It's not like landing on a huge aircraft carrier. Diana was going nuts, but Ozzie Virgil, Jr. is a top gun and a great pilot. Ozzie is a survivalist and he owns .50 caliber guns. Ozzie is an amazing guy." And that Ozzie Virgil, Jr. is, and a whole lot more, too.

Ozzie Virgil, Jr. briefly was Bill Lee's catcher in Montreal, long before he was the Spaceman's "pilot." Ozzie has also caught Bill in Senior Leagues, in other semi-professional leagues, and in charity games, but most importantly, Ozzie Virgil, Jr. has been Lee's close friend for decades. If you are either stranded on a desert island or in some godforsaken foxhole, Ozzie is the guy you want at your side.

Ozzie's father, Oswaldo Jose Virgil y Pichardo, Sr. was the first Dominican to play major league baseball. This historic event took place on September 23, 1956 when Ozzie, Sr. started at third base for the New York Giants at the Polo Grounds versus the Philadelphia Phillies, who were the last National League team to integrate. This is also significant because 21 months later, Ozzie Virgil, Sr. became the first player of African descent to play for the Detroit Tigers. The date was June 6, 1958, breaking the "color line" for still another major league team, ELEVEN YEARS after Jackie Robinson! Ozzie, Sr. was also a proud member of the U.S. Marine Corps from 1950-1952 and one wonders if that is where his son perhaps inherited his survivalist skills. Ozzie, Sr. married a Puerto Rican woman and their son, Ozzie, Jr. was born in Mayaguez, Puerto Rico on December 7, 1956.

Ozzie Virgil, Sr.'s family moved to the Bronx, New York when he was thirteen years old. The future groundbreaking major leaguer would attend DeWitt Clinton High School in the Bronx.*

> * The author actually saw Ozzie, Sr. appear at a clinic in Crotona Park in the Bronx after Virgil had joined the New York Giants.

The elder Virgil went on to a distinguished major league career, one which lasted 17 seasons, as both a player and coach. He was the favorite coach of Hall of Fame manager Dick Williams for several years. As for Bill Lee's buddy, Ozzie Virgil, Jr., he was born in Arizona and starred at Moon Valley High School in Phoenix. Lee's "pilot" set many state records as a slugging catcher in high school and even forced a taller fence to be erected on the Moon Valley field due to his tendency to use nearby houses as target practice.

As the Spaceman attested to, Ozzie became very adept at a different type of "target practice." Ozzie, Jr. performed in 11 outstanding seasons for the Philadelphia Phillies, Atlanta Braves, and the Toronto Blue Jays from 1980 to 1990 and was named to two All-Star squads. To this day, Ozzie Virgil, Jr. has keys to Bill Lee's home in Vermont. *Mi casa es su casa.*

As the Spaceman described, "Once we went to St. Maarten's to do a clinic when my shoulder was bad and we got drunk as hell in Mayaguez at Rincon Beach and my arm was so bad I had to play centerfield with one arm." Ozzie was most likely running ballplayers out of Cuba on his plane, but that's another story.

One of Ozzie's former bosses and friends was the no-nonsense manager of the Philadelphia Phillies, Dallas Green, who was the man who would lead the Phillies to their initial World Series title in 1980. Green would also go on to be a successful general manager. In a horrific event that occurred at a supermarket in Tucson, Arizona on January 8, 2011, Arizona Congresswoman Gabrielle Giffords was shot by a crazed gunman. Tragically, Christine-Taylor Green, the granddaughter of Dallas Green, was killed. She was nine years old and Dallas Green never recovered from the horrid episode.

In a circumstance that Lee described was indicative of just how far we have NOT come as a species, Ozzie traveled to Arizona in order to pay final respects to Dallas Green's granddaughter, but as the Spaceman explained: "Ozzie was nearly thrown out by the white cops because he looked like a bandito to them."

We had mentioned that a fence had to be constructed at Ozzie's high school field in order to prevent him from breaking windows with towering home run blasts as if he was using them for target practice, and that Virgil had become quite adept with another form of target practice. Up at Lee's home in northern Vermont, hard by the Canadian border, Bill described Ozzie as using Lee's .270 Elk Rifle and "shooting at a flock of geese that had landed on the 'Black River' across Route 14. I told Ozzie that if he could hit anything from five hundred yards that he was definitely sniper material. However, Ozzie wasn't actually attempting to hit anything."

CHAPTER FIFTY-ONE

Revenge is Best Served Cold.

Aw, Nuts!

God Bless You Mrs. Wohlford, a Nation Turns Its Lonely Eyes to You

"Punishment deferred is punishment wasted."
—Bill "Spaceman" Lee

"Man does not control his own fate. The women in his life do that for him." *—Groucho Marx*

Suffice to say that most ballplayers if asked, couldn't tell you when their wife's birthday is or cannot explain why the socks they're wearing that particular day don't match, but ask a pitcher (especially the southpaw of the species) about a specific batter they faced forty-one years ago and the response is generally, "Oh, John Smith? Yeah, it was the sixth inning on a Friday night in Baltimore. I hung a one and two curveball and he looped it for a two-run double, that son of a bitch!" It is that rare occasion, however, when the wife of a ballplayer holds a grudge against her husband's opponent for over four decades. That is a woman clearly not to be messed with.

In July of 2017, the earthling known as William Francis Lee, III, found himself in Cooperstown, New York to honor his former Montreal Expos teammate, Tim "Rock" Raines. The occasion was a party at a meeting hall feting Raines, who had just been elected to the Baseball Hall of Fame. Tim Raines was a terrific hitter and one of the greatest base-stealers in baseball history. Raines had also overcome major drug issues, ones which literally forced him to briefly take a sabbatical from the game.

Not surprisingly, Tim Raines' drug of choice was cocaine, one which was prevalent during that era in baseball. During the famous Pittsburgh baseball drug trials in September of 1985, Raines freely admitted snorting cocaine before games, on occasion between innings during games, and nearly invariably in his car following games. Raines' testimony was not only courageous, but his memory was apparently much greater than that of Keith Hernandez who had claimed that although he had used illicit drugs with several teammates, he could only recall Bernie Carbo. For the record, Hernandez also stated under oath that he had merely taken the playing field on only one occasion during the time he was under the influence.

Tim Raines not only resurrected his career, but obviously, as his Hall of Fame credentials attest to, became a superstar. Pete Rose, a great player, but a man of dubious character, was one of the first practitioners of the headfirst slide, a way of attaining a base that is commonplace these days, but often scorned by the purists of the game who claim it's simply not the correct or most effective fundamentally sound approach. However, there was a reason to Tim Raines' method, since as Raines' friend Bill Lee told me many years ago, "Raines slid headfirst into bases because he had a vial of cocaine in his hip pocket."

In 1982, Tim Raines entered treatment for substance abuse. At one time, Rock told those at the trial, he was spending up to $40,000 a year on cocaine. But on July 30, 2017, a fully rehabilitated Tim Raines was enshrined at the Hall of Fame in Cooperstown and the Spaceman was there to pay tribute to his friend.

At the aforementioned bash in the picturesque quaint little town, the peaceful serenity of the party honoring the new Hall of Fame inductee was suddenly interrupted by what appeared to be a screaming banshee. A rather inebriated woman charged at the unsuspecting Spaceman, her fists flailing and spewing invective like Tommy Lasorda at a postgame press conference. The meeting house at which this event took place was sandwiched between two bars, and the woman in question had apparently patronized both and in significant fashion prior to her assault. As Bill Lee turned to see the source of the commotion, he was assailed by the shrieking woman who immediately proceeded to kick the Spaceman in the balls.

As numerous well-dressed shocked onlookers witnessed, Lee, to defend himself from the crazed woman, took drastic action. As the Spaceman described:

"After she kneed me in the nuts, she was preparing another kick, but I grabbed her by the ankles and she went down on the ground. Then I dragged her across the floor like she was a wheelbarrow. Someone yelled out, 'Bill Lee's beating up on a girl,' but one of the French Canadians visiting from Montreal shouted, 'No, no. He's being very gentle.' It was so fucking funny.

I tossed her up on my shoulders L'il Abner style and began walking her out the door of the meeting hall. When I got outside, Jim Wohlford yells, 'Hey, put down my wife!' I looked at Wohlford and yelled, 'Come get "Daisy Mae" and while you're at it, take your balls out of your wife's purse!'"

As the crowd on the sidewalk looked on in a silenced shock, Lee gently placed the infuriated inebriate back on her feet, but she once more hit the ground. As Lee stated:

"She rolls onto her stomach and knees. God, she was sloshed! What a sight! Here she was wobbling away on her spiked heels. You have to admire a woman who holds a grudge for forty-one years."

Upon the author asking the first name of his assailant, he replied:

"I don't know, probably 'Honey' or 'Meat,' she was a typical '4-H' girl from Visalia, California. She almost got the blue ribbon at the 4-H Club, but the only problem is that she couldn't keep her calves together. I'm telling you, she was a pistol!"

Jim Wohlford, the would-be assassin's husband, was an outfielder with several major league teams from 1972-1986. Upon learning of the ineffectual assault inflicted upon the Spaceman from Wohlford's enraged and totally plastered spouse, the story becomes even more hilarious. On May 4, 1976, Jim Wohlford of the Kansas City Royals had the misfortune of facing the Spaceman at an inopportune time. You see, Bill Lee was not having a good day. On that day, Lee had given up an uncustomary 6 runs in 5 innings, and the carnage included two home runs by Amos Otis. Upon K.C. catcher Buck Martinez driving in two runs with a double, Lee's conviviality decreased commensurately. Therefore, seeing Jim Wohlford step into the batters' box, a man who had significant success versus the Spaceman in the past did not exactly provide inspiration or provide Lee with an overt warm fuzzy feeling. A fastball to the ribs was in order.

It should be noted that Wohlford, who obviously realized that Lee's errant toss was not exactly "errant," did not charge the mound in order to initiate hostilities with the larger Spaceman. Wohlford merely took his base rather than confront his already troubled foe.

Seriously though, had Wohlford and his tipsy wife discussed some sort of revenge for forty-one years? That scenario would be considered bizarre, but nothing seems uncustomary when examining the world of the earthling known as William Francis Lee, III.

CHAPTER FIFTY-TWO

When Swordfish Go Bad

"We are what we imagine ourselves to be." —*Kurt Vonnegut*

During the time that the earthling known as William Francis Lee, III, was playing amateur ball, he managed to get himself thrown out of a game by a deaf umpire. This amusing incident occurred at Hohokam Stadium in Mesa, Arizona with the Spaceman's parents in attendance.

"I hadn't suspected that he was deaf, but I certainly suspected that he was blind," said Lee. "It was only when I got in his face that he ejected me from the game," explained the Spaceman, as he continued, "He must've been a great lip-reader. My mom and dad were so mad at me that they wouldn't even drive me back to the hotel."

Bill Lee has always loved the southwest, with its red rocks, its desert, and spectacular sunsets, especially when in the wilderness. During the time Lee was "trying out" for the San Francisco Giants in Scottsdale, Arizona in the spring of 1983, a bogus audition because the Spaceman had been unofficially blackballed from the game he so loved, as Lee explained:

"We drove our Volkswagen down through Visalia and decided to drive through the San Carlos Apache Indian Reservation in southeast Arizona, but first was a stop in the Gila National Forest in New Mexico, a protected area which prohibits the intrusion of roads or the evidence of human presence. As we were coming out of the national monument, we were skinny-dipping in a hot springs pool that Cochise and Geronimo used to hang out on the middle fork of the Gila Wilderness and I'm with a guy named Ben Benson, who is a federal park ranger down there. Ben was in fact, a park ranger at the cave dwellings. Ben, a really cool guy, was also a fish pilot out of Machias, Maine, at least until he lost his load of fish during the 1975 World Series."

Obviously, I was incredulous upon hearing Bill describe this tale, but then I remembered exactly whom I was speaking with. As the Spaceman elaborated:

"Ben, a great fan of baseball, had planned to deliver his catch of fish to Machias, Maine, where his boat was supposed to dock, but by the time he got there, his swordfish had gone bad and Ben wound up losing his job as ranger in the Gila Wilderness."

But it was why the fish went bad that told the tale. Ben had tickets for game six of the epic 1975 World Series between the Spaceman's Red Sox and the Cincinnati Reds, but the game was rained out for three consecutive days! Therefore, Ben Benson's boat was moored in Boston Harbor until Bernie Carbo and Carlton Fisk's historic home runs freed the ranger from Fenway Park! By the time Ben got his boat up to Machias, one of the favorite fishing spots of the great Ted Williams, as Bill Lee stated, "the fucking fish had gone bad." But at least Ben Benson had witnessed baseball history.

A little history of the San Carlos Apache Indian Reservation in southeast Arizona reveals that it was established in 1872 as a reservation for the Chiricuhua Apache tribe, as well as surrounding Yavapai and Apache bands that had been forcibly removed from their homelands under a strategy devised by General George Crook of using an Apache to catch an Apache.

The Spaceman also learned that Ranger Benson had also worked at the Sugarbush Resort in a country club in central Vermont and had "stolen a Volkswagen and driven it all the way from Vermont to fucking New Mexico." The friends and acquaintances of "Spaceman" Lee are not the usual run-of-the-mill neighbors of yours.

"Spaceman" Lee, and nothing should surprise you by now, was once driving through the San Carlos Apache Reservation, which of course, is basically in the middle of nowhere. As Lee explained:

"I was on my way to Phoenix to try out for the Giants. My car starts conking out. There were two Indians in this little garage and they see my car come limping in. They immediately see that it's a fuel filter, smile and say, 'Oh, you're fine.' One of them takes a #2 lead pencil and he sticks it through the fuel filter and breaks the seal. I'm back on the road and I drive all the way to fucking Phoenix!"

But it was what happened upon the Spaceman's arrival in Phoenix that makes this story even more improbable.

"I drove all the way to Phoenix/Scottsdale and the car conks out again on a corner that had these apartments with a swimming pool in the middle. My car literally stopped in front of the property manager's door. I go inside and the manager tells me he's got a place for rent, so I rent a bungalow that borders on a stone wall fence, and behind the fence is the right field corner of the Giants ballpark I was supposed to report to! I drove all the way with the pencil repaired fuel filter and incredibly it conks out upon my arrival. I mean what are the odds? This was the same ballpark that the Red Sox had used when they held their spring training in Arizona. Then it got even weirder. I found out that Ted Williams lived in that same house!"

CHAPTER FIFTY-THREE

Bush League

> "There are a great many people who have a vested interest in maintaining the stupidity of the American public." —*Gore Vidal*

The earthling known as William Francis Lee, III recently told the author that he often frequently awakes the following morning and exclaims, "What the fuck just happened?" Such is life when you are Bill "Spaceman" Lee, whose surrounding existence is often unexplainable even to him, sort of a delayed reaction culture shock.

If Bill Lee has one weakness other than an occasional hanging curveball, it would be regularly attempting to explain the unexplainable. It is virtually impossible to arrive at any sort of rationale upon viewing less intelligent members of his species, but it still takes far too much of the Spaceman's allotted time on planet Earth in endeavoring to even remotely comprehend the actions of imbeciles and nitwits.

Consider that during the time Bill Lee was still an impressionable student at the University of Southern California, he would spend time studying at Stoner Hall (sounds like it belonged in John Belushi's 'Delta Tau Chi fraternity in Animal House) while merely a few hundred yards away, the man who would become the Spaceman's idol, Buckminster Fuller, would be lecturing Lee's fellow students. The author has resisted grabbing Lee around the shoulders, shaking him, and scolding him much like one of the "Budweiser Lizards" while attempting to coax him to "Let it go, Louie, let it go." Bill Lee's college coach Rod Dedeaux seemed to realize this long before during the days he frequently exhorted, "Don't think, Tiger, it will only hurt the team."

One such inexplicable morning, Bill Lee awoke and discovered that on only the day before he had somehow become entangled at a Republican re-election event. Not only that, but as he reclined in a corner downstairs where a Tyrannosaurus Rex majestically towered above him, he found himself smoking weed with the future President of the United States, the less than capable George W. Bush, while just above them, Lee's wife Mary Lou was deep in conversation with another future president, George

Walker Bush, and the future First Lady, Barbara Bush. George Walker Bush prior to becoming president of the United States would head the Central Intelligence Agency.... The Spaceman also pointed out that while serving in the army, much like himself, George W. Bush was also classified as an REMF (Rear Echelon Mother Fucker), perhaps supporting the theory that there is indeed, at least some sense in the universe.

"George W. Bush," spoke Lee, "was not really a bad guy, but merely one of those guys with a name like 'Chauncey Gardner,' Peter Sellers' character in 'Being There.' He was just a guy that's not going to piss everyone off, someone who can come up with a term like 'compassionate conservative.' It sounds non-threatening, and that was his motto. It pretty much got him elected president."

Lee described the event at the Museum of Natural History in Boston as follows:

"What got me was not that I was smoking dope with the son of the future president of the United States, but what the hell was I doing there in the first place? I had taken my son Mike in a stroller and there was Mary Lou, Senator Ed Brooke of Massachusetts, and a whole bunch of other people and George W. and I decided to go off in a corner to smoke some Thai weed."

I should point out that Bill Lee's dearest friend for many years has been Mike Mulkern, a staunch conservative, and of course, Bill is the polar opposite. However, it also speaks volumes that both friends can engage in partisan political discussions sans the bitter diatribe and invective, something apparently impossible in the year 2020. Mike Mulkern recently told Bill, "You remind me of my father." Lee responded, "And you remind me of my father!" (Lee's dad was a Goldwater Republican).

Recently, Bill Lee asked the author, "How many ballplayers do you know that can quote *The Rape of Europa*?"

"One," was my immediate response.

As for smoking weed with a future President of the United States while his Miss Alaska wife sat upstairs deep in dialogue with another future President and First Lady? Well, it was just another day in the life of the earthling known as William Francis Lee, III.

CHAPTER FIFTY-FOUR

Cool Breeze

"Bill, you're the only white guy allowed on the back of the bus."
—John Milner, teammate of the Spaceman

"Hammer, I didn't know I was white." *—Bill "Spaceman" Lee*

John "Hammer" Milner, a slugging first-baseman and outfielder, who as Lee said, "died way too young at the age of fifty-one because he smoked too many goddamned cigarettes," alluded to the fact that Bill Lee was "color-blind." Ironically, Lee would literally eventually be blackballed from baseball for his stance in defending two minority ballplayers, both of whom had been royally screwed by the system, Bernardo Carbo and Rodney Scott. However, the Spaceman did not single them out because one was Hispanic and the other African American, but because they were simply friends and teammates. Lee would have done the same for a white athlete if they had come under similar injustices.

Rodney "Cool Breeze" Scott, who hails from Indianapolis, Indiana, and whom we mentioned earlier in this tome, was an outstanding defender, one who saved his pitchers many runs by utilizing his enormous range and soft hands, and Rodney was also a fundamentally sound player, a throwback to the days when players knew how to bunt, advance runners, and steal bases. He was an asset to the Montreal Expos at the time he was released, and as Lee stated, "If the problem was drugs, 'Breeze' was the only one who merely indulged in only marijuana. Many of our other teammates, me included, were into far more banned substances. To this moment, the Expos never had the balls to say exactly why he was released."

Lee and Rodney Scott remain good friends to this day, and Breeze's initial trip to Lee's home in the wilds of Vermont was hilarious. As the Spaceman described:

"Rodney is such an urbanite that he stayed up all night and binge-watched the seven-part series, 'Lonesome Dove.' Breeze was afraid to go to sleep because he was convinced a bear would come into the house!"

There will be much more on the release of Rodney Scott later on, the final act in Bill Lee's career, the one that was the final nail in the coffin for his career.

Bill Lee, and rightfully so, has always been critical of how often disreputable jerks are rewarded by the higher-ups, but those that truly respect the game of baseball are subjected to its slings and arrows. Take the former utility infielder Jerry Terrell, for instance. To Terrell's credit, he was a slick fielding, decent enough hitting and hustling middle infielder. To his discredit he was a contemptuous unethical ballplayer, and as an alleged Christian, likely a hypocrite.

On May 29, 1974 in a game at Fenway Park, Terrell's Minnesota Twins were in town to play the Red Sox. In a tight contest on a getaway day, the game remained tied as it went into extra innings. It remained 4-4, in fact, entering the thirteenth inning. The Red Sox were a bit short on pitching and the durable starter/reliever Diego Segui had come on in the eighth inning. From that point on, Diego threw shutout ball. In the top of the thirteenth inning, the Twins had runners at first and third place and Terrell stepped to the plate. As Segui began his windup, Terrell suddenly bent over in the batters' box and appeared to be picking up a handful of dirt. Segui, wary of hitting the unprotected Terrell, ceased his windup. The umpire, and again, rightfully so, called "Balk!" The lead run and the one which would be the winning run were both allowed to score. What Terrell committed was cheap and underhanded and went against the ethics of the game, but since timeout had not been called, it was at least according to the rules, "legal." But it was what Terrell stated to the media following the game that irked the Red Sox even more. Terrell, in his holy righteousness, announced for all to hear, "God told me to do it."

Bill Lee, God bless him, pun intended, wanted desperately to face Terrell following that at bat, but it was getaway day for Terrell's Twins, and getaway he did. As Lee stated, "I was going to drill him in the ribs with a fastball and shout, 'God told me to do it.'"

This was not the lone occasion that Terrell aroused the ire of his fellow players. In April 1980, the membership of the Major League Baseball Players Association voted 582-1 in favor of a strike. Union head Marvin Miller said the lone dissenter did so because of his "religious convictions." While neither Terrell nor Miller confirmed it was Jerry Terrell who issued the lone dissenting vote, it seemed to be common knowledge that it was Jerry Terrell.

Perhaps to Terrell's credit? Terrell was given the 1980 "Danny Thompson Award" for "exemplary Christian spirit." Thompson was a courageous Minnesota Twins shortstop who tragically succumbed to cancer during his playing career. It is not known if the presenters of the award balked upon handing Terrell the award.

In 1981, Peter Gammons wrote an article about Ferguson Jenkins in which Peter stated that morality was not a prerequisite for induction into Cooperstown. "If it were," wrote Gammons, "Babe Ruth (and many others) would have to be dropped to make room for Jerry Terrell." All the Spaceman desired to do was to "drop" Jerry Terrell, who incidentally, batted .231 (9-39) with 0 home runs and 1 RBI versus Lee during his entire career.

CHAPTER FIFTY-FIVE

Guns 'n Tobacco

Don't Bite off More Than You Can Chew

"All family life is organized around the most damaged person in it."
—*Sigmund Freud*

On August 10, 1977, the earthling known as William Francis Lee, III found himself sitting in the bullpen at Fenway Park as he watched a wild ballgame between the Angels and Red Sox unfold. Don Zimmer, Lee's manager and longtime adversary, was not expecting to be called into the wild fray, but his left-handed mound mate Ramon Hernandez had been warming up to enter the game.

In the top of the seventh inning, the Angels had scored three runs and Zimmer waddled out of the dugout to bring Hernandez into the game. Ramon Hernandez was a veteran left-handed reliever who hailed from Carolina, Puerto Rico. Hernandez would play 9 major league seasons and compile a respectable 3.03 ERA and his 337 games (that's "Lee" upside down, incidentally) did not include even a single start.

As a crowd of 34,869 looked on, Zimmer signaled to the bullpen with his left arm to summon Hernandez. Within moments, Bill "Spaceman" Lee leaped over the bullpen fence and began trotting to the mound. Upon arriving at the pitching rubber, Zimmer squawked at his least favorite person, "Who the hell called you?! I called for Hernandez!"

It was then that Lee informed his beloved manager of the sad truth: "Ramon can't pitch. He's blowing his lunch in the shitter." And that he was. Ramon Hernandez had swallowed his chaw of tobacco and was in the process of heaving everything he had eaten into the porcelain toilet bowl.

"Don't worry, Zim," said the Spaceman, "it's only Rance* Mulliniks, and I can get him out on one pitch." Moments later, Lee indeed got Mulliniks, the pride of Visalia, California out on that one pitch, a soft ground ball to first base. For the record, the Red Sox won the wild game 11-10. As you read in an earlier chapter, Lee always seemed to be able to successfully vanquish those from Visalia, including the enraged inebriated wives of outfielders.

> * It should be noted that was the lone time the Spaceman faced Rance Mulliniks in a major league game.

One would have thought that Don Zimmer, genius manager that he was, should have been well-schooled to the fact that Ramon Hernandez did not always answer the call. On one such occasion during a 1967 winter league doubleheader, Zimmer was managing a team in San Juan. On that occasion, Zimmer requested the presence of Hernandez by calling the bullpen but was told he was not present in the vicinity. Zimmer's catcher, incidentally, was a nineteen-year-old youngster named Johnny Bench.

A perturbed Zimmer—he despised pitchers, especially the left-handed member of the species—went looking for Ramon and located him in the clubhouse where he found Hernandez seated in front of his locker wearing shorts and downing a cold brew.

Apparently, Zimmer was afraid of approaching his reluctant hurler because he had allegedly heard that Ramon was packing a gun and a knife.

"Knowing Zimmer," said Lee, "he most likely suspected that of all Hispanic players."*

Only "Spaceman" Lee could possibly draw an analogy to one of the greatest motion pictures of all time, the great 1948 classic written and directed by John Huston, *The Treasure of the Sierra Madre,* starring Humphrey Bogart, Tim Holt, and Walter Huston, John Huston's father.

In the movie, the three American gold miners are in Mexico and they are approached by three native Mexicans, and the three gringos ask for the Mexicans' credentials. One of the Mexicans, who is wearing a gold hatband (actor Alfonso Bedoya) answers, "We don't need no stinking badges!"

Bill Lee was no doubt looking into Zimmer's mind and what his poor manager was thinking at the time. "Zimmer probably believed that Ramon Hernandez was one of the banditos who approached Walter Huston."

Somehow, Zimmer's team reaches the playoffs, but the feisty skipper went to the general manager of the ball club to demand that Ramon Hernandez be released. Zimmer had allegedly told his bosses that Hernandez had been bringing a gun and a knife into the locker room. The following day, the general manager indeed released... Don Zimmer. He handed Zimmer a letter informing him that his services were no longer required.

Young Johnny Bench had allegedly told Zimmer that he was leaving, too, but was talked out of it.

* Note: The author learned from his friend David E. Diaz, a fellow Bronx native whose knowledge of the game is unsurpassed, that Ramon Hernandez indeed, carried a gun and a knife! You see, Hernandez owned a liquor store and kept the weapons as protection.... Holy crap, this time Zimmer was right!

CHAPTER FIFTY-SIX

The Spaceman Live at San Quentin

"I am in a cage, in search of a bird." —*Franz Kafka*

"Never invest in a brokerage firm at which one of the partners is named 'Blackie.'" —*Woody Allen*

In the 1960s, 1980s, 1990s, 2000s, and 2010s, the earthling known as William Francis Lee, III appeared at San Quentin Prison, the iconic and infamous penitentiary on the San Francisco Bay. The prison, constructed in 1852, is the oldest prison in the state of California. Resting north of San Francisco, it offers spectacular views of the Bay and many "permanent" rooms since it is a maximum-security prison containing numerous hardened criminals, many of whom are serving life sentences.

Bill Lee, much like Johnny Cash before him, is a frequent visitor to the institution, a place at which he plays exhibition games versus the inmates. As the Spaceman stated, "It's not a place you want to play a home game. The key is to be on the visiting team. There is no home field advantage."

Bill Lee also joked, "I've been in San Quentin longer than anyone except perhaps Caryl Chessman." Lee also stated:

"There's an inmate on their team, a Native American from up on the Klamath River. He's there for murder one, so he's not going to enter into free agency. Scott Boras won't be calling. This guy has more tattoos than Ray Bradbury's 'the Illustrated Man.'"

Lee described the playing field as being "tucked away in a back corner and you hit your home runs to right field." Bill continued: "Outside of the prison, they have a shower and a sweat lodge out for the Native Americans and they'd be out there naked in the shower while we're playing the ballgames. It's not a pretty sight to see. We have a back screen and a path where you ran around and above a wall there's a prison guard up in a turret with a gun. Every time a foul ball would go out of the park, all of the inmates would say, 'I wish I was that ball.'"

Bill Lee also provided the author with some fascinating history in regard to the greatest prison baseball player of all time, and the enthralling tale can be told in Eric Stone's fine 2005 book, *The Life of Blackie Schwamb: The Wrong Side of the Wall.*

Ralph Richard "Blackie" Schwamb was a 6′ 5″ fire-balling right-handed pitcher, who at the age of twenty-two reached the major leagues with the St. Louis Browns. Blackie's major league career was shortlived, however, because he developed this annoying habit of murdering people.... No, really. As the Spaceman remarked, "They don't call it film noir for nothing."

Following the 1948 season, Schwamb gravitated back to his home in Los Angeles to return to his off-season occupation, which was "hitman for the mob." Apparently, one of Blackie's bosses was the notorious mobster, Mickey Cohen, who also acquired a fondness for killing people. Hey, it's a hobby. Get over it.

Therefore, when the St. Louis Browns' rookie hurler ended the life of a prominent Long Beach doctor, his baseball career was ostensibly over. In addition, the doctor's medical career also ended abruptly. As "Spaceman" Lee pointed out, "Blackie's pitching career indeed, continued, but at San Quentin Prison. Don Zimmer, who didn't like pitchers to begin with, I would suspect, would not have invited Mr. Schwamb to his home, either."

Schwamb, therefore, became the ace of the San Quentin Pirates team, the ball club that played all its games at its home field. "Blackie" Schwamb was sentenced to life in prison in 1949, thereby missing his sophomore season in the big leagues, but he did develop quite a reputation at the "Big House." Schwamb, however, was granted parole in 1960, but succumbed at the age of sixty-three in 1989.

The earthling known as William Francis Lee, who of course, never faced Schwamb, made a rather astute observation. Said the Spaceman:

"Schwamb was only 1-1, 8.53 in his only partial major league season but he did HIT .300 (3-10). He was just at the wrong position. After all, Blackie was a HITTER."

CHAPTER FIFTY-SEVEN

Rogelio

"I hate to advocate drugs, alcohol, violence or insanity, but they've always worked for me." *—Dr. Hunter S. Thompson*

On Sunday afternoon, July 27, 1975, the earthling named William Francis Lee, III, found himself at Shea Stadium in Queens, New York for a doubleheader versus the Yankees.... Yes, you read that correctly. With a "new" Yankee Stadium under construction, the Bronx Bombers briefly became residents of Flushing, New York. The struggling Yankees were in the midst of a nosedive and the surging Red Sox were in town to place a further damper on their fading hopes. Bill Lee took to the hill in the first game of the doubleheader against legendary Hall of Fame pitcher, Jim "Catfish" Hunter in still another epic matchup.

On that sunny afternoon, both the Spaceman and Catfish pitched in front of 53,631 fans including the author of this tome. Lee and Hunter staged an epic pitchers' duel and both men hurled shutout ball versus two formidable lineups for eight scoreless innings. In the top of the ninth inning, however, the Red Sox finally broke through for a run, but it wasn't due to a failure on Hunter's part, but an error led to a two-out RBI single by Rick Miller that scored Fred Lynn, who had reached on that miscue and then stole second base with two out.

The Spaceman, however, still had to shut down the Yankees in the ninth inning to secure the victory. With one out and no one on base, Graig Nettles hit a long line drive blast to left-centerfield. Fred Lynn got a great jump on the ball and made an incredible diving catch while running full speed and crashing to the ground, but holding onto the ball. Lee then retired Chris Chambliss on a foul pop to Red Sox third baseman Bob Heise and gained his thirteenth victory, on his way to his third consecutive 17-game season. The Spaceman's catcher that day was Tim Blackwell, a backup catcher who Lee loved pitching to because of his ability to provide a great target while allowing Bill to pitch at his favored rapid pace. The pitching duel took a mere 1:59 minutes, a rarity during modern day baseball.

In the second game of the doubleheader on that afternoon, Rogelio

"Roger" Moret took the ball for Boston. Moret, like Lee, was a left-handed pitcher. Rogelio was born in Guayama, Puerto Rico and spoke little English. The Spaceman befriended the gifted southpaw and attempted to hang out with him as much as possible. Back then, the author told Lee that if he could surgically graft Moret's arm onto Lee's shoulder, you would have a Hall of Fame pitcher.

In that second game of the doubleheader, just as Lee had done in the first game, Roger Moret shut out the Yankees with the final score being 6-0. The Yankees season was ostensibly over, and the Red Sox would be on their way to an epic World Series against the Cincinnati Reds.

Following the doubleheader, Yankees owner George Steinbrenner fired his manager Bill Virdon and once more rehired the fiery Billy Martin as his manager, but the Red Sox had buried the 1975 Yankees for good.

Despite going 13-2 in 1973, 9-10 in 1974, and 14-3 in 1975, Moret could not sustain his success. By 1976 he was jettisoned off to Atlanta and to virtual obscurity. Many thought Moret to be childlike, and most likely they were at least partially correct, but the Spaceman referred to Roger as "precious." Lee loved the playful youngster and felt that his difficulties mastering the English language led many to believe that Moret was completely ignorant. Lee explained that oft-times Moret had difficulty ordering food and once upon being asked at a restaurant how he would prefer his eggs, he answered "Over large." Then upon looking at the menu, he pointed to it and offered, "I'll have this, too." When the waitress asked what he was referring to, Moret replied, "Thank you very much."

Moret's difficulty in being understood also caught the attention of Red Sox manager Eddie Kasko, who approached his Hall of Fame Venezuelan shortstop, Luis Aparicio and asked, "Luis, can you do me a favor. Can you hang with Rogelio for a few days because I'm having difficulty in communicating with him? Perhaps it's a language problem."

After three days, Aparicio informed Kasko, "It's no use Skip, he's just as dumb in Spanish as he is in English." However, as Lee explained, "Aparicio was Venezuelan aristocracy. Poor Roger was 'El Barrio Puerto Rican' and that's probably why Luis did not provide the proper guidance. Let's put it this way. There was no way that Roger knew who Simon Bolivar was."

Within a few years, Moret drifted into ambiguity and wound up back in Puerto Rico where several reported that he had suffered mental issues. After both Lee and Moret's career had ended, the Spaceman reached out to him and offered to put him on his traveling "Grey Sox" team.

When Rogelio arrived to join the team, he was a mess. As Lee described, "Roger showed up with white hair, a white beard, and appeared scared to death."

Upon seeing Rogelio arrive, the legendary Mark Belanger, one of the greatest fielding shortstops in major league history, asked Lee, "Are you paying Moret for this trip?"

Lee responded, "No, I just invited him down."

Mark Belanger then informed Bill, "You shouldn't pay him because he's collecting $70,000 in deferred payments for medical disability because he's been diagnosed as insane." The Spaceman replied, "He's getting $70,000? Well, apparently then, he's not the one who's crazy!"

Bill Lee gave his old friend Rogelio Moret an additional $1,000, got him cleaned up, and got him to buy a new suit. It was, according to the Spaceman, the equivalent of seeing Lee Marvin's gunslinger character in "Catballou," when they roll the aging drunk gunslinger out of the stagecoach and he winds up wearing a black velvet suit and is wielding pearl-handled revolvers. To further welcome Roger Moret back, the ever thoughtful Bernardo Carbo dyed his hair as a tribute to Rogelio.

Upon his sartorially splendored return to the team, Roger smiled and asked Lee, "Do you want to see my friend, Juan Beniquez?" Note: Beniquez was a teammate of Lee and Moret in Boston.

With that, a somewhat confused Bill Lee asked Roger, "You brought Juan Beniquez with you?"

Rogelio Moret, delightful as always, then reached into his pocket and pulled out a flask of J&B Scotch and winked at Lee. Lee then stated: "When you pull a flask of J&B Scotch out of your pocket and call it 'Juan Beniquez,' how can you not love Roger?

"He was crazy like a fucking fox," the Spaceman continued. "I thought I was watching Señor Wences on the old *Ed Sullivan Show*." Bill closed out by stating, "I love Roger."

Bill Lee reported that once Rogelio Moret had fallen asleep in his girlfriend's Audi while driving to New Haven after a night game. "He fell asleep at the wheel and the Audi slid under a parked truck and a trailer, and the truck and trailer sheared the roof right off the top of Roger's car. It turned the Audi into a convertible." Amazingly, Rogelio Moret was not seriously injured.

INTERLUDE

Since we are well into *The Spaceman Chronicles*, I hope you are enjoying the biography of the unimitative earthling known as William Francis Lee, III and that perhaps you are either entertained and/or fascinated that Lee is perhaps a practitioner of "Santeria," or at least a believer that he has the highest number of wins of any rasta in baseball history and was a fraternity brother of a renowned superstar murderer, had a trainer who was the nephew of one of the most infamous killers in U.S. history, was greatly influenced by iconic authors and sociologists, had his first girl-friend pilfered by the son of a Hollywood legend, was taught how to pitch by his beautiful aunt, was invariably challenged by smaller men with even tinier brains, signed his initial professional contract illegally, smoked dope with a future president of the United States, married a Miss Alaska in the Miss Universe Pageant, was photographed by *Sports Illustrated* wearing astronaut Allan Shepherd's spacesuit on the mound at County Stadium in Milwaukee, had a great grandfather who founded the University of Southern California, nearly had his second son born at Fenway Park, had a close one-eyed friend who was nominated for a Pulitzer Prize in Literature for a pornographic essay, had at least two songs written about him by the great Warren Zevon, had poems written about him by renowned poet Tom Clark, had a teammate who was Elvis Presley's cousin, was given uniform #37 because his behavior was reminiscent of the only player to have ever undergone shock treatments and whose story became a major motion picture, was only one of two pitchers in baseball history to have won 17 games for three consecutive seasons, had one of the greatest African American civil rights leaders and legendary comedians as a good friend and had that friend resurrect his career, was one of the few white players allowed on the back of the bus, is perhaps the only open-minded Marxist on planet Earth, often defeated the mighty New York Yankees with relative ease, quotes the likes of Kurt Vonnegut, Ray Bradbury and Buckminster Fuller and in the next breath, Yogi Berra, pitched the longest time-wise complete game in major league history (including rain delays), got into a tug of war over a rain soaked tarpaulin with an enraged Hall of Fame midget manager, got a sneak preview of the immense stupidity of a Los Angeles Dodgers high ranking team executive, worked as a locksmith at his uncle's shop where his uncle would often be called in the middle of the night to change the locks on Howard Hughes' doors, gave up home runs on two successive pitches using the same baseball, told bizarre stories about his eccentric former college teammate Dave Kingman (Kingman confirmed them), publicly battled a racist congressman who strongly opposed desegregation in Boston, frequently rubbed elbows with some of the greatest journalists of the twentieth century at a famous Greenwich Village watering hole in New York City, while inebriated, "tried out" for the New England Patriots punter position outside of a famous bar on Boston's Massachusetts Avenue in front of heavy traffic and so impressed the sober Patriots general manager that he invited him to Foxboro for an actual tryout, was with the young star quarterback of the Patriots when the youngster seriously and mysteriously suffered a serious knee injury, walked into a Cleveland bar with a teammate after a shootout and had to step over at least two bodies, pitched two games in arguably the best World Series of all time and left with leads in both, prevented his dear friend and teammate Bernie Carbo from committing suicide, the same man whose pinch-hit three run homer made it possible for Carlton Fisk's iconic game-winning home run, became part of a counter-culture gang of misfits known as "The Buffalo Head Gang," a group of players who were outcasts, but productive players, was endorsed by comedic anarchist Abbie Hoffman, when Lee ran for president of the United States on the Rhinoceros Party ticket, walked out in protest after the release of two minority teammates, traveled to China and attended Premier Zhou Enlai's funeral, hilariously fended off an attack by the drunken enraged wife of an opponent over an incident that occurred forty-one years prior, along with George W. Bush was a REMF (Rear Echelon Mother Fucker) in the U.S. Army, had previously changed the locks of the bungalow at which John Belushi died of a massive overdose of cocaine and heroin, locked Bob Dylan out of his house, snorted mescaline in the clubhouse after a rainout in Minnesota, had friends who helped fugitive Patty Hearst elude capture, and even inspired this, the longest run-on sentence in literary history!*

Then there was this thing about his having a famous friend whose father most likely assassinated President John F. Kennedy.

* This is for you, Professor Anita V.

It should be noted that the author, either Scott Russell or Kilgore Trout, had been mesmerized in his misspent youth by an attractive English Composition Professor (she had the legs of a goddess), who once told him during his freshman year that he had a "gift for writing." I did not believe her at the time. I am not certain if I do now. But I do recall, however, that she told me that my essays were rife with too many commas. Therefore, the above run-on sentence is dedicated to Professor V, wherever she may be.... God, she had legs that went up to the sky!

CHAPTER FIFTY-EIGHT

Unlikely Convergences

"It should be noted that before writing the following chapter that the author, either Scott Russell or Kilgore Trout, had rediscovered a long lost video of a round table discussion at a ski resort in Oslo, Norway, one in which Bill Lee discussed amnio synostosis with a group of renowned scientists and scholars that included Neil degrasse Tyson, Kurt Vonnegut, James Baldwin, Javed Ahmad Ghamidi, Timothy Berners-Lee, Steven Hawking, Noam Chomsky, Jane Goodall, Carl Sagan,* and Don Zimmer. This now epic assembly was emceed by numerous Christian theologians who included Bernie Carbo and Dennis 'Oil Can' Boyd." *—Scott Russell (or Kilgore Trout). Take your pick, they are both ugly motherfuckers.*

* Sagan, who wrote "Broca's Brain," was present to examine Don Zimmer's brain, but after a futile and disappointing seven days attempting to locate it, left the conclave disconsolately.

"A nickel ain't worth a dime anymore." *—Lawrence Peter "Yogi" Berra*

In the spring of 1977, the author found himself "celebrating" his honeymoon with his first wife in the unlikely locale of Winter Haven, Florida. The ill-fated marriage at least served as a precursor to the groom that bizarre circumstance often occurs on planet Earth. At the Holiday Inn in Winter Haven, the author found himself in the "Honeymoon Suite" next door to… Don Zimmer.

The author and his bride, an erudite often sarcastic literate from the "nutmeg state" called Connecticut, were there to enjoy sunshine, libations, and to hang out with the aforementioned renowned iconoclastic counter-culture journalist George Kimball, the son of a career army military officer who had made the grievous mistake of introducing the newlyweds to each other. Semi-functional thugs from the South Bronx are no match for such refined members of the female species, apparently.

Upon my arrival in Boston from my birthplace and home in New York some forty-seven years ago, I settled in the Back Bay. At the time I felt as if I was Valentine Michael Smith from Robert Heinlein's *Stranger in a Strange Land*. In Heinlein's masterpiece, Valentine Michael Smith was a human who arrived on Earth in early adulthood after being born on the planet Mars and being raised by Martians. Boston, in truth, may as well have been Mars to me back then. I was a young thug from the South Bronx, the son of an illiterate semi-functional father and a conniving, deceitful, certifiably insane mother. I say that without bitterness or intended malice, it's just who and what I am. I am the sum of all parts.

Boston in the early '70s was in the process of a great upheaval. Busing desegregation which took place from 1974-1988 resulted in riots that occurred from 1974-1976. It was mind-blowing to me because I had always envisioned Boston as a liberal city and nothing like Horrific Birmingham in the '50s and '60s. Man, was I wrong. My being a huge baseball fan, I gravitated to Fenway Park and immediately was in for another shock. Upon attending games in New York City, I never once considered the racial demographics at the local stadiums. One can only imagine the culture shock of seeing 30,000 white faces at the ballpark near Kenmore Square. I wondered if I had entered some sort of time warp. Shortly thereafter I befriended the aforementioned legendary journalist, George Kimball... whose dear friend, of course, was the earthling known as William Francis Lee, III. For some reason still unknown to me, they both took a liking to the crude, unrefined, semi-educated newcomer from the Bronx.

My introduction to my first wife was a pisser. One day, I received a phone call from George at my apartment at 83 Marlborough Street:

"Scotty, can you do me a huge favor?"

I responded, "I'll do my best."

George then replied, "Can you take a class for me tonight?"

I hesitated before asking, "Aren't you a bit old to be taking classes?"

George laughed and answered, "Actually, I'm teaching a class. It's called 'Sports in Boston' and I thought you'd be perfect. I have a deadline to beat so I can write my column (for the *Phoenix*) and I really need you to conduct the class. Just wing it. You'll do fine."

Foolishly, I acquiesced, but in truth, upon arriving at 5 Commonwealth Avenue near the Boston Public Garden, I reasoned that both George and the Spaceman were merely pulling my leg and just attempting to get me to attend some sort of party. Therefore, I arrived at 7:00 p.m. entirely unprepared. Upon arriving at the address, I noticed the sign on the building read, "The Boston Center of Adult Education." I walked in.... Holy crap! There was indeed a class. The "students" included the young woman who would become my wife.

I "taught" the class for nearly an hour and a half. We were having a blast. I believe the class was amused by my Noo Yawk accent. At approximately 8:30 p.m. the door flew open and a significantly inebriated George Kimball staggered in. Even his glass eye appeared bloodshot.

George, a bear of a man, threw a huge arm around my neck and shoulders and exclaimed to the throng, "I want to introduce you to Scott Russell, the most incredible motherfucker you'll ever meet!"

"Um, George," the young lady countered, "we've already met Scott. He's been here for nearly two hours."

Within two years, we had entered into a marriage destined for failure. That was as much my fault as anyone's. At the time I arrived in Boston, I was still reeling from a prior failed relationship. Back in New York City and presumably back to Ireland, there was this young woman with an Irish brogue. The young lass who waddled like a duck, quoted Shakespeare, Tennyson, Keats and Behan and would down an inordinate amount of Bushmill's Irish Whiskey, and then waddled out of my life, breaking a heart that has since healed. It took decades to get over her.

The mere suggestion that I marry the young woman from Connecticut was akin to asking, "Hey, do you want to go bowling?" My bad, as in the vernacular of today's youth.

Here I was, a delinquent from the Bronx tenements and alleyways, hanging with a woman who rubbed elbows with the Kennedys.... Yeah, she worked for Kevin White, the Mayor of Boston. I was barely sentient. Upon meeting my ex's co-workers, I was often humiliated. The greater part of my vocabulary in those days was, "Yo Vinny, trow me da ball!" I must have appeared as someone that belonged on a short leash.

Back in Florida, in addition to loitering with the oft-times controversial writer, our mutual friend, the earthling known as William Francis Lee, III was also on hand to engage in the time-tested rigors of spring training, an exercise pertaining to members of the sport called baseball purportedly getting them in some sort of decent physical condition. Kimball, an absolutely brilliant writer, had on numerous occasions run afoul of Red

Sox management, as he had the temerity and unmitigated gall to actually refuse to not bow down in order to kiss their rear ends as required by the lords of the game. It was no surprise then, that the outlaw, Bill Lee, would have the outrageously witty Kimball as his friend.

George Kimball III was, as I attested to, one of the greatest writers of his times. As the son of an army veteran, George had lived all over the world, including stops in Taiwan and Germany. George graduated high school in San Antonio, Texas and then attended the University of Kansas on an ROTC scholarship, but soon participated in many anti-war movements, several of which landed him in jail.

In 1970, the Spaceman's buddy ran a controversial and often hilarious campaign for Douglas County Sheriff in Kansas and nearly defeated the incumbent. While attending the University of Kansas, George was the fraternity brother of the great running back, Gale Sayers.

Kimball became such an outstanding writer that he contributed to "The Paris Review," "Rolling Stone," "The Realist" and "Scanlan's Monthly." Upon moving to Boston, he became the sports editor of the "Boston Phoenix," where his colorful columns often featured the adventures of his friend, Bill "Spaceman" Lee.

While at the *Phoenix*, George worked with other journalistic legends such as Joe Klein, Jon Landau, and Janet Maislin, and he nurtured the careers of Mike Lupica, Michael Gee, and the incomparable Charles P. Pierce, who the Spaceman agrees is "the best fucking writer in the country."

As I had earlier mentioned, Kimball had written several books including the classic *Four Kings*, a magnificent journal about four of the greatest professional fighters in history, Sugar Ray Leonard, Marvin Hagler, Thomas Hearns, and Roberto Duran. The tome was preceded by a forward by my idol, the singular novelist and columnist, the great Pete Hamill. George, who had covered nearly 400 world championship boxing matches, united with two other terrific journalists, John Schulian and Colum McCann, in writing "At the Fights."

George Kimball contracted cancer in 2005. After George went into hospice, he messaged yours truly on Tuesday, March 15, 2011.

"Hi Scott, thanks. Yes, I'm at Sloan Kettering, though now in home hospice and it is my firm intention never to go back into the hospital. I just spent eight days there last week. I'm probably realistically looking at a month or two now, but it was diagnosed in 2005 and I've had a pretty good run, since I wasn't supposed to last more than a year then. Fortunately, insurance covers everything. I haven't totaled it up, but I'm probably closing in on a million by now. What happens to these poor fucks that have no insurance at all? —G

George succumbed to cancer on July 6, 2011. He was sixty-seven years old.

One morning during either the spring of 1977 or 1978, my ex and I arrived at the home of the mayor of Winter Haven to pick up the precocious sixteen-year-old nephew of Kimball's, a youngster named John. We were headed to such tourist sites as Busch Gardens and Disneyland, and we believed that such diversion would be appreciated by the youth. Therefore, we stopped for breakfast at a restaurant called "Stuckey's." I was immediately impressed by John Kimball upon hearing him remark, "What is the excuse for the existence of this place?" I really liked the kid.

Upon arriving to pick George's unpretentious nephew up, we left George's dad, George E. Kimball, Jr. who was a career military veteran, alone in a recliner at the house. Alongside Mr. Kimball was a table that had a full bottle of rye and a single shot glass. There was also a pile of newspapers and the conservative father of his rebellious son was already immersed in them.

Upon arriving back at the house at approximately 9:00 p.m., the bottle of rye was nearly empty, and George's dad was stone-cold sober. George Kimball, the writer, was soon to become persona non grata with the conservative establishment of major league baseball. It should have served as a harbinger for his friend, "Spaceman" Lee.

CHAPTER FIFTY-NINE

Mean People Suck

"If you attack the establishment long and hard enough, they will make you a member of it." *—Art Buchwald*

Journalists such as George Kimball have always been considered threats to narrow-minded assholes with agendas. It is traditional among those that run professional baseball that those members of the Fourth Estate merely serve as nothing more than mouthpieces and publicity lackeys for the organizations they are covering. Thankfully, there are those such as the late Will McDonough of the *Boston Globe* and his protégé, Dan Shaughnessy, who despite having his newspaper, the *Boston Globe,* owned by John Henry, the CEO of the Boston Red Sox, invariably is critical of the franchise, going as far as to write "The Red Sox have no leadership," recently. How is that for sticking it to the man?

Throughout George Kimball's tenure in covering the local Boston sports franchises, the award-winning journalist often ridiculed the hypocrisy of the Red Sox, especially their front office. The situation finally reached the point of no return to the conservative obstinate executives who took umbrage to the pointed biting criticism offered by "Spaceman" Lee's close friend. How dare he tell the truth? The imbeciles did not even attempt to disguise their bias in literally attempting to ban George from the press box.

The following letter was written by the noble executive sports editor of the *Boston Herald,* Joe Fitzgerald on July 23, 1980, upon learning that George was no longer permitted to enter the press box. The missive was addressed to Bowie Kuhn, the officious, arrogant "Commissioner of Baseball," and was sent to his offices at 75 Rockefeller Plaza in New York:

Dear Commissioner Kuhn:

Columnist George Kimball, a member of my staff, was banned from the Red Sox press room yesterday by team management for what vice president Bill Crowley termed "the totally negative tone of what he has written."

Crowley retains that the press room is a "privilege" granted by the club, and I'd be inclined to agree with that if we were only referring to consumption of the food and beverages. Indeed, if the Sox had simply taken away Kimball's right to eat or drink there, I'd have to concur that they were properly, if ungraciously, exercising their prerogative.

But that press room also happens to be the source of considerable news flow. General manager Haywood Sullivan, for example, frequently holds court with a small group of writers there. It's a gathering spot for scouts, minor league officials, visiting press and assorted sports figures.

I challenge the Sox's right to deny a fully accredited member of my staff any access to the things that are said in that room, and I strongly urge your immediate intervention, not just in Kimball's behalf, but also in behalf of the principle that a free press should not—and MUST not—be made to knuckle under the self-serving policies of an organization like the Red Sox.

I anxiously await your reply.

Respectfully,
Joe Fitzgerald
Executive sports editor
Copies: Bill Crowley, Haywood Sullivan,
Lee MacPhail, Larry Whiteside

I should note that the reason *Boston Globe* journalist Larry Whiteside was copied was because Larry was the head of the Boston Baseball Writers Association, and for the record, Whiteside, too, was outraged by Kimball's banishment. Larry Whiteside, indeed, insisted that the Red Sox reinstate Kimball's credentials, something they did, albeit displeased that they had been publicly called out.

In those days, two highly conservative nitwit writers who also hosted a Boston radio show, "Clif and Claf," (Clif Keane and Larry Claflin), brazenly suggested that Kimball was a "freeloader" in the press box and was only there to "eat and drink for free." Keane particularly was known as "Poison Pen" and was often accused of racism by Boston's Hispanic community. During one radio program following a costly fielding error by the normally slick fielding African American first baseman, George "Boomer" Scott, Clif Keane remarked on the air, "He would have fielded it cleanly if it was a chicken wing."

As for their claim that George Kimball took advantage of his "privileges" by merely eating and drinking in the press room, the highly respected longtime press box steward Tommy McCarthy came to George's defense upon stating:

"If there were any freeloaders up there, I can assure you that Kimball was not one of them. In fact, many of the other writers were the ones taking advantage, but not George. George would not only thank me for the beverages he drank, but would always tip me generously."

George Kimball, of course, was reinstated as a member of the Fourth Estate and he continued to write the truth, as he saw it.

As for his friend, the earthling known as William Francis Lee, III, he had already been banished to Montreal for a "hypoglycemic" poor hitting, poor fielding, and possibly nutty infielder, but Bill Lee, too, would eventually be banned, but unlike George Kimball, whose exclusion was temporary, the Spaceman's would be permanent and leave an embarrassing stain on the face of the game referred to as "the National Pastime."

CHAPTER SIXTY

Faith

"Midget, midget, midget, how he struts and winks, for he knows a man's as big as what he hopes and thinks!" —*The Book of Bokonon*

In Kurt Vonnegut's masterpiece *Cat's Cradle*, "Newt," when told he talks like a Bokononist, replies, "Why shouldn't I? As far as I know, Bokononism is the only religion that has any commentary on midgets."

As the earthling known as William Francis Lee, III recalls:

"I was in a Catholic church in Malibu in 1976. I've got Katie in a baby bucket, she had just been born on December 18, and Katie was delivered to us in the hospital in a Santa stocking. We arrived at church about ten minutes late and we wind up in the front row. It's an amphitheater and Mary Lou and I have Mike and Andy with us, but they're getting restless and obnoxious and we're trying to calm them down. Kate the baby is not crying, she's quiet, but the boys are making a racket. Andy's got a 'Bert and Ernie' doll, I think it was Ernie, and the service seemed to be taking forever. Finally, the priest gets there, and he finally announces that the mass had ended, and he makes the sign of the cross and says, 'Go in peace.' Andy yells out, 'Yahoo!' and throws the Ernie doll way up in the air, and the doll goes end over end and lands at the feet of the priest. That's the last time I was in a Catholic church. I'm telling you, the Malibu days were a complete haze."

However, the author, whether it was Scott Russell or Kilgore Trout—and does that matter at this point anyhow?—invited the Spaceman to another church in 1978, and the southpaw graciously accepted the invite. I had received a rather formal letter which read in part:

Dear Scott,

My daughter, LouAnn, has often talked about you regarding your knowledge of baseball, awareness of my nephew, Butch Alberts' position in Triple A ball under a Toronto contract, and your being a friend of Bill Lee, which has prompted this letter.

We at the Community Church of Boston would like very much to have Bill Lee speak at a Sunday morning service. It would be great because of whom he is as a person. LouAnn said that among other things he is against nuclear weapons, for the rights of all people including gay persons, and dared to speak out on behalf of his friends at the risk of being traded. I've also been informed that he visited China. He speaks his mind which is so refreshing these days.

If Bill Lee were able to speak, he would naturally choose his own subject. I look forward to your response.

Sincerely,
William E. Alberts, PH.D
Minister
Rev. Donald Lothrop
Minister Emeritus

The letter was dated July 9, 1978.

AUTHOR's ADMISSION: Under normal circumstances, I would've most likely chosen to not even bother to contact the Spaceman, however Reverend Albert's daughter, with whom I worked, was this absolutely stunning green-eyed blonde and I am not an atypical member of the male species. To be entirely truthful, if she had invited me to a Bulgarian midget and pet yak convention, I would have eagerly brought wine to the affair... and perhaps a blanket for the yak.

Upon inviting the earthling known as William Francis Lee, III to the Community Church of Boston, he, of course, politely accepted. In fact, Bill asked if they had shower facilities at the church. Upon learning they indeed, did, on a bright Sunday morning, Lee ran from his home in Belmont, showered, and ran back home following the service. To this moment, I cannot recall exactly what the Spaceman chose as his subject matter and for all I know it could've been a dissertation on Bulgarian midgets and yaks, but I remember that the congregation was quite pleased.

At one point during the church service, our mutual friend, the great, late George Kimball, took a seat behind me, put his arm on my shoulder, and whispered, “Scotty, do you know what this place is?”

I naively (redundant, no doubt) responded, “Yes, it's the Community

Church of Boston."

"Yes," George replied, "but it's also a front for the Communist Party of Boston."

"Jesus, George," I answered, "I'm sorry. I had no idea."

Kimball laughed and said, "No, no, Bill loves this. He's eating it up!"

And that it was. In fact, the Community Church in Boston, to their credit, was the very first church in Massachusetts to have married gay couples.

CHAPTER SIXTY-ONE

Human Rain Delays & Marshmallows

> "If I worked at Starbucks, instead of writing people's names on their coffee cup, I'd write the following:
>
> One day, you and everyone you love will die
> And beyond a small group of people for an extremely brief
>   period of time,
> Little of what you say or do will ever matter.
> This is the Uncomfortable Truth of Life.
> And everything you think of or do is but an elaborate
>   avoidance of it.
> We are inconsequential cosmic dust, bumping and milling
>   about on a tiny blue speck.
> We imagine our own importance.
> Enjoy your fucking coffee."
> —*Mark Madson in* Everything is Fucked.

Billy Martin was a fiery, combative player and manager, quick-tempered and even quicker fisted, especially when someone was holding onto his "opponent." Martin got into battles with his own teammates and even several of his own players when he managed. On one occasion, he punched out a marshmallow salesman (you can look it up) in a barroom brawl in Minnesota. On August 4, 1960, the then player Martin seriously injured an opposing pitcher named Jim Brewer, who wound up requiring two surgeries to repair a fractured orbital bone near his right eye. Martin precipitated the melee by flinging his bat at the hurler.

Nothing like getting an unfair advantage, but Billy Martin, the manager Bill Lee described as a "no good dirty rat," sought advantage no matter how repugnant he appeared to civilized humans. After the "marshmallow salesman" incident, Yankees CEO George Steinbrenner fired Martin for the second time.

In 1980, however, Martin, who always seemed to get second, third, and fourth chances, brought his new team, the Oakland A's, to Bloomington,

Minnesota to play the Twins. During the first inning, a Minnesota fan in an attempt at humor (I thought it to be funny) began throwing marshmallows at Martin when he approached the dugout after removing his pitcher. Martin glared at the fan. In the ninth inning, the fan returned and once more began pelting an infuriated (Martin seemingly lived his entire life being infuriated) Martin with marshmallows. This time, however, Martin commenced to go after the fan by climbing over the railing, but umpires and others prevented an ugly scene. After the game, however, the imbecilic, homophobic manager addressed the press:

"It was a young kid with a French queer's hat on. When I went up there, I didn't know whether to kiss him or punch him. I thought he would have caressed me. He was a big, fat fag. It had to be a fag because he was throwing marshmallows."

On May 24, 1952, an already mentally troubled Jimmy Piersall was jumped from behind by Billy Martin in a runway leading to the Red Sox dugout and beaten mercilessly.

In another drunken escapade appearing earlier in this tome, in August 1969 in Detroit at the Lindell AC, Martin's pitching coach, Art Fowler, another less than admirable person, ratted out his pitcher, Dave Boswell for not running between starts, to rookie manager Martin. Inebriated as was his wont, Martin went after Boswell, who was even more sloshed than his manager. Outfielder Bob Allison attempted to intercede by leading Boswell away, but anyone capable of being punched was suitable to Martin, who sneakily clobbered Allison by sucker-punching him. At that point, Martin continued his pursuit of the nearly helpless drunk Boswell, and punched him out too. Upon this incident being uncovered by the press, Martin attempted to paint himself as the victim.

In 1985, Martin got into an altercation with another of his pitchers, Ed Whitson, this time in a restroom at a Baltimore hotel. A fistfight ensued, but this time Martin had his arm broken and George Steinbrenner once more fired the animalistic moron, Martin.

Patrick Reusse, the fine writer who has covered the Twins for several seasons, reported on April 6, 2020, that he had seen a wire service report that police were summoned to a residence in Orange County, California. It was there that Martin was "removed from the property." As Reusse reported, "Police took this action because Bill was lying on his back on the front lawn, drunk and 'screaming about a horse.'"

Billy Martin despised the earthling known as William Francis Lee, III. Firstly, Lee routinely beat his Yankees teams. Secondly, Bill often challenged Martin to "join him" on the mound. While Martin would spew invective from the safety of his dugout, Bill would smile at him and beckon him to engage him in combat. However, Martin did not like the odds of taking on a larger man, especially one he couldn't cold-cock with a cheap shot, which was Billy Martin's specialty.

Incredibly, the Spaceman got Martin fired from his job as the manager of the Texas Rangers! This occurred during the 1975 season. They had just installed the "twenty second rule" in order to speed up the games, but not only wasn't it enforced rigidly, but the Rangers had a first baseman named Mike Hargrove, who was nicknamed "the human rain delay." As Lee explained:

"Hargrove stepped into the batters' box and began his routine of adjusting his 'thumb thing,' hitching up his pants and continually stepping out. My catcher, 'Pudge' Fisk was ridiculously slow, too, and he'd spend half the game crouching and moving around before he'd even provide a sign. So, I began counting from one to twenty and when I reached nineteen, I'm shouting at the umpire, 'Nineteen! Twenty!' And I'm banging a bat on the top step of the dugout and I'm yelling, 'Strike one! Strike two!' Martin hated me and he began to hang from the roof of the dugout swinging around like a chimpanzee. It was 'the Slow Tango in Arlington.' Billy Martin got fired shortly afterwards!"

On Christmas day, 1989, Billy Martin died in a one vehicle accident, and yes, alcohol was involved. The lone dispute was whether he or his inebriated friend, Bill Reedy, was driving the car. Billy was sixty-one years old.

Perhaps Minnesota Twins writer Patrick Reusse, put it best upon writing:

"I never could figure out the public's love of Martin. Where baseball fans and loyalists saw a wolverine, I saw a weasel."

Montreal '79, "Playing with myself."

Annabelle throws left, hits right, and has beautiful legs.

Josh Duhamel and Bill on the hill at Conoga Winnitka field.

"Sniper shot me at White Sox game—maybe ex-relative."

Bill and grandson Brandon at spring training.

Josh Duhamel sitting on his bus.

"If Henry David Thoroux was Indian he would be Gandhi."

"Russell—fan mail on my fridge."

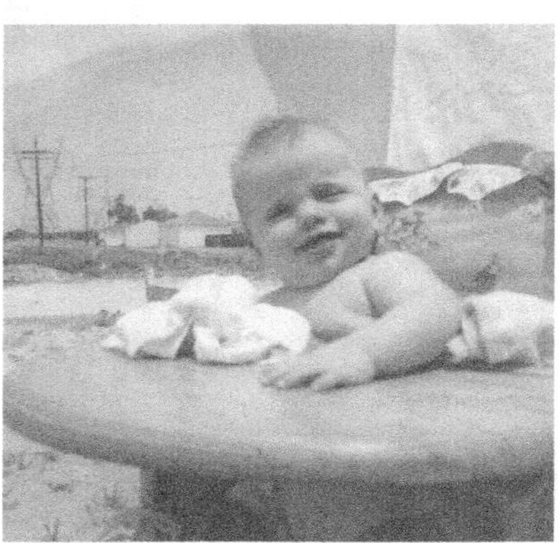

How 'bout another creamie?

El Tiante and the Spaceman.

"Us at our fireplace."

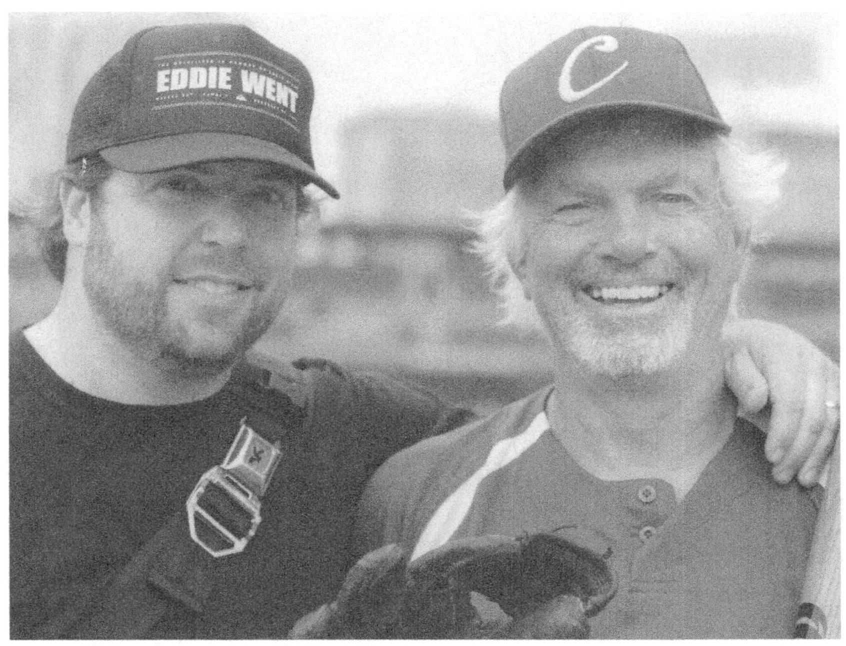

"Our adopted son—wine partner Jeff Whitman."

Being put in the same regard
as Jose Luis Borges.

Eephus pitch in Charlotte.

"Maybe we should get the heat put back on."

BL 1963 with a fine Pendleton.

"Rube Waddell—my wife's drinking buddy."

William Francis Lee III
Executive Vice President

N.E. Baseball Inc.
RFD 1 Box 145
Craftsbury, Vermont 05826
802.586.9977

The last barn stormer Birdie Tebbetts.

First yellow birch bat.

Bill wearing Alan Shepard's spacesuit.

Chuck!

"First marriage to Diana."

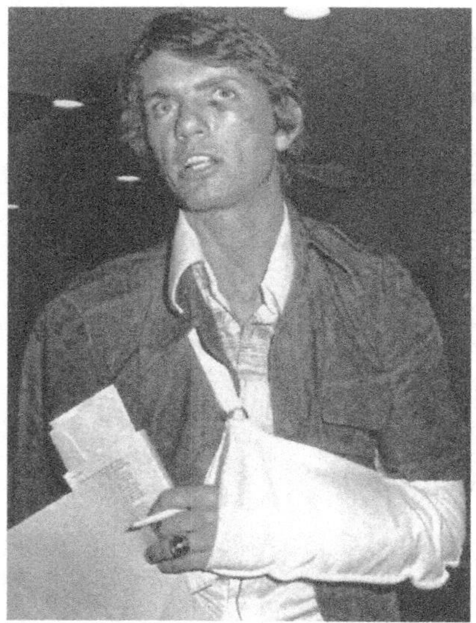

"My three favorite things—
a book, a joint, and a beer."

"My second baseman in Cuba."

"Zim questioning my integrity."

Anna's first visit with the Lees.

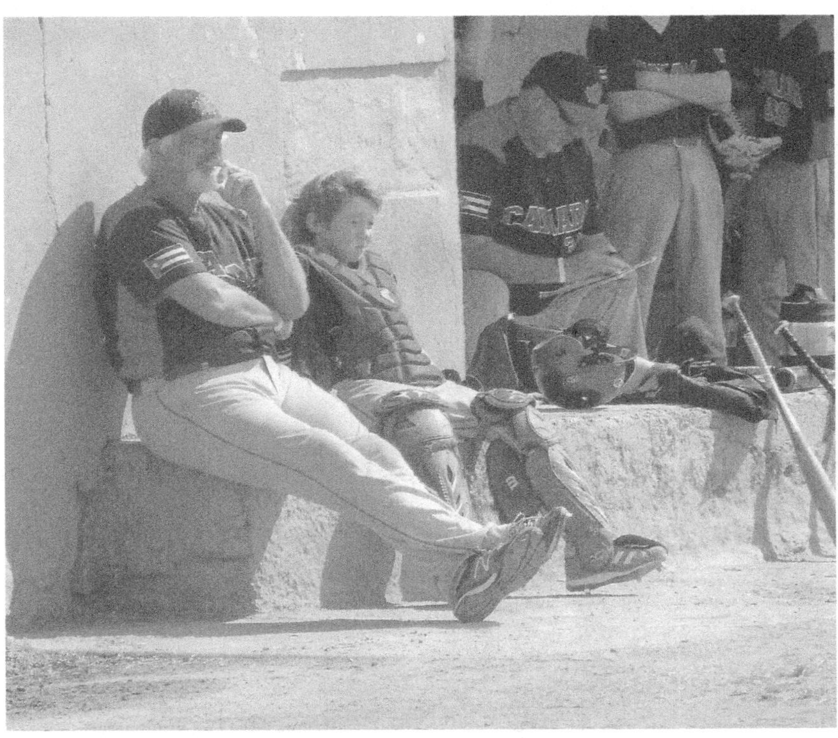

Bill and his Canadian catcher in Cuba.

"Proof I can still knock myself out with my knee."

"I don't know, I'll ask you."

Hanging deuce for Kenny Burns.

"Anna—the best result of the trade with Montreal."

Annabelle's team.

"Best friend, best man, best wife."

Katie in Maui.

Bill Lee, Jr. Indian Valley.

"Last time I caught Chuck."

Lee with his new teeth in '74.

The Buffalo Heads.

Benny Carbeau—beautiful swing.

"Papillon—butterfly in Belle's beard."

"Out of a stretch, always in trouble."

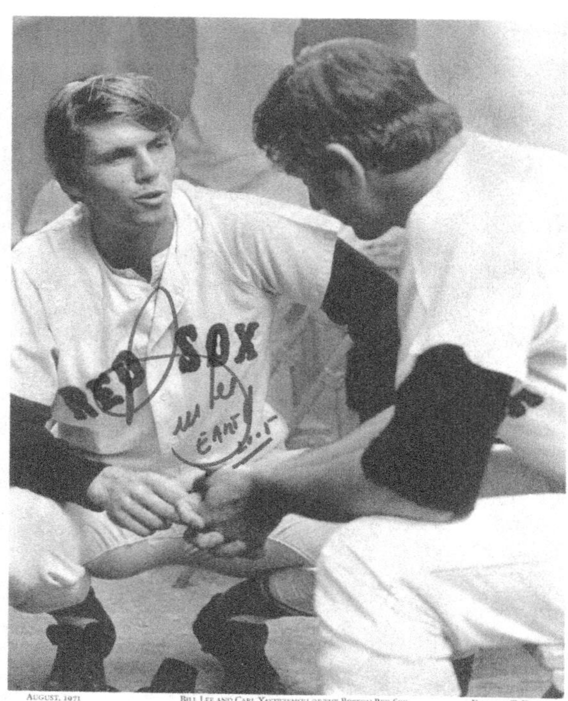

August, 1971 Bill Lee and Carl Yastrzemski of the Boston Red Sox Donald T. Young

Herald-Traveler Photo Collection
of the
Boston Public Library

"Trying to explain to Yaz the finer points of Bridge."

Keep your eye on the ball.

"Proof I could have been a Giant except I was too flexible."

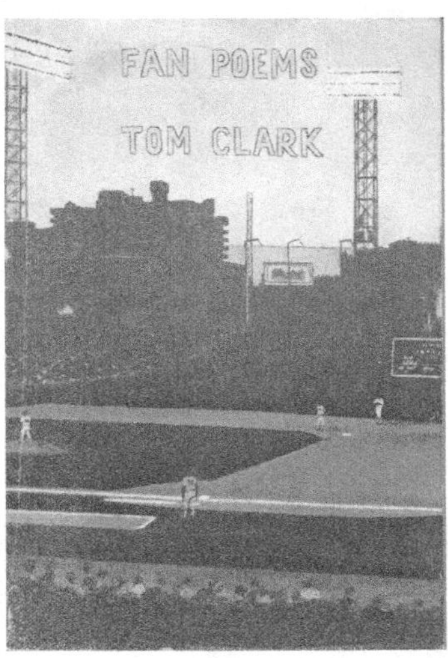

"Best poem ever written about me."

Scuz and the Spaceman.

Jocks: Ross Grimsley, Gary Carter, Bill Lee.

"Annie, Diana, and me."

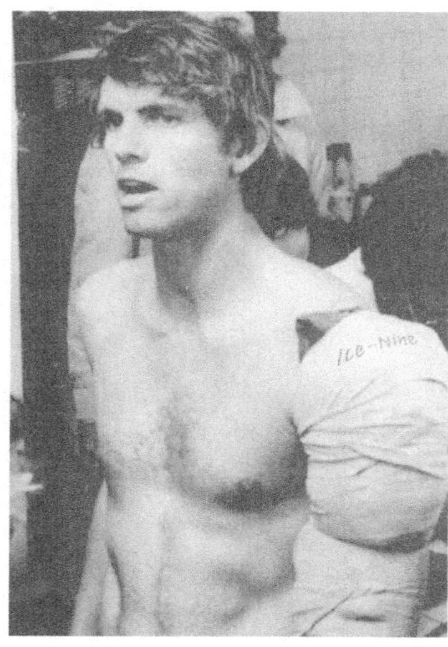

Ice-Nine.

"#1 son Michael."

"Dad with future College Coach of the Year Andy."

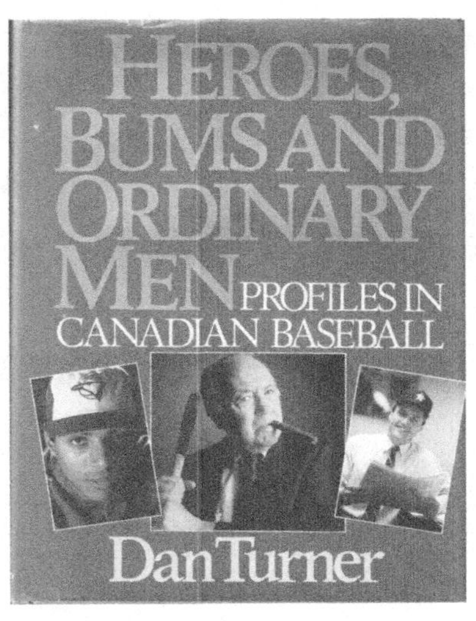

Bill Lee in Moncton, New Brunswick.

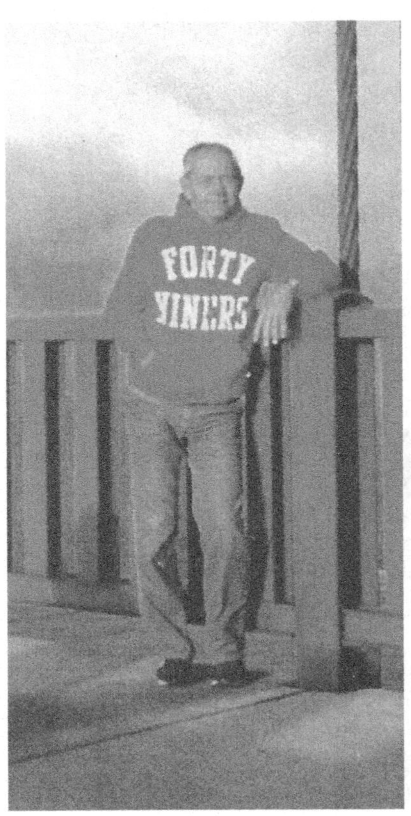

Bud Bachman.

Old Testament left-hander.

"The view north from Anna's room."

Bill & Perry.

"Crazy Grandma Hazel."

"Hitting during the COVID crisis."

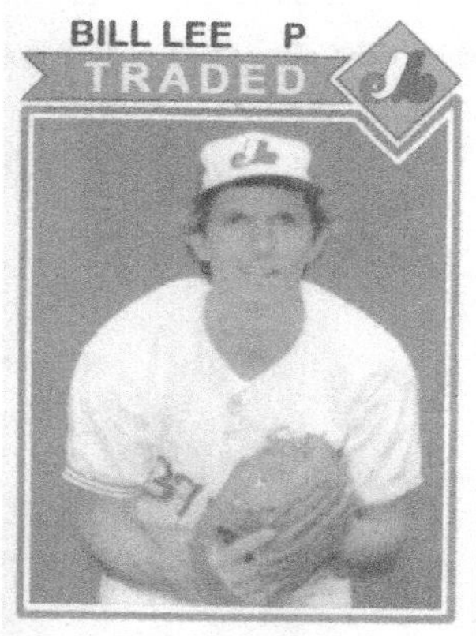

"Bill Lee, 1979: clean-shaven, never won a game."

Jack Billingham and Bill.

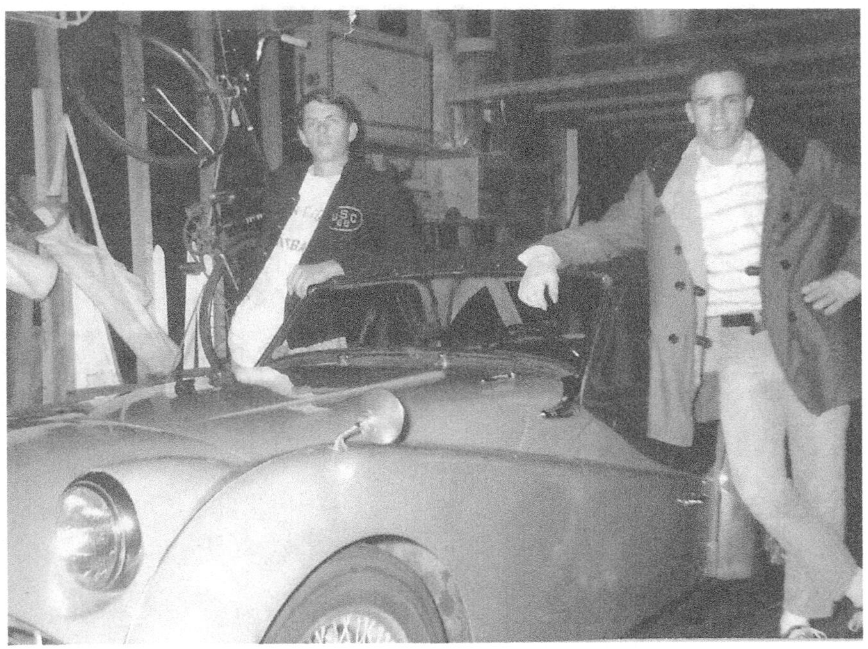

"A triumph in the garage in Terra Linda with my brother Paul."

Bill Lee, Sr. (Grandpa).

"In trouble again."

"The usual suspects, 1923."

Perry Barber and Annabelle.

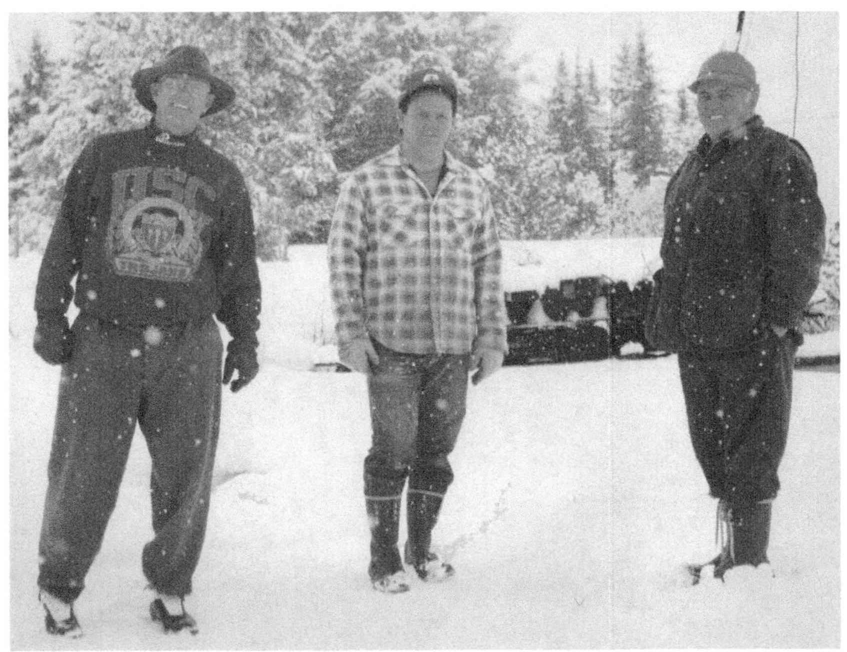

"The Reeds—two Vermonters and a Trojan."

"Midnight Sun phenome."

Mike and Bill, New Years 2020.

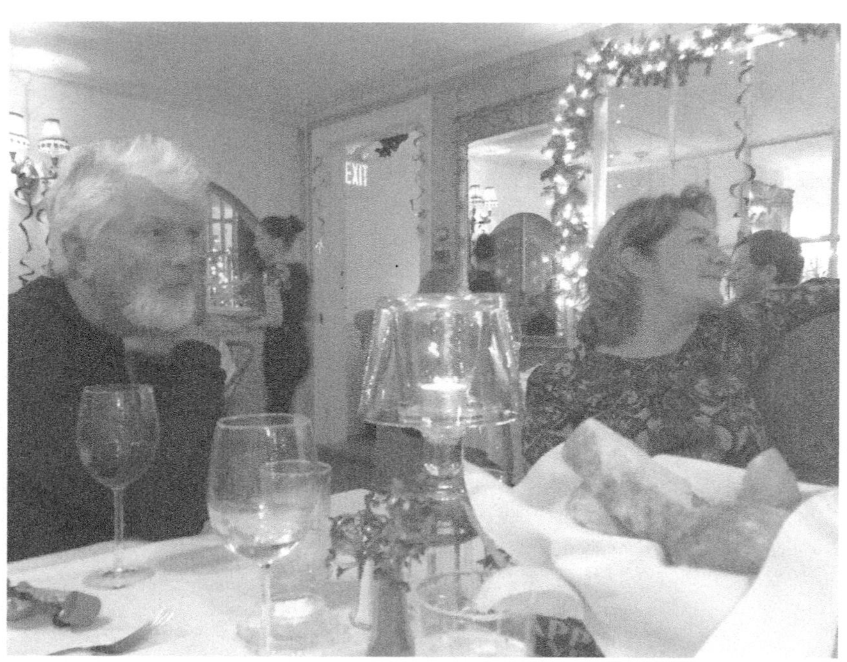

Bill and Diana, New Years 2020.

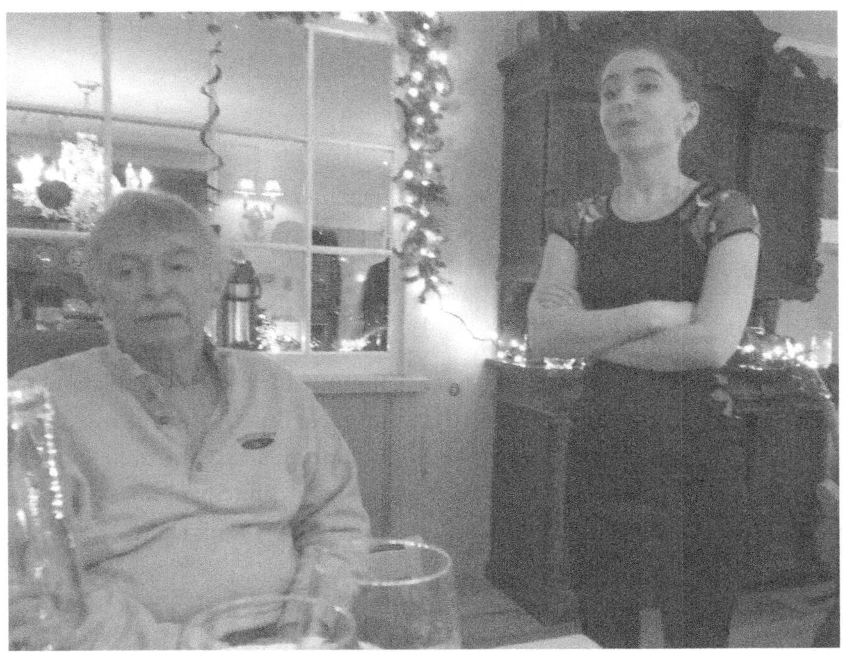

Mike and Miss Moldova, New Years 2020.

Bill and Killgore Trout.

CHAPTER SIXTY-TWO

Kindred Spirits

> "Dan Shaughnessy has pissed off management, the players, and the fans. Therefore, he must be writing the truth."
> —*Bill "Spaceman" Lee*

Note: Dan Shaughnessy has been a columnist for decades. He is famous (infamous?) for often raising the ire of local Bostonians for his sometime critical assessments of local Boston sports teams and their ownership. What the author finds most refreshing regarding Shaughnessy is that his newspaper, the *Boston Globe,* is literally owned by John Henry, the CEO of the Red Sox.

Shaughnessy has written several books including *Seeing Red,* the biography of Red Auerbach, *Senior Year* and most notably, *The Curse of the Bambino.*

The author recently spoke with Shaughnessy, who is enshrined at the writers' wing of the National Baseball Hall of fame in Cooperstown, a locale he has also recently accused of "brokering backroom deals for admission." It's called integrity. The following are Dan Shaughnessy's words:

"The 'marriage' between Peter Gammons and Bill Lee was a great fit because they both arrived at the big-league level at about the same time. They were approximately the same age and I think they were aligned intellectually and politically, and Peter was able to bring out Lee's character. It was fun and made for great reading.

"I was a bit younger, but I really enjoyed that period in Red Sox history, and it was good that Bill was both a colorful and funny character. Bill would playfully shag balls in the outfield and he really enjoyed being a baseball player. He always seemed to be with his glove. He'd even have his glove while in Central Park in New York, he just wanted to play and even now you can see that he just wants to pitch. I love that purist in him and obviously all his goofball and oddball theories.

"Some of Lee's quotes included calling George Steinbrenner's Yankees 'brown shirts.' When he had that brawl with the Yankees and called the

Yankees 'nazi brown shirts,' I mean, who talks that way? It went into the history books and what he talked about was so unusual for baseball. Bill is an avid reader and thoughtful, and yes, he was full of shit a lot, but who cared? He was a great character and a great competitor, but also a complete ballplayer. He could hit, he could field, he could do all things and he understood the game he played 90 feet at a time. He was really ahead of his time.

"I found Lee's theories to be sound. He worked quickly; get the ball and throw strikes. He was fundamentally sound, it all worked. Just on the surface that was a special time in Red Sox history, the team was very attractive and colorful. Peter (Gammons) brought that out and having Bill to write about was a huge factor in that it made it fun and easier for us readers.

"I loved the fun part of it and as I came into being a Boston-based sportswriter, and that occurred just about the time Bill was being traded to Montreal and at the time I had my first book coming out. Here was Bill being photographed with a propeller on his head and with 'L'Homme de Espace'; the timing was perfect. It was all good fun. Subsequently, when you have the job I have and you encounter a lot of Bill Lee as I did, Bill was helpful in *The Curse of the Bambino*. In the book, he talks about digging up Babe Ruth's coffin and apologizing to him for sending him to New York, where Ruth became an alcoholic.

"I can't say for certain if Bill would like to take credit for *The Curse of the Bambino*, but George Vecsey (N.Y. Times) and I have wrestled over that for years, but I acquired the title of the book from my editor. While, of course, Bill Lee was helpful with the book, he certainly was not the inspiration for it, but it's been fun.

"The whole thing about Lee not pitching in that four game* 'massacre' (the Yanks swept the Red Sox 4-0 during the critical time the Zimmer managed team was in the process of blowing a 14 game-lead to the Yankees) was that Yaz* (Carl Yastrzemski) told me he went to 'Zim' and begged him to pitch Bill Lee. Zimmer just reacted by showing Yaz the clippings of him calling him a 'gerbil.' He allowed Lee's personality to get in the way of winning and that's unfortunate.

"Then there was the 1975 World Series, the Tony Perez home run, the Eliot Lounge and all of the other things that became part of the culture around here, and I appreciate Bill Lee for that."—*Dan Shaughnessy*

I also asked Dan if he'd ever been to the raucous Lindell AC (see Chapters 21 & 22) in Detroit and his response was:

"Earl Weaver would take me to the Lindell AC (Dan covered the Orioles before coming to Boston) with his coaches. My wife, Marilou is from St. Claire Shores, Michigan. It wasn't the kind of place you'd ask for a wine list."

Upon my asking Dan if he ever spoke to Zimmer regarding his least favorite pitcher, Shaughnessy replied, "I never spoke to Zim about Lee. Bill was a 'hot button' topic and I wasn't going to go there."

> * For the record, by the time the Yankees arrived at Fenway Park in Boston on Thursday, September 7, 1978, the Red Sox, with Don Zimmer's "revamped" starting rotation, had already blown 10 games off of their allegedly insurmountable 14 game lead over the New Yorkers. By the time the four-game "massacre" that Dan Shaughnessy alluded to was finished, the Red Sox had squandered their entire lead, and even the Hall of Fame veteran Carl Yastrzemski could not convince his obstinate manager, Don Zimmer, to put his ball club's wellbeing in front of his disdain for his name-calling southpaw.

To make matters worse for Zimmer and for the legions of Red Sox diehards, Bill Lee was, of course, an accomplished "Yankee killer." The results of that four-game debacle in front of the Fenway faithful still stick in the craw of Red Sox Nation some forty-two years later, and the statistical facts surrounding what occurred on the field still amaze baseball historians. Despite their differences, "Spaceman" Lee could have been and more importantly, SHOULD have been, Don Zimmer's life raft, but Zimmer chose several leaking inner tubes instead. Please consider the following:

On Thursday, September 7, the Yankees clobbered Boston 15-3.

On Friday, September 8, the Yankees annihilated the Red Sox 13-2. On top of that, once Red Sox rookie Jim Wright and a reliever had been blasted out in the second inning, Zimmer finally brought in the Spaceman in the third inning. Lee mopped up, pitching 7 innings, allowing 1 earned run!

On Saturday, September 9, the Yankees won 7-0.

Presumably, this is when Captain Carl Yastrzemski pleaded with Zimmer to pitch Lee, to no avail. Instead of the Spaceman, he started rookie Bobby Sprowl on Sunday, who did not make it out of the first inning! With the Red Sox trailing 7-3 in the seventh inning, Zimmer once more brought Lee into the game. Of course, Bill threw 2 & 1/3 innings of scoreless ball. Bobby Sprowl, the inexperienced novice hurler that Yaz had strongly suggested Zimmer skip for the veteran Lee, never won a major league game during his career. It is highly likely that Zimmer "ruined" the youngster.

To fully comprehend what Don Zimmer's decisions had wrought, one must merely glance at their devastating effect on the 1978 Boston Red Sox. The starting Boston pitchers in that four-game sweep were pummeled for a combined 19 runs in 6 & 2/3 innings. That is not a typo. Bill Lee, merely called upon to "mop up" after the horse had left the barn, wound up hurling 9 & 1/3 innings while allowing 1 earned run. If the despised evil despot George Steinbrenner ran the Red Sox, Don Zimmer would have been gone after the fourth game of that weekend debacle, if not before. However, with Mike Torrez struggling in that notorious Bucky Fucking Dent final game of the season, Zimmer, in his infinite wisdom and vast knowledge, told Lee to sit down as he warmed up on his own in the bullpen, and Zimmer's dog track acumen had once more chosen a loser.

Incredibly, in Zimmer's "autobiography" with award-winning journalist Bill Madden, Zimmer said he was most proud of leading the Red Sox to one of their most thrilling seasons in 1978. Hell, the Red Sox relinquished a seemingly insurmountable 14 game lead! As Bill Lee stated, "It was akin to bragging about being the lookout on the *Titanic*."

There is no doubt that Zimmer's oversensitivity to being ridiculed by both the frustrated Fenway faithful, and in particular by the unforgiving Boston sports talk radio, contributed even further in regard to his disdain for Bill Lee, who was unrelenting in his being passed over. The one thing that Lee has in overabundance is an undying competitive spirit. When it was all on the line, he wanted desperately to be out there and Don Zimmer denied him that privilege, something that the Spaceman, and rightfully so, believed he had earned.

Things got so bad for Don Zimmer that he in fact telephoned the producer of the most popular sports talk show in Boston, WHDH's "Sunday Night Sports Huddle," and foolishly insisted that the show never again mention his name. This, of course, only fanned the flames. The host of the show was a hilarious innovative ball-busting gentleman named Eddie Andelman. Andelman knew he had a captive and loyal audience, so he further belittled the besieged Zimmer by informing his listening audience to obey Zimmer's edict.

Upon Eddie Andelman informing his tens of thousands of avid followers to never again mention the name "Zimmer," but to refer to him as "Chiang Kai-Shek," the then leader of Nationalist China, the abuse became even more absurd. If a caller to the program forgot the hilarious directive and mentioned the name "Zimmer," Andelman immediately would scold, "No, no. You mustn't use that name." One can only imagine a new listener tuning in to a sports talk show and repeatedly hearing, "Chiang Kai-Shek should've never allowed Reggie Cleveland to pitch to Reggie Jackson in that situation."

Seriously, what the fuck?!

> * It should be noted that the Spaceman and Hall of Famer Carl Yastrzemski often did not see eye to eye, but that no one doubted either man's commitment to winning. There is no doubt that when Yaz approached Zimmer in his futile attempt to convince him to pitch Bill Lee in that critical four-game series, Captain Carl had the best interests of the team at heart. The author has always felt that criticism without solutions is pure bullshit. By 1978 Carl Yastrzemski knew that his lengthy illustrious career was in its twilight and that he would have loved to have added an elusive World Series trophy to it. Therefore, he pleaded with Zimmer to allow Lee to pitch, knowing fully that Bill Lee's proclivity to master the Yankees would likely have ironically saved the season and therefore, Zimmer's managerial career. Obviously, his plea fell on deaf ears. All Zimmer could see was the word, "gerbil."

If Don Zimmer had merely allowed his hatred for his gifted southpaw to not interfere with the overall goals of the collective ball club, Yaz might have had his championship, Lee might have literally saved Zimmer's job, and Don Zimmer's legacy would not have been perceived by most to have been a failure.

CHAPTER SIXTY-THREE

Hole in One

> "Gerber makes the greatest tequila in the world which may explain the smile on the baby's face." —*Bill "Spaceman" Lee*

> "Spaceman take off! Spaceman take off! You know, Billy Lee jes' a whole bunch of fun!" —*George "Boomer" Scott*

The earthling known as William Francis Lee, III once found himself in the unlikely locale of Hartford, Connecticut at a charity game. Before the game, the Spaceman was entertaining the crowd, and as often occurs a group of small children followed him around as if he were the Pied Piper, Buck O'Neal style.

Bill was showing off one of his self-made wooden bats, ones which were manufactured from the trees on his own property in Vermont. This bat, however, was a weighted in-loaded practice bat used for training. With dozens of youngsters looking on, Bill was about to demonstrate his swing, but first he walked three hundred feet away and placed a small bucket over the outfield fence. He then returned, tossed a baseball in the air, and clobbered it three hundred feet... into the bucket! It was a million to one shot at best, the sort of thing that his old manager, Don Zimmer, would bet on and lose at the dog track.

However, this was Bill "Spaceman" Lee we are talking about. Incredibly, the ball landed IN THE BUCKET ON THE FLY! A small African American boy approximately ten years old excitedly shouted at Bill Lee, "Hey, Mr. Lee, do it again!"

CHAPTER SIXTY-FOUR

You've Got Mail

"We choose not randomly each other. We meet only those who already exist in our subconscious." —*Sigmund Freud*

The following article appeared in *The Players' Tribune* on August 19, 2016:

LETTER TO MY YOUNGER SELF
By BILL "SPACEMAN" LEE

Dear Recently Born Bill Lee,

(For the record, it's Bill Lee, not "Billy." Your first memory of rejection will be in kindergarten, when you come to class on your first day and your kindergarten teacher asks, "What's your name?" You'll respond "Bill Lee." She'll say, "Oh, well what's your last name?" You'll say, "Bill… Lee." She'll say, "Don't be smart with me. What's your last name?" It will be humiliating.)

(Eventually, she'll realize her error, but the damage will have already been done.)

The first time you'll ever drive a truck will be to take a load of elk and deer meat over the pass up on Route 80. You'll be with your grandfather coming back from Tahoe after a snowstorm. He'll say to you, "It's getting slippery, you better drive." And you, somewhat scared, somewhat intrigued, will respond, "Grandpa, what do I do?"

His response will be simple, but profound: "Don't accelerate, but don't brake."

Good luck with that, kid.

Right now, things might seem slow for you. You're a really shy kid. People think you're weird, or that you're dumb because you struggle with dyslexia. You're probably a little scared about what's to come. But as you move forward in life, try to remember your grandpa's advice. Don't accelerate and be obsessed about what awaits in the future, but at the same time don't brake and be consumed by the past. There's nothing you can do about the future, either. You might as well do the best you can right here in the present.

Also, this is unrelated to the metaphor, but keep two hands on the wheel. It's really icy.

As you embark on your journey through life, here are a few bits of advice that you might want to keep in the recesses of your mind:

- Ask questions. Always. If you don't ask questions you're never going to learn anything.

- That being said, don't be satisfied with the answers you get. Embrace the Socratic Method. Have the courage to dig deeper, to seek more and more information. There's so much to learn. Never be satisfied.

- When you play YMCA football Father Crow will come to the house and yell at you because it's a Protestant sport that he says you shouldn't be part of. He'll tell you that you're going to hurt yourself. The next game you play, you'll punt a ball off the back of a kid's helmet and have it come back and hit you in the fucking teeth. Now, at the time you'll wonder, "How did Father Crow know that was goin' to happen?" But don't over think it. The universe unfolds as it should. That football was always destined for your teeth, Bill. You didn't do anything wrong.

- You're destined to be a pitcher. But you already know that. Your grandfather played pro ball, your aunt played pro ball and your dad played semipro ball. Hell, when you were a baby, you had these blocks with A-B-C and 1-2-3 on them, and whenever you fell down on their sharp edges, it would hurt. So you threw those fuckers out of the playpen. Pitching is in your blood. Don't overcomplicate it by letting your mind get in the way. Throwing a baseball is feeling, not thought. It should be like a religious experience every time you go to the hill. Approach this game with sound mind, sound body and controlled emotions. When you think you only fuck it up.

- You'll get your tenacity from your father, but when it comes to pitching form, listen to your aunt. There's a reason she was the first woman to throw a perfect game in the All-American Girls Professional Baseball League. She'll teach you your fundamentals and delivery. When you do pitch professionally, you'll have the same movement as her, the same pitches and the same arm slot. Most baseball players might be hesitant to learn from a woman, but guess what? Most baseball players suck.

- Oh, and on a side note here: It's amazing what you'll know one day about volcanology, climatology and sedimentology.

- The most important thing in life is attitude. The lining of your stomach changes constantly—every four hours you produce a new layer of cells. So if you're ever feeling upset, just wait around a bit, take a good shit and you'll be fine.

- A big turning point for you will come when you decide to go to college. You'll want to go to Oregon, but your family will push you toward USC. Your dad will sit you down one day and ask, "Son, do you want to be a big fish in a small pond, or a small fish in a big pond?" You won't know the answer, so you'll continue, "Well, if you're a big fish in a small pond, you're never gonna grow. But if you're a small fish in a big pond, you have a chance to grow a lot." You'll scratch your head, and then you'll ask, "What does that even mean?" He'll say, "It means you're going to USC."

- Just a heads-up: You're going to get kicked out of Shanghai in '75 for smoking dope. But hey, it's better than being hanged!

- On that note, let's discuss marijuana because you'll get asked about it a lot as you get older. It's in the nature of man to try and alter his state of consciousness, whether it is with alcohol, peyote or religious ceremonies. The only problem with any of these things is if you become reliant on them and use them as a crutch. You don't need pot to pitch, but you recognize that it helps you. Many of the drugs you'll encounter in the big leagues, such as amphetamines, are meant to speed you up. But marijuana slows you down, and allows you to focus. Some of your greatest athletic feats will occur while you're high, but not BECAUSE you're high. Understand that distinction.

- Thomas Malthus was wrong, Bill! Malthusian economics surmise that goods and services grow arithmetically and population grows exponentially, therefore there's not enough to go around. That's bullshit.

- Think twice before you decide to climb up to a second-story balcony to say goodbye to that girl in Montreal. Your heart is in the right place because you don't want to disturb the whole house by going through the front door, but when you slip and fall you'll be placed on the 21-day disabled list and feel like a total asshole.

- Throwing hard is overrated. Pitching is all about movement and location. Guys who throw the same speed are only pitching in two dimensions. A guy who can throw the ball at different speeds is pitching in three dimensions. He can add or he can subtract, and he can move it every which way. Always pitch in 3-D.

- During your playing career, you'll be mostly a loner. Not everyone has the same outlook as you, and that's fine. But in Boston, you'll become part of a group called the Buffalo Heads, which will include Ferguson Jenkins, Jim Willoughby and Rick Wise. The buffalo is the dumbest animal on the face of the earth. As Fergie used to say, and pay close attention, because he'll be your idol one day—"We don't even use arrows to kill them, we just run them off a cliff and go pick 'em up." The Buffalo Heads will understand that, in the grand theme of things, we know very little of the universe that surrounds us. But that's not a reason to be upset. Instead, be close with those who embrace the unknown and revel in it. Those who fear what they do not know have little room for growth.

- If you seek revenge, dig two graves, get mad early, and get over it early.

- "Don't accelerate, but don't brake," would become the equivalent of Don Zimmer instructing his favorite pitcher, "Don't give him anything good to hit, but don't walk him."

CHAPTER SIXTY-FIVE

Spaceman Takes Off, Orbits, and Splashes Down... Hard

"And I think it's gonna be a long, long time
Till touch down brings me 'round again to find
I'm not the man they think I am at home
Oh no no no, I'm a rocket man
Rocket man, burning out his fuse up here alone." —*Elton John*

"A black cat crossing your path signifies that the animal is going somewhere." —*Groucho Marx*

In Chapter Sixty-Four of this superb and magnificently written biography (the author will graciously accept plaudits), you read the following from Bill Lee's letter to his younger self:

"Think twice before you decide to climb up to a second-story balcony to say goodbye to that girl in Montreal. Your heart is in the right place because you don't want to disturb the whole house by going through the front door, but when you slip and fall you'll be placed on the 21-day disabled list and feel like a total asshole."

Perhaps we owe you (after all, you were kind enough to either purchase or steal this book) an explanation. Therefore...

In 1980, during Bill Lee's sensational albeit brief career with the Montreal Expos, there may have been an "incident." All right, there WAS an incident. Here then, is a brief synopsis of the events surrounding that incident as best as it can be explained.

The earthling known as William Francis Lee, III fresh off his sensational 1979 inaugural Montreal season, as was his wont, decided to go for a run one early morning. Therefore, Lee donned a pair of brand-new, great looking Nike running shoes and left Olympic Stadium for a six-mile run. The fact that the shoes were not Lee's to begin with is immaterial to those of us that know the Spaceman.

The events surrounding that memorable run by "Spaceman" Lee have been debated for several decades. After the following "explanation" provided by Lee, they may be discussed for several additional decades:

"It had rained that morning and the Montreal streets were slick, so while I was at Olympic Stadium, I picked out a pair of Nikes I thought would give me good traction, but when a black cat jumped out in front of me, I hydroplaned and lost my balance, but I continued on.* The Nikes were one of those expensive running shoes with a waffle sole. As I continued on my run, I thought I'd be a gentleman and stop at a three-decker on Rue de Marseille to say goodbye to a girl, but I didn't want to bother anyone and I began to climb the outside of the building.

"I made it to the second story of the building, but those wedged soles had bottoms that extended from the bottom of the shoes and they were bigger than the top of the shoe. There was mortar outside and when I reached the second story and attempted to swing around and grab the railing to pull myself up and swing my hips around in order to pull myself up, the railing broke. As I plummeted to the ground I was thinking, 'So far, so good.'"

After taking a deep breath, the Spaceman continued:

"Thank God the edge of the balcony wasn't spiked, or I would have impaled myself. I can imagine what Don Zimmer would have told the press back in Boston. The left side of my head hit my left knee as I was bent completely over. I landed on my back. I was knocked unconscious. When I came to, I was in agony. I then walked all the way to the hospital. I had a 360 degree bruise around my entire body."

All right, some of you have questions, but this author, whether it be Scott Russell or Kilgore Trout, will leave some things to the imagination, but leave others hanging. If you require more information, well, ask the Spaceman. However, this is what I did ascertain:

The Nike shoes belonged to John McHale, the general manager of the Montreal Expos. "You see," explained the southpaw, "it was slick out and as I said, I thought they'd provide good traction."

"Was McHale aware you had 'borrowed' his shoes?"

"Well," spoketh Lee, "I borrowed them in the manner Huckleberry Finn borrowed the watermelon."

As for the girl on the second floor of the balcony, well, stuff happens. GM McHale's shoes, as I understand, were perhaps "appropriated" army style. I believe it is referred to as "requisitioned."

> * Since this tome is nothing less than at least educational, the author has done some research (you didn't think I was just a pretty face, did you?) on that magnificent pair of Nike running shoes. The shoes were designed by Nike co-founder Bill Bowerman. If the name sounds familiar, Bowerman was the legendary track and field coach—although he abhorred being called "coach"—at the University of Oregon for 24 years. Bowerman trained 31 Olympic athletes during the time that the likes of Jim Ryun, Frank Shorter, and Bill Rodgers ruled the world of track.

The shoes that the Spaceman nearly died while wearing was Bowerman's famous invention the "Waffle Shoe." Bowerman, a genius, used his wife's waffle iron to create a waffle patterned sole to help improve running speed. However, he apparently neglected to add a feature that would prevent left-handed pitchers from falling off second story balconies. Imagine what Michael Jordan would have charged for one of those puppies.

Perhaps Bowerman's most famous pupil was an incredible record-breaking long-distance runner named Steve "Pre" Prefontaine, a hard-headed youth from Coos Bay, Oregon. At first, Pre and his coach clashed over Prefontaine's style of running, which invariably included jumping out ahead and not properly pacing himself, but the obstinate but iconoclastic Pre eventually won his coach over.

There is a powerful motion picture titled *Without Limits* based on the all too brief and tragic life of Steve Prefontaine, who was portrayed by Billy Crudup. Donald Sutherland stars as Bill Bowerman and the absurdly beautiful Monica Potter stars as Pre's girlfriend. Prefontaine perished in an automobile accident on May 30, 1975. He was twenty-four years old.

CHAPTER SIXTY-SIX

Women in Baseball

> "Let others pride themselves about how many pages they have written. I'd rather boast about the ones I've read." —*Jose Luis Borges*

The earthling known as William Francis Lee, III has always and will continue to always pay homage to his late aunt, the great Annabelle Lee, the woman who taught him how to pitch. She taught him how to change speeds, maintain the proper arm slot and delivery. Lovely Annabelle, as we have learned, was the first woman to ever pitch a perfect game in the All American Girls Professional Baseball League, a league which helped heal our nation during the years from 1943-1955 and was featured in the great motion picture, *A League of Their Own* in 1992.

Another beautiful pioneer woman who has crossed paths with Bill Lee on occasion is a legendary baseball umpire named Perry Barber. Perry, as it is prominently displayed at the National Baseball Hall of Fame in Cooperstown, New York, was the first woman to ever umpire a major league game. That occurred during spring training and Perry has also umpired in Japan, Hong Kong, Guam, and the Caribbean. Perry Barber also frequently umpires in Roy Hobbs Leagues and at several other professional baseball venues.

On one of the occasions Perry was umpiring, the Spaceman came up to hit. As Perry stated:

"On the first pitch to him, I called 'Strike two!' Bill stepped out and gave me a look that cracked me up."

In addition to Perry's career as an umpire, she has been a great mentor and friend to countless women attempting to enter the sport and Perry's promotion of that wonderful cause recently garnered Ms. Barber a prestigious award, as she was named as the first recipient of "The Dorothy Seymour Mills Lifetime Achievement Award." Perry has been umpiring since 1981. Perry also conducts clinics.

The most fascinating thing about Perry Barber, however, is that most people would have thought her unlikely to ever become an umpire. Perry and her identical and equally stunningly beautiful twin sister were debutantes… no, really.

Perry and her twin sister were also terrific singers and musicians and they literally appeared on "Dodger Dugout" before a game and performed one of their compositions. How good is/was Perry as a singer-composer? She was the opening act for the likes of Billy Joel, Bruce Springsteen, Jerry Jeff Walker, and other notable legends.

One of Perry's dearest friends was the incomparable Steve Goodman, one of the greatest singer-songwriters of the twentieth century. Among other memorable songs, Goodman, whose personality was off the charts, penned "City of New Orleans." Sadly, Goodman lost a lengthy battle with leukemia, but his songs live on, and they include "Go Cubs, Go," which is played and sung by the entire crowd at Wrigley Field following each Cubs victory.

As Perry Barber told the author several years ago, "Steve was like my brother. When he was undergoing chemo at Sloan Kettering in New York, he would come to my apartment afterwards and lie on my couch and play my Morgan until he felt strong enough to leave. I live right around the corner from the hospital." The author fondly recalls seeing Steve Goodman perform live at Passim's in Cambridge, Massachusetts on several occasions.

Perry and her identical twin sister, Warren, were debutantes, but they both absolutely loved baseball. Although they were both discouraged by many of the thick-skulled males of the species, they nevertheless decided to attend "umpiring school" and the rest is history. Perry, a brilliant woman, also was a winner on the game show *Jeopardy*.

Recently, Ms. Barber offered the following when asked about Bill "Spaceman" Lee:

"Last November while I was out in Arizona umpiring the Men's Senior Baseball League (MSBL) World Series, I turned around while I was working the plate one game and saw Ozzie Virgil, with whom I had recently become friends through some APBPA events. Ozzie waited until I was done, then grabbed me by the hand and steered me toward the field right across from mine and said, 'There's someone I want you to meet.'

"As we walked past the opening of the fence, all disheveled and sweaty in my plate gear, I spotted Bill Lee sitting in the dugout and started giggling a little, thinking that Ozzie obviously had no idea that Bill's and my paths had crossed quite a few times before. Ozzie called out to Bill as he approached, and he kind of stared at me and did a double take, which surprised me. I wasn't sure he'd remember me personally, since I had only seen him in Florida at the Roy Hobbs, but I was pretty sure he'd remember a woman umpire. So his reaction to seeing me was a bit odd, but as I walked over to him and stood in front of him to shake his hand, this weird unsanitary custom that Americans used to engage in, he said, 'You remind me so much of my aunt, Annabelle.' I about fell on the dugout floor, I was so caught off my guard and overwhelmed, because I knew he was referring to Annabelle Lee, one of the stars of the AAGPBL, who threw the first perfect game in the league's history. I thought that was one of the sweetest things anybody ever said to me."

Tragically, Perry Barber's beautiful identical twin sister succumbed to cancer several years ago.

CHAPTER SIXTY-SEVEN

Blast Off

Tales of Red Sox Fantasy Camp

"Yaz was my bridge partner for my first three years in the big leagues. He cost me half of my meal money." —*Bill "Spaceman" Lee*

The earthling known as William Francis Lee, III has always enjoyed himself at numerous Red Sox fantasy camps, and some of his teammates have been wondrous characters. Consider Art Edwards, who also doubled as the head of public relations at Cape Canaveral before it became known as the Kennedy Space Center.

As Lee explained, "Art's a really good guy and a good friend. Art took Diana and I on a tour of the entire facility and I signed the giant hangar where the space shuttles were. Afterwards, another friend, Jack Loveday, who is one of our pitchers, and I were walking on the beach just north of Cape Canaveral and we found the wingtip from the *Challenger*."

Bill Lee then continued, "Jack 'Lucky' Loveday has a 'stop and go' fastball, the slowest fastball I've ever seen. He throws it 30 mph, but it never changes altitude. On that fantasy camp team, we had a cop, 'Chick' Rodenbush at third and a bookie, Terry Mansullo at first base. Terry could hit, but he couldn't run and the cop, Chick, is a really good ballplayer.

"One day, Mansullo, the bookie, is playing on teams in the younger division and the older division. Once we were in Arizona for a championship series and Teddy, the bookie, goes a combined 6-8 in the doubleheader. He had a good day on both fields. While he was playing, he booked $4,000 on the Patriots game. He had a captive audience. After the games we went to a bar and there was a cop show on television. In the show, there's a cop with a hat with a light on it, and he's sneaking into a bar in Brockton called Teddy's Lounge. While we're watching the show a cop came in and arrested Teddy's daughter. You can't make this shit up. Our teams would play great at the beginning of the tournaments, but by the finals, we would be missing three guys who were arrested for DUI."

The great NHL star, Bobby Hull, perhaps as big of a character as the

Spaceman, once joined the Lees at Cape Canaveral. As Lee stated, "Thanks to Art Edwards, we had access to every inch at the space center and the Mercury sites. Diana and I walked every square inch of the facility. I always loved the place. Well, one time we had Bobby Hull with us and the sheriff of the county was driving us around and keeping us out of trouble, day and night. One time, Bobby came up to Vermont to visit us."*

> * Note: Bobby "The Golden Jet" Hull and Bill "Spaceman" Lee are the embodiment of "double trouble." Hull is one of the greatest players in NHL history.

Bill Lee laughed and continued, "Bobby came up to my house. He was selling freckled face Herefords.** All of the farmers in the area came over in their John Deere tractors and they were all over my pasture up here. Before long, they were all drunk as shit and trying to get back down from my hill. Not that Bobby and I would lead anyone astray."

> ** "Freckled-face Herefords are terrific animals. They tend to be more maternal and are renowned for their higher milk flow and great fertility.

The Spaceman also pointed out that both Bobby Hull and Bill's wife Diana are from Belleville, Ontario and Diana's aunt used to date the Golden Jet.

Bill Lee then said, "Visitors to the town of Belleville, Ontario will see a sign as they drive into town. It reads, 'Welcome to Belleville, Home of Bobby and Dennis Hull.' Dennis Hull, the brother of Bobby, was a less successful hockey player, but Bobby, never allowing a ball-busting opportunity to get by him, always gets out of his car and crosses out Dennis' name upon returning home."

Once during a fantasy camp game, the Golden Jet's wife came down to the dugout to get one hundred dollars from her husband, and as the Spaceman described "waddled away with her little duck feet, she's a dancer." Bobby gave his wife a one hundred dollar bill and remarked, "I should put the one hundred dollar bill on my dick, because she can blow one hundred dollars faster than any woman alive."

The Spaceman and the Golden Jet together. As the great, late Hall of Fame Red Sox broadcaster, Ned Martin would say: Mercy!

CHAPTER SIXTY-EIGHT

The Real Conspiracy "Theorists"

The Truth Hurts, but Lies Are Worse

> "I'm not upset that you lied to me, I'm upset that from now on I can't believe you." —*Friedrich Nietzsche*

We began Chapter Twenty-Seven with "It is highly likely that the father of one of the Spaceman's friends assassinated President John F. Kennedy." In truth, that possibility is actually even greater than "highly likely." It is pretty much a fact. Let's put it this way: For those that claim Lee Harvey Oswald "acted alone," and that the Warren Commission "investigated" the assassination of President John F. Kennedy, well, the facts indicate otherwise.

Please consider that Charles Harrelson, the father of the superb actor Woody Harrelson, ADMITTING to the crime, having photographic evidence to substantiate his claim, his being arrested at the scene, his being convicted of murdering a federal judge, his being convicted of a prior contract killing, his admission that he committed a total of 12 contract killings and numerous other corroborating evidence, seems rather compelling. It sure beats the hell out of dragging someone named Lee Harvey Oswald out of the back of a movie theater, immediately claiming he had murdered the president, not to mention a police officer, without evidence of either alleged "fact," and then having a commission appointed to investigate the assassination by designating a man recently fired from his position as head of the Central Intelligence Agency by the now deceased president, and then claiming that the assassin who killed the prior assassin did so on his own, too, a killing that left no witnesses alive, except for the second assassin, who is also killed, but not before being interviewed by a renowned columnist who also mysteriously "dies." If you believe the findings of the Warren Commission, I have a bridge to sell you.

Not only does the earthling known as William Francis Lee have the renowned actor Woody Harrelson as a friend, but Woody realizes that his father was likely one of the two killers on that fateful day at Dealey Plaza on November 22, 1963. All points lead to Harrelson and one of his accomplices, Charles Rogers, as the shooters. Chauncey Holt was also arrested at the scene by the Dallas police, but after being "interrogated" by the FBI, the three men were mysteriously released. It is also interesting to note that at the time of Charles Harrelson's arrest, the contract killer had the business card of a R.D. Matthews, a mobster who was a known Jack Ruby associate.

The Warren Commission, to be brutally honest, was a complete joke. To appoint the deposed leader of the head of the most powerful military industrial complex in the world, Allen Dulles, a man fired by President Kennedy shortly before the assassination, should seem absurd to any sentient human being. That fact alone is a powerful conflict of interest. But the American public bought it, for the most part.

Even to the then eighteen-year-old author, I was amazed at how quickly a full dossier on the alleged assassin, Lee Harvey Oswald, became available to the media merely hours after his arrest. Those were not the days of quick dissemination of information. It smacked of some significant preparedness. This was clearly a well-organized script.

The fact that the alleged assassin, Lee Harvey Oswald, was characterized as a radical communist just did not wash. Seriously, how many communists enlist in the Marines, get access to classified information during the "Cold War," and receive a visa to travel to Russia, but get turned down afterwards for another visa in order to travel to Cuba... by the Cuban government?! Then there was this "minor" detail about his widow, Marina Oswald, receiving a check for $25,000 from the State Department shortly after his death... for reasons that remain "classified." Sorry, but I am not buying the "lone assassin" theory. Charles Voyde Harrelson, hitman for both the mob and CIA, seems much more credible.

Anyone of a certain age would recall a popular television game show in the 1950s and 1960s called *What's My Line*. One of the esteemed panelists was a highly respected nationally known columnist named Dorothy Kilgallen, a humorous and trusted investigative journalist not given to hyperbole. Ms. Kilgallen was the ONLY journalist (she had connections, of course) who somehow engineered her way in to visit Jack Ruby, the man who had killed Oswald, thereby eliminating the only witness to the assassination of the president. Even more impressive is that Dorothy Kilgallen visited Ruby's cell TWICE!

Jack Ruby was a famous or infamous manager of numerous night clubs, strip clubs, and dance halls in Dallas, Texas. Ruby developed close ties with many Dallas police officers who frequented his establishments, places where the police were provided free alcohol, prostitutes, and other "favors." It should be noted that there were no transcripts of any conversations between the "assassin" Lee Harvey Oswald and his interrogators during the two nights he was held in custody. On the morning of November 24, the police were in the process of relocating the "assassin" to another facility when Jack Ruby stepped out from behind a group of reporters and killed Oswald at close range with a single shot to the abdomen from a .38 colt cobra revolver. There would be no questioning of the man who allegedly killed the president of the United States.

It would be natural to ask how Jack Ruby got into the building, and with a gun. But reconsider his relationship with law enforcement. He had a "job" to do, and he did it well. The Dallas police admitted that they "mistakenly" removed a couple of security guards from UNLOCKED entrances to the building. Think about that.

So, let us get back to highly admired columnist Dorothy Kilgallen, who had somehow wangled her way in to interview Jack Ruby on two occasions. In one of Ms. Kilgallen's final columns, she stated that she was "going to blow the case wide open."

It should also be known that Jack Ruby had pleaded with Chief Justice Earl Warren, who had appointed the deposed former CIA Director Allen Dulles to lead the investigation, to allow him to visit Washington, D.C. Ruby claimed that he had critical information while stating "My life is in danger here." Ruby requested that opportunity on numerous occasions. Chief Justice Warren denied Jack Ruby access to those in Washington and replied to Ruby:

"Too many legal barriers and public interest in the situation would be too heavy." It was reported that Dorothy Kilgallen privately told a few select people that Ruby feared he was being "injected with live cancer cells." On January 3, 1967 Jack Ruby died in his Dallas cell... of cancer.

Jack Ruby lived longer than the prominent columnist, Dorothy Kilgallen. Ms. Kilgallen was found dead in her New York City apartment on November 8, 1965, of an "apparent alcohol and barbiturate combination overdose." Kilgallen, who was merely fifty-three, had been in excellent physical condition.

A gentleman named Clarence Carlson reported that Dorothy Kilgallen had been found in bed in a room she did not sleep in, wearing clothing she seldom slept in, her makeup still on, a book lying next to her, a book she had finished weeks before, her reading glasses not in the vicinity, and that an autopsy revealed that the amount of alcohol and drugs in her system was not particularly high. Perhaps it was also quite indicative that her notes on the assassination had mysteriously vanished....

So, do you still believe the Warren Commission? Who are the REAL conspiracy theorists? I would say Charles Harrelson's admission, his presence at the scene of the crime, and the fact his job was "contract killer," and a damned good shooter, have a bit of credibility. Bill "Spaceman" Lee's friend, Woody Harrelson, a great person, incidentally, had a father who most likely assassinated perhaps our most beloved president. Never blame the sons and daughters for the sins of their fathers.

Speaking of the Spaceman, whose Uncle Grover, as we have already documented, owned Malibu Lock and Key back then. One day, "The Band," one of the greatest musical groups in history, required the locksmith service. As Spaceman recalls, "I'm not sure, but I think they stored their band equipment inside the building." Grover's son, Buddy, still has the bounced check from the group, a check totaling $142. No, really. As Bill says, "With interest from over forty years, they probably owe us a ton, but I'll settle for a four hundred pound pig for my farm."

Speaking of "The Band," their iconic last performance, which of course became part of the now legendary motion picture *The Last Waltz*, produced and directed by the great Martin Scorcese, Bill Lee recalled lead guitarist Robbie Robertson's description of a venue they appeared at in Fort Worth, Texas. As Robertson stated in *The Last Waltz*:

"We got to this place, a joint in Fort Worth, Texas. It was burned out, bombed out. The roof wasn't even on the place anymore and that's when they decided to call it 'The Skyline Lounge.' We got there and set up, it was a big place. There was a huge bar way at the back and a big dance floor, really old. So, we set up the first night and go in, and in this huge place, there's about three people in the audience, a one-armed go-go dancer, and a couple of drunk waiters. A couple here, a couple there, and someone fires tear gas. A fight starts and there aren't even enough people in the place to get angry. We found out a few years later it was Jack Ruby's club."

The life of the earthling known as William Francis Lee incorporates various "tentacles."

CHAPTER SIXTY-NINE

Say What?

Bill Lee Simply Played for the Wrong Managers

> "See that fella over there? He's twenty years old. In ten years, he's got a chance to be a star. Now, that fella over there, he's twenty years old, too. In ten years, he's got a chance to be thirty."
> —*Casey Stengel*

> "Committee—a group of men who individually can do nothing, but as a group decide that nothing can be done." —*Fred Allen*

Life often takes illogical bounces. Consider that Bill Lee's mom was raised right down the street from Casey Stengel, and that the Spaceman's legendary coach at USC was Rod Dedeaux, who had been Casey's neighbor for several years. Imagine the possibility of Casey Stengel managing Bill Lee! The two eccentric #37's would have made for the greatest duo in major league history.

Unfortunately, after USC, Bill was on his way to Waterloo, Iowa and Rac Slider, another man who no one knew what he was talking about; however, in Rac's case, it was not intentional. Casey Stengel and Bill Lee were masters of non-sequiturs. Both Stengel and Lee delighted in ball-busting. For those listening to Casey, however, for the initial time, one would never imagine he was the brilliant president of a bank in Glendale, California.

Bill Lee recently said, "Joining professional ball and having Rac Slider as an immediate roadblock was a harbinger of things to come." Far too many in professional baseball had been promoted to positions of authority and in charge of several younger men, including Bill Lee, who were vastly more educated. Obviously, very few of these athletes had the brain power of the precocious Bill Lee, who could quote the likes of Buckminster Fuller as well as Casey Stengel. The Don Zimmers were waiting in the wings and they comprised hindrances, not only to Lee, but to themselves, as well.

To fully appreciate the ball-busting genius of Charles Dillon "Casey" Stengel, who long before becoming the manager of several World

Championship New York Yankee teams, was a clown prince outfielder in the major leagues, one would only have had to be present at the July 8, 1958 United States Senate Anti-Trust and Monopoly Subcommittee Hearing, conducted to investigate major league baseball's anti-trust laws.

In the twilight of Stengel's managerial career, he was given the reins of the New York Mets 1962 expansion team, and Casey was perfect for the part. The team was a collection of washed-up major league veterans and younger players, who were at best marginal players. Casey was the biggest attraction as he entertained writers and fans in describing the futility of his sinfully bad ball club.

Why exactly, the U.S. Senate believed they would receive anything less than abject avoidance of their questions directed at Casey Stengel, is still unknown, but Casey's responses were both hysterical and intentionally nonsensical. The following is an actual transcript of the great Casey Stengel's "testimony" to the Kefauver Subcommittee. Some sixty-two years later, it is still as mind-numbingly hilarious:

Senator Kefauver: Welcome Mr. Stengel. We eagerly await your testimony.

Casey: Well, I started in professional ball in 1910. I have been in professional ball, I would say for forty-eight years. I have been employed by numerous ballclubs in the majors and in the minor leagues. I started in the minor leagues with Kansas City. I played as low as class D ball, which was at Shelbyville, Kentucky, and also class C ball, and class A ball, and I have advanced in baseball as a ballplayer.

I had many years I was not so successful as a ballplayer, as it is a game of skill. And then I was no doubt discharged by baseball in which I had to go back to the minor leagues as a manager, and after being in the minor leagues as a manager, I became a major league manager in several cities and was discharged, we call it "discharged," because there is no question I had to leave. (Laughter). And I returned to the minor leagues at Milwaukee, Kansas City and Oakland, California, and then returned to the major leagues.

In the last ten years, naturally, in major league baseball with the New York Yankees, the New York Yankees have had tremendous success and while I am not the ballplayer who does the work, I have no doubt worked for a ball club that is very capable in the office. I must have splendid ownership, I must have very capable men who are in radio and television, which is no doubt you know that we have mentioned the three names—you will say they are very great.

We have a wonderful press that follows us. Anybody should in New York City, where you have so many people. Our ballclub has been successful because we have it, and we have the Spirit of 1776. We put it into the ball field and if you are not capable of becoming a great ballplayer since I have been in as a manager, in ten years, you are notified that if you don't produce on the ball field, the salary that you receive, we will allow you to be traded to play and give your services to other clubs.

The great proof was yesterday. Three of the young men that were stars and picked by the players in the American League to be in the All-Star-Game were Mr. Cerv, who is at Kansas City, Mr. Jensen, who was at Boston, and I might say Mr. Triandos that caught for the Baltimore ball club, all three of those players were my members and to show you I was not such a brilliant manager they got away from me and were chosen by the players and I was fortunate enough to have them come back to play where I was successful as a manager.

If I have been in baseball for forty-eight years there must be some good in it. I was capable and strong enough to do any kind of work but I came back to baseball and I have been in baseball ever since. I have been up and down the ladder. I know there are some things in baseball, thirty-five to fifty years ago that are better now than they were in those days. In those days, my goodness, you could not transfer a ball club in the minor leagues, class D, class C ball, class A ball. How could you transfer a ball club when you did not have a highway? How could you transfer a ball club when the railroads then would take you to a town you got off and then you had to wait and sit up five hours to go to another ball club?

How could you run baseball then without night ball? You had to have night ball to improve the proceeds to pay larger salaries and I went to work, the first year I received $135 a month. I thought that was amazing. I had to put away enough money to go to dental college. I found out it was not better in dentistry, I stayed in baseball.

Any other questions you would like to ask me? I want to let you know that as to the legislative end of baseball you men will have to consider that what you are here for. I am a bench manager. I will speak about anything from the playing end—in the major or minor leagues—and do anything I can to help you.

Senator Kefauver: Mr. Stengel, are you prepared to answer particularly why baseball wants this bill passed?

Mr. Stengel: Well, I have to say at this present time, I think that baseball has advanced in this respect for the player help. That is an amazing statement for me to make, because you can retire with an annuity at fifty and what organization in America allows you to retire at fifty and what organization in America allows you to retire at fifty and receive money?

I want to further state that I am not a ballplayer, that is, put into that pension fund committee. At my age, and I have been in baseball, well, I say I am possibly the oldest man who is working in baseball, I would say that when they start an annuity for the ballplayers to better their conditions, it should have been done, and I think it has been done. I think it should be the way they have done it, which is a very good thing.

The reason they probably did not take the managers in at that time was because radio and television or the income to ball clubs was not large enough that you could have put in a pension plan. Now, I am not a member of the pension plan. You have young men here who are, who represent the ball clubs. They represent them as players and since I am not a member and don't receive a pension from a fund, which you think, my goodness, he ought to be declared in that too but I will say this is a great thing for the ballplayers. That is one thing I would say for the ballplayers they have an advanced pension fund. I think it was gained by radio and television or you could not have enough money to pay anything of that type.

Now the second thing about baseball that I think is very interesting to the public or to all of us that it is the owner's fault if he does not improve his club, along with the officials in the ball club and the players.

Now what causes that? If I am going to go on the road and we are a travelling ball club and you know the cost of transportation now—we travel sometimes with three Pullman coaches, the New York Yankees and remember I am just a salaried man and do not own stock in the New York Yankees, I found out that in travelling with the New York Yankees on the road and all, that it is the best, and we have broken records in Washington this year, we have broken them in every city but New York and we have lost two clubs that have gone out of the city of New York.

Of course, we have had some bad weather, I would say that they are mad at us in Chicago, we fill the parks. They have come out to see good material. I will say they are mad at us in Kansas City, but we broke their attendance record.

Now on the road we only get possibly 27½. I am not positive of these figures, as I am not an official. If you go back fifteen years or if I owned stock in the club I would give them to you.

Senator Kefauver: Mr. Stengel, I am not sure that I made my question clear. (Laughter).

Mr. Stengel: Yes, sir. Well that is all right. I am not sure I am going to answer yours perfectly either. (Laughter)

Senator Kefauver: I was asking you, sir, why it is that baseball wants this bill passed.

Mr. Stengel: I would say I would not know, but would say the reason why they would want it passed is to keep baseball going as the highest paid ball sport that has gone into baseball and from the baseball angle, I am not going to speak of any other sport. I am not here to argue about other sports, I am in the baseball business. It has been run cleaner than any business that was ever put out in the one-hundred years at the present time. I am not speaking about television or I am not speaking about income that comes into the ball parks: You have to take that off. I don't know too much about it. I say the ballplayers have a better advancement at the present time.

Senator Kefauver: One further question, and then I will pass the other Senators. How many players do the Yankees control, Mr. Stengel?

Mr. Stengel: Well, I will tell you: I hire the players and if they make good with me, I keep them without criticism from my ownership. I do not know how many players they own as I am not a scout and I cannot run a ball club during the daytime and be busy at night and up the next day and find out how many players that the Yankees own. If you get any official with the Yankees that is here, why he could give you the names.

Senator Kefauver: Very well. Senator Langer?

Senator Langer: Mr. Stengel?

Mr. Stengel: Yes, sir.

Senator Langer: What do you think is the future of baseball? Is it going to be expanded to include more clubs than are in existence at the present time?

Mr. Stengel: I think every chamber of commerce in the major league cities would not change a franchise, I think they will be delighted because they have a hard time to put in a convention hall to get people to come to your city and if it is going to be like Milwaukee or Kansas City or Baltimore, I think they would want a major league team, but if I was a chamber of commerce member and I was in a city, I would not want a baseball team to leave the city as too much money is brought into your city even if you have a losing team and great if you have a winning ball team.

Senator Langer: You look forward then, do you not, to say, ten years or twenty years from now this business of baseball is going to grow larger and larger and larger?

Mr. Stengel: Well, I should think it would. I should think it would get larger because of the fact we are drawing tremendous crowds, I believe, from overseas programs in television, that is one program I have always stuck up for. I think every ballplayer and everyone should give out anything that is overseas for the Army, free of cost and so forth. I think every hospital should get it. I think that because of the lack of parking in so many cites that you cannot have a great ballpark if you don't have parking space. If you are ancient or forty-five or fifty and have acquired enough money to go to a ballgame, you cannot drive a car on a highway, which is very hard to do after forty-five, to drive on any modern highway and if you are going to stay home you need radio and television to go along for receipts for the ball club.

Senator Langer: That brings us to another question.

Mr. Stengel: Yes, sir.

Senator Langer: That is, what do you think of pay-as-you-go television?

Mr. Stengel: Well, to tell you the truth, if were starting in it myself I would like to be in that line of business as I did not think they would ever have television and so forth here but they have got it here now. (Laughter). Forty years ago you would not have had it around here yourself and you would not have cameras flying around here every five minutes but we have got them here and more of them around here than around a ball field, I will give you that little tip.

Senator Langer: You believe the time is ever going to come when you will have pay-as-you-go in the World Series, which would be kept from the public unless they had pay-as-you-go television in their homes?

Mr. Stengel: I think you have got a good argument there and it is worthy of you to say that. I am not thinking myself of anybody that is hospitalized and anybody who cannot go to a ball park, I should think if they could pass that they should try to pass it, but I don't think they will be able to do it because they have gone in television so far that they reach so many outside people, you have to have a sponsor for everything else you do, go pay television and that is going to run all the big theaters out of business where you have to use pay television. All the big theaters and all the big movie companies went broke. We know that. You see that now or you would not have a place to hold a television for pay. I don't know how they would run that of course. I am not on that side of the fence. I am paid a salary.

Senator Langer: Just one further question. You do not have to answer it unless you want to. That is, is there any provision made whereby the team owners can keep a racketeer out of the baseball business?

Mr. Stengel: Well, sir?

Senator Langer: Can the owners of the New York Yankees, for example, sell out to anyone who may want to buy the club at a big price without the consent of the other owners?

Mr. Stengel: That is a very good thing that I will have to think about but I will give you an example. I think that is why they put in as a commissioner Judge Landis, and he said if there is a cloud on baseball I will take it off, and he took the cloud off and they have had only one scandal or if they had, it is just one major league city.

How can you be a ballplayer and make twenty-five ballplayers framed without being heard? It is bound to leak, and your play will show it. I don't think, an owner possibly could do something, but he can't play the game for you. It is the most honest profession I think that we have, everything today that is going on outside.

Senator Langer: Mr. Chairman, my final question. This is the Antimonopoly Committee that is sitting here.

Mr. Stengel: Yes, sir.

Senator Langer: I want to know whether you intend to keep on monopolizing the world's championship in New York City.

Mr. Stengel: Well, I will tell you, I got a little concerned yesterday in the first three innings when I say the three players I had gotten rid of and I said when I lost nine what am I going to do and when I had a couple of my players. I thought so great of that did not do so good up to the sixth inning I was more confused but I finally had to go and call on a young man in Baltimore that we don't own and the Yankees don't own him, and he is going pretty good, and I would actually have to tell you that I think we are more the Greta Garbo type now from success.

We are being hated I mean, from the ownership and all, we are being hated. Every sport that gets too great or one individual, but if we made 27½ and it pays to have a winner at home why would you not have a good winner in your own park if you were an owner. That is the result of baseball. An owner gets most of the money at home and it is up to him and his staff to do better or they ought to be discharged.

Senator Langer: That is all, Mr. Chairman. Thank you.

Senator Kefauver: Thank you, Senator Langer. Senator O'mahoney?

Senator O'mahoney: May I say, Mr. Stengel, that I congratulate you very much for what happened on the field at Baltimore yesterday. I was watching on television when you sent Gil McDougald up to bat for Early Wynn. I noticed with satisfaction that he got a hit, knocking Frank Malzone in with the winning run. That is good management.

Mr. Stengel: Thank you very much. (Laughter).

Senator O'mahoney: Did I understand you to say, Mr. Stengel, at the beginning of your statement that you have been in baseball for forty-eight years?

Mr. Stengel: Yes, sir; the oldest man in the service.

Senator O'mahoney: How many major league teams were there in the United States when you entered baseball?

Mr. Stengel: Well, there was in 1910, there were sixteen major league baseball teams.

Senator O'mahoney: How many are there now?

Mr. Stengel: There are sixteen major league clubs but there was one year that they brought in the Federal League which was brought in by Mr. Ward and Mr. Sinclair and others after a war, and it is a very odd thing to tell you that during tough times it is hard to study baseball. I have been through two or three depressions in baseball and out of it.

The first World War we had good baseball in August. The second World War we kept on and made more money because everybody was around going to the services; the larger the war, the more they come to the ballpark, and that was an amazing thing to me. When you were looking for tough times, why, it changed for different wars.

Senator O'mahoney: How many minor leagues were there in baseball when you began?

Mr. Stengel: Well, there were not so many at that time because of this fact: Anybody to go into baseball at that time with the educational schools that we had were small, while you were probably thoroughly educated at school, you had to be. We had only small cities that you could put a team in and they would go defunct. Why I remember the first year I was at Kankakee, Ill., and a bank offered me $550 if I would let them have a little notice. I left there and took a uniform because they owed me two weeks' pay. But I either had to quit but I did not have enough money to go to dental college, so I had to go with the manager down to Kentucky.

What happened there was if you got by July, that was the big date. You did not play night ball and you did not play Sundays in half of the cities on account of a Sunday observance, so in those days when things were tough, and all of it was, I mean to say, why they just closed up July 4 and there you were sitting there in the depot. You could go to work someplace else but that was it. So, I got out of Kankakee, Ill., and I just go there for the visit now. (Laughter).

I think now, do you know how many clubs they have? Anybody will start a minor league club but it is just like your small cities, the industries have left them and they have gone west to California, and I am a Missourian—Kansas City, Missouri—but I can see all those towns and everybody moving west and I know if you fly in the air you can see anything from the desert, you can see a big country over there that has got many names. Well, now why wouldn't baseball prosper out there, with that many million people?

Senator O'mahoney: Are the minor leagues suffering now?

Mr. Stengel: I should say they are.

Senator O'mahoney: Why?

Mr. Stengel: Do you know why? I will tell you why. I don't think anybody can support minor league ball when they see a great official, it would be just like a great actress or actor had come to town. If Bob Hope had come here or Greta Garbo over there half of them would go see Greta Garbo and have Bob Hope but if you have a very poor baseball team they are not going to watch you until you become great and the minor leagues now with radio and television will not pay very much attention to minor league ballplayers. Softball is interesting, the parent is interested; he goes around with him. He watches his son and he is more enthusiastic about the boy than some stranger that comes to town and wants to play in a little wooden park and with no facilities to make you interested. You might rather stay home and see a program.

Senator O'mahoney: How many baseball players are now engaged in the activity as compared to when you came in?

Mr. Stengel: I would say there are more, many more. Because we did not have as many cities that could support even minor league baseball in those days.

Senator O'mahoney: How many players did the sixteen major league clubs have when you came in.

Mr. Stengel: At that time, they did not have as many teams. They did not have near as many teams as below. Later on Mr. Rickey came in and started what was known as what you would say numerous clubs, you know in which I will try to pick up this college man, I will pick up that college boy or I will pick up some corner lot boy and if you picked up the corner lot boy maybe he became just as successful as the college man, which is true. He then had a number of players.

Now, too many players is a funny thing, it cost like everything. I said just like I made a talk not long ago and I told them all when they were drinking and they invited me in I said you ought to be home. You men are not making enough money. You cannot drink like that. They said, "This is a holiday for the Shell Oil Company", and I said, "Why is that a holiday?" and they said, "We did something great for three years and we are given two days off to watch the Yankees play the White Sox," but they were mostly White Sox rooters. I said, "You are not doing right." I said, "You can't take all those drinks and all even on your holidays. You ought to be home and raising more children because big league clubs now give you a hundred thousand for a bonus to go into baseball." (Laughter). And by the way I don't happen to have any children but I wish Mrs. Stengel and I had eight, I would like to put them in on that bonus rule. (Laughter).

Senator O'mahoney: What I am trying to find out, Mr. Stengel, is how many players are actively working for the major league teams now as was formerly the case? How many players do you suppose"

Mr. Stengel: You are right, I would honestly tell you they naturally have more, and they are in more competition now. You have to buck now a university — anyone who wants to be a hockey player"

Senator O'mahoney: Let's stick to baseball for a minute.

Mr. Stengel: I stay in baseball. I say you can't name them. If you want to know get any executive, you have got any names, bring any executive with the Yankees that is an official in the ball club and he will tell you how many players the Yankees have. And there is his jurisdiction — every ball club owner can tell you he is an official, they have enough officials hired with me with a long pencil, too.

Senator O'mahoney: I recently saw a statement by a baseball sportswriter that there were about four-hundred active ball players in the major leagues now. Would you think that is about correct now?

Mr. Stengel: I would say in the major leagues each club has twenty-five men which is the player limit. There are eight clubs in each league so you might say there are four-hundred players in the major leagues, you mean outside of it that they own two or three hundred each individual club, isn't that what you have reference to?

Senator O'mahoney: I was coming to that, but is that the fact?

Mr. Stengel: Well, I say that is what you would say (laughter) if you want to find that out you get any of those executives that come in here that keep those books. I am not a bookkeeper for him. But I take the man when he comes to the big league. They can give it to you and each club should. That does not mean, and I would like to ask you, how would you like to pay those men? That is why they go broke.

Senator O'mahoney: I am not in that business.

Mr. Stengel: I was in that business a short time, too. It is pretty hard to make a living at it.

Senator O'mahoney: But the stories that we read in the press.

Mr. Stengel: That is right.

Senator O'mahoney: Are to the effect that the minor leagues are suffering. There are no more major league teams now than there were when you came into baseball, and what I am trying to find out is, what are the prospects for the future growth of baseball and to what extent have the sixteen major league teams, through the farm system, obtained, by contract or agreement or understanding, control over the professional lives of the players?

Mr. Stengel: That is right. If I was a ballplayer and I was discharged, and I saw within three years that I could not become a major league ballplayer I would go into another profession. That is the history of anything that is in business.

Senator O'mahoney: Do you think that the farm system keeps any players in the minor leagues when they ought to be in the majors?

Mr. Stengel: I should say it would not keep any players behind or I have been telling you a falsehood. I would say it might keep a few back, but very few. There is no manager in baseball who wants to be a success without the ability of those great players and if I could pull them up to make money in a gate for my owner and for myself to be a success, I don't believe I would hold him back.

Senator O'mahoney: The fact is, is it not, Mr. Stengel, that while the population of the United States has increased tremendously during the period that you have been engaged in professional baseball, the number of major-league teams has not increased; it remains the same as it was then. The number of players actually engaged by the major-league teams is approximately the same as back in 1903, and there is now, through the farm system, a major league control of the professional occupation of baseball playing. Is that a correct summary?

Mr. Stengel: Well, you have that from the standpoint of what you have been reading. You have got that down very good. (Laughter). But if you were a player."

Senator O'mahoney: I am trying to get it down from your standpoint as a forty-eight-year-man in baseball.

Mr. Stengel: That is why I stayed in it. I have been discharged fifteen times and rehired, so you get rehired in baseball, and they don't want a good ballplayer leaving, and I always say a high-priced baseball player should get a high salary just like a moving-picture actor. He should not get the same thing as the twenty-fifth man on a ball club who is very fortunate he is sitting on your ball club, and I say it is very hard to have skill in baseball.

Senator O'mahoney: You are not changing the subject; are you, sir?

Mr. Stengel: No. You asked the question and I told you that if you want to find out how minor league baseball is; it is terrible now. How can you eat on $2.50 a day when up here you can eat on $8.00 or better than $8.00? Now how can you travel in a bus all night and play ball the next night to make a living? How can you, a major league man, make it so that you can't? Is he going to fly all of them to each place?

Senator O'mahoney: I am not arguing with you, Mr. Stengel.

Mr. Stengel: I am just saying minor league ball has outgrown itself, like every small town has outgrown itself industrially because they don't put a plant in there to keep the people working so they leave.

Senator O'mahoney: Does that mean in your judgment that the major league baseball teams necessarily have to control ball playing?

Mr. Stengel: I think that they do. I don't think that if I was a great player and you released me in four years, I think it would be a joke if you released a man and he made one year for you and then bid for a job and then played the next year, we will say, out of Washington, he played in New York the third year, he would play in Cleveland and put himself up for stake. I think they ought to be just as they have been.

A man who walks in and sees you get fair compensation and if you are great, be sure you get it because the day you don't report and the day you don't open a season you are hurting the major league and hurting yourself somewhat, but you are not going to be handicapped in life if you are great in baseball. Every man who goes out has a better home than he had when he went in.

Senator O'mahoney: Did I understand you to say that in your own personal activity as manager, you always give a player who is to be traded advance notice?

Mr. Stengel: I warn him that. I hold a meeting. We have an instructional school, regardless of my English, we have got an instructional school.

Senator O'mahoney: Your English is perfect and I can understand what you say, and I think I can even understand what you mean.

Mr. Stengel: Yes, sir. You have got some very wonderful points in. I would say in an instructional school we try you out for three weeks and we clock you, just like — I mean how good are you going to be in the service; before you go out of the service we have got you listed. We know if you are handicapped in the service and we have got instructors who teach you. They don't have to listen to me if they don't like me.

I have a man like Crosetti, who never has been to a banquet; he never would. He does a big job like Art Fletcher; he teaches that boy and teaches his family: he will be there. I have a man for first base, second base, short; that is why the Yankees are ahead.

We have advanced so much we can take a man over to where he can be a big-league player and if he does not, we advance him to where he can play opposition to us. I am getting concerned about opposition. I am discharging too many good ones.

Senator O'mahoney: Mr. Chairman, I think the witness is the best entertainment we have had around here for a long time and it is a great temptation to keep asking him questions, but I think I better desist. Thank you.

Senator Kefauver: Senator Carroll.

Senator Carroll: Mr. Stengel, I am an old Yankee fan and I come from a city where I think we have had some contribution to your success, from Denver. I think you have many Yankee players from Denver. The question Senator Kefauver asked you was what, in your honest opinion, with your forty-eight years of experience, is the need for this legislation in view of the fact that baseball has not been subject to antitrust laws?

Mr. Stengel: No.

Senator Carroll: It is not now subject to antitrust laws. What do you think the need is for this legislation? I had a conference with one of the attorneys representing not only baseball but all of the sports, and I listened to your explanation to Senator Kefauver. It seemed to me it had some clarity. I asked the attorney this question: What was the need for this legislation? I wonder if you would accept his definition. He said they didn't want to be subjected to the ipse dixit of the Federal Government because they would throw a lot of damage suits on the ad damnum clause. He said, in the first place, the Toolson case was sui generis, it was de minimus non curat lex. Do you call that a clear expression?

Mr. Stengel: Well, you are going to get me there for about two hours.

Senator Carroll: I realize these questions which are put to you are all, I suppose, legislative and legal questions. Leaning on your experience as manager, do you feel the farm system, the draft system, the reserve clause system, is fair to the players, to the managers, and to the public interest?

Mr. Stengel: I think the public is taken care of, rich and poor, better at the present time than years ago. I really think that the ownership is a question of ability. I really think that the business manager is a question of ability. Some of these men are supposed to be very brilliant (sic) in their line of work, and some of them are not so brilliant (sic), so that they have quite a bit of trouble with it when you run an operation of a club in which the ownership maybe doesn't run the club. I would say that the players themselves — I told you, I am not in on that fund, it is a good thing. I say I should have been, to tell you the truth. But I think it is a great thing about that fund.

Senator Carroll: I am not talking about that fund.

Mr. Stengel: Well, I tell you if you are going to talk about the fund you are going to think about radio and television and pay television.

Senator Carroll: I do not want to talk about radio and television, but I do want to talk about the draft clause and reserve systems.

Mr. Stengel: Yes, sir. I would have liked to have been free four times in my life; and later on I have seen men free, and later on they make a big complaint "they wuz robbed," and if you are robbed there is some club down the road to give you the opportunity.

Senator Carroll: That was not the question I asked you, and I only asked you on your long experience"

Mr. Stengel: Yes, sir. I would not be in it forty-eight years if it was not all right.

Senator Carroll: I understand that.

Mr. Stengel: Well, then, why wouldn't it stay that?

Senator Carroll: In your long experience"

Mr. Stengel: Yes.

Senator Carroll: Do you feel, you have had experience through the years?

Mr. Stengel: That is true.

Senator Carroll: With the draft system, and the reserve clause in the contracts. Do you think you could still exist under existing law without changing the law?

Mr. Stengel: I think it is run better than it has ever been run in baseball, for every department.

Senator Carroll: Then, I come back to the principal question. This is the real question before this body.

Mr. Stengel: All right.

Senator Carroll: Then what is the need for legislation, if they are getting along all right?

Mr. Stengel: I didn't ask for the legislation. (Laughter).

Senator Carroll: Your answer is a very good one, and that is the question Senator Kefauver put to you.

Mr. Stengel: That is right.

Senator Carroll: That is the question Senator O'mahoney put.

Mr. Stengel: Right.

Senator Carroll: Are you ready to say there is no need for legislation in this field, then, insofar as baseball is concerned?

Mr. Stengel: As far as I'm concerned, from drawing a salary and from my ups and downs and being discharged, I always found out that there was somebody ready to employ you, if you were on the ball.

Senator Carroll: Thank you very much, Mr. Stengel.

Senator Kefauver: Thank you very much, Mr. Stengel. We appreciate your testimony.

Senator Langer: May I ask a question?

Senator Kefauver: Senator Langer has a question. Just a moment, Mr. Stengel.

Senator Langer: Can you tell this committee what countries have baseball teams besides the United States, Mexico and Japan?

Mr. Stengel: I made a tour with the New York Yankees several years ago, and it was the most amazing tour I ever saw for a ball club, to go over where you have trouble spots. It wouldn't make any difference whether he was a Republican or Democrat, and so forth. I know that over there we drew 250,000 to 500,000 people in the streets, in which they stood in front of the automobiles, not on the sidewalks, and those people are trying to play baseball over there with short fingers (Laughter), and I say, "Why do you do it?"

But they love it. They are crazy about baseball, and they are not worried at the handicap. And I'll tell you, business industries run baseball over there, and they are now going to build a stadium that is going to be covered over for games where you don't need a tarpaulin if it rains.

South America is all right, and Cuba is all right. But I don't know, I have never been down there except to Cuba, I have never been to South America, and I know that they broadcast games, and I know we have players that are playing from there.

I tell you what, I think baseball has spread, but if we are talking about anything spreading, we would be talking about soccer. You can go over in Italy, and I thought they would know DiMaggio every place. And my goodness, you mention soccer, you can draw fifty or a hundred thousand people. Over here you have a hard time to get soccer on the field, which is a great sport, no doubt.

Senator Langer: What I want to know, Mr. Stengel, is this: When the American League plays the National League in the World Series and it is advertised as the world championship."

Mr. Stengel: Yes, sir.

Senator Langer: I want to know why you do not play Mexico or Japan or some other country and really have a world championship.

Mr. Stengel: Well, I think you have a good argument there. I would say that a couple of clubs that I saw, it was like when I was in the Navy, I thought I couldn't get special unless they played who I wanted to play. So, I took over a team. When they got off a ship, I would play them, but if they had been on land too long, my team couldn't play them. So, I would play the teams at sea six months, and I would say, "You are the club I would like to play." I would like to play those countries, and I think it should be nationwide and governmentwide, too, if you could possibly get it in.

Senator Langer: Do you think the day is ever going to come, perhaps five years from now or ten"

Mr. Stengel: I would say ten years, not five.

Senator Langer: When the championship team of the United States would play the championship team of Mexico?

Mr. Stengel: I really think it should be that way, but I don't think you will get it before ten years, because you have to build stadiums and you have to have an elimination in every country for it, and you have to have weather at the same time, or how could you play unless you would hold your team over?

Senator Langer: Do you not think these owners are going to develop this matter of world championship of another country besides the United States?

Mr. Stengel: I should think they would do that in time. I really do. I was amazed over in Japan. I couldn't understand why they would want to play baseball with short fingers and used the same size ball, and not a small size, and compete in baseball. And yet that is their great sport, and industries are backing them.

Senator Langer: In other words, the owners someday, in your opinion, Mr. Stengel, are going to make a lot of money by having the champions of one country play another country and keep on with eliminations until they really have a world championship?

Mr. Stengel: That is what I say. I think it is not named properly right now unless you can go and play all of them. You would have to do that.

Senator Langer: That is all, Mr. Chairman.

Senator Kefauver: Mr. Stengel, one final question. You spoke of Judge Landis and the fact that he had rather absolute control over baseball. There was a clause in Judge Landis' contract which read:

We, the club owners pledge ourselves to loyally support the commissioner in his important and difficult task, and we assure him that each of us will acquiesce in his decisions even when we believe they are mistaken, and that we will not discredit the sport by criticism of him or one another.

This same clause was in Mr. Chandler's contract, but we do not understand it to be in Mr. Frick's contract. Do you think the commissioner needs to have this power over management?

Mr. Stengel: I would say when there was a cloud over baseball, like any sport, you have to have a man that has the power to change things. Now, when Landis was in, that was the situation with baseball. You were bucking racetracks. We don't have a tote board. We are playing baseball for admission fees. Now, we don't have a tote board in baseball. Who would? That would be great, if you have that out there, and you could go out there and, you know, use a tote board and say, "Does he get to first or won't he get to first?" and so forth.

Now Landis was an amazing man. I will give you an example of him. It is a good thing you brought him in. I was discharged one year, and I was the president of a ball club at Worcester, Mass., so I discharged myself, and I sent it in to Landis and he O.K.'d it.

Why was I president? Then I could release my player, couldn't I? And I was the player. So, I was the only player ever released by the president, and that was in Worcester, Massachusetts, so I got discharged.

Senator Kefauver: Do you think the present commissioner ought to have the same power?

Mr. Stengel: There are sixteen men in baseball who own ball clubs. We will say that an individual can hardly make it anymore unless he is wealthy. That is how it has grown. I would say the biggest thing in baseball at the present time now, and with the money that is coming in, and so forth, and with the annuity fund for the players, you can't allow the commissioner to just take everything sitting there, and take everything insofar as money is concerned, but I think he should have full jurisdiction over the player and player's habits, and the way the umpires and ball clubs should conduct their business in the daytime and right on up tight up here.

Senator Kefauver: Thank you very much, Mr. Stengel. We appreciate your presence here.

Senator Kefauver: Mr. Mantle, do you have any observations with reference to the applicability of the antitrust laws to baseball?

Mr. Mantle: My views are about the same as Casey's (laughter).

Note: The following is a remembrance by Bill Lee:

"My parents sat with both Casey Stengel and Rod Dedeaux at the field at which I was playing for the Hollywood Stars. I still have my jersey from that game, jersey #4."

INTERLUDE #2

Bokononism

"Beware of the man who works hard to learn something, learns it, and finds himself no wiser than before." —*Bokonon*

"A child of five would understand this. Send someone to fetch a child of five." —*Groucho Marx*

The following requires verification.

The author, and there remains confusion as to his identity, wishes to convey that he began this tome somewhat confused, but has since been rendered entirely bewildered. There is now sepulchral (I promised myself I would fit that word into my Holy Writ) evidence that my condition may be permanent, but I digress.

The subject of this biography, the earthling known as William Francis Lee, III is not your average citizen. For one thing, he is left-handed. For another, according to the Spaceman, "Jesus was a southpaw." Incredibly, there is empirical evidence to support that "fact."

To fully, or at least to even partially understand Bill Lee, requires patience, dictionaries (that's plural, there are numerous languages involved), a tolerance of the absurd, and perhaps to even consider the usage of a mind-altering substance or three.*

| * Note: the author finds Grey Goose vodka to be effective.

To truly follow the wisdom of the sage, Bill Lee, reading a few novels by the likes of Kurt Vonnegut, Ray Bradbury, and researching Buckminster Fuller, would not be a bad idea.

In an attempt to master the teachings of the Spaceman, I will admit to being at an advantage, since Number One, I have known the man for over four decades; and Number Two, I read Vonnegut religiously... and yes, there's that word "religiously."

Firstly, consider that Bill Lee is a lapsed Catholic who refers to himself as a "compassionate misanthrope." Please understand that contradictions, plus-minus theories, and other mind-numbing "elements" comprise a large portion of Lee's mind. While pitching for the Red Sox, upon visiting New York City, Bill would often visit with Jewish scholars in Long Island (doesn't every lapsed Catholic?) and down drinks with priests at the Lion's Head in Greenwich Village, and this was before becoming a rasta (Rastafarian) and perhaps even an atheist. The reason I say perhaps is that the Spaceman also whistles past graveyards. Hey, why take chances? When in Rome....

There exist two beings that served and continue to serve as mentors for Lee. One exists and the other is perhaps extant in another dimension, for lack of a better word. You see, Kurt Vonnegut may have left planet Earth, but his characters are immortal. Vonnegut's words will live on through eternity.

Bokonon, and it is highly likely that the Spaceman is a devout Bokononist, was/is a black man from the island of Tobago who became shipwrecked on the Isle of San Lorenzo. What better place to start your own religion, and one that pays homage to midgets? The author will admit to also being a follower of the great Bokonon.

Bill Lee has also come under the influence of another oracle of sorts, a young man named Mark Manson, the author of several books including the hilarious *Everything is Fucked*. However, before we introduce you to young Mr. Manson, I will leave you with the words of Kurt Vonnegut, who stated eloquently:

"If what Jesus said was good, what can it matter whether he was God or not?"

The following are the words of Mark Manson:

"HOW TO START YOUR OWN RELIGION—STEP FOUR

RITUAL SACRIFICE FOR DUMMIES—So easy, anyone can do it.

"Growing up in Texas, Jesus and football were the only gods that mattered, and while I learned to enjoy football and not being terrible at it, the whole Jesus thing never made sense to me. Jesus was alive, then he died, then he was alive again, and he died again. He was a man and also a god and some kind of god-man spirit thing. He loved everyone eternally except gay people depending on who you asked.

"It all struck me as kind of arbitrary and I'm not sure how to say this, but I thought people were making this shit up. Don't get me wrong, I can get behind most of the moral teachings of be nice, love your neighbors and all that stuff. Youth camp was actually tons of fun, Jesus camps were probably the most underrated summer activity of all time and the church had 'special' cookies hiding around in 'special' rooms. Sunday was exciting, but to be totally honest I didn't like becoming a Christian. I didn't like it for really dumb reasons. My parents made me wear really lame clothes. That's right, and I became an atheist at the age of twelve because of suspenders and bowties.

"I remember asking my parents about it. I asked if God is so forgiving, why can't I wear anything I want then? Things never panned out for me, I was sneaking Nine Inch Nail T-shirts into school before my balls had completely dropped, and a couple of years later I struggled through my first Nietzsche book. From then on it was all downhill. I started acting out, I bailed out of Sunday school, I smoked cigarettes in the parking lot. I was a little heathen." *—Mark Manson*

We close "Interlude, Part Two" with some advice from the earthling known as William Francis Lee, III, who exclaimed:

"*Everything is Fucked* by Mark Manson is four years of psychiatry and you don't even have to attend college for one year. Merely reading this book and the first chapter of Buckminster Fuller's *Operating Manual for Spaceship Earth* and Kurt Vonnegut's *Cat's Cradle* and *God Bless You, Mr. Rosewater*, will save you a lot of time and money."

CHAPTER SEVENTY

Guileful but Delightful Deception

"In Chapter Seventy we will attend Adolph Hitler's bar mitzvah and learn how to make malignum steel." —*Scott Russell*

In Chapter Sixty-Nine we witnessed how a great man named Casey Stengel, a predecessor of "Spaceman" Lee, was called upon to provide enlightenment to a group of United States senators regarding anti-trust laws in baseball, but offered a soliloquy so prescient that it precluded any hope of ever even ascertaining what the fuck the question was in the first place. Some sixty-two years later there are debates as to what Casey Stengel implied or was attempting to explain, or if he even was attempting to explain anything. "Spaceman" Lee, the "son" of Casey Stengel is a practitioner of the art form. Suffice to say that both Aristotle and Plato would have just moved on and attributed Casey's remarks to pure genius, but these were U.S. senators, which should explain their bewilderment.

Recently the author, either Scott Russell or Kilgore Trout, and for all we know they are the same being, came upon the earthling known as William Francis Lee, III, who was in the process of engaging in strengthening and conditioning. Some fifty-one years after performing in his initial major league game, Lee still pitches, and in fact, at a high level. Lee informed the author that he was in the process of creating malignum steel. Malignum steel, as I would learn (at least Lee attempted to explain the process) initiated in Bessemer, Alabama and therefore the effect is called "the Bessemer Process." I immediately acquired a migraine upon imagining how Don Zimmer might have reacted upon hearing Lee's lecture.

I also learned that Henry Bessemer of England is credited for its discovery; at least that is what I thought I heard the Spaceman state. Bill Lee's favorite word, as I also discovered, is "synergy." Synergy, as the southpaw explained, is "achieving the benefit which results where two or more agents work together to achieve something either one could not have achieved on its own. These agents produce a combined effect greater than the sum of their separate effects." My only wish at that point, was to somehow resurrect Casey Stengel, who would have not only agreed with the Spaceman's explanation, but would no doubt, have offered some additional thoughts regarding the subject matter.

As further proof of Bill Lee's commitment to synergy, he further expounded as follows:

"The cobalt/Bessemer technique began in Bessemer just south of Birmingham. Adding malignum to the Bessemer process creates high tensile steel which is five times stronger. This process dates back to the Vikings who went to Damascus and brought the method back up to the Baltic Sea. That's when they made their own swords and controlled the world." Somewhere, Casey Stengel, I thought, was smiling.

Unfortunately, we have somehow morphed from the likes of Casey Stengel and "Spaceman" Lee into a world of Lenny Dykstras and Blake Snells. Thank God for an occasional Trevor Bauer, the young right-hander of the Cincinnati Reds, an outstanding pitcher and a "descendent," as it were, of Bill Lee. I am thrilled upon hearing the outstanding Bauer's dissertations regarding synaptic plasticity. Not that I know what the fuck he's talking about, but it sure beats the hell out of the current malaise.

CHAPTER SEVENTY-ONE

Code-Talkers and Cow Whisperers

"I am not a hero, but the brave men who died deserve this honor."
—Ira Hayes upon being feted at a banquet

The earthling known as William Francis Lee and his beautiful wife, Diana, have always paid homage to our Native Americans and have spent considerable time on their reservations. Many of their experiences have been rewarding and educational. However, one meeting with Native Americans wound up being both poignant and hilarious. It started out a bit dicey, however. As Lee explained:

"Diana and I were at an In and Out Burger in Tucson and two drunk Indians were looking at her while she was putting condiments on her burger and commenting in Navajo about her breasts. Diana turned to face them and said, 'I know what you guys are talking about.' Diana brought her food back to the table and I could see the reflection of the two Indians in the window overlooking the University of Arizona. One of them works up enough courage and approaches our table and apologizes. One of the Indians who appeared to be an elder spoke:

'I'm sorry, sir. I recognize you and I think you're a very learned man. May I sit down?'"

Bill Lee then continued:

"We had a great conversation for well over a half-hour. We discussed all the great Indians including Ira Hayes*, including Hayes' famous 'death mask.' I told him I'd gladly visit him on the reservation at the Four Corners Reservation in Farmington up in the area of the cliff dwellings. I finally asked his name, but he was hesitant about it and said, 'I hate my name.' Eventually I learned his name was 'Gene Simmons,' the same name as the guy in "Kiss!"

* Ira Hayes, the gentleman Bill Lee and Gene Simmons were discussing was a Pima Indian who was born in Sakaton, Arizona. On August 26, 1942, Hayes enlisted in the U.S. Marine Corps Reserves and after training, Ira Hayes volunteered to become a Paramarine. During World War II, Hayes fought at both Bouganville and Iwo Jima.

In the now iconic photograph, Ira Hayes is one of the six Marines raising the American flag atop Mount Suribachi while the war still raged on. It was Ira Hayes who reported that he and the other five Marines present were not the original ones that raised the flag. Earlier that morning during the battle, the original members of Hayes' outfit had raised the flag, but it was not photographed at that time. Hayes and their fellow Marines returned to the top of Mount Sirabachi later that morning to record the historic event.

Ira Hayes was a legitimate AMERICAN hero. Although Ira returned a hero, the emotional scars of war remained embedded in his heart and mind. Ira was feted at countless banquets, and the alcohol combined with his memory of the brutal conflict left him an alcoholic. On January 24, 1955, Ira Hayes died drunk in a ditch in Bapchula, Arizona. The cause of death was hypothermia. He was thirty-two years old.

Ira's courage and tragic end were magnificently described in Patrick Sky's "The Ballad of Ira Hayes." Patrick Sky was one of the most renowned folk singers in history, and himself, a Native American.

Another of Bill "Spaceman" Lee's noteworthy friends was the great W.P. Kinsella. William Patrick Kinsella is one of the greatest journalists of our times. Kinsella, a native of Hope, British Columbia wrote a superb novel titled *Shoeless Joe,* a masterpiece that was adapted into perhaps the greatest baseball motion picture of all time, *Field of Dreams*. The Canadian author's works especially concerned baseball and First Nation people.

Bill Lee spoke of his friend, W.P. Kinsella:

"W.P Kinsella was a friend of mine. Once, Kinsella and I dedicated a wiffleball field called Putkee Park in western Massachusetts. Putkee was the name of a local's dog. The dog is buried at home plate. Up in Kinsella's territory in Hope, British Columbia, the Canadian government passed legislation that prohibited cattle from travelling from place to place. There was this inventive Native American named 'Frank Fence Post.' He kept finding loopholes in the laws. He got a whole trainload of cows and he stampeded them down Main Street near the reservation, and they were tearing up all kinds of shit. Friggin' cow whisperer! He was great."

The Spaceman continued:

"There was this woman RCMP (Royal Canadian Mounted Police) named Bebe Ribowski and she was as tough as nails. She was apparently in charge of Indian affairs. Kinsella's description of her was great. He wrote,

'She's so tough that she would roll her own tampons and she kick-starts her dildo.'"

Bill Lee said that many years ago he, Mary Lou, and the boys would go to Hope to fish and see all the wood carvings on Main Street. On occasion, W.P. Kinsella would join them as they fished on the Coquihalla River. As Lee described:

"The Coquihalla River is at the confluence of the Coquihalla and Frazier River at the start of the Coquihalla Highway, which is a cutoff into the interior of British Columbia. The television program *Highway to Hell* near the Othello Caves is filmed there."

CHAPTER SEVENTY-TWO

First Impressions

"I feel sorry for people that don't drink. When they wake up in the morning, that's as good as they're going to feel all day." *—Joe E. Lewis*

"We have only two rules during our concerts. #1—There will be no drinking during gospel songs. #2—No gospel songs!" *—Billy Gibbons—ZZ Top*

While in the Army Reserve, the earthling known as William Francis Lee, III, as we had stated, was an REMF. You already know what that designation stands for and that Lee and his former dope smoking friend, George W. Bush, shared that distinction. Lee, of course, was already a major league hurler and had already had his fill of vertically challenged authority figures with Napoleonic complexes, so adding another to his collection of contemptible midgets did not particularly surprise him.

"I had this superior, a Sergeant Green Feather," as Lee recalled. "He was this 5' 5" nasty Cherokee Indian and he hated me because he knew I wasn't going to 'Nam. This crazy little bastard could do one hundred one-armed push-ups. He would take the bill of his Smokey the Bear First Sergeant hat, and he would poke me on my breastbone with it, the little prick. Those types of people really piss me off. He was not on the Indians' side."

In recalling those incidents, the author was reminded of the approximate time he became friends with the Spaceman. I was new to Boston and began attending many Red Sox games. I had not yet met Lee but would read of his hilarious exploits in the *Boston Phoenix* columns penned by the great, late George Kimball. I would usually be seated in the grandstand behind home plate in Section 20. On occasion, I would also be seated at field level directly behind the screen, a place where major league scouts congregated with their notepads, stop watches, and other accoutrements of the trade. These were the days before iPhones and other electronic devices.

One day in 1973, I found myself seated next to a group of scouts, many of whom were legends. There was Howie Haak, Ray Scarborough, Hugh Alexander and several others. As was my wont, being a baseball junkie, I was charting pitches for my own amusement. Seated directly to my left was a gentleman in a straw hat, spitting tobacco juice into a coffee cup which was nearly filled to the brim with his spittle. It was slightly gross, but I had seen worse. He appeared to have stepped out of central casting in an audition for a major league scout. He interrupted the serenity by asking yours truly, "Who are you with?"

"Pardon?" I responded.

He repeated his query, "Who are you with? What ball club?"

I replied that I was merely a fan. Joe Reilly, that was his name, was astonished, as he remarked:

"I've never seen a fan chart pitches before."

Joe Reilly, an advanced scout for the Philadelphia Phillies, began asking me a few questions including my favorite restaurants in the area. Eventually, Reilly asked me if I had seen anyone on the Red Sox, other than the known stars, that impressed me. I mentioned that I really liked Rick Miller, who despite a lack of power was a fundamentally sound player and a great defensive outfielder. I them told him that I really liked the young southpaw, Bill Lee. I stated, "Lee is a bit flaky, but he's a great competitor and although he's not overpowering, he has an assortment of pitches, changes speeds and eye-levels and keeps hitters off balanced."

It should be noted that at the time Joe Reilly made his inquiry, Bill was still in the bullpen.

Joe Reilly then told me, "Wow, that's surprising. We had a cross-checker scout Bill in Clearwater, Florida in spring training, and he filed a report telling us to avoid considering acquiring him. He wrote that during the exhibition game, they were lining shots all over the field, Lee was getting his ass kicked, and the more they pounded him, the more Lee smiled.

It was then that I informed Joe Reilly that I had read an article (George Kimball, who else?) that the Spaceman had just returned from an Army Reserve meeting and afterwards had gotten sloshed with a few other military members and had then joined the club in Clearwater, not expecting to be called on to pitch that day. Thus, Lee getting pounded and grinning from ear to ear.

Phillies scout Joe Reilly laughed and replied, "You really seem to know your stuff, Scott. Thanks for the info."

Lee, of course, had a breakout year in 1973, and by July had been named to the American League All-Star team. Joe Reilly soon began to seek me out at the ballpark and often left his fellow scouts behind the screen to join me in the grandstand. By then, however, I had befriended the Spaceman. Reilly came over to where I was seated one day and thanked me profusely, telling me that he was grateful for me praising Bill Lee.

"I filed a glowing report on Lee, and it made me look great with the Phillies front office. We're interested in acquiring him." Note: The Phillies DID acquire Rick Miller!

One evening, I informed the Spaceman of my hilarious interaction with the Phillies scout and that the Phillies had expressed interest in obtaining his services.

"Shit! I don't want to play for Philadelphia!"

Joe Reilly had absolutely no idea that I had befriended Lee, of course.

Therefore, the next time I saw Joe Reilly behind the screen at Fenway, I told him that I had heard rumors that Lee had a sore arm, was hanging out in various dens of inequity and there was even an unconfirmed rumor that he was gay. Reilly stared incredulously at me. It was then that I turned to return to my seat in the grandstand. Keep in mind that the players' wives are generally in close proximity to the major league scouts.

As I climbed the runway past the box seats, Mary Lou Lee called out, "Hi, Scott!" My cover was blown. Joe Reilly smiled, nodded his head, and peered at me as if to say, "Gotcha!" I wonder if the Spaceman would've enjoyed playing in the "City of Brotherly Love."

CHAPTER SEVENTY-THREE

Preventive Medicine

Kerlan and Jobe & Pray for Rain

"I don't think the robots are taking over. I think the men who play with toys have taken over, and if we don't take the toys out of their hands, we're fools." *—Ray Bradbury*

The infamous brawl at Yankee Stadium in 1976 was not exactly included in the list of Bill Lee's fondest memories. Having been an established major league star and winner of 17 games for three consecutive seasons, the fracas in the Bronx resulted in Lee having an injured and weakened arm. What the hell, he thought, since Dr. Robert Kerlan and Dr. Frank Jobe had performed "miracles" with other renowned hurlers, Lee thought it was certainly worth a visit at the very least.

Dr. Kerlan had become the team doctor for the Dodgers in Los Angeles immediately following their move from Brooklyn in 1958. As the Spaceman explained:

"I went to see Dr. Kerlan, he was the head guy, and Dr. Jobe was his associate. I had never met Jobe and didn't know what he looked like. I arrived at Kerlan's office and he's an arthritic, hunched over seventy-five year-old man. He looked at me and he asked, "So, what's your problem?"

The Spaceman replied, 'After seeing you, I don't think I have one.' He examined my elbow and he told me I had a lot of micro-tears in there, and that they were all in 'little bundles.' He told me that they get all inflamed and instructed, 'We've got to calm them down, and to not throw so hard.'" The following Lee admitted that he made up:

"My father told me to not throw so hard, keep the ball down, throw strikes and don't alibi. He had written that on my 'Mike McCormick' glove in high school."*

* Mike McCormick was a southpaw with the San Francisco Giants. McCormick's teammate with the Giants was another southpaw named Ray Sadecki. McCormick and Sadecki once made a pact in

> spring training that upon being asked for autographs, they would sign each other's name. Apparently, no one ever caught on and therefore, anyone in possession of a Mike McCormick signature most likely has one signed by Sadecki and vice versa. This makes sense to Lee, who remarked, "They're southpaws."

Bill Lee also stated, "The last guy to ever stick a needle in my arm was Red Sox team physician, Arthur Pappas. I went to see him in Worcester and he gets me on this surgeon's table. He's standing over me and holding me down. He's got a syringe that looks like something he'd need for a fucking cow, he injects my elbow. My elbow got better, but when I read all the shit he injected in there, I thought I'd wind up like Sandy Koufax. Do you know what I mean? I said to myself, the fuck with this, and that's went I decided to try acupuncture. I continued with acupuncture in China when I was ill, but I got worse. The Chinese doctor asked 'Are you left-handed?' I answered yes, and he replied, 'I yinged you when I should have yanged you.'"

Said Lee:

"I've always gone for the drug treatment, not the fucking knife. When I badly injured my knee in high school at a take-out slide at second base, a doctor recommended surgery, but I went to another doctor. This guy was wearing a T-shirt and he had a drink in one hand and a cigarette in the other. He examined my knee and said, 'Nah, I'll just drain the fluids and let it rest for a week or two.' I was playing in three weeks."

The Spaceman told me that he thought it was because of Zimmer that he was being injected with a needle of that size. Said Lee: "I thought I was Dustin Hoffman in *Marathon Man,* and that Pappas was 'Zell' (Laurence Olivier). Is it safe?"

CHAPTER SEVENTY-FOUR

Arrivederci Roma

"All time is all time. It does not change. It does not lend itself to warnings or explanations. It simply is." —*Kurt Vonnegut*

Wilhelmus Abraham "Win" Remmerswaal pitched briefly for the Red Sox in 1979-1980. Win was the first European trained major league baseball player. Born in the Hague, the Dutch native was the first because Hall of Famer Bert Blyleven, although also born in the Netherlands, was raised in California. The earthling named William Francis Lee, III, although jettisoned to Montreal by 1979, had his paths cross with Remmerswaal several years later.

With the Spaceman blackballed from playing major league baseball in the United States, Lee attempted to join an Italian League, but as he explained, "They chose Win Remmerswaal over me. Remmerswaal used to drive around in a 1962 Chevrolet Biscayne. Remmerswaal used to drink twenty-six Heinekens a day, and one day he just didn't wake up."

Upon researching Remmerswaal's checkered history, I learned that the Spaceman was correct. Despite playing five years in Italy, Remmerswaal has been confined to a Dutch nursing home since 1997. He entered the facility at the age of forty-three. Win is sixty-six now and is still confined there.

Bill Lee auditioned for San Marino in Italy, but Remmerswaal beat him out for the job. As Lee explained:

"I spent two weeks in Parma, Italy doing clinics. I was there with my ex-wife Pam, and Rod Dedeaux and his wife. We were staying in this fancy mansion. All you saw there were Ferraris and Maseratis, and these trysts were going on between men and women from Milan and Parma. There was one Contessa who was swimming naked in the pool. She was a bag of bones. We offered her an expensive bottle of champagne if she put her clothes back on."

Bill Lee recalled a trip to Jamaica during his playing career:

"I woke up the following morning after an alcohol induced coma. When I woke up, there were several Jamaicans applauding me. I found out that I had won a case of beer. All I remember, though, is that George Kimball was involved."

CHAPTER SEVENTY-FIVE

The "Real" Big Lebowski

One Less Legend

"Some may live, but the crazy never die." *—Dr. Hunter S. Thompson*

"Crazy people don't sit around wondering if they are nuts."
—Jake Gyllenhaal

"We are all born mad. Some remain so." *—Samuel Beckett*

The earthling known as William Francis Lee, III was thrown out of the "Legends Suite" at Fenway Park because of "The Big Lebowski." No, not Jeff Bridges, the Spaceman was tossed out by uniformed police because of the REAL "Big Lebowski." Such is the life encircling Bill Lee, erstwhile southpaw of the Boston Red Sox.

There was a time in the not too distant past that Bill "Spaceman" Lee, who is enshrined in the "Red Sox Hall of Fame" incidentally, that Lee was not persona non grata in the Legends Suite. Bill would often be invited to the elite locale since he remains one of the most beloved characters, albeit perhaps the most eccentric of the group, to Red Sox games, ones at which he'd be introduced to the crowd in the seventh inning. The possibility of Lee receiving that privilege in the future was greatly decreased by the actions of a man named Jeff Dowd.

Jeff Dowd was the inspiration behind the hilarious and somewhat twisted cult classic motion picture, *The Big Lebowski.* In the movie, Jeff "Dude" Dowd is portrayed by the award-winning Hollywood legend Jeff Bridges. In that film, Jeff Dowd is named "The Big Lebowski," a rather slovenly, drunk, slacker and bowler. In real life, however, "The Big Lebowski" is a rather slovenly, drunk, slacker and bowler... and that is the reason Bill "Spaceman" Lee is no longer welcome in the Legends Suite at Fenway Park. Please allow me to explain.

Bill "Spaceman" Lee arrived with the Big Lebowski to enjoy a Red Sox game. Bill also brought along Peter Vogt, the director of his 2007 Lee documentary, *High and Outside,* as well as Bill's friend Jim Brown (not that "Jim Brown"), a publisher and former Microsoft executive from Seattle. Of course, the Big Lebowski's entourage included a few characters of questionable repute.

In the now iconic motion picture *The Big Lebowski,* the director and producer, Joel and Ethan Coen, decided to pay homage to the aforementioned Jeff "Dude" Dowd. The premise behind the movie is that Dowd—Jeffrey "The Dude" Lebowski, a poor slob is attempting to get a replacement for a rug and he somehow manages to hook up with another Jeffrey Lebowski, a millionaire with a sexy young wife named "Bunny," portrayed by Tara Reid. The movie stars Bridges, John Goodman, and Julianne Moore.

As Bill Lee explained:

"So here we are with the real Big Lebowski, a real loser. Why the fuck the Coen Brothers decided to do a movie based on the life of this prick is behind me. Before heading to Fenway Park, we toured the Freedom Trail. It was before Obama was elected. As we toured the Freedom Trail, Dowd (the Big Lebowski) was basically just yelling at people and going into lengthy diatribes. I think he mumbled something about white supremacy, the man was clearly nuts. The Big Lebowski actually got us thrown off of the *U.S.S. Constitution* by Ed Foley, who was a friend of mine. Foley took care of that entire area and he was an employee of the federal government.

"Then we went to Charlestown where Lebowski began speaking to a bunch of girls and they ran away from him at the Bunker Hill Monument. A flat-out lunatic."

Eventually the entire group headed to Fenway Park to enjoy a Red Sox game and to witness Spaceman's final appearance in the Legends Suite. As Lee reported:

"After the motion picture, Dowd (Lebowski) attempted to embezzle funds from the two filmmakers (the Coen Brothers). We learned that Lebowski had been living in the streets in Santa Monica. The guy was a bum. How the hell did the Coen Brothers even get involved with this guy, and to think of it, created a great movie based on this idiot? They must have caught him on his only good day. In the motion picture business, they glorify pricks and assassinate the Gandhis and the Gunga Dins.

"We go to Fenway, and we have this really good 'sound man,' a nice kid who's all tattooed. The kid had a dyed rainbow mohawk, and we're in the Legends Suite. Of course, Lebowski's group is acting up, they're all anarchists, and the police arrive and ask us all to leave because the group is too 'radical.' My old teammate and Red Sox broadcaster, Dennis Eckersley, is with us too, and Eck and I are holding court. I was thrown out of Fenway Park because I have 'the Big Lebowski' with me and he's a raving lunatic. I felt sorry for the sound man with the mohawk, he was the best behaved of all of us, but they just didn't like his look, I guess."

Of course, Jeff Dowd, aka "The Big Lebowski," is all worked up. As Lee explained, "I do bring stuff upon myself and because of my entourage and the stuff we get into, but how can the Coen Brothers make a movie about a complete asshole?"

The Spaceman's description of Jeff Dowd (The Big Lebowski) was perfect:

"He looked like a giant doughboy. He looked exactly like Ignatius J. Reilly in *A Confederacy of Dunces*. When the police arrived to throw us out, they probably thought they had walked into a Star Wars bar."

"And now," the Spaceman concluded as he quoted the immortal words of Paul Harvey, "you know the rest of the story. Good day!"

The author of this book would like to dedicate the above chapter to the great, late George Kimball, who would have loved to once more have been heaved from Fenway Park.

CHAPTER SEVENTY-SIX

This Ship Be Sinkin'

"Just the facts, ma'am." —*Jack Webb as "Joe Friday" on* Dragnet.

The earthling known as William Francis Lee, III, may have been unlike most other (all right, ALL other) major league players, but the one thing that anyone other than his manager in 1978 could not deny is the fact that he was an accomplished and successful hurler. The Spaceman may have been into Tibetan Buddhism, a few herbal "remedies," be capable of a dissertation regarding mohorovicic discontinuity, and quote from *The Rape of Europa,* but he was also proficient at getting major league hitters out, that is, if his then manager, Don Zimmer, had provided him the opportunity.

After Don Zimmer's removal of the Spaceman from the Red Sox starting rotation after action had been completed on August 19, 1978, the results of the aftermath of that decision are irrefutable. As the Red Sox, who were already well into the process of blowing their 14-game advantage over the Yankees began play on August 20, all hell broke loose.

Beyond Hall of Fame hurler Dennis Eckersley and the great Luis Tiant, the balance of the rotation sans Bill Lee was pathetic to say the least. The numbers do not lie. In perhaps an attempt to resuscitate what was left of his chances to salvage the season, Zimmer added his outstanding reliever, Bob Stanley, to the starting rotation on September 22. Stanley went 7 terrific innings in a no-decision, a game the Red Sox eventually lost. Then on September 29, Stanley delivered another 7 innings in a stellar victory, but the other starters were the primary reason Zimmer will forever be reviled by the Fenway Faithful.

Rather than swallow his gerbilistic pride, Zimmer continued to trot out disaster after disaster, that is, anyone other than Bill Lee, who was permanently banished to the bullpen for the remainder of the season. Lee was brought on as a "mop-up" reliever in games that had already been decided. He was clearly a non-entity and so deep in Zimmer's doghouse that he could not see daylight.

Other than Eckersley, Tiant, and the converted reliever, Stanley, the other five starting pitchers Zimmer utilized combined for a 3-11, 4.74

ERA. Bill Lee, the proven major league winner, was not even an afterthought to Zimmer. The rotund former middle infielder simply hated Lee. Please keep in mind that if the Red Sox had won ONE more game after Lee's removal from the rotation, they would have won the pennant, and that covered 41 games!

One of the remaining Red Sox starters was Mike "Taco" Torrez, a strong durable right-hander from Topeka, Kansas. Torrez was of Mexican descent and had been acquired by the Red Sox before the 1978 campaign. Torrez pitched for a total of seven major league teams, but will be forever recalled as the man who gave up the Yankee Bucky Fucking Dent's three-run home run, the blow that cost the Red Sox the pennant on the final day of the season, and to rub salt in the wound, it had occurred moments after Zimmer had told an anxious Bill Lee to cease warming up in the bullpen.

Torrez, a handsome man who married a beautiful actress, was a flamboyant and flashy guy (at least off the field) who wore expensive suits and jewelry. However, none of this impressed the irrepressible and hilarious Luis Tiant. Tiant, never noted for his political correctness, once told Torrez, who had arrived at the ballpark looking like a movie star, "When you take off that expensive suit, you (sic) just one more spic!"

In those final 41 games of that fateful 1978 season, "Taco" Torrez started 10 games and went 1-7 with a 4.31 ERA. Respectable, but not particularly effective. It should be noted that Lee, who had been called upon to mop-up in merely 4 relief appearances, hurled 16 innings with a 2.81 ERA.

Despite these IRREFUTABLE FACTS, Don Zimmer still has his defenders. Oh, if only the Spaceman had not referred to his manager as a "gerbil." That, of course, mattered little. Zimmer would have just found something other than his rodent designation to be offended by.

One of Lee's teammates who was in Zimmer's corner was the immensely popular curmudgeon, Jerry Remy, the second baseman on that unfortunate team. Lee refers to Remy as "a tough little SOB and a good ballplayer," and that he was. "But," said Lee, "there's this thing about middle infielders. They're all fucking hares. To this day, if Remy sees me at the ballpark, he hides around a corner to avoid me. The shortstop Rick Burleson was another terrific ballplayer, but he had some of Billy Martin's tendencies. I once had to pull Burleson off some poor guy on an elevator in Minneapolis. He was pounding the shit out of the guy and he wouldn't even let him fall to the ground. He must've thought he was a marshmallow salesman. All middle infielders have this fucking Eddie Stanky mentality. It's inherent. All except for Bobby Doerr and Phil Rizzuto, two good guys. Doerr and 'The Scooter' were exceptions."

Note: The author recalls Jerry Remy's early days as the Red Sox color analyst. Remy, for some reason, was getting all over Ellis Burks, the young Red Sox outfielder for "missing a cutoff man." Upon hearing that, I was incredulous. There was a man at second base and none out. The hitter flew out to right field and Burks uncorked a throw to the third baseman on the fly. According to Remy, "Burks missed the cutoff man." Now I ask you: Who the hell should Burks have attempted to prevent from advancing, the batter who had just been retired, or the guy in the on deck circle? No wonder he liked Don Zimmer.

CHAPTER SEVENTY-SEVEN

Endings and Awakenings

> "When I was younger, I wanted to be a vet or a tightrope walker, but I have no sense of balance, and I can't bear animals dying, so I abandoned both ideas." —*Georgia May Jagger*

On March 22, 1978, the earthling known as William Francis Lee, III, awoke after a rather raucous evening and the first thing he saw was the body of the great Karl Wallenda lying below his San Juan hotel room window. As Lee recalled:

"I was on the sixth floor of the Holiday Inn in San Juan and I heard a commotion. I was hung over. We had played a ball game the night before and we went out and got drunk afterwards. George Kimball joined me on that trip and we both got shitfaced. We were in Puerto Rico for an exhibition game and we were going to fly back that morning. I looked out of my window and saw the two towers of the ten-story Condado Plaza Hotel. The crowd noise woke me up. I looked down out of my window and saw Karl Wallenda lying dead on top of a '57 Chevy cab.

"I had just watched a thing on television about another aerialist named Philippe Petit walking on a tightrope across two skyscrapers in New York City and his being arrested by about forty-seven policemen, and as they brought him down there were thousands of people cheering and clapping and every person in the tower was applauding the trapeze artist while he was being arrested. I did not see Karl Wallenda fall, but I sure saw its awful aftermath. I learned afterwards that high winds and improperly secured wires were the cause of his fall. It's a hell of a sight I'll never forget."

Note: At seventy-three, Karl Wallenda was the founder and senior member of the world famous "Flying Wallendas" who performed daredevil circus acts on skywalks across towers.

CHAPTER SEVENTY-EIGHT

"Scuz" and the "Spaceman"

"Dr. Filth, he keeps his world inside of a leather cup, but all his sexless patients, they are trying to blow it up.

"Now his nurse, some local loser, she's in charge of the cyanide hole, and she also keeps the cards that read 'Have mercy on his soul.'

"They all play on the pennywhistle, you can hear them blow, if you lean your head out far enough from Desolation Row." —*Bob Dylan*

Upon the earthling known as William Francis Lee, III, arriving in Montreal in 1979, he acquired a veteran teammate, a man from Topeka, Kansas, the home of Mike "Taco" Torrez, except that Ross Grimsley was no Mike Torrez. Grimsley, a fellow southpaw, may very well have been as off-the-wall eccentric as the newcomer to Quebec, Bill "Spaceman" Lee.

The 6′ 3″ 200 lb. Ross Grimsley pitched for Cincinnati, Baltimore, Montreal, and Cleveland from 1971-1980.

As Lee recalls:

"Grimsley was a great character and a damned good pitcher who won 20 games for the Expos in 1978. We called him 'Scuz' or 'Crazy Eyes.' He wore these turquoise contact lenses. Sparky Anderson had him in Cincinnati at the beginning of his career, but Grimsley didn't follow the Reds dress code. Sparky didn't allow facial hair or anything other than a conservative look. But the last straw for Sparky was because of who Grimsley communicated with. Sparky warned him to stop communicating with a witch. So Sparky traded Scuz to Baltimore at the end of the '73 season. Grimsley was only twenty-three years old."

It should be interesting to note that Ross Grimsley, despite his long-flowing hair, full mustache, and overall greasy appearance, finished his big-league career with a record 124-99, he was a winner.

Lee also explained why Scuz needed to retain his greasy look:

"Scuz didn't need Brylcreem, his grease came from the loads of KY-Jell (KY Lubricating Jelly) in his hair. He had a heck of an afro. In 1977 Billy

Martin accused Scuz of throwing spitballs, and he was sort of right. Scuz would load up by just running his hand through his hair. When Scuz was pitching, our shortstop Chris Speier would field ground balls and he'd throw the ball away because it had so much KY-Jelly on it. Grimsley's hair was greasy to begin with because he wouldn't shower for days at a time. Scuz was superstitious and he wouldn't shower during a winning streak. Scuz was a good guy, but he wasn't pleasant to be around during a hot streak."

CHAPTER SEVENTY-NINE

A Cardiologist Named "Boom Boom"

Wasting Away in Margaritaville

"As knowledge increases, so does the circumference of that which you don't know." —*Bill "Spaceman" Lee*

It is a distinct possibility that the earthling known as William Francis Lee, III may have taken his instruction to "keep his eye on the ball" to unnecessary lengths. As the southpaw was pitching in a senior league circa 2001, he was struck just above the right eye by a ground ball. As the Spaceman explained:

"We were playing a game in Chelsea, Vermont when I got clobbered by a bad hop. We had only nine guys on our club and the umpire told us that if I could not continue, we'd have to forfeit the game. I needed stitches. They wound up duct-taping my eye shut 'cause I was bleeding so bad. I wound up hitting two home runs, and after the game we drove to a hospital in Berlin (Vermont) and they needed fourteen stitches to close the wound."

The bizarre tale—and are there any that are not bizarre in the life of Bill Lee?—continued:

"In Cuba (one of the Cuban tours), we had our friend, 'Boom Boom' with us. Boom Boom traveled with me because they thought I may have had an irregular heartbeat. He was taking care of Ross Grimsley's wife, 'Bird.' 'Boom Boom' is Dr. Brian 'Boom Boom' Hummel, a great cardiothoracic cardiologist from Fort Myers, Florida.

"Boom Boom is sitting at the shallow end of the pool with his feet dangling in the water. Well, it was time to remove my stitches and Boom Boom is holding a mojito with a scalpel in it. He took the stitches out and then finished off the mojito."

CHAPTER EIGHTY

Back in the U.S.S.R.

Boris and Natasha Meet the Spaceman

Долбаеб

"Well, I flew in from Miami Beach B.O.A.C.
Didn't get to bed last night
On the way the paper bag was on my knee
Man, I had a dreadful flight
I'm back in the USSR
You don't know how lucky you are, boy
Back in the USSR." —*Paul McCartney*

The earthling known as William Francis Lee, III was arrested three times in one night in Moscow. Bill Lee's travels brought him to the then Soviet Union to play baseball against Russian teams. The following is Bill Lee's detailed description of the improbable, albeit hilarious events surrounding one rather tumultuous evening in the U.S.S.R:

"I had just beaten the Russian team on a Thursday. I went seven innings during which I picked off five players. After the game, we were doing all kinds of stuff and the Russians had no idea I had grey hair until I took my cap off for the team picture. They couldn't believe how fucking old I was! The Russians had the entire foundation wrong in the outfield. They had the footing on the outside of the fence rather than the inside, so if you dove for a ball you had a good chance of getting decapitated. They also never fixed the holes on the pitchers' mound. An entire Panzer Division could be swallowed up in those holes.

"They asked if they could play me again, and of course, I said yes. We played them again on Saturday and I shut them out again and picked another five guys off base. Not only that, but I hit three doubles. We had a few beers afterwards and as we're leaving the park, we cut off a Russian diplomat's car that had the flags on it. It was a West German car. Alcohol may have been involved.

"We all wound up going to a nightclub and outside the restaurant we saw the diplomat's car parked outside, the one we had cut off. I saw the diplomat at a table in the restaurant and he was pretty pissed off when we had cut him off. When I saw him, I told him that if I had my VFW I'd drive it right up his fucking ass! The diplomat was seated with a real beautiful woman. They got up and left the restaurant!

"In the restaurant, they had this real unique food. I'm sure it wasn't what the Russian citizens eat. Later that day, we were shooting pool in this place underneath an old subway station. I noticed that the pool balls were all white. The key was to knock in two balls at one time. I told the Russians, 'You guys will never win anything. In America we call that a scratch.' We were smoking dope and this little guy ran in two balls and began jumping up and down. I yelled at him, 'that's a scratch, you little Azerbaijani!' He shouted, 'No, no! No Azerbaijani. Georgia!' That's where Stalin came from.

"Afterwards we went out and got DUI'd. It cost us 200 rubles. 200 rubles for the first DUI, 200 more rubles for the second DUI, and the third time we're at a discotheque, and as we left there was a plainclothes car outside. I was hammered and I staggered and bumped into it. It turned out to be a cop. He stuck a billy club in my chest, but I took the nightstick away from him with a deft maneuver. I just backed off and ripped it out of his hands. The guy starts backing off and the two Russians I'm with, Andre and Andre, began laughing and shouting, 'Michael Jackson! He's doing the fucking moonwalk!' That cost me another 200 rubles.

They put me in a car and drove me back to the hotel. The cop said, 'You (sic) no come out again, you Dalbayob!'"*

* долбаеб—as it is written in Russian. And you folks thought this book was not educational! (in Russian, "the word "dalbayob" is not a compliment. There is no English to Russian translation for "motherfucker," however, this is as close as it gets. For the record, and there are a few interpretations, "dalbayob" can be translated to "retard," "moron" or "pound-fucker," but as far as the author has ascertained, the Spaceman was basically called a "fucking lowlife woodpecker prick!") For true scholars, we advise calling your nearest Russian embassy.

The Spaceman continued:

"The entire trip was arranged by a professor at the University of California at Davis. I went over with my buddy, Bob Wagner, and a bunch of other guys. We never lost a game over there. One of the two 'Andres' was actually my catcher. Andre Artimov was born in Russia but has lived in the U.S. and has caught me for years. The other Andre was a guy the Russians assigned to me, another good guy. I had a great time in Russia."

The games were arranged by Lee's friend, Bob Wagner of the famed "Wood Bat Classic." The games were played at Joseph Stalin Field in Moscow.

The Spaceman informed the author that Brian O'Halloran, the executive vice-president of the Boston Red Sox, speaks Russian fluently. O'Halloran is a graduate of Colby College and majored in political science and Russian studies. O'Halloran also has the distinction of being the very last American to leave the country of Georgia after one of its civil wars.

CHAPTER EIGHTY-ONE

Cheers... Where Everyone Knows Your Name

(Except for the producers of the show)

"I would rather have written an episode of *Cheers* than anything I've ever written." —*Kurt Vonnegut*

"I find television very educating. Every time somebody turns on the set, I go into another room and read a book." —*Groucho Marx*

The main character on the award-winning television comedy program *Cheers* was styled after the earthling known as William Francis Lee, III. No, really.

Cheers, was one of the most popular weekly sitcoms in television history. The show's creators were Glen and Les Charles and James Burrows. Since the creators hailed from Nevada, they originally considered filming the show out there in the desert, but soon felt that since the chief romantic character, Sam "May Day" Malone, was a former Red Sox pitcher, the gentlemen scouted out and found the "perfect" location in Boston.

Ironically, the actor chosen to portray Sam Malone, former Red Sox pitcher, lothario, and bartender, Ted Danson, knew little about sports. His romantic interest would be beautiful actress Shelley Long, who was an owner of the bar. The successful show ran from September 30, 1982 and closed on May 20, 1993, an eleven-year run.

Bill Lee and his beautiful wife, Diana once watched the producers of the show discuss the show's derivation. On the wall behind them was a photograph of the REAL Sam "May Day" Malone, the irrepressible Bill "Spaceman" Lee. Bill and Diana immediately recognized the photograph as being Bill going through his pitching motion with Lake Saint Louis in southwestern Quebec in the background. Bill and his ex-wife, Pam, would spend considerable time at that location at the confluence of the Saint Lawrence and Ottawa Rivers. The Saint Louis Seaway passes through the lake. You would think that having that eclectic photograph over their shoulders would spur some interest in the inspiration behind "May Day"

Malone, but the world of Hollywood is seldom rational.

Bill "Spaceman" Lee? Who? Instead, the creators of *Cheers* stated that their original intent was to have the Boston bartender perhaps be a former football player, but then realized that Ted Danson, the actor, was a bit too frail looking, so rather than that, they switched to a former "OBSCURE Red Sox relief pitcher named Lee." When the Spaceman heard that, he didn't know whether to laugh or be angry. Bill Lee is a lot of things, but none of them "obscure."

Cheers became must-see for lovers of comedy and the popular show took on various risqué elements seldom seen on prime-time television. Sam "May Day" Malone was portrayed as a recovering alcoholic. There were 275 full half-hour episodes and many stars heretofore relatively unknown became household names. The show starred Ted Danson, Shelley Long, Nicholas Colasanto, Rhea Perlman, George Wendt, John Ratzenberger, Kelsey Grammar, and eventually Woody Harrelson, Kirstie Alley, and Bebe Neuwirth.

Cheers won 28 Primetime Emmy Awards from 117 nominations and ranked #18 on TV Guide's 50 greatest shows of all time. Celebrities who appeared included Luis Tiant, Wade Boggs, Kevin McHale, Alex Trebek, Arsenio Hall, Dick Cavett, Robert Urich, Johnny Carson, Speaker of the House, Tip O'Neill, and Harry Connick, Jr. But as for the ACTUAL inspiration for the main character Sam "May Day" Malone, portrayed by Ted Danson, Bill "Spaceman" Lee, not a whisper. As Lee exclaimed:

"I was apparently not even a thought in the minds of the creators of the show. I was just some "obscure Red Sox relief pitcher" who inspired the role. Not only didn't I get an invite, but they never even considered contacting me for a cameo appearance. If they had, I would've suggested that I'd be face-down drunk at the bar, smoking a doobie and having a beer with my friend 'Woody Boyd' (Woody Harrelson) and I'd be mumbling, 'They should've never taken Willoughby out.' It would've been a hell of an episode."

The Spaceman concluded with:

"Although I was ignored by the creators of the show, at least I wound up making a good friend in Woody Harrelson, whose father committed this slight impropriety of assassinating the president of the United States."

CHAPTER EIGHTY-TWO

Dear Mr. Fantasy

"I never forget a face, but in your case I'll be glad to make an exception." —*Groucho Marx*

"Dear Mr. Fantasy, play us a tune
Something to make us all happy
Do anything, take us out of this gloom
Sing a song, play guitar, make it snappy
You are the one who can make us all laugh"
—*Chris Wood, Jim Capaldi, & Steve Winwood*

"Bill Lee, Ferguson Jenkins, and Rick Wise were mean-spirited in their criticisms of the way I handled them. Lee was the ringleader, but the other two willingly joined in with them as clubhouse lawyers. In the case of all three, they were previously effective major league pitchers who were generally pitching lousy and blamed me for their inability to get hitters out anymore." —*Don Zimmer*

Bill Madden, the long-time *New York Daily News* columnist is one of the finest sports journalists of my lifetime. In writing *Zim, A Baseball Life*, the autobiography of Don Zimmer, however, I would suggest relocating it from the sports biographies section in libraries and bookstores, to "fiction." I don't even know where to begin. Perhaps at Fenway Park for the 1979 home opener for the Boston Red Sox.

As Don Zimmer described in the *New York Times* bestseller:

"On opening day 1979, we were playing the Cleveland Indians. I'll never forget the look on the face of Indians manager Jeff Torborg when I came out to home plate to exchange lineup cards. The boos from the Fenway crowd were so loud I'm sure you could hear them all the way to Cape Cod.

"'Wow!' Torborg exclaimed. 'This is one tough audience. You win 99 games and go to a playoff and they boo you like that? I'd hate to ever work in this town!'"

Well, there was this little thing about blowing a 14 game lead to the Yankees, having a roster with four future Hall of Famers (another, Luis Tiant, who belongs), removing a proven winner, Bill "Spaceman" Lee from the rotation at a critical juncture in the season, not listening to Carl Yastrzemski who pleaded with Zimmer to reinstate Lee, and having removed Ferguson Jenkins (after 1977) and Rick Wise (1977) from the pitching rotation in a two-year period and replaced them with retreads and quite frankly, bums. Yeah, I was booing, too.

What is particularly sad about Zim's attitude is that to his dying day, he could not face the fact that (gulp) perhaps he was the one that fucked up. The numbers and the FACTS certainly indicate that, and 35,000 booing fans are a strong testimony to that "possibility."

In Madden's well-written tome, Zimmer stated, and I cannot make this up, "Over the winter, we signed free agent righthander Steve Renko, who had been 6-12 with the A's in '78, as a fifth starter. He essentially (c'mon, Bill Madden, Zim used the word "essential?") replaced Bill Lee, who we traded to the Expos for a utility infielder named Stan Papi. I'd have taken a utility garden hose for Lee,* but I was glad to get a useful player."**

> * "Finally," stated Lee, "some truth!"

> ** Stan Papi, the "useful" player, batted .188 with 1 home run, 6 RBIs, slugged .282 and had an OBP of .221.

Zimmer stated that Renko had "essentially" replaced Bill Lee. That was an actual admission. Consider then that entering that 1979 season, the Spaceman's lifetime record was 94-68, .580, while Renko's had been 104-121, .462.... That "essentially" is the difference between replacing a proven winner with, quite frankly, an established loser. And Zimmer was wondering why he was being booed?

Zimmer "wrote":

"I wish we could have picked up in 1979 where we left off in '78 with a resolve to get that one more win." Um, Zim, that's why 35,000 were on their feet booing. Where "we left off?" You mean when Bucky Fucking Dent blasted a three-run shot to left immediately after you called the bullpen to have Lee sit down?! Wait, it gets worse.

In Chapters Twenty-Five, Twenty-Six, and Seventy-Six, we described how Zimmer's spiteful actions led to the historic collapse and demise of the 1978 season, especially in regard to Bill Lee and Bernie Carbo, but now we'll further explain how Zimmer's prior moves began the slow and painful death. The jettisoning of Bill Lee was planned and calculated, but even before then, Don Zimmer wanted both Ferguson Jenkins and Rick Wise gone because, well, Zimmer is thin-skinned and that had NOTHING to do with the ability of either Jenkins or Wise, but more with Zimmer's proclivity of loathing pitchers, especially intelligent ones, and as is unfortunately the case with "arguments" these days, if there aren't facts to substantiate one's argument, just make a few up.

In *Zim*, the manager is quoted, "Jenkins took a lot of shots at me, which is okay. The man is in the Hall of Fame. I only wish he'd been a Hall of Fame pitcher for me."

In 1977, Zimmer had removed Fergie Jenkins from the rotation and put him in the bullpen. Zimmer was also quoted, "The fact is, Ferguson Jenkins was a great pitcher who pitched away. In Fenway Park especially, you have to pitch in (inside). After we traded Jenkins to Texas for a non-prospect minor league pitcher in December, 1977, he ripped me for sending him to the bullpen. He said, 'I got shoved to the bullpen by a fat, ugly bald man who doesn't know anything about pitching.'"

Incredibly, Zimmer wasn't through as he definitively proved Jenkins' latter comment. Zimmer concluded:

"Jenkins' best pitch was a slider on the outside corner and he simply couldn't adjust to pitching in Fenway Park. When we traded him to Texas after the '77 season, he won 18 again. But he couldn't win in Boston and he blamed me for his problems there."

Sounds good, right? Unfortunately for Don Zimmer, his statements, as they nearly invariably were, are completely incorrect. Here are the FACTS:

Ferguson Jenkins, who "couldn't win at Fenway Park," had a lifetime record of 18-8, a .692 winning percentage in Boston, covering 231 & 2/3 innings pitched over 35 games, 33 of which he started. Coincidentally, the Hall of Famer who was no longer good enough for Zimmer's rotation wound up exactly 18-8 with a 3.04 ERA in Texas in 1978. If that ERA sounds familiar, upon Zimmer ridding himself of Bill Lee, the Spaceman posted a 3.04 ERA with a 16-10 record in Montreal in 1979 on his way to winning the N.L. Left-Handed Pitcher of the Year Award by the wire services. Rick Wise, another member of the bane of Zimmer's existence, the Buffalo Head Gang, went 15-10 3.73 in Cleveland in 1979, another Zimmer reject. Zimmer's statement that Jenkins could not pitch at Fenway Park is even more absurd upon further examination, as Jenkins in his final in Boston finished at 6-2 at home! But let us not allow facts to get in the way of *Zim, a Baseball Life*. Perhaps the letter "F" should be removed from the title.

Speaking of facts, the following are the records of Jenkins, Lee, and Wise's in their final Boston season. You know, the guys that could not "get hitters out anymore."

> FERGUSON JENKINS—1977—10-10, 3.68
> BILL LEE—1978—10-10, 3.46
> RICK WISE—1977—11-5, 4.77

The three "washed-up" hurlers combined for 591 victories during their illustrious careers.

In addition to his failure to blame himself for the collapse of the 1978 Red Sox, Zimmer was quick to point fingers at others to blame for his poor decisions regarding his starting rotation. Consider the following:

"By September 7 of '78, our lead had been shaved to four games by the Yankees as they came into Boston for a four-game series. We were reeling, but I refused to lose faith in this team. The Yankees pounded us 15-3, 13-2 and 7-0 in the first three games, and for the fourth game I had Bobby Sprowl, a rookie who had pitched only one other game, as my starter. There was a hue and cry from Lee and his supporters (Yastrzemski had begged him to start Lee!) and when Sprowl failed to get out of the first inning, I was blamed for letting personalities get in the way of winning. Believe me, my decision to start Sprowl had nothing to do with personalities. I didn't throw him out there on a 'hope.' Podres (Johnny Podres) had told me that Sprowl had big league stuff, and I had confidence the kid could give us five or six innings. If I didn't, I would have started a relief pitcher. It turned out I was wrong, but there was no reason to think that Lee would have done any better."

In truth there was reason. As we have stated, Bill Lee owned the Yankees, and in fact was brought in by Zimmer after the horse had left the barn. Of course, it's also not surprising that Johnny Podres was mentioned as being blameworthy for the decision to start Sprowl, who never won a major league game during his entire career!

The earthling known as William Francis Lee, III uses trees on his own property to manufacture wooden bats for his friend, Louis Ledoux, the owner and operator of "Axis Bats." Sadly, a few years ago, the Spaceman ran into his old manager Don Zimmer at a celebrity golf tournament. As Lee stated:

"We were selling bats at Tropicana at the spring training complex down at Port Charlotte and Zimmer drove by on a golf cart. Zim really seemed to like the bats, so I went over to say hello to him. Zim turned to face me and began stammering, 'I know who you are! I know who you are!' Zim kind of stumbled and staggered and climbed back into his golf cart. As he drove off, he was mumbling to himself. I thought he was going to have a heart attack. That was the last time I ever saw him. I really felt sorry for him."

CHAPTER EIGHTY-THREE

Pot-Smoking Sensitive Guy

The Tarpon Lodge—Where Worlds Converge

"The reason I was never on *Cheers* was because I was too busy with reality." *—Bill "Spaceman" Lee*

The earthling known as William Francis Lee, III may not have been formally recognized as the inspiration behind Ted Danson's character on *Cheers,* but he most definitely received recognition as the inspiration for the character "Tomlinson" in a series of *New York Times* best-selling thrillers and crime novels.

Bill Lee's good friend, Randy White, is a prolific award-winning novelist of a magnificent series of thrillers, many of which have been *New York Times* bestsellers, and one of the chief characters in those novels is a charming character named "Tomlinson." Each winter upon Bill and Diana returning to Pine Island, Florida, the author, Randy Wayne White, does not greet the Spaceman with a "Hi, Bill," but rather with a "Hi, Tomlinson!" Art imitating life or perhaps vice versa.

Randy White's "Tomlinson" character is a generally inebriated and/or stoned character (how is that for method acting?) who in his lucid state assists the protagonist, "Doc" Ford, with exciting and dangerous adventures. The eccentric "Doc" Ford is a retired NSA agent in these wondrous crime-fiction tales, and Randy White has written numerous books based on the thrilling adventures of "Doc" Ford. Randy White has not only been critically acclaimed for his books, but the series was featured in a television documentary.

This spellbinding series of books include *Sanibel Flats, Deep Shadow, The Heat Islands, Captiva, Ten Thousand Islands, The Man Who Invented Florida, Shark River, Hunter's Moon, Black Widow,* and *Tampa Burn.*

It would be sensible, therefore, to ask how Bill "Spaceman" Lee and author Randy White became friends. Well, just as everything else in the Spaceman's life seems to be "tied together," this instance is no different. You see, Randy White, who based the character Tomlinson on Bill Lee, served as a bullpen catcher for the Fort Myers Sun Sox in the "Senior League" during the time that Lee pitched in the league.... You can't make this shit up, not even in a thrilling crime novel.

One of the factors in the Spaceman and author Randy White becoming such fast friends is that Lee invariably sought out the "non-pros" who made the squads because it was obvious that they were in it for the love of the game. As Lee stated:

"Randy White is one of my four favorite catchers and none of them are named Fisk."

During the winter months, Bill & Diana stay at the Tarpon Lodge in Pine Island, Florida. The Tarpon Lodge is a historic landmark in a breathtaking environment. Literally right across the street from the Tarpon Lodge are the pre-Colombian Indian mounds of the ancient Calusa civilization. The lodge is situated in the Pineland Marina, and by boat, the islands of Cabbage Key, Useppa Key, Boca Grande, Sanibel, Captiva, and the beautiful beaches on Cayo Costa are a short boat ride away from the lodge.

In addition to his bullpen catching duties, the Spaceman's author friend, Randy White, is also involved with the operation of "Doc" Ford's Rum Bar and Grille on Sanibel Island, Captiva Island, and at Ft. Myers Beach. White was born in Ashland, Ohio. Author White recently married a young woman named Wendy Webb from Saskatchewan, where songstress Joni Mitchell performed many years earlier, and not surprisingly, Wendy is an accomplished singer and pianist and a Joni sound-alike. The Whites recently moved to Sanibel Island. The Spaceman often takes care of the Tarpon Lodge, and in fact, recently repainted it.

As for the aforementioned Useppa Key, Cabbage Key is famous for the "Old Florida" restaurant which many believe was the inspiration for Jimmy Buffett's "Cheeseburger in Paradise."

The history of Useppa Key includes none other than explorer Ponce de Leon! Juan Ponce de Leon, of course, was a son of Campos, Spain, and in the year 1511, his expedition first landed somewhere on the western side of the Florida peninsula. On that initial European expedition, de Leon first founded the oldest settlement in Puerto Rico, and then he landed on the mainland of North America, a region he named "la Florida." Subsequently, Ponce de Leon returned in 1521, but upon landing in Useppa Key, his group was attacked by Calusa warriors and de Leon was struck by one of the tribe's "poison arrows." The ship sailed on to Havana, where de Leon died from the injuries he had suffered. He was perhaps forty-six or forty-seven years old.

Ponce de Leon is interred inside of the Cathedral of San Juan Batista in San Juan, Puerto Rico. The tomb is a popular tourist attraction. Incredibly, it is believed that thirty percent of the modern population of Puerto Rico descended from Ponce de Leon and his wife, Leonor.

Some history books have claimed that Ponce de Leon was in search of "The Fountain of Youth," but that is as unfounded as some statements made by Don Zimmer centuries later. What is known is that the earthling known as William Francis Lee, III, may have indeed, located "The Fountain of Youth" in the area, since he is still pitching at the age of seventy-three.

The Spaceman recently stated: "Once we were hosting a group of Russian Little Leaguers, and while they were there, my car battery died and about twelve of the Russian kids helped push my Pathfinder down the street in order to get it restarted with a new battery. As for the adults, I played with my Russian team down there for five years with my friends Igor and Sasha, and of course, my catcher, Andre Artimov, who joined me in Moscow, all great guys. Hurricane Charlie came through and destroyed most of the homes in the area, but both the Tarpon Lodge and the Mound House remained intact because they are old Floridian structures. Igor owns the Siberian Coal Company and the Russians rent this motel down there. The Mound House is the oldest house on Pine Island and it was also home to Bobby Kennedy and Jimmy and Rosalynn Carter. It was originally a sanitarium. Peter Matthiessen, who wrote *In the Spirit of Crazy Horse,* stayed there."

Bill Lee drew an analogy to the Vortex in Sedona, Arizona upon stating:

"The Mound House is one of those points on Earth where everything converges. All elements come together like at the vortex in Sedona. Imagine being at the origin of the Calusa Indian Civilization, and at a house built atop a shell mound where the tribe would sit and look at the sunset."

The Spaceman laughed as he recalled his Russian buddies cavorting in the gulf waters off the coast:

"The Russians all get into their thongs and swim out to the bull sharks about a half-mile off-shore. No Floridians swim that far out. The Russians swim halfway to Havana! They drink vodka, they swim and are not afraid of the bull sharks. The bull sharks are afraid of them!"

It should also be noted that by merely peering out of the window from the Tarpon Lodge, you can not only see the Indian mounds of the ancient Calusa, but the Mound House, the exact location legendary mobster Al Capone used for bringing his illegal liquor into the area to avoid detection, an offloading place during prohibition. Not only that, but the Tarpon Lodge was used for storing the illegal contraband. The area around "Wilson Cut" not only provides breathtaking views but is home to some incredible historical significance. It is also a winter home for Bill "Spaceman" Lee, aka "Tomlinson," who has been known to be worthy of author Randy White's epic character. The character "Doc" Ford invariably saves the damsel in distress, with help, of course, from "Tomlinson," aka Bill "Spaceman" Lee.

INTERRUPTION

The Spaceman Explained... Sort of

"Politics: A strife of interests masquerading as a contest of principles. The conduct of public affairs for private advantage."
—Ambrose Bierce

"Instead of giving a politician the keys to the city, it might be better to change the locks." *—Doug Larson*

"Politics is too serious a matter to be left to politicians."
—Charles deGaulle

Since we have managed to interrupt this magnificent volume twice in order to insert a couple of "interludes," it stands to reason that on the third occasion, rather than an "interlude," a brief intrusion should be called an "interruption." Therefore...

To fully understand, or perhaps to partially understand the earthling known as William Francis Lee, III, it is suggested that we begin to examine, but not too closely, his relationship with his closest and dearest friend, Michael Mulkern. Mike is an exceptionally intelligent conservative, and that is not necessarily a contradiction.

In the author's opinion, be it Scott Russell or Kilgore Trout, Bill "Spaceman" Lee's mind is like a sponge, with the exception that a sponge can be squeezed to alleviate the overflow of content. You see, Lee retains everything he learns and much of what he does not learn. Bill Lee does not view a glass as half full or half empty, he does not see the glass. The Spaceman views the glass in another dimension.

Bill Lee can be best described as a lapsed Catholic, a Rastafarian, a devoted follower of Bokononism, a Hindu, a Tibetan high priest, an atheist—albeit a confused one who whistles past cemeteries while making the sign of the cross—a Muslim, a Jew, but above all, a southpaw and admittedly one "with an occasional black eye." It is also highly possible that as a follower of Bokonon, that the Spaceman worships midgets, or at least admires them.

Bill Lee, it says here, is politically bipolar and often describes himself as a "compassionate misanthrope." The author believes the subject of this book, the Spaceman, to be blessed with innate decency. Lee is a friend to the less fortunate unless the less fortunate have evil intent.

Is the Spaceman insane? How can he not be? Look around you! Bill Lee sees a flawed species, one in which, as he quotes from one of his favorite books, *Everything is Fucked, a Book About Hope* by Mark Manson, a sequel to Manson's *The Subtle Art of Not Giving a Fuck,* there is little hope. No, wait. It is my belief that Bill Lee sees hopelessness in hope and hope in hopelessness. Is that clear?

Despite Bill Lee's positive-negative theories as well as his plus-minus hypotheses and his seeing hypocrisy in partisanship, he still finds solace and humor in man's failure to even attempt to salvage what is left of our doomed species. Bill Lee, in short, pun intended, may very well be the midget (Newt) in Kurt Vonnegut's *Cat's Cradle* or perhaps even the nine-foot monster, Dr. Wilbur Daffodil-11 Swain, a former president of the United States, who stands barefoot in the ruins of the Empire State Building while wearing a purple toga, alongside his granddaughter who is significantly pregnant.

This scenario, of course, was painted in Kurt Vonnegut's epic novel, *Slapstick,* of which the author proudly acknowledged was "as close to an autobiography as anything I've ever written."

I am hopeful, therefore, that there exists some light on what has thus far been written. Again, the concept of this book is as Bokonon attempted to teach us, "Live by the foma!"

The author also suspects that many of you have no idea what the next chapter will bring. This is a good thing, but of course, it is also highly likely that you have yet to learn what the fuck occurred in the initial eighty-three chapters. This is perfectly all right because, to be truthful, neither does the author.

I will now attempt to explain Bill "Spaceman" Lee in one brief sentence: This book explains the Spaceman while failing to explain him because, well, he is unexplainable.

As for Mike Mulkern, Lee's closest friend for decades, Mike's beautiful wife, Deirdre's family came over on the *Mayflower*. Upon Deirdre's rather matronly (not that she was old at the time) meeting her daughter's beau for the initial time, she immediately noted that Mike did not appear to be, shall we say, of the elite class. He must have appeared rather slovenly that day, to be kind. The concerned prospective future mother-in-law asked her intruder, "Tell me, are you penniless?"

Mike Mulkern, God bless him, reached into his pocket, fumbled around for a few moments, and pulled out approximately fifty-three cents and proudly displayed his largesse by holding out his palm and exclaiming, "Not quite."

Deirdre's mom smiled broadly. She liked Mike immediately.

CHAPTER EIGHTY-FOUR

Gauchos y Vaqueros

> "See the shootout at the cantina
> Down below the Rio Grande
> See them hang him by a Douglas fir
> See the preacher take his silver spurs
> Man, I'd like to have that pinto pony." —*Paul Siebel*

Mike Mulkern, the closest friend of the earthling known as William Francis Lee, III, absolutely loved his horse, "Gaucho," unconditionally. Gaucho, a gift from Mike's beautiful wife, Deirdre, had been Mike's sidekick and confidante for many, many years. On their rides together, Mike and Gaucho would discuss various topics, the state of the planet and other worldly events. Gaucho was also an Argentinian polo pony. They were inseparable friends, man and beast.

As is life in our universe, Gaucho got old, lame, and eventually rolled his ankle, broke his leg, and had to be "put down." Mike Mulkern was heartbroken and for several years, he never mounted another horse. Gaucho was truly special. Then one day, Deirdre decided to search for a worthy successor to Mike's noble steed. Deirdre had heard there was a wonderful horse at the horse club, an easy ride and a colt with a mild and friendly personality. Mike Mulkern, meet "Colonel." Deirdre acquired Colonel as a gift to her husband.

Mike Mulkern's ball-busting best friend, the Spaceman, delights in the fact that Mulkern's farm in Ipswich is called "The Not Too Stable Farm." Lee also reminds Mike that H.L. Mencken was quoted as saying, "The horse is the dumbest animal on the planet except for the horse owner."

Mike Mulkern and his new equine pal, "Colonel" became instant friends. They discussed the Red Sox, the Celtics, the Bruins and the Patriots, the weather, and all other pertinent and impertinent subjects. Then one day, Mike was notified by the horse club that a woman named "Nan," another member of the horse club, visited the paddock where Colonel resided and immediately fell in love with the horse. Through the proprietors of the club, she asked Mike if she could perhaps ride his horse on occasion. Mike, of course, responded yes, but only if she would be gentle with Colonel and that his horse did not object.

Nan, of course, a horse lover herself, accepted those conditions and Colonel had made a new friend. After Nan had ridden Colonel three times, in appreciation she sent the Mulkerns two steaks from the famous restaurant "The Butcher Boy" in North Andover, Massachusetts. It was then that Mike Mulkern checked the register at the stable at the horse club. He immediately noticed that Nan's full name was "Nancy Yastrzemski." Yes, Carl's wife, and the Spaceman's longtime teammate!

Mike Mulkern laughed as he told Lee:

"Two steaks from the Butcher Boy? Hell, Yaz gets free steaks at that restaurant, and so can I. Yaz smokes cigarettes on the back deck of the restaurant and plays golf with the owner at the Haverhill Golf Club. If they really want a free trade, Yaz and Nancy own a boat up on the Parker River. If Nancy Yastrzemski gets to ride my horse, we should be able to ride his boat!"

CHAPTER EIGHTY-FIVE

Inevitabilities

Brothers in Arms

"Disbelief is catching. It rubs off on people." —*Ray Bradbury*

Although a statistician of sorts, the author is of the opinion that most of today's baseball statistics and metrics are pure unadulterated bullshit. Consider this recent crap regarding "launch angles," "exit velocities," and especially this absurd "catch probability."

Recently our sensibilities have been assaulted with such nonsense as "Based on the trajectory of the ball and the ground the outfielder had to cover, he had a twenty percent chance to catch that ball! What a remarkable catch!" Seriously, how fucking stupid is that?! The play happened! It already occurred! Therefore, at that SPECIFIC time and space, the player had a one hundred percent "probability" of catching the damned ball! These self-appointed scientific "experts" cannot even predict the past! He caught the ball. Get over it.

In the world of the earthling known as William Francis Lee, III, the odds of his paths crossing with a former fellow eccentric Red Sox left-handed pitcher named Maurice "Mickey" McDermott was predestined. Such convergences are inexorable in our universe.

Mickey McDermott was Bill "Spaceman" Lee before Bill "Spaceman" Lee. While in high school, McDermott was voted, "Most Likely to be Found Dead in a Hotel Room" by his classmates. Quite obviously, an eventual meeting with the younger version of himself was preordained.

For the record, McDermott was a highly touted southpaw who was considered by many to be the greatest hitting pitcher since some guy named Babe Ruth. McDermott was also a terrific pitching prospect, and much like Bill Lee, well, he was bat shit crazy. McDermott and Lee were also approximately the same height and had similar bodily builds. He was also seventeen years older than the Spaceman.

How eccentric was Mickey McDermott? There were numerous parallels between the two pitchers' careers. When McDermott's major league career ended, he was signed to a Triple A contract to pitch for legendary innovator Bill Veeck's Miami Marlins. Two of his teammates were legends. One was the colorful Leroy "Satchel" Paige, arguably the greatest hurler of all time and a hero of Bill Lee's. The other was the eccentric Virgil "Fire" Trucks, who was another off-the-wall major league star who, coincidentally, beaned Don Zimmer in a major league game, an incident that precipitated a brawl. Trucks also pitched two no-hitters in one season!

Just as controversy always seemed to follow the Spaceman, strange occurrences and McDermott were synonymous. Consider that while playing in winter ball in Cuba in 1959, McDermott's team was at bat at the precise time when Fidel Castro's "26th of July Movement" overthrew the regime of Fulgencio Batista! Several people on the field and in the stands were shot, including McDermott's teammate Leo Cardenas, the future Cincinnati Reds shortstop. Even Graig Nettles would not have resorted to that.

As for Fidel Castro's takeover, not only was Mickey McDermott there that day, but the Spaceman's manager in Puerto Rico, Cal Ermer, a baseball veteran, was present during that very same game in Havana! As Lee explained:

"Cal Ermer's wife was in the stands during the takeover. One of the guards told her, "If this guy tries to steal home, I'm going to shoot him before he reaches home plate!"

During the time that McDermott's major league career was hanging by a thread, and much of his problems were alcohol related, he was attempting to make the St. Louis Cardinals roster in 1961. It was then that he met a woman named Linda Biggio, who would become his second wife. After being out late one night, he invited Ms. Biggio to his hotel room. The hotel detective noticed that Linda was wearing a Hawaiian muumuu and scolded McDermott, "You can't bring that hooker into your room!" Naturally, McDermott punched out the hotel detective and Mickey was released by the Cardinals. I assume that the detective was not invited to any future Hawaiian luaus. Mahalo!

In 2003, Mickey McDermott, along with outstanding author Howard Eisenberg, penned his autobiography, *A Funny Thing Happened on the Way to Cooperstown.*

The following is what McDermott and Eisenberg wrote about his inescapable meeting with "Spaceman" Lee:

"University of Southern California coach Rod Dedeaux, he's famous for bringing along Mark McGwire and a lot of other major leaguers, woke me up one morning to invite me to play in the annual USC vs. Ancient Warriors game at the college.

"The USC ace, a kid named Bill Lee, later to famously wear a Red Sox uniform in the seventies and join the Expos as Bill "The Space Man" Lee, was on the mound. I leaned into a fastball and drove it over the fence. Being upset when someone does that to you is par for the course. I should know. But Lee looked more than upset.

"After the game, the coach came over to our bench with a big grin on his face. 'The kid is going crazy,' he said. 'He's saying, you know who hit that home run off me? Some fucking gateman, an old man taking tickets at the Santa Anita clubhouse. I recognized him. I was there a couple of weeks ago. I can't believe it. A sonovabitch ticket-taker hit a homer off me!'

"I had a Mickey McDermott trading card in my pants pocket. I wrote him a message:

"'I hit home runs off better pitchers than you'll ever be.' I gave it to the coach to give to him.

"Some years later, I was doing a fantasy camp with a bunch of other players and Lee was one of them. He apologized. 'How the hell would I know you were a famous pitcher?' he says. 'All I knew is that I saw you taking tickets at the racetrack.'

"There was a big party at the end of the week, and here came the Space Man, who I found out was more genius than Space Man and a helluva guy. He was wearing a tux with a pair of sneakers. 'You gotta be comfortable,' he explained. I understood completely. Another McDermott. A nutcase just like me. But with my tux I wear patent leathers."

Oh, and get this: While Bill Lee was pitching in the College World Series in Omaha, Nebraska, Mickey McDermott was one of the major league scouts! Then again, another scout on hand during that NCAA tournament was Jim Fanning. One good guy, McDermott, and the other, Jim Fanning.

There, of course, was a one hundred percent "probability" that Lee and McDermott would eventually meet.

CHAPTER EIGHTY-SIX

Cuba Libre!

"Scientists now believe that the primary biological function of breasts is to make men stupid." —*Dave Barry*

"There are two theories to arguing with a woman. Neither works." —*Will Rogers*

Unlike his predecessor Mickey McDermott, who also visited Cuba to play baseball, at least the earthling known as William Francis Lee, III, did not have to dodge bullets.

Bill "Spaceman" Lee's consecutive 19-year streak of playing baseball in Cuba ended this year, due to the horrific COVID-19 Virus, or as the Spaceman refers to it, "COVID-Freddie Lynn." That, of course, is not a criticism of Lee's former teammate, but that Lynn wore #19 on the back of his uniform.

Since Lee creates bats from the trees on his property for his partner, Louis Ledoux, the Spaceman was kind enough to bring a load of bats to legendary Cuban slugger, Omar Linares, considered by many to be the greatest ballplayer in Cuban baseball history. Linares, a third baseman, wore #10 and he hailed from Pinar del Rio Province. Linares played for both Pinar del Rio and Vegueros in the Cuban National Series. Linares won two gold medals in the World Baseball Cup, two gold medals in the Summer Olympics, three gold medals in the Pan American Games, another in the Goodwill Games, and several other medals in many other international competitions. As Bill Lee stated, "Linares was some kind of good!"

Bill Lee, ever so gracious, wanted to honor Omar Linares by presenting him with several of the bats he and Louis Ledoux had manufactured. It was their way of paying homage to one of the great baseball players in history. However, despite Linares' popularity amongst his fans and peers, on occasion the spouses of heroes do not share in the warm glow of unabashed affection. As the Spaceman reported:

"While in Havana, I decided to take a side trip to Pinar del Rio in order to pay respect by giving Linares some great bats, but apparently he wasn't at home. Linares had also taken a trip to Havana in order to 'spark' some young woman, and it was apparent that Linares' wife was aware of where he was and what he was doing. His wife reacted to the gift by heaving the bats out into the street where they were stolen." I wonder if his gold medals met the same fate.

During one of Lee's trips to Cuba, he became aware of another Cuban legend, this one a pitcher named Perfidio Perez. Perez was heralded in Cuba as "The man with a hundred moves." As the Spaceman described Perez:

"He'd hide the ball behind his kneecap, turn his back on the hitter and twirl like Luis Tiant; he had an incredible number of moves. No one could hit him. He was a fucking magic man. The next day we found out most of our equipment was gone, and we then realized he had 101 moves!"

CHAPTER EIGHTY-SEVEN

Progenies

> "A friend of mine once described parenthood as 'basically just following around a kid for a couple of decades and making sure he doesn't accidentally kill himself, and you'd be amazed how many ways a kid can find to accidentally kill himself.'" —*Mark Manson*

It would stand to reason that the earthling known as William Francis Lee, III, would wind up marrying a Miss Universe Alaska and produce three progenies, two of them being the male of the species, thereby rendering them the mentally lamer of the species.

Michael, the elder son of Bill "Spaceman" Lee and the former Mary Lou Helfrich, fortunately took more after his mother and therefore, wound up more sedate and less calamitous than his father and younger brother, Andrew. Michael, in fact, became a teacher and also has a wonderful website called www.thechurchofbaseball.com. It pays homage, of course, to his dad, "The Spaceman." For several years, Mike worked for Hamilton Studios and the owner was born in Burbank, California on December 28, 1946, the exact date of Bill Lee's birth. Hamilton Studios is a photography and graphic design studio which specialized in the terracotta soldiers manufactured in China. Eventually, Mike went into independent work involving photography and graphic design.

Bill Lee remarked about Mike, his older son:

"Mike always internalized everything, much like my grandfather, William Lee the first. Michael and Andy are the result of the opposite sides of my neuroses."

As for the younger son, Andy, as mentioned in Chapter Five, Andy Lee was nearly born at Fenway Park; since then however, things got even more interesting for Andy Lee. Just yesterday, yesterday being Sunday June 7, 2020, for those reading this tale, the Spaceman received a telephone call from his carbon copy son. As Lee explained:

"Andy got into a fight with a captain on a ship, and now he's forced to wear sunglasses because he's got a black eye. He was out on a boat, he got drunk and got into a brawl with a sea captain who punched him out and now he has a big shiner. Andy should not have been on the boat in the first place because there was this big old tropical depression out there in the Gulf. Unfortunately, Andy has always taken after me. Another time he got into a fight with Keith Tkachuk, a damned good NHL player. At the time, Andy was pitching for the Falmouth Commodores in the Cape Cod League* during the summer, and Andy was cleaning pools for some rich folks that were part of an elite country club in Sandwich where Bobby Orr, Tkachuk, and Derek Sanderson all resided. Andy's summer job was reminiscent of mine when I played in the Alaskan Summer League. I worked at a Safeway Supermarket stocking shelves and helping out at the register. Andy told Tkachuk he had a 'real cushy job,' and the next thing, they were both grappling with each other. They were both drunk, of course."

Lest you think that Andy Lee, son of the Spaceman is merely some sort of a drunken lout, think again. Andy Lee holds a bachelor's degree from Delta State University in Mississippi, where he was a star pitcher, one so good that he was invited to pitch in the prestigious Cape Cod League. Andy Lee was not done with his education, however, as he attained his master's degree in education from Jackson State University, a predominantly black school. Andy also signed a professional contract to pitch for the Boston Red Sox, his dad's old team, and spent two years in their minor league system.

Perhaps just as impressive as his educational achievements, Andy became the head softball coach at Hinds Community College and then at LSU-Eunice, where his team won six national championships, and if that isn't enough, Andy was voted NCAA coach of the year three times! Recently, Andy accepted the head coach position at Northwest Florida State University. Despite their season being suspended due to the coronavirus, in between brawls and getting his ass kicked, Andy is recruiting players. As the Spaceman exclaimed:

"Andy can spot talent from a moving train."

As Andy's dad, the Spaceman stated, "He's driving around and has way too much free time. He is a piece of work. The apple didn't fall far from the tree and just like his dad, he didn't win too many fights, either, but he's the only one with a doctorate in the family."

The Spaceman once offered to put on his uniform as an instructor for Andy's players. Andy's response was hilarious:

"Dad, I wish you wouldn't. We already have a team mascot."

While pitching at Delta State University, one of Andy Lee's coaches was Dave "Boo" Ferriss, a terrific pitcher for the Red Sox and a teammate of Ted Williams. Bill described Ferriss and Bobby Doerr as the two nicest ballplayers of all time. Boo also had the most beautiful shoes in the world.

The marriage between Bill and Mary Lou also produced perhaps the most remarkable of their three offspring, their absurdly beautiful daughter, Katie Lee, who is the spitting image of her Miss Alaska mother. The Spaceman spoke of Katie, the youngest child, as follows:

"Katie is a special needs teacher at St. Richard's Parish Church. She works with autistic and disabled kids. Katie was also a great veterinary technician and was voted as the best vet tech in all of Memphis, Tennessee. Katie's a dog and cat whisperer who is renowned for pairing up people with rescue animals. Katie's so good at it that once this guy's animal passed and he was so stressed out that he dug its grave with his fingernails. Katie has an amazing knack for communicating with animals."

Athleticism did not bypass Katie either. She won several tournaments as a high hurdler in Mississippi and was the only white girl in the state championship finals. Bill described her one day as leaping over a ping pong table and said:

"She can step over a clothesline and not even have to leave her feet."

Obviously, like her mom, the former Miss Alaska, Katie is stately and stunningly attractive. Bill recalled an incident when a young man got drunk and arrived at their house:

"This guy got hammered and stole a floral arrangement from a Jimmy Fund (Dana-Farber Children's Cancer Institute) function we had attended. He banged on her door at 2:00 a.m. and asked if Katie could come out. I nearly threw the floral arrangement in his face."

Speaking of the Spaceman's youngest son, Andy Lee, the author once had the honor of baby-sitting him one afternoon during spring training. Lee was not scheduled to pitch in the actual game but had to get his in-between-starts throwing in during a game at Joker Marchant Field in Lakeland, Florida. Therefore, Bill and my ex-wife and I drove over while Bill headed out to the bullpen. Mary Lou had remained back in Winter Haven for a function involving the team wives. Mary Lou's instructions were to take a bottle of juice with us. Andy was a mere tyke. "He'll ask for it when he's thirsty," said Mary Lou, and he indeed, did.

"Jew!" declared Andy Lee. I peered at the son of Spaceman and replied, "Why, you little anti-Semite!" It was hilarious.

Earlier, I mentioned that Mike, the older son, internalized everything much like the Spaceman's grandfather, William Lee the first . However, William Lee the first's wife, Hazel Lee, was a gregarious and outgoing individual, the opposite of her husband. As the Spaceman recalled his grandmother:

"Grandma Hazel was a pisser. Hazel Ruth Stevenson Lee was one of a kind. She taught me how to crochet! Hazel would crochet poodles for whiskey bottles, but one winter she taught me how to crochet penis warmers. They even had the little ball-sacks in 'em."

William F. & Hazel Lee

The Spaceman's grandfather and grandmother get their own unnumbered chapter!

The grandfather and grandmother of the earthling known as William Francis Lee, III, are worthy of their own chapter in this unlikeliest of tomes. William F. Lee and his wife, Hazel Lee, were, well, different. Amazingly different.

"Spaceman" Lee's grandfather, William F. Lee, worked for Gilmore Gas in North Hollywood, California. Incredibly, many years before his grandson would be blacklisted from major league baseball, Bill Lee's grandfather was forever banned from the L.A. Zoo... honest. The lives of the Lee family are all connected, and oft-times bizarrely so.

During his days being employed by the aforementioned Gilmore Gas Company, Grandpa Lee was a lion trainer. That is not a typo. It seems as if Gilmore Gas's symbols were these two rather impressive lions. However, when Gilmore Gas merged with Mobil, they dropped the lions as their symbolic identity. So, what seemed to be the problem? Well, these specific lions were living in the back of William F. Lee's house in North Hollywood. Again, you cannot make this shit up.

Grandpa William F. Lee was given an ultimatum: Ditch the lions or lose your job. Well, being a fellow cat lover, and for the record, the author has been feline owned for decades, the Spaceman's grandfather sadly took his beloved cats to the L.A. Zoo. However, of course, as any responsible cat-owner would do, he decided to visit them at the popular enclosure. Upon the lions seeing their beloved "daddy," they began roaring so loudly that the other animals at the zoo practically went berserk and Mr. Lee was asked to leave the zoo, with or without his cats. Permanently. The kitty cats had been pining for their owner. Goodbye to his job with Gilmore/Mobil Gas.

In 1957, Grandpa Lee also was the winner of the Sun Valley to Los Angeles "Mobil Gas Economy Run" for getting the most miles per gallon in a 1950 Ford.

If you think the Spaceman's grandfather was eccentric, now you are about to learn a bit more regarding Mr. Lee's wife and Bill Lee's grandma, Hazel Lee. If you thought it entertaining that she taught the Spaceman how to crochet penis-warmers, you have not heard anything yet.

Hazel Lee, as a small child, appeared on the cover of the *L.A. Times* as she sat atop a bar under the heading, "Baby Craves Beer." But she was, above all, eccentric. Consider:

After Grandpa died, Hazel would take the Spaceman's legendary baseball playing aunt, Annabelle, drinking. After Annabelle had her fill, Hazel, considerably older than Annabelle, would take her home and then return to drinking emporiums and stay out all night. One evening, Hazel told her grandson the Spaceman that she knew of a terrific establishment that had great pizza, beer, and popcorn. As the Spaceman recalls:

"All the waitresses wore blue and white G-strings and there was a Dallas Cowboys game on the television. The pool table had been covered with plywood; we were all drinking margaritas and shooting the un-popped kernels from the popcorn at helium balloons that were hung from the ceiling with the straws from our margaritas. I aimed at a bottle of Dos Equis and I hit it squarely, but the kernel ricocheted off the bottle into some poor guy's neck and Hazel yelled, 'Do it again, Billy!' I've got a photograph of Grandma Hazel drinking a margarita at the age of ninety-nine. She was a pisser!"

The author also learned that Hazel had preceded Annabelle as a ballplayer, and in fact had broken her leg sliding into second base at the age of forty-seven!

The Spaceman also recalled that his grandmother, the former Helen "Hazel" Ruth Stevenson had married and divorced three men and had them all over for Thanksgiving dinner, drawing a parallel to the Spaceman's personal "interesting" Thanksgiving.

CHAPTER EIGHTY-EIGHT

Slapshot

"They brought their fuckin' toys with 'em." —*Paul Newman as "Reggie Dunlop" in* Slapshot.

"Well, I'd rather have 'em playin' with their toys than playin' with themselves." —*McGrath*

"They're too dumb to play with themselves." —*Reggie Dunlop*

"Live by the Foma!" —*from the book of Bokonon*

You simply do not fuck around with a man's autographed photo of the Hanson Brothers. Some things are just off-limits. Poisoning his food is bad. Hurling his clothing out into the street is thoughtless and mean-spirited. Flushing his iPhone down the toilet is most definitely a no-no. Kicking a guy's dog is most definitely a despicable act. But fucking around with a man's autographed photo of the Hanson Brothers is a heinous and unspeakable crime worthy of retaliation of the utmost degree.

The 1977 hilarious and profane motion picture *Slapshot* is a film classic. One of its many stars is Hollywood legend Paul Newman, who stars as "Reggie Dunlop," a washed-up hockey player and coach who inherits a terrible hockey team and teaches it to play dirty. The movie also stars Michael Ontkean, Martin Strother, and Jennifer Warren, among other notables. You would be hard-pressed to find a red-blooded American or Canadian boy or man who does not love this epic comedy. Bill Lee is no exception.

During the final days of Bill Lee's marriage to his second wife, Pam, the divorce was a Fait Acompli, for reasons we will not get into, Pam unexpectedly arrived, or perhaps expectedly, take your pick, at the Spaceman's home in Craftsbury, Vermont, and her appearance was eerily similar to Graig Nettles' arrival upon greeting him at home plate during a memorable game at Yankee Stadium in the Bronx in 1976. Pam, a stormy beauty, who Bill described as an "Ann Margret lookalike, but with square shoulders like Richie Allen," approached much alike Mike Tyson answering the bell for the first round of a heavyweight championship fight.

Ironically, the initial victim of the assault was a book of poetry written by the great peaceable writer, Kahlil Gibran, author of *The Prophet,* which was Diana's book.... Yes, Bill's now wife. I believe you see where this is going. Next, the "victim" was one of Diana's sweaters. However, the third target was the Spaceman's autographed photo of "The Hanson Brothers," the stars of perhaps Lee's favorite sports movie of all time, *Slapstick*. The enraged Pam, who had been with Lee for nineteen years, then removed her newly "acquired" merchandise, threw them all out onto the driveway, and (gulp) set them afire! The Hanson Brothers' autographs gone up in a blaze of smoke!

It should be noted that Bill arrived at the house to retrieve a few items, since at the time Pam was still living there. But what occurred next is perhaps one of the funniest things you will ever hear. As the highly agitated Pam looked on, her soon to be ex-husband mournfully witnessed the embers of his prized holy photograph of the Hanson Brothers fill the night sky, and she pointed to the road and shouted to the besieged southpaw, "Get out of here! I'm calling the State Police!"

Again, I must remind you that the life of Bill "Spaceman" Lee is not what most would call mundane. The telephone then rang. The Vermont State Police officer was calling from the State Police Barracks to ask Bill if he would consider playing in a charity game.... No, really, and they had never called Bill before! The timing was magical.

Bill Lee graciously accepted the invitation and then informed said officer that his soon to be former wife would like to speak with him. As Pam looked on incredulously, the State Police officer offered the following suggestion to the earthling known as William Francis Lee, III. The State Trooper said, "If I were you, I would leave the premises immediately."

Bill "Spaceman" Lee honored his commitment and played in that charity game. As for his beloved autographed photo of the Hanson Brothers, its fate, as Bob Dylan once stated, is blowin' in the wind.

You simply do not fuck around with a man's autographed photo of the Hanson Brothers.

CHAPTER EIGHTY-NINE

Diana Donovan Lee

Up on Cripple Creek

"Up on Cripple Creek, she sends me
If I spring a leak, she mends me
I don't have to speak, she defends me
A drunkard's dream if I ever did see one"
—Jaime "Robbie" Robertson

The earthling known as William Francis Lee III recalls the first time that he met Diana Donovan:

"She was at Kayleigh's, her brother's bar in Calgary. It was late at night and Kayleigh's was closing, so we walked across the street to another bar called Cowboys. Diana was dancing on my buddy Ozzie Virgil's shoes. Cowboys had these barmaids who had can openers in their cleavage. These barmaids were given breast implants by the owner of the joint. Free hooters! They would open bottles of beer with their tits, the can openers were between their breasts. Everything was served in a bottle. You should have seen them push those caps off! Suddenly, Diana's ex-husband walked in and they left together. I was completely hammered, but I felt elated. I walked back to my hotel on Eighth Street. I didn't see her until exactly 365 days later."

There is nothing dull in the life of Bill "Spaceman" Lee. Consider the following:

"When I first took Pam, my second wife, to meet my parents, we went to Bay Meadows Racetrack. Pam's former boyfriend was named 'Jeff' and there was a horse running named 'Charming Jeff.' She bet on the horse to win. There was another horse named 'West Coast Willie,' and of course, I bet on my namesake. 'West Coast Willie' came out of nowhere and nipped 'Charming Jeff' at the wire. That should've been a sign."

The Spaceman continued:

"Exactly 365 days after meeting Diana, I ran into her again in Calgary. By this time, both Diana and I were "free agents." She was dancing with my former Red Sox teammate, Rick Miller, Carlton Fisk's brother-in-law.

I remembered her from the prior year. I leaped over a table and tossed Miller out of the way so I could dance with her. After a road trip, I wrote her a letter and called her from Jasper, Alberta up in the Athabasca Ice Fields, and asked her if she'd join me in Vancouver. The rest is history."

It should be noted that Bill Lee picked Diana up in an unmarked Vancouver police car! In fact, it belonged to "The Drug Detachment of the Vancouver Police." Don't ask.

The Spaceman recalls that his team played against those police:

"The caps of the Vancouver Police we played against had a giant marijuana leaf on it and they were marked 'Drug Enforcement.' Diana and I went for a walk in Vancouver one time in a park right next to Nat Bailey Stadium. The great Brooks Robinson played at that stadium in 1959 when he was with the Orioles AAA team. It was the middle of the summer and the flowers in the park were beautiful. There must have been twelve weddings going on at once as well as a Hindu celebration. Then we went over to Vancouver Island and there were several more weddings going on. We kinda got married seventeen times that weekend."

Pay It Forward

One of the most wonderful adventures experienced by Bill and Diana Lee occurred just outside of beautiful Diana's Calgary. In the region they filmed the *Jason Bourne* trilogies, originally starring Matt Damon, based on the great books by Robert Ludlum, the Spaceman and his bride found themselves at Elbow River Falls in Alberta. Elbow River Falls is located at the end of the road outside of Bragg Creek going into Kananaskis Country. This is some beautiful wilderness. As Bill recalled:

"We decided to take a hike in early December after a light early December snowstorm. There were no footprints or tire tracks, it was serene. We had brought a large submarine sandwich to share, but we didn't bring any beverages. We were just there for a brief walk. In the middle of nowhere we see a picnic table and there's a twenty-four ounce bottle of unopened Carlsburg Beer sitting on the middle of the table. Diana looked at me and said, 'We're not touching that until we complete our walk. If it's still there, then we'll enjoy it then.'"

The Spaceman continued:

"We got back and the beautiful cold bottle of Carlsburg was still there.

It's as if it dropped down straight from fucking Tralfamadore. It was a sign. The beer was perfect! We returned a year after and we took another twenty-four ounce Carlsburg with us and just left it there on the same picnic table. We had paid it forward. It was inevitable."

Elbow River Falls is used as a thirty-mile ski-trail in the winter.

Bill Lee admitted to the author that he followed Diana around "like a puppy dog." Lee also recalled how when he tossed Rick Miller aside to dance with Diana that "it was sort of like a Jackson Browne song. That girl came home with me."

Beautiful Diana Donovan Lee is the Spaceman's lover, confidante, and often his drinking partner. Diana is also often Lee's "babysitter" when he requires such supervision. As the author told his friend, the Spaceman, as we would say in the Bronx, "You done good!"

CHAPTER NINETY

Chuck

> "Outside of a dog, a book is man's best friend. Inside of a dog, it's too dark to read." —*Groucho Marx*

It was love at first sight upon the earthling known as William Francis Lee, III, meeting "Chuck." Chuck was Diana's dog, but perhaps more accurately, Chuck belonged to the world.

Chuck could best be described as the "Bill Lee of dogs" and therefore, it was little wonder that the Spaceman would immediately grow fond of the wayward Siberian husky pup, who was perhaps as prolific a nomad as Lee. The itinerant pooch never saw a direction he did not hesitate to explore, and he had evasive moves that would have impressed Barry Sanders or Gale Sayers.

The Spaceman described several of Chuck's numerous adventures:

"That dog would just look at you and wink, and then once more be on his way, you wouldn't see him for days. We had to save his ass so many times, the dog had suicidal tendencies. Once we were on a road trip with the Edmonton Police and we were visiting Lethbridge and Medicine Hat, Alberta. On an early morning walk, Chuck got into it with a fifty-pound porcupine near a coulee wash. Chuck had over two hundred quills in him and he was bleeding badly. A little Scotsman came along in his Lincoln, and he tossed Chuck in the backseat on his leather seats and drove him to his veterinarian. The vet refused to open, but the little Scotsman insisted he operate on the dog and the vet finally agreed to take care of Chuck. The vet saved Chuck but had to sedate him. We went back to the bus and we tossed him on a rug underneath the front seat of the bus. He was out cold for a long time. Chuck didn't awake until we reached Medicine Hat. When he awoke, every cop on the bus gave him a standing ovation.

"Another time we had to save him because he was running around in an area where a bunch of brand-new calves were being born. There was this trucker in a 4 X 4 and he was shooting at Chuck. We had to save his life because he was disrupting the breeding season of the Black Angus in Alberta. If there was trouble, Chuck would find it. They once caught Chuck trying to dig his way into the Siberian tiger's cage at the Calgary Zoo. Chuck was a lot like me. I really loved that dog."

INTERLUDE #3

Welcome to the Waters of Babylon

For greater "awareness," the author suggests you read this "interlude" with the accompaniment of the voices of "The Melodians" or Jimmy Cliff singing "The Rivers of Babylon." A little weed wouldn't hurt, either.

Listen: The author—and does it really matter if such person is Scott Russell or Kilgore Trout?—after writing the thoughts and actions of one William Francis, Lee, III for ninety chapters, has finally arrived at the conclusion that the Spaceman is even deeper than I originally believed.

I even considered adding a subtitle to *The Spaceman Chronicles* by attaching "READING BETWEEN THE LINES AND PLAYING BETWEEN THE LINES," however rejected it because it detracts from what will no doubt become a *New York Times* bestseller, or at the very least be distributed at AA meetings throughout our planet.

What I find most enlightening but also regretful, is that neither the Spaceman's 1988 Rhinoceros Party presidential run, nor his 2016 Vermont gubernatorial run for the Liberty Union Party, resulted in victory. If Lee had won either or both of those elections, our planet would either have been much better off, or perhaps just immediately spun off its axis and hurtled towards the sun.

One can only imagine what the Spaceman's press conferences and addresses to the nation would have produced. I have now arrived at the conclusion that Bill Lee's words should be placed inside a time capsule. In fact, perhaps this book is indeed that "time capsule." Can you imagine journalists from the *New York Times,* the *Washington Post,* and Animal Planet attempting to decipher the Spaceman's most recent diatribe? President Lee's addresses to the nation would have been must-watch television, sort of "Fireside Chats from Space."

By listening closely to the musings of William Francis Lee, III but not too closely unless you wish to be fitted for one of those fancy jackets without sleeves, you (at least yours truly) can hear the faraway "Code of Hammurabi" in the distance. I believe that President Lee would begin each address to the nation with, "Welcome to Mesopotamia." It is written. (Actually it is typed, but I digress).

The Code of Hammurabi, which certainly predates the pitiful "Designated Hitter Rule," was, of course, a wonderful code of laws, and most certainly pertinent, especially upon drawing an analogy to Bill Lee's very existence. Consider:

CODE OF LAWS:

1. If anyone ensnares another, putting a ban upon him,* then he that ensnared him shall be put to death.

2. If anyone brings an accusation against a man, and the accused go to the river, if he sink in the river, his accuser shall take possession of his house.

| * The Spaceman, of course, was indeed, banned, so this is applicable.

As it is in the "Code of Hammurabi," it was the gods who dictated the laws to men for handling a deeper sense of spirituality and balance, so the laws have a divinity character.

For some ungodly reason unknown to mankind, this resulted in the Spaceman conjuring up thoughts of a brief discussion he experienced with his former pitching teammate, Mike Nagy. This meeting of the minds apparently took place as Lee and Nagy sat around the pool in Winter Haven in the early 1970s. The Spaceman was in the process of attempting to explain the "Code of Hammurabi" to the right-hander and as the word association turned to the "Hanging Gardens of Babylon," Nagy, a hurler who had attended the University of Connecticut, suddenly blurted out, "That was Nebba Kadinosaur." I did not seek additional information for fear I'd receive it.

The author also notes that "The Code of Hammurabi" was written in 1754 BC. Why is this significant? Well, the Spaceman won 17 games for 3 consecutive seasons and the numbers 5 and 4 add up to 9 innings. The author shall rest now. His head hurts.

The Spaceman reminds us that in Rastafarian, the Babylonians are the police.

Welcome to Babylon.

CHAPTER NINETY-ONE

Royalty

Dr. John Finley recalled stitching Gordie Howe up during a game and being asked to work quickly so he could get back to the action. The cut sewn up, Howe headed toward the ice. As he exited the door of Dr. Finley's infirmary, Howe paused for a moment. "You might want to wait here," Howe told the doctor. "The guy who did this to me is going to be right in."
"I am just a hockey player." —*Maurice "The Rocket" Richard*

Yes, and Igor Stravinsky was just a piano player.

The earthling known as William Francis Lee, III played on some superb teams during his career in major league baseball, but upon being questioned as to the greatest team he ever played on, he didn't hesitate to list its players:

"At first base, we had Frank Mahovlich, who won six Stanley Cups. At second base, we had Henri Richard, who won eleven Stanley Cups. At shortstop, we had Yvan Cournoyer, who won eight Stanley Cups. Steve Shutt was my third baseman, and he won five Stanley Cups. Our left-fielder was Larry Robinson, and he won six Stanley Cups. My center-fielder was Gaston Gingras, and he won a Stanley Cup. My catcher was Jean-Guy Talbot, and he won seven Stanley Cups. Our pitcher was Maurice 'The Rocket' Richard, and he won eight Stanley Cups. I was the right-fielder. I didn't win any Stanley Cups. If you're counting, that's fifty-four Stanley Cup rings! And the best baseball player who ever played for the Montreal Canadians, Doug Harvey, wasn't even on the team! That's easily the greatest team I ever played on."

The ball club the Spaceman was referring to took the field at "The Wanderer's Grounds" in Halifax, Nova Scotia. The Spaceman recalled an NHL goaltender once remarking:

"The scariest thing in the world was to be in net and seeing Maurice Richard's eyes as he skated towards you."

One of the greatest players in NHL history was the immortal Doug Harvey, who won six Stanley Cups and was named to the NHL All-Star team for eleven consecutive seasons. While with Montreal, Harvey was awarded the James Norris Memorial Trophy on seven occasions, that honor bestowed upon the best defenseman in the NHL. Harvey is generally recognized as perhaps the greatest defenseman in NHL history. But what most folks do not know is that Harvey was also a terrific baseball player.

Doug Harvey's baseball exploits are also quite impressive. While playing third base for the Ottawa Nationals baseball team, he led the Ontario League in runs scored, RBIs, and won a Silver Bat from Hillerich and Bradsby for leading the entire league in hitting! He was offered a contract to play major league baseball with the Boston Braves, but decided to concentrate on hockey.

Bill "Spaceman" Lee describes himself as a hockey "Dadaist." Say what?

"Dada art," said Lee, "came into being during the awful days of World War I in Europe. It included music, literature, paintings, sculptures, performance art and puppetry, and it was intended to provoke and offend the political elitists. Some of the art depicted someone wearing half an Allied uniform and half a Nazi uniform. It started out in Zurich, Switzerland and at the Cabaret Voltaire and it reached New York in 1920 after it had flourished in Paris."

Well, are you confused? I was, too, until the Spaceman explained:

"The reason I consider myself a devotee of 'Dadaism' is because I'm half a Boston Bruins fan and half a Montreal Canadians fan."

When told by the author that was not possible, Lee elaborated:

"The guys on the Canadians have always been great to me. They gave me my first pair of ice skates. I recently donated them to the Craftsbury, Vermont Center."

Although Doug Harvey did not play on Bill's baseball team, as it often does in the life of the Spaceman, they were destined to eventually meet. As Lee explained:

"Doug Harvey was living in St. Andrew, New Brunswick. One day Diana and I are sitting on the side of a hill in Salisbury, New Brunswick and this guy sits down next to us. He has a ten-day growth of beard and he has a fishing knife on his hip. As I would l later find out, he was waiting for Eddie Feigner (The King and his Court, more on him later). I had no idea who this guy is. Suddenly, he looks at me and says, 'You're Bill Lee, aren't you?'

"I answered, 'Yes, I am? Who are you?'

"The man with the stubble answered, 'I'm Doug Harvey.'"

Of course, the Spaceman was familiar with the great Doug Harvey and Bill continued as he addressed the Montreal legend:

"'You're the greatest defenseman in history.

"Soon, we began talking about what we were up to and Harvey asked, 'When the Expos released you, did they fine you, too?' I told him they did. Harvey, who was always a fighter for players' rights while he was in the NHL, advised me, 'They can't do that! You should get your money back! They're not allowed to do that.' Pretty soon Harvey, a great guy, began telling me hilarious stories. He said that he would pay close attention to the exchange rate at the borders and take advantage of the fluctuation. He would grab handfuls of quarters and buy beer in either New Brunswick or the U.S. dependent on the exchange rate. Then Doug Harvey told me a great story:

"'Once, we had played a tough game in New York and afterwards, a sea captain asked me if I'd join him for a few drinks. I never turned down an opportunity to down a few brews, but I got hammered. By the time I woke up, we were six hundred miles off the coast of Nova Scotia! We finally docked at Halifax so I could return to the team.'"

CHAPTER NINETY-TWO

No Crime, but Punishment

"If the world were perfect, it wouldn't be."
—Lawrence Peter "Yogi" Berra

In Chapter Fifty-Four, we wrote about the release of Bill Lee's teammate, Rodney "Cool Breeze" Scott, a terrific fielding second baseman with great range, terrific hands, a formidable base-stealer and perhaps the best high school baseball player to ever come out of Indianapolis, Indiana. Therefore, when the Montreal Expos suddenly released Rodney, the earthling known as William Francis Lee, III, was once more reminded of the inequities in both baseball and life.

It mattered little to Bill Lee that Rodney Scott was African American, but only that he was a good ballplayer as well as his friend and teammate. The move just made no sense, just as it did not when his friend Bernardo Carbo was jettisoned by the Red Sox some four years earlier. So, in May of 1982, upon learning that Rodney Scott had been released, Lee left the ballpark in full uniform, went to a bar across the street from Olympic Stadium in Montreal, had about four beers, and returned to the bullpen in the eighth inning.

It should also be noted that the Spaceman's seven inning hiatus from the ball club not only cost him a huge fine and a lifetime ban from major league baseball, but it also resulted in Lee losing five dollars to a wheelchair-bound pool shark. As Bill Lee explained:

"So, I'm pissed off that my friend Rodney got screwed by the Expos, and as I'm downing a few beers to drown my sorrow, there's this paraplegic in a wheelchair who challenges me to a game of billiards. The guy has cerebral palsy and I figured, what the hell, let's shoot some pool. The guy is shaking as he stood up in his wheelchair, but when he pulled the pool cue back, he was steady as a rock and he'd run the table. I couldn't believe the little SOB could shoot pool like that."

On the way out of the locker room, Lee paused for a second and took his frustrations out on a chalkboard in the locker room. To this day there are indelible spike marks approximately 6 & ½ feet where Lee leaped to attack the inanimate object. Lee offered, "Several Montreal Alouette football players who use the locker room have been amazed at the marks and ask who the fuck did that?!"

The Spaceman was already on the shit-lists of major league baseball Commissioner Bowie Kuhn, his own manager, Jim Fanning, and the Expos general manager, John McHale. Lee's admitted marijuana usage, his outspokenness and his pro-union stance and his intolerance of the narrow-minded people running the game, all rankled the nerves of the conservative gatekeepers of the "National Pastime." Collectively, the establishment of major league baseball had explored for ways to punish who they considered to be a nuisance and this time Bill Lee had provided them with an excuse. He had once more stepped over their imaginary line of demarcation.

It should be noted that in 1981, Bill had shifted to the bullpen where he compiled an outstanding 2.94 earned run average in 31 games, but also batted .364! Also keep in mind that left-handed pitchers are an invaluable commodity in major league baseball, especially those savvy enough to change speeds, deceive hitters, and are flexible in their roles. Therefore, many were surprised, but not shocked, when Lee was called into John McHale's office the following day and was given his release. Little did the Spaceman realize that he had thrown his very last major league pitch, and all allegedly because he had defended his teammate, Rodney Scott, who had also been royally screwed.

Bill Lee and Marvin Miller, the executive director of the Major League Baseball Players Association, had worked hand in hand regarding many issues. The Commissioner Bowie Kuhn had also crossed swords with Lee on numerous occasions, and the fact that Marvin Miller was a perfect 10-0 versus Kuhn in labor disputes did not exactly result in the Spaceman being revered by the powers that be. Then there was this little fact that Lee's boss, John McHale, also served as the vice president of the National League! The Spaceman was soon to learn that he'd been blacklisted from the game he so loved, the one he had played since childhood, but his exclusion was more sneaky, clandestine, and intentionally humiliating than any thoughtful fair-minded person could even imagine.

To fully understand the magnitude of Bill Lee being blacklisted from participating at what had been his livelihood since leaving the University of Southern California, imagine what it must have been to have been a performer during the heinous McCarthy witch hunt during the 1950s, a truly dark era in which a misguided "investigation" of those in politics and the entertainment industry, one that was headed by a previously obscure senator named Joe McCarthy, forever ruined the careers of numerous innocent people, and in some instances, their lives. In Bill Lee's case, however, there was no trial. The Spaceman was "convicted" behind closed doors in a gentlemen's agreement, although those that condemned Bill Lee could in no way be described as "gentlemen."

To fully "appreciate" what happened to Bill Lee, imagine a successful Hollywood actor or singer no longer being able to be gainfully employed in his or her industry, because, well, the right-wing estate wanted him gone. No explanation given. No rooms for rent. Whites only. No Jews allowed. No Muslims allowed. Get the picture? And if you believe that is a harsh analogy, Lee, who knows more about the art of pitching and is a great instructor, has not been offered a job in baseball for five decades. The Spaceman has been sentenced to a lifetime suspension, but in his case, there has never been a formal announcement. Such a declaration would indicate integrity and character.

At one point, Marvin Miller spoke with Lee about the possibility of initiating litigation against the Expos, but Miller also advised, "It's tough to prove collusion, and I doubt we'd win the case." Bill realized then that a conspiracy to ban him from the game was an almost certainty. Wonderful journalists such as Jane Gross of the *New York Times* and Dick Schaap pointed out the inequity, but Lee was not about to get a fair trial, or a trial at all, for that matter.

In Bill's book *The Wrong Stuff* with Dick Lally, there is a poignant reminder of what occurred during the following off-season. A highly respected Atlanta Braves scout named Joe Anselmo had watched Bill work out and what resulted convinced the Spaceman that his major league playing days had concluded. Here it is verbatim:

"I worked out at USC for a couple of days, pitching to their junior varsity team. I was unaware that some scouts from the Atlanta Braves were watching me throw. Apparently impressed with what they saw, they called Henry Aaron, the Braves director of player development, and told him I was worth taking a look at. Henry called me at my father's home in California. He told me that the Braves were interested in possibly having me come to spring training with them and that they would reach a final decision on the matter after discussing it at a meeting of the team hierarchy. Henry was very cordial, assuring me that he would call back within a few days. There had to be something wrong with the telephone system in Atlanta because he never got back to us.

"After a week of waiting for his call, I decided to go to Phoenix, Arizona. I wanted to see if I could hook up with Dick Williams and the San Diego Padres. The day after I left, my father called Henry to ask why we hadn't heard from him. When we reached him, he found Henry was not quite as friendly as he had been in our earlier conversation.

He said, 'We told Bill we'd get back to him.' My dad reminded him that ten days had passed since that phone call. That's when Henry got tough, saying, 'The Braves don't owe Bill Lee anything.' When I heard that, I flipped out. I mean, Jesus, they were the ones who called me! Henry's last line was the topper. My father had told him that the Braves might be a bit leery of signing someone with my reputation. Henry replied, 'I don't know anything about that. That's something Bill will have to talk over with baseball.'

The Spaceman continued:

"Talk over with baseball! What did that mean? Was someone going to lead me into the royal court of the Emerald Palace and bring me before a giant baseball perched on a throne? What would I talk to it about? I guess I could bow down to it and ask, 'Gee, baseball, what did I do to make you angry at me? Did I let you get hit over the fence too often, or squeeze you too hard on the mound? What's your problem?'

"That was the last I heard from Henry Aaron, and it convinced me more than anything else that the fix was in."

Note: The author recalls Bill Lee's dad recalling his telephone conversation with the great Henry Aaron and how upset he was because Henry had somehow been transformed from a cordial affable person to someone who had been told in no uncertain terms that Bill was persona non grata.

Henry Aaron is one of the most beloved icons in the annals of sports history, and for good reason. However, just as any of us—and that includes the victim here, Bill "Spaceman" Lee—he made some poor decisions based on circumstance. Lee acknowledges his poor decisions, on and off the field. I suspect that if Henry Aaron were asked today about this particular injustice, and that it was, he'd simply say, "I really don't recall. It was a long time ago." And that itself would be an error in judgment.

CHAPTER NINETY-THREE

The Keepers of the Key

"You wouldn't have hurt me like this for nothing. So, what have I done? How have I wronged you? Tell me." —*Fyodor Dostoevsky*

For several years, the *Providence Journal* has featured columns by an arts and entertainment critic named Channing Gray. Since my long-suffering bride, Peg, and I often attend stage plays and musicals at the Providence Performing Arts Center, we would invariably read Mr. Gray's "reviews" before attending the latest show... that is, we used to.

Channing Gray's "reviews" became rather tiresome and repetitive. If one were to believe what Channing Gray had written, one would have to be convinced that each theater production that had arrived in town was not worth seeing. We have spoken to various employees of the theater that we have come to know throughout the years, and we always jokingly ask if Mr. Gray "enjoyed" the show. Mr. Gray, I suspect, would complain that Audrey Hepburn had a zit on her ass. The man is the penultimate curmudgeon, but why?

I am about to draw an analogy to Channing Gray, theater critic, and Bill "Spaceman" Lee's last major league manager, Jim Fanning. It is my opinion that both men are/were bitter fools. First, I will explain what I feel is obvious. Channing Gray, the youngest of three sons, is a failed actor. What better way to "get even" with those that rejected him than to belittle those that achieved success in the endeavor at which he failed miserably? Channing Gray's oldest brother is the legendary late, great Spalding Gray, a successful actor, playwright, and teacher. His works include *Swimming to Cambodia, Monster in a Box*, and *Gray's Anatomy*. His younger brother, Channing Gray, has written mean-spirited, sarcastic, and often irrational critiques of stage plays that have received high honors and lengthy standing ovations. Which brings us to the Spaceman's critic: former player and manager, Jim Fanning.

Before I elaborate regarding the similarities between theater critic Channing Gray and Jim Fanning, it may interest you to know that Fanning's propensity for cruelty had been firmly established by another pitcher, one whose best-selling autobiographical book, *A False Spring*, a respected journalist named Pat Jordan. Jordan's magnificent tome was, as "Spaceman" Lee described, "A noble and humble tale of his failures. It takes a lot of integrity and strength to admit failure, as Pat Jordan so courageously did."

For the record, Pat Jordan was a highly regarded hard-throwing pitching prospect in the Atlanta Braves organization. Despite his averaging 11 strikeouts per game during his third and final minor league season, he also walked 8 men per nine innings, and there was no one around to PROPERLY instruct him how to harness his control, certainly not his last manager, Jim Fanning, and Jordan did NOT blame Fanning for his own shortcomings... something Fanning never accomplished himself.

Jim Fanning caught for 11 seasons in minor league baseball and never established himself as "big league material." When he finally reached the major leagues with the Cubs, he was nothing more than a third string catcher, sort of a bullpen catcher.... I'd like you remember that fact.

In four rather poor partial seasons in the major leagues, Fanning batted a pathetic .170 with 0 home runs and a total of 5 RBIs. In other words, pitcher Bill Lee was a better hitter. That is hardly breathing. For some reason, he was eventually promoted to "management."

Pat Jordan was frustrated. Although blessed with a great arm, he just could not harness his control and he was banished to the bullpen where he was merely brought in occasionally to mop up in hopelessly lost games. He had asked his coaches for help, but for the most part, they just avoided him. His manager, Jim Fanning, had not spoken to Jordan in a week.

The following was an example of Jim Fanning's "humanity," or lack thereof, as described by Pat Jordan in *A False Spring*:

"Finally, I confronted him in our deserted clubhouse one night. I demanded that he pitch me. 'I haven't pitched in two weeks! Everyone pitches but me! When am I gonna pitch?' He looked at me curiously. Then warily. His features clouded—narrow eyes, long sharp nose, lipless grin, all slanting upward toward his temples like the features of a fox. He was a catcher in the Chicago Cubs farm system, he had never risen higher than the American Association (AAA). There he was a bullpen catcher, who made good use of his idle time. He pasted newspaper photographs of prominent players in action on plywood and cut out their silhouettes. During each game, young boys hawked these mementos in the stands for one dollar.

"Fanning called his business 'Jim Fanning Enterprises,' and in truth, he was an enterprising man. Even at Eau Claire he had the distracted air of a man who had no intention of remaining a lowly minor league manager for very long."

The players on the club knew that Fanning had plans much higher than his floundering minor league career. As Pat Jordan wrote:

"Today, Jim Fanning is the general manager of the Montreal Expos."

Pat Jordan recalled what Jim Fanning had told him that evening when he practically begged him to pitch:

"Sure, you're gonna pitch, Pat. Just calm down. I was gonna start you in Winnipeg on Sunday."

Sunday arrived and as Pat Jordan recalled, "Jim Fanning tossed me a ball and told me to go to the bullpen. 'But don't warm up yet,' he said. I sat in the right field bullpen and watched our team take infield practice. I grew anxious as the game drew near. Finally, one of my teammates came sprinting toward me. I stood up, flexed my shoulders, touched my toes twice. It was Hummitzch. He tossed me a catcher's mitt. 'Jim wants you to warm me up,' he said. 'He can't spare a catcher right now.'

"'But I thought... he told me I was starting.'

"'I only know what he told me,' Hummitzch said, and stepped onto the mound. I caught him until he was warm, each pitch a blur through my tears. When he returned to the dugout I remained in the bullpen for a few minutes, and then I walked across the outfield to our clubhouse. I changed into my street clothes without showering, packed my blue canvas bag with 'Braves' stenciled in white at both ends, and walked to the bus stop. I took a bus into town, got my other bags at the hotel and took a Greyhound bus from Winnipeg to Eau Claire.

"I reached the Eau Claire bus terminal at nine o'clock in the morning and found my wife there, crying. 'I didn't know what happened to you,' she said."

I believe that explains my analogy between theater critic Channing Gray, a failed actor, and Jim Fanning, a failed baseball player. I believe it speaks volumes that Fanning belittled Pat Jordan by sending him to the bullpen. What better way to humiliate someone by not only lying to him, but to relegate him to the job he himself so hated? Jim Fanning sucked at baseball, and Pat Jordan failed at it, too, but at least he had the courage to admit it.

Long before Jim Fanning attempted to tear down Bill "Spaceman" Lee, his cruel and sadistic tendencies were experienced by Pat Jordan, a great writer. There are those in this world, as both Pat Jordan and Bill Lee learned, who believe they are building themselves up by tearing others down. Jim Fanning and John McHale are practitioners of the art form. Jim Fanning ended Pat Jordan's once promising career, but in a cruel manner. Jim Fanning, John McHale, and others put an end to Bill Lee's major league career, but they failed miserably in their attempts to break either man.

What should be obvious to any discerning baseball fan is that those in charge of the grand old game had built an impenetrable wall in order to "protect" themselves from the free-thinker and colorful character, the earthling known as William Francis Lee, III.

CHAPTER NINETY-FOUR

Speaking Ill of the Dead

"He's a Jew, isn't he?" With that accusation, the author was "introduced" to the vile woman who would become his mother-in-law. "He's a Jew, isn't he?"

The words emanated from the kitchen of the home in Meriden, Connecticut and could easily be heard from where I sat in the living room I had just entered for the initial time in my lifetime.

"He's a Jew, isn't he?"

From the intonation and inflection of the brief and cogent inquiry, it was not too difficult to ascertain that my presence was not appreciated by the strange little woman who would shortly become my mother-in-law. In truth, the stinging words did not have a negative effect on me; this, despite the fact that their intent was to both humiliate and offend me. My immediate reaction was to realize that my then fiancee had not even bothered to notify her family that she was bringing her "love interest" home for the Christmas holidays. However, the mere fact that "Suzie,"—and that's what her mother called her, but I had never heard that name before that sojourn—had kept our relationship a secret because she knew how her vile mother would react.

The reason I am bringing this "incident" up is to perhaps draw an analogy to what is going on around us in the year 2020. Our world is currently in the middle of major upheaval and hopefully, change, but my point is that by denying the past, we are eliminating the "necessary" contrasts that clearly demonstrate the sins of the past. How can we differentiate between good and evil if we eliminate all signs of prior injustice?

The author is apolitical, and in truth, ANTI-political, but is often dismayed by the methods "chosen" to make amends. Intolerance begets intolerance. Having been raised in South Bronx tenements, I was hardened to harsh reality early on. The reason I am bringing this up:

In the prior two chapters, we have strongly criticized John McHale and Jim Fanning, two folks who are not around to defend themselves. Earlier we were critical of Don Zimmer, an often "admired" baseball lifer. Zim, too, is deceased. Let it go, Louie, let it go. Sorry, but no. I will now draw an analogy.

The author's favorite columnist is his idol, the incomparable Pete Hamill, a superb author and chronicler of our times. As an impressionable young man, I would eagerly anticipate reading every word Hamill wrote, and I would fervently hope that something had significantly pissed him off that morning. You see, the greater the injustice, the sharper the wit and the more pointed his arrows would be.

One afternoon, I had just picked up the evening edition of the *New York Post* as I began my daily commute home from Manhattan to my apartment in the Bronx. I quickly turned to Pete Hamill's column, one in which the headline read "Dirksen."

Senator Everett Dirksen, to his credit, was a great civil rights advocate and in fact, helped write the Civil Rights Act of 1964. Dirksen, who hailed from Illinois, served in the United States Senate from 1959 to 1969. It was during that period that he aroused the ire of Pete Hamill who strongly opposed the war in Vietnam. Hamill would often accuse Dirksen of sending our young men off to die in what he felt was an unjust war, a conflict I had grown to also despise. Therefore, upon seeing the headline above Pete Hamill's column, the one which read "Dirksen," I immediately thought, "Oh, no, just because the man died has Pete written a glowing tribute?" Trust me, he did not.

My point was, and remains, death does not somehow convert bad deeds into good deeds. Yes, we have "attacked" John McHale and Jim Fanning and perhaps somewhat ridiculed Don Zimmer. As for the great Henry Aaron, one of the most beloved men on planet Earth and one of the first minorities to become a major league front office executive, it is my belief that Mr. Aaron was simply instructed by the powers that be to continue to deceive and withhold the truth from the erstwhile southpaw. And thirty-eight years later, Bill "Spaceman" Lee is still blackballed from major league baseball. There were/are people responsible for that injustice. I have merely identified them. It should also be a point of interest that the earthling known as William Francis Lee, III is NOT in the least, bitter. Shortly, we will elaborate regarding that fact.

CHAPTER NINETY-FIVE

Recessive Genes

A Lesson Not Learned

"Talent skips a generation." —*Bill "Spaceman" Lee*

Hal Lanier, the manager of the Ottawa Champions of the Independent Can-Am League, approached the earthling known as William Francis Lee, III and announced, "Don Zimmer was my friend." This was not, as the Spaceman immediately ascertained, a cordial, "Hi, we have a mutual friend," but rather had the intonation of Mandy Patinkin in the motion picture *The Princess Bride*, spewing, "Hello! My name is Inigo Montoya! You killed my father! Prepare to die!"

The location of this somewhat veiled warning was the Wanderers Ground in Halifax, Nova Scotia and the occasion was a baseball game in which former major league infielder, coach, and manager Hal Lanier was managing the Ottawa ball club. Lanier, much to his chagrin, was managing his last game for the "Champions," as his services would no longer be required. I suspect that Hal Lanier was thinking, and that's a stretch to even consider that the man engaged in actual thought process, that why not go out with a bang by punishing the then seventy-two year-old "Spaceman" Lee, who incredibly was still playing professional baseball at his advanced age.

Hal Lanier was a middle infielder—and that particular species has nearly invariably been the bane of Bill Lee's existence—who had a poor lifetime batting average of .228 during his playing career with the San Francisco Giants (1964-71) and New York Yankees (1972-73), although he was a slick fielder. His lifetime batting average was eerily similar of that of his "friend," Don Zimmer, and his attitude was also alike. Lanier had also briefly managed the Houston Astros from 1986-88.

Rather than showing appreciation for a septuagenarian who so loved the game by still honoring it and playing it against men less than half his age, Hal Lanier chose to remind Bill Lee that his friend Don Zimmer took his hatred for Lee to his grave. Initially, Lanier informed the Spaceman that he was starting him that day, but Bill truthfully informed him that his arm was killing him, which it was. Bill inquired, "Don't you want to win this game?" Therefore, Lanier, in his holy wrath, decided to install Lee as the designated hitter, a position the Spaceman loathed, and penciled him in the third spot of the batting order against a young hard-throwing left-handed pitcher with a 90 mph fastball and as Lee elaborated, piss-poor control. "In other words, he was trying to kill me," said Lee. Attempting to stave off instantaneous death versus the flame-throwing southpaw, Bill batted right-handed in his final at bat, and if it were not for an outstanding play by the opposing shortstop, would have finished with a base hit.

It should be noted that in September of 2010, Bill pitched 5 & 2/3 innings for the Brockton Rox, making him the oldest pitcher to ever appear in or win a professional game. The Spaceman also took part in the "100 Innings of Baseball Game" hosted by the Boston America Baseball Network to raise money for ALS (Lou Gehrig's Disease) on October 8, 2011. None of that mattered to Hal Lanier, who proudly exclaimed, "Don Zimmer was my friend." Or was it, "Hello! My name is Inigo Montoya! You killed my father! Prepare to die!"

Hal Lanier requires a lesson in history, and if he is reading this, or perhaps gets someone to read it to him, he is about to receive a long-overdue education.

It should be noted that earlier (Chapter Sixty-Nine) we included Casey Stengel's hilariously witty and intentionally evasive testimony regarding major league baseball's reserve clause to the Kefauver Committee on July 8, 1958. This time, however, we will not engage in elusiveness, but rather in a clarity that perhaps everyone can understand, perhaps even the son of a gentleman named Max Lanier.

Some thirty-six years before Hal Lanier displayed his disdain for Bill "Spaceman" Lee, the player who had been blackballed from major league baseball, Hal Lanier's father, Max Lanier, had been———blackballed from major league baseball. No, really.

Hal Lanier, self-proclaimed friend of Don Zimmer, a man who told Bill Lee he'd never wear a major league uniform again, was the son of one of the men who ORIGINALLY challenged the reserve clause, the officious baseball "law" that prohibited its athletes from choosing who to be employed by, has little or no sense regarding what his noble late father initiated.

Much credit, and rightfully so, has been given to Curt Flood, Andy Messersmith, and others for challenging baseball's now archaic reserve clause, but it was Hal Lanier's father and a handful of others major league players who began the process in 1946, the same season that Jackie Robinson began his professional baseball career. Coincidentally, 1946 was the same year that a thirty-nine year-old Mexican multi-millionaire named Jorge Pascuel, who along with his brothers who owned the Mexican League, decided to go after Major League players by offering them considerably more money. One of those players was Hal Lanier's father, Max Lanier.

Max Lanier, like Bill Lee, was a left-handed pitcher and a damned good one. Max Lanier was an integral part of three consecutive St. Louis Cardinals championship teams from 1942-1944, a ball club that defeated the New York Yankees in the 1942 World Series. During three seasons from '42-'44, Max won a total of 45 games and compiled a N.L. leading 1.90 ERA in 1943. He was damned good.

By May of 1946, Max Lanier had gotten off to a fabulous start. He was 6-0 with a 1.93 ERA when he "jumped" to the Mexican League. Major League Commissioner Happy Chandler, of course, was livid and he called the Mexican League an "outlaw league." Except the Mexican League had been established in 1925 and was well-respected by some of the greatest players in baseball history, many of whom were the great black players who were intrinsically blacklisted, no pun intended, from playing in the "major leagues." Who were some of these African American Mexican Leaguers? Well, try Leroy "Satchel" Paige, Roy Campanella, and Monte Irvin on for size. One of the stars who jumped was legendary right-handed pitcher Sal Maglie. The great Hall of Famer, Monte Irvin, who would go on to star for the New York Giants, referred to Jorge Pascuel as "dynamic!" "Outlaw League?" Hardly.

Commissioner Happy Chandler, in his holy wrath, immediately imposed a five-year suspension on all those "major leaguers" who accepted the largesse offered to them, and in most instances, these men were at least doubling their salaries. Again, for the great black players, so-called major league baseball was unavailable to them anyhow.

Max Lanier was joined by his St. Louis Cardinals teammate and fellow pitcher, Fred Martin as well as New York Giants infielder Danny Gardella. How serious were the Pascuel Brothers in bringing even greater baseball south of the border? Overtures were made to Ted Williams, who ironically would be discovered as being Mexican many years later, a three-year $300,000 deal. Stan Musial was offered a five-year $650,000 contract, and Phil Rizzuto, a one-year $10,000 pact with a Cadillac thrown in as a bonus. Contracts were also tendered to major league stars Bob Feller, Joe DiMaggio, Whitey Kurowski, Enos Slaughter, and others. Oh, and there was this Babe Ruth fellow. The Pascuel Brothers offered him a ONE MILLION DOLLAR contract to become league president!

Within a few seasons, many of the men who took the money and ran attempted to return home to the United States and return to their prior jobs, but were blacklisted. However, Max Lanier, Fred Martin, and Danny Gardella all filed federal lawsuits challenging the major league's reserve clause. The twenty-two major league players that had jumped were branded with five-year suspensions.

During the 1948 season, Danny Gardella brought a claim against Commissioner Happy Chandler and league presidents Ford Frick and Will Harridge. In 1949, Gardella won a major appeal against baseball's reserve clause in the federal courts. This SUCCESSFUL attempt is now recognized as the first major early step towards baseball's free agency.

Upon players such as Max Lanier and Sal Maglie being reinstated, they had to agree to drop their lawsuits against major league baseball which challenged the reserve clause. However, in a move that was a clear indication that it would be many years before Marvin Miller would bring MLB to its knees, Danny Gardella, who had successfully challenged baseball's reserve clause, had his five-year suspension lifted in 1950. Gardella, a much better hitter than Max Lanier's son, Hal, had batted .272 with an OPS of .775 in his final season with the New York Giants, was "reinstated" in 1950. After appearing in ONE GAME and having one at bat for the New York Giants, Gardella, still a young player, was released in a move that was blatantly symbolic. He never again played in a major league game.

It may also interest you to know that those players who "jumped" to the Mexican league were denied their major league pensions and health benefits.

Apparently, the only espanol Hal Lanier can speak is:

"Hello! My name is Inigo Montoya! You killed Don Zimmer! Prepare to die!"

Meanwhile, back on planet Earth, Hal Lanier, the son of the true baseball pioneer Max Lanier, told "Spaceman" Lee that he was a friend of the late Don Zimmer. Perhaps Hal Lanier should have concentrated more on his father's accomplishments than disparaging a latter-day player, who much like his honorable dad, had been unjustly blackballed from major league baseball. I believe the earthling named William Francis Lee, III, may have put it best upon stating:

"That's what Max Lanier gets for raising a son who is not only right-handed, but a middle infielder at that. Danny Gardella died for our sins."

CHAPTER NINETY-SIX

Prevarications

"I never deny. I never contradict. I sometimes forget."
—Benjamin Disraeli

"How can I miss you if you don't go away?" *—Dan Hicks*

In an article written by Don Amore of the Hartford Courant dated April 12, 2001 titled "Zimmer Vents on Lee," Amore writes:

"In Zim: A Baseball Life, Don Zimmer calls Bill Lee 'a jerk' and says he's the only man he wouldn't let into his home."

As Amore continued:

"'Bill Lee is the biggest scumbag,' and at one point said, "What do I care what Bill Lee says? Bill Lee, scum of the earth.'"

Don Amore then wrote, "Zimmer insisted in his book and to reporters Wednesday that he never let his personal feelings toward Lee dictate his decisions."

In Chapter Sixty-Two, the *Boston Globe*'s Dan Shaughnessy wrote of the time during a critical series at Fenway Park how Red Sox Hall of Fame captain Carl Yastrzemski begged Zimmer to pitch the "Spaceman" in order to prevent a four-game sweep by the Yankees at Fenway, but was denied by the burly manager who instead waved newspaper articles in front of Yaz while decrying, "He called me a gerbil!" Sounds to me that Zimmer had zero intention of even considering utilizing his Yankee killer. It also appears as if Zim was not exactly being forthright in his autobiography with Bill Madden.

As the superb journalist Leigh Montville penned in the *Boston Globe*:

"Zimmer was one of those old-fashioned guys who ran the ship as it always had been run. But now there were bells and whistles all over the ship, and he didn't want to deal with the bells and whistles. He just wanted to run the ship."

As the award-winning columnist Bill Reynolds wrote in the *Providence Journal*:

"Not that Lee was the only member of the '78 Sox who thought Zimmer was a dinosaur in double knits, often referring to him as a 'gerbil,' there was a cadre of them. They referred to themselves as 'Buffalo Heads,' and suffice to say they treated Zimmer as if he was some relic, someone to make fun of, someone to ridicule. The counterculture was not always kind."

Bill Reynolds pretty much concluded that at the time, "Zimmer was the wrong man at the wrong time for the '78 Sox."

Seriously though, to call someone "scum of the earth," to maintain that he was the only player he'd ever known he wouldn't allow in his home, and to react to a fervent plea from his respected Hall of Fame captain by pointing to printed insults levied at him like some six year old, and then claim that he never allowed his personal feeling towards Lee to dictate his decisions, is obviously pure unadulterated bullshit.

It should be noted that at the time Zimmer issued the statement that he wouldn't allow the Spaceman in his home, Lee responded, "That's all right, I really didn't want to see furniture from the 1950s anyhow."

Again, the counterculture members of the Red Sox Buffalo Head Gang, may have indeed unfairly maligned their manager on occasion, but consider that Zimmer had not only removed successful veteran pitchers Rick Wise, Fergie Jenkins, and Bill Lee from the rotation while telling the media that "they could no longer get major league hitters out," and by then had jettisoned both Wise and Jenkins to other ball clubs where they once more resumed their success, and resorted to alleged "facts," which were fabricated, even in retrospect, and in truth the vast majority of the fans and media in Boston were certainly not pleased with the manager (an understatement) and had considered the Spaceman and others critical of the oversensitive Zimmer to be in the right. Some forty-two years later you would be hard-pressed to find members of Red Sox Nation that recall Don Zimmer fondly, after his "leadership" resulted in blowing a historical 14 game lead over the Yankees.

INTERLUDE #4

Interruption #2

> "From the moment I picked up your book until I laid it down, I was convulsed with laughter. Someday I intend reading it."
> —*Groucho Marx*

> "Live by the foma that make you brave and kind and healthy and happy." —*Bokonon*

It is imperative, or perhaps inessential, I forget which, that anyone reading this book is aware that both the author, and there remains confusion as to his identity, and the subject of this otherworldly volume, are both essentially insane. In fact, we both discussed this fact the other day and arrived at the conclusion that we will both be institutionalized at some point during the not too distant future. And so it goes.

The subject of this magnificent tome, the earthling known as William Francis Lee III, suggested that we be placed in adjoining rooms with padded walls. I am hoping that in his case, his room contains baseballs, ones he can throw at specific targets on the walls of his chamber, so that he will feel at home. I am hoping that both rooms resemble libraries, as we both wish to continue to be surrounded by books.

The author also envisions that the substance of this work be placed in a time capsule, one which would perhaps describe his existence here on planet Earth. Archeologists would then discover that the author may have postdated John Kennedy Toole by seeing similarities in their methods, i.e., the existence of innumerable and nearly undecipherable dog-eared yellow-lined notepads in the capsule. Or perhaps they will just arrive at the conclusion that he visited Staples frequently. Either way, it is all good.

Speaking of books, it may surprise you, or perhaps not, that both the author and the subject are currently in the process of rereading the entire works of Kurt Vonnegut. Which brings me to Haile Selassie, who to my knowledge was not a subject in any of Vonnegut's books, but should be. You see, the Spaceman believes, as many do, that Selassie, the former Emperor of Ethiopia, is a direct descendant of Jesus Christ.

It should also be noted that both the author and the Spaceman are devout followers of Bokonon, and that we spend great amounts of time quoting this great black orator who hailed from Tobago and settled on the Caribbean Island of San Lorenzo, a place he began a new and worthy religion. Bokonon's original name was Lionel Boyd Johnson, not to be confused with Wallace Johnson, a good-hit, no field infielder on the Expos baseball club, and the man who replaced Rodney "Cool Breeze" Scott, whose barbaric banishment from Montreal resulted in the Spaceman's being blackballed from the sport called "baseball." I should note that Bokonon won me over by paying homage to midgets.*

In this lengthy tome, one that will no doubt offend many of Bill Lee's fellow earthlings, many of whom are currently "dead," the author and the subject have detailed that many listed in this literary masterpiece, are what the inhabitants of planet Earth often refer to as "assholes." Please keep in mind that being identified as an "asshole" is purely subjective and can be debated ad infinitum. In fact, at the end of this tome, we will actually provide a list of perceived assholes and present them in a manner which "registers" each with a ranking similar to a countdown of popular songs, motion pictures, and books, as it were. They will be listed from ten to one and upon reaching the pinnacle of assholeism, those recipients of that honor will be forever entered into the annals of planetary deities, and in so doing will have attained immortality.

Again, there is a fine line between being an asshole and a good person, and in fact, there are a few individuals who will be included on both lists! Yes, we will also have a countdown on the non-assholes. As both the author and subject are impartial observants of the human species, there are various assholes we retain both disdain and admiration for.

Neither the author nor William Francis Lee, III approve of the politics of exclusion. Therefore, in order to prevent even further dismay on our planet caused by individuals who anxiously anticipated seeing their names prominently displayed on the "Wall of Assholes," only to find they didn't quite make the grade, we have decided to include an official wall titled, "The Honorable Mention Register of Assholes." After all, there are countless people who find us both rather repulsive.

We can certainly commiserate with those disappointed at finding their level of repugnancy somewhat inadequate. Imagine for instance, of how Lenny Dykstra would feel if he awoke one morning to learn that he had somehow inexplicably brought joy to someone the prior day.

Again, we wish to offend everyone, not merely the upper echelon of ignoble disreputable boors.

> * It should be noted that the author claims to be living in sin with fourteen Dominican nuns, three women of questionable repute, a Bulgarian midget, and a pet yak.

CHAPTER NINETY-SEVEN

Oleg Cassini Meets Goodwill Industries

"Clean shirt, new shoes
And I don't know where I'm goin' to
Silk suit, black tie (black tie)
I don't need a reason why
They come runnin' just as fast as they can
'cause every girl's crazy 'bout a sharp dressed man"
—Frank Beard, Dusty Hill, Billy Gibbons—ZZ Top

Hall of Fame ballplayers can be assholes, but in a good way. Carl Yastrzemski and Luis Aparicio are no exceptions, although "Little Louie" at least had a modicum of taste in haberdashery. As the earthling known as Bill "Spaceman" Lee said about his teammate, Hall of Famer Carl Yastrzemski, "Even Goodwill Industries would turn down Yaz's clothing. I think Yaz's greatest influence was "Ratso Rizzo" in *Midnight Cowboy*.

During the 1970s, many men were attempting to make fashion statements. Carl Yastrzemski was not one of them, that is, unless he was going for the "Recently Fallen Upon Hard Times," look. Yaz appeared like someone who can be seen at bus terminals and train stations checking phone booths in hope of discovering if anyone left any loose change in the coin slot. Yastrzemski looked like an overgrown poster child for the Salvation Army. In the '60s and '70s, the androgynous look was in vogue for many men, much of it the influence of the British rock invasion. However, Yastrzemski's countenance more resembled the discovery of a lost tribe of indigents found in the remote mountains of an ancient Balkan civilization. Enter sharp-dressed Venezuelan Luis Aparicio, a dapper and flashy shortstop.

Luis would wear stylish silk suits from Oleg Cassini along with Gucci shoes and Yastrzemski would arrive in the clubhouse at Fenway Park appearing for all intents and purposes that he had recently shopped at a dumpster in a back alley of the Back Bay. While Aparicio looked as if he routinely visited "Men's Warehouse," Yaz looked as if he acquired his duds someone had left behind on a rack in a soup kitchen. As the Spaceman explained, "Yaz looked like a reject from Saturday Night Fever."

Being a ballplayer, the Spaceman was not kind upon describing Yastrzemski's outerwear:

"Yaz had this ungodly blue London Fog jacket he would wear every fucking day. The thing got grayer and grayer and dirtier and dirtier. He looked like Sergeant Columbo (Peter Falk). The damned coat wouldn't have burned if you threw it into a fire."

Luis Aparicio attempted to "educate" Yastrzemski concerning his sartorial failures, to no avail. After all, Yaz was team captain. Therefore, Luis would sneak into Yastrzemski's locker and tie Yaz's offending clothing into knots. Yaz would just untie the knots in his ugly chinos and jacket, unsuccessfully attempt to remove the permanent wrinkles which were present before Aparicio's intervention, and simply put them back on. Often, they looked better after Luis' hilarious "attacks."

Obviously, being an asshole in his own right, Yastrzemski would sneak into Luis' locker and wrinkle his much more expensive clothing. Both men would resort to some sort of vigilance and remember to place locks on their private compartments.

On the final day of the 1973 season, Yastrzemski finally got his revenge. As numerous players do, Aparicio was flying home to his native Caracas immediately after the Sunday afternoon game at Fenway Park. Since it was the last game of the season, Luis had shipped his clothing in advance to his home in Venezuela rather than taking it onboard the flight. All Aparicio had was the expensive Oleg Cassini suit he had worn to the ballpark that morning. I believe you see where this is going.

Being fully aware that his friend and teammate, Carl Yastrzemski, would at least attempt some subterfuge, Aparicio made sure to thoroughly prevent such an event from occurring. To this day, some forty-seven years later, no one knows how Captain Carl managed to get into "Little Luis'" locker, but he did. Upon returning to the clubhouse following the game, Aparicio found his locker open, his Gucci shoes nailed to the floor and his silk Oleg Cassini suit cut off at the knees, his suit jacket sliced off at the shoulders and his silk shirt hanging in his locker, sans its buttons.

As "Spaceman" Lee described it:

"Aparicio left for Logan Airport looking like 'Little Lord Fauntleroy.' He looked ridiculous wearing what amounted to Oleg Cassini shorts."

I can only imagine what the flight attendants thought.

CHAPTER NINETY-EIGHT

I Am the Way

The following chapter requires verification.

"Dynamic tension is a sense of a priceless equilibrium between good and evil." *—Bokonon*
It was Bokonon's belief that good societies could only be built by pitting good against evil and by keeping the tension between the two high at all times.

"I can walk on the water and I can raise the dead
It's easy... I'm the way
(This song has a romantic part to it)
Don't tell nobody, but I kissed Magdalene
Right on the mouth
I said, Mary, it's okay, I'm the way"
—Loudon Wainwright, III

"We are ALL the way." *—Bill "Spaceman" Lee*

If Don Zimmer were not already deceased, this chapter would no doubt have killed him. In their unholy wrath, the blasphemous heathens that run major league baseball may have forever blackballed a direct descendant of Jesus Christ, the earthling known as William Francis Lee, III.

Several years ago, Bill and Diana Lee found themselves back at The Sullivan Bed and Breakfast, a wonderful inn at the head of the bay in Boothbay Harbor, Maine. It was there that Bill met Richard G. Brown, the father of an author named Dan Brown... yes, that Dan Brown, the renowned author of the highly controversial novel, *The Da Vinci Code,* a remarkable book that was adapted to a magnificent and equally controversial but successful motion picture by the same name, starring Tom Hanks and Audrey Tautou. Among the topics "Spaceman" Lee and the father of the best-selling author discussed were the unsuccessful lawsuits brought against his son, claiming that he had plagiarized their prior works. The courts in both the United States and the Court of Appeals of England rejected the plagiarism claims and in fact, the plaintiffs were ordered to pay legal expenses of nearly six million dollars in England.

Dan Brown's father, Richard G. Brown, is also an author, a writer of mathematics books including several on algebra. The conversation between the southpaw pitcher and Dan Brown's father turned to religion, since that was the historical basis behind his son's amazing book. As it was, Bill "Spaceman" Lee is a follower of Rastafarian and a firm believer that the former Ethiopian Emperor, Haile Selassie, was a direct descendant of Jesus Christ; however, Bill's own ancestry dates back to Mary, Queen of Scots! Therefore, the Spaceman is convinced that he, too, is a direct descendant of Jesus Christ since the lineage of Christ, according to many theologians, ends with Mary, Queen of Scots, and Bill Lee is a descendant of the Stuarts!

Listen: As I stated, this chapter requires verification, and lots of it, but the Lees are indeed descended from the Stuarts of Scotland. The possibilities are, of course, infinite, as is the brain of Bill Lee, but at the same time, delicious. The Knights of Templar, Mary Magdalene, Bishop Manuel Aringarosa, Jacques Sauniere, Sophie, the Priory of Sion and Opus Dei. Hey, I am not going to explain it to you, read Dan Brown's literary masterpiece or at least watch the motion picture.

Sacrilege? I will leave that to a higher judge. The Spaceman belongs to "The Church of Baseball," and in fact, the initial time he entered the hallowed grounds of Fenway Park, he immediately remarked, "Where do they keep the holy water?"

While up in Boothbay Harbor, where Bill Lee met the father of Dan Brown, I asked the Spaceman the following:

"Was Diana your cryptographer on the trip?" A lengthy conversation ensued, most of it reminiscent of Casey Stengel's 1958 testimony to the Senate regarding major league baseball's reserve clause. I should have known better.

This I can tell you, however. After learning of the possibility that the Spaceman could possibly be a direct descendant of Jesus Christ, I experienced a rather disturbing dream later that evening. In the dream, Don Zimmer had been eavesdropping as Lee held court with a few reporters, informing them that he was indeed a descendant of Jesus. Zimmer immediately flew into a rage and spewed: "Did you hear that?! Now he's telling people that Christ was his grandfather!"

At that point in the dream, Lee walked over to Zimmer and replied, "No, Jesus is way older than that. He was my great grandfather." Fortunately, I awoke immediately, soaked with sweat.

Back to reality, or at least what passes for reality on those occasions I converse with the southpaw. Upon my asking Bill Lee, descendant of Jesus Christ, if he had encountered any frightening albinos, such as the evil "Bishop Silas" in *The Da Vinci Code*, the Spaceman replied, "When I see the albino, I'll know the end is near."

Author's note: The earthling known as William Francis Lee, III, direct descendant of Jesus Christ, informed me that among his favorite characters from that lineage was Dagobert, King of the Franks (Lee believes that Yogi Berra is a descendant of DAGObert), King of Austrasia from 623-634 and King of Neustria and Burgundy from 629-639. Dagobert was the last Merovingian dynast to wield any real royal power.

The Spaceman also admired King Charlemagne, who was the eldest son of Pepin the Short (Lee did not mention if Pepin was an ancestor of Freddy Patek) and Bertrada of Laon, born after their canonical marriage. He became King in 768 following his father's death, initially as co-ruler with his brother Carloman (It is not known, however, if Carloman was an ancestor of Carl Yastrzemski, although it is suspected he had a better tailor.)

CHAPTER NINETY-NINE

Blasphemy—Part Two

At Least Give Me My Sword

"I sit, I shake, a silent palsy in hand with extended reading glasses. Who thought I'd see seventy-one? Fear not, grab your Viking sword and jump into the pit. Those aren't the howls of wolves down there, it's your sled dog team to Valhalla."
—Bill "Spaceman" Lee

"The only way to entice enlightenment is to dance and spin around in a circle." *—G.I Gurdjieff*

Big Rock Brewing Company owns three breweries in Calgary, Vancouver and Etobicoke, Ontario. Its founder was a gentleman named Ed McNally, who is noted for his hilarious beer commercials. Ed McNally is also a descendant of "Dr. Zoom" (don't ask) who was the man who introduced Bill Lee to Diana. McNally was the Spaceman's closest friend in Calgary.

After many years of practicing law, being a farmer, and raising cattle, McNally, a philanthropist, decided to enter an industry dominated by Molson, Labatt, and Carling O'Keefe and set out to brew the kind of beer that he himself wanted to drink. That is how the renowned "Big Rock Brewing Company" came to be. Ed McNally's idea of using the clean water of Alberta and the golden barley he so loved quickly produced magnificent beers and ales.

In addition to being a visionary as a brewer, McNally instituted an annual promotional event, a contest called "The Eddies," in which beer drinkers would submit commercials for the products, enabling money to be raised for Calgary arts beneficiaries. Some of these entries were hilarious, and of course, intentionally so.

As Lee stated:

"Dr. Zoom was Dr. Hunter S. Thompson before Hunter S. Thompson. Ed McNally decided that I should film a commercial for Big Rock Beer with Dr. Zoom. 'Dr. Zoom,' whose real name was Gordy Grayburn, was McNally's in-law. Grayburn's sister was married to McNally. Grayburn's great grandfather was the first RCMP officer to be killed in the line of duty. He's got a mountain named after him."

Somewhere, according to the Spaceman, there is a photograph with a young Gordy Grayburn and his Little League coach in Toluca Lake, a man who happened to be Bob Hope.

The Spaceman explained:

"In the commercial they're stoning this poor woman. Jesus walks over and spreads his arms and exclaims, 'Let he who has not sinned, cast the first stone!' Suddenly a huge bottle of Big Rock Beer comes hurtling down from space and crushes everyone. Then Jesus ends up walking away with Mary Magdalene, and as they are leaving you can see that Mary Magdalene is wearing a thong that has 'MF' tattooed on her ass. Jesus stops, looks to the heavens and shouts, 'You know, Dad, sometimes you piss me off!'"

Bill Lee, slightly disappointed, informed the author that the commercial had been rejected, although it was runner-up. The Spaceman never did tell me who he had portrayed in the commercial and I was not about to ask in fear of getting an honest answer.*

> * Note: As I learned shortly thereafter, Bill Lee portrayed a man standing on a rock, wearing a kilt, and playing bagpipes. As they zoom in on his kilt, you can see two McNally's Ale bottles hanging from his balls beneath the kilt.

The commercial that was chosen as the winner that year was titled, "Beer Hound." The commercial was filmed from a low perspective and as they pan in, you can see overturned empty beer cans strewn all over the floor and there are ashtrays everywhere, and you can hear the sounds of what appears to be an animal making sniffing noises. Finally, you see an inebriated woman crawling around on all fours searching for any possible remnants in the beer cans.... They really know how to make great beer commercials in Canada.

How this possibly segues into Bill Lee's next thought, I have absolutely no idea, but the Spaceman told the author about a one-eyed doe he had on his property a while ago. As Lee explained:

"We had a one-eyed pet doe on our property. She was amazing. She gave birth to six consecutive sets of twins. We named her 'One-Eyed Fiona' from the song by Lyle Lovett. I guess with her one eye, she could never see the buck approaching her from behind."

CHAPTER ONE HUNDRED

Persistent Asshole

In Chapter Fifteen we described the stupidity of baseball "lifer" Al Campanis during the time the sage told Lee, then a senior in college, that he did not have Sandy Koufax's fastball, curveball, command, or poise. Yes, and Bill wasn't Jewish, either. Many years later, during the time the Spaceman had not yet entirely given in to the fact that he had been blackballed, Bill was pitching in an alumni game at USC. As Lee described:

"I wound up pitching three no-hit innings against some terrific hitters. Coach (Rod) Dedeaux was there as well as my aunt Annabelle and my grandmother, Hazel. A few members of the Dodgers front office were impressed with my performance and they peered up into the stands where Al Campanis sat like a warlord or a dictator of a fascist nation. Campanis immediately answered the inquiry by giving a 'thumbs-down' signal. I fully expected the lions to be released. Grandma Hazel witnessed the nitwit Campanis gesturing his thumbs down and immediately ran up the steps, got directly in the moron's face and began poking him in his chest. Hazel was an amazing woman."

During the time that Bill Lee was a senior All-American at the University of Southern California, he was chosen along with several other elite senior collegiate to pitch in the Alaska summer league, and in fact, pitched for the Alaska Goldpanners. The famous league is still going strong these days and one of its most heralded attractions is "The Midnight Sun Game" held annually in Fairbanks, Alaska, a game played at midnight without lights! That is, of course, because of the "Midnight Sun Season," a time during which the sun never sets. The season runs from April 22 through August 20 and comes to a peak on either June 20 or 21, marking the beginning of the Summer Solstice.

During those summer months, the Goldpanners also play games in California and it was there that the earthling known as William Francis Lee, III, found himself engaged in a game at Eureka some fifty years ago. As the Spaceman recalls:

"There was a play at second base. I take the guy out and flip him into the air. It was a clean play, just a good, hard slide and I was safe. The kid gets up and the umpire shouts, 'You're out!'

"So help me God, the second baseman looks at the umpire and says, 'Nice call, Dad!' I yell, 'What?!' I'm mad as hell and the umpire throws me out of the game! His father was the fucking second base umpire! They put me on the team bus outside of the stadium.

"Fifty years later, I'm at a Eureka-Humboldt Crabs game at the same ballpark. A shortstop had gone to Terra Linda High School and I was there to support him. I had Anna and Diana with me. Between games, this kid comes running out of the stands and onto the field. We find out he was celebrating his twenty-first birthday and he got hammered. He's drunk and he runs around the bases and he runs around the bases as if he had hit a home run and he slides into home plate. It was harmless fun. Then he gets up and tries to do it again, but when he slides into home plate, a player for the Southern Cal Roadrunners knocks him over. The player actually hurt himself a little. The drunk gets up again and runs around the bases a third time and slides into home plate, but this time the ground crew beats the crap out of him.

"They carried the kid off the field and the sheriff arrives to arrest him. Diana looked at me and said, 'Bill, you can't let that happen.' I went down to the general manager and asked to cut the kid some slack and they throw me out of the same stadium again! Fifty fucking years later!"

CHAPTER ONE HUNDRED ONE

Baseball 101

National Unplugged Day

"The right side of the brain controls the movement of the left side of the body, and the left side of the brain controls the right side of the body. Therefore, only left-handers are in their right minds."
—Bill "Spaceman" Lee

"I feel so akin to Trevor Bauer, it's unbelievable." *—Bill "Spaceman" Lee*

The earthling known as William Francis Lee, III, believes he has a kindred spirit in young Cincinnati Reds right-hander Trevor Bauer, a delightful iconoclast in his own right. Not only that, but Bauer is also one hell of a pitcher.

While the Spaceman speaks of Santeria, Bokononism, seeks psychological guidance from mystics, quotes Kurt Vonnegut and Buckminster Fuller, is a believer in comfrey root, speaks about Mohorovicic Discontinuity, can quote from *The Rape of Europa*, knows how to create malignum steel and studies the Calusa Indian civilization, Trevor Bauer is one of the few younger athletes around these days that the Spaceman truly admires.

A while ago, the author, either Scott Russell or Kilgore Trout, and that is irrelevant, wrote a brief essay, as it were, regarding the possibly of the older eccentric Lee meeting up with the younger nonconformist, Trevor Bauer. I wrote the following to acknowledge some foolish annual occasion referred to as "National Unplugged Day." The following was my rambling dissertation:

NATIONAL UNPLUGGED DAY

So, have I got your attention? No? Good. You're not supposed to be online today, remember?

I am about to discuss Trevor Bauer, the iconoclastic pitcher, currently toiling for the Cleveland Indians, although it is 99% likely that he will be elsewhere in 2020, and good for him. Have you ever been to Cleveland?

Let me begin by saying that I have been a fan of Bauer's since I read his comments regarding the absurdity of how modern-day pitchers are "handled." Bauer is a throwback to the days of Gaylord Perry, Don Drysdale, Tom Seaver, Warren Spahn, Juan Marichal and those of their ilk (what the hell is an "ilk?" Is it anything like an elk?). Before the days of pitch counts, before the days of babying modern day hurlers into injuries created by some sort of deranged "evolution," men like Leroy "Satchel" Paige roamed the Earth, often pitching three games in one day at three different venues. If "sore arms" existed, they were seldom acknowledged.

Now, if you believe for a moment that I am about to claim that I "understand" Trevor Bauer, you are completely mistaken. Those of you who have read my plus-minus, positive-negative theories are cognizant that it is my belief that to be understood, you first must be completely misunderstood. Follow? No? Good, because if you do not follow, you are "following" to a degree.

I am about to draw an analogy between my old friend Bill "Spaceman" Lee and Trevor Bauer, this despite the fact that no such analogy could possibly exist, at least to a sentient being. Briefly, I will touch on a conversation between Lee and the immortal Ted Williams, arguably the greatest batsman in the history of baseball. I'm almost certain that when Bill approached Teddy Ballgame to discuss hitting in Winter Haven, Florida many years ago, that Williams, an eccentric character in his own right, was hesitant, for lack of a better word, to enter into a discussion with someone Williams most likely believed was not playing with a full deck of cards.

Bill wanted to discuss his "left eye-right eye dominance" theory as it applied to hitters. Incredibly, the great Ted Williams, who knew more about the art and science of hitting than any man in history, was actually enthralled by the Spaceman's theories.

So, now there's Trevor Bauer, an equally seemingly eccentric modern day hurler, apparently espousing some equally seemingly delirious theories about physical conditioning and pitching.... First of all, a disclaimer. I have absolutely NO FUCKING CLUE as to what Trevor Bauer's "theories" are, how he applies them or if anyone other than a handful of people on this planet are capable of comprehending them. If I met Bauer I would simply say, "Have a nice day" and move on. I can barely pronounce "Transcanial Direct Current Stimulation," let alone hope to discuss it with young Mr.

Bauer, nor would he want to engage me in such a forum.... Perhaps Bill Lee would enjoy speaking with Bauer.... I suspect that they'd dislike each other immediately and therefore become good friends...which brings me to...

"The Spaceman," in my opinion, longed to be misunderstood to be understood. Trevor Bauer, on the other hand (in my opinion) desires to be understood to be misunderstood, and by doing so, he would NOT be bothered by the likes of inquiring minds. Such minds would only deter him from his goal(s), which are considerable. Young Mr. Bauer is too busy attempting to master methods that would increase his "synaptic plasticity" to be bothered by such mundane things such as life... life, as it were, or will be, will arrive at the time that Bauer has concluded his current project(s). Capish? No? Good, we are making progress.

So, on a day we are "unplugging," so to speak*, I am honoring those individuals such as Bill Lee & Trevor Bauer, homo sapiens who have been virtually "unplugged" the majority of their adult lives.

I am sort of hoping that Trevor Bauer's career finds him in either New York or Boston next season. That way, I can observe him more closely, but not too closely. It is best to allow nature to take its inexorable course towards God knows what. I would not want to interfere with progress, nor would I understand it. I do not desire to be a nuisance.

Sadly, I believe that young Mr. Bauer will eventually fall prey to the feminine wiles of a beautiful young woman. At that time, another unicorn shall perish.

Note: It should be added that this missive was sent to young Mr. Trevor Bauer, and that his response was, "I love this."

CHAPTER ONE HUNDRED TWO

Home Field Advantage

Infidels!

"I drink too much. The last time I gave a urine sample it had an olive in it." —*Rodney Dangerfield*

Daisy Buchanan's, as you read earlier, was one of the best watering holes in all the northeast. It was not only home to local athletes, but it was also a home away from home for those opponents arriving in town to play versus the Boston teams.

On many occasions, visiting teams arriving to play versus the Red Sox at Fenway Park would no sooner have their bags checked in at the Sheraton, than they would walk a few blocks in order to enjoy some libations and perhaps whatever else Daisy's was "offering." Boys will be boys.

As was pointed out in Chapter Twenty, one of the owners of Daisy's was former Boston Bruins great, Derek Sanderson, who the author discovered face down on the bar on his initial excursion to the popular nightspot. Sanderson, as was his wont, had sampled a bit too much of his own merchandise. Sanderson, along with Joey Cimino and Jimmy McDonough, were the three original owners of Daisy Buchanan's.

Daisy's saw many superstar athletes and entertainers pass through its doors, including Reggie Jackson, Thurman Munson, Leslie Nielsen, Ellen Degeneres, Bobby Orr, Phil Esposito, John Havlicek, and other legends. Daisy's first opened its doors in 1970.

The earthling known as William Francis Lee, III, recently told the author that Daisy's was instrumental in making him a much better pitcher, and not from his own frequent imbibing at the location, although he certainly often indulged in enjoying a brew or ten at the establishment. However, what really enabled the Spaceman to become a greater pitcher were opposing players getting sufficiently plastered at the den of inequity. As Lee explained:

"Those girls! They'd run them in and out of there. There was a back alley that connected to Daisy's and a 'speakeasy,' too. You'd go out the back alley and take a right and you'd be in Daisy's. It was a friggin' highway. It was hard to win in Boston, our opponents would be hammered all the time. I loved to pitch on 'getaway days' (the last game of a home series) because all the hitters would be blind. They all had a twinge in their back and their swings were fucked up."

Lee elaborated that after spending three or four nights drinking and then having to carry their suitcases out of the team hotel, the Red Sox' rivals would be too exhausted to play. As the author told Bill from the outset, I would be researching and corroborating all information he would offer. Once more, the Spaceman was accurate.

During Lee's two initial seasons as a starting pitcher, 1973 & 1974, the Spaceman started a total of 11 series ending games on getaway day and compiled a won-lost record of 8-2 with a 2.70 ERA! Not only that, but Lee hurled an incredible 8 complete games out of those 11, an absurd amount. For the period between 1973 and '75, which comprised three consecutive 17-win seasons, Bill Lee was 11-4 in 16 starts on getaway day, and that included 10 complete games! The names of the young ladies who assisted in those victories have been withheld.

Of course, the Red Sox also went on the road and their records, especially during lengthy west coast trips, were nothing to write home about, both literally and figuratively. The Spaceman would often climb into the cockpit with the pilots and get on the intercom and spew, "Hi, this is Captain Lee speaking. We'll be landing at Logan Airport shortly," and then he'd refresh his teammates' memories as to what their wives' names were and to remind them to slip their wedding rings back on their fingers.

CHAPTER ONE HUNDRED THREE

Unrequited Love

"Bill Lee is a jerk." —*Don Zimmer*

"Looking back over a lifetime, you'll see that love was the answer to everything." —*Ray Bradbury*

The earthling known as William Francis Lee, III, actually attempted to offer an olive branch to Don Zimmer, but the Spaceman's former manager was determined to never accept a peace offering from the man he clearly stated was the only player he'd ever known he would never allow in his home.

The attempt at an accord came at Wrigley Field in Chicago during the summer of 1984. At the time, Zim was the third base coach of the Chicago Cubs and since Lee was in Chicago, he figured he might as well stop in and say hello to his former Red Sox teammate Dennis Eckersley. As Lee recalled:

"Both Eck and former Red Sox pitcher Chuck Rainey were Cubs and thought it would be a good thing if they brought me into the Cubs locker room and try to patch things up with Zim, but Zimmer became apoplectic at the mention of my name and had the clubhouse security guards prevent my entering the locker room. As soon as Zim saw me attempting to enter the locker room, he shouted at me, 'Get out of here, I'm not going to shake your hand, you California faggot!'"

Since the Spaceman was already in Chicago, albeit not in the Cubs clubhouse, he reasoned he may as well hang around and enjoy a ballgame. Therefore, Lee ventured out into the bleachers and within minutes was joined by the Hall of Fame great, Bill Veeck, whose ownership of teams such as the Cleveland Indians, St. Louis Browns, and Chicago White Sox provided fans with some of the most memorable and hilarious moments in baseball history. Veeck was not only a great person, but a great promoter of the game of baseball. Veeck, who had planned to integrate the game even before Branch Rickey, was the first American League owner to field a black player, Larry Doby in 1947. As the Spaceman recalled:

"After Zim threw me out of the clubhouse, I went out to the bleachers. What a great guy. I would've loved to have played for Bill Veeck. As we watched the game, Veeck took off his wooden leg, and as he smoked his cigarettes, he would put out the smoke in an ashtray in his hollow leg. I recalled what Veeck had answered to a woman who called the front office of the St. Louis Browns. The Browns weren't good in those days and they weren't even drawing flies. The woman asked, "What time does the game start?" Bill Veeck answered, 'What time can you get here?"

What the author still finds amusing in Zimmer's biography is his mentioning that he had managed both the Cubs and Red Sox "in two of their most exciting seasons." Yes, and I'm sure that Mary Todd Lincoln was "excited" upon attending that play at the Ford Theater and that the captain of the *Titanic* was "excited" upon seeing rather large icebergs.

During the time that Bill Lee had still not entirely abandoned his hope of returning to the major leagues and attempting to convince himself that someone in power would recognize the abject iniquity of his situation, Lee was pitching at an MSBL (Senior League) Game at Scottsdale Community College. Red Sox southpaw ace Bruce Hurst was several hundred yards away and saw the unmistakable delivery of "Spaceman" Lee. As Bill recalled:

"Hurst noticed me and turned to Jim Lefebvre who was in the San Francisco Giants front office and told him that was me pitching on that field. Lefebvre said, 'No way! I'll bet you a hundred dollars that's not Lee!' Hurst accepted the wager. Lefebvre still owes Hurst a hundred dollars to this day. Lefebvre was nothing more than a hatchet man for the Giants, a real asshole. He was the guy who released me after I had pitched 10 scoreless innings for the San Francisco Giants in 1984 in spring training.

"Let me give you a contrast: During a game I was pitching during that same spring, the veteran catcher Tony Pena was coaching a bunch of minor league players. He interrupted their workout and brought them over to watch me pitch. Pena turned to them and said, 'Come over and watch how Bill Lee works if you want to see a real pitcher!' One guy (Pena) honoring me and the other, the asshole Lefebvre, was nothing more than a hatchet man for the Giants. Lefebvre and Tom Haller, two assholes."

During the spring of 1984, Bill Lee was told unequivocally by those in the game that he had been forever blackballed.

CHAPTER ONE HUNDRED FOUR

A Stone's Throw Away

"I don't have a short temper. I just have a quick reaction to bullshit."
—Elizabeth Taylor

By 1984 it was apparent to nearly everyone that the earthling known as William Francis Lee, III had been forever blackballed by baseball. In 1982, Bill had sent out letters to all twelve National League teams, but merely two took the time to respond. One response came from Pittsburgh Pirates general manager Harding Peterson, who wrote, "We have enough problems with our roster without adding you to our ball club." Hey, at least the man attempted humor.

San Francisco Giants general manager Tom Haller also replied, but his reaction offered little if any reason for optimism. According to Lloyd Herberg of the Arizona Republic, Haller answered, "Don't call us, we'll call you." Pretty sarcastic. However, in 1984, hope finally arrived from an unlikely source, an old friend of the Spaceman.

In the early 1970s, the Boston Red Sox had a batting practice pitcher named Martin Stone. As Bill recalled, "Marty was a terrific batting practice pitcher because he threw a good hard sinker and had a rubber arm. Marty's love of the game was obvious because the guy was a millionaire, but he loved being around the game."

That love of the game resulted in Marty Stone purchasing the Triple A farm team of the San Francisco Giants, the Phoenix affiliate. Marty Stone invited the Spaceman to spring training with the hope that Lee could somehow either make it onto the big league roster or at the very least, as Bill stated, "All I want is a chance to play baseball and have the possibility of moving up to the majors."

As Lloyd Herberg wrote, Haller was then quoted as saying, "Our concern is whether he'd help the Phoenix Giants win and whether he'd help the rest of our system. This is something we'd have to seriously discuss. But his history is history."

Herberg also quoted Phoenix Giants manager Jim Lefebvre as follows: "I'm not concerned about a guy's past. I'm concerned about where his head is now, what his goals are, his intentions, his motivation. What I'd like to do is sit down and have an exchange, find out what his ideas are, tell him our ideas, and hopefully, they're compatible. Then we'll go from there."

In 1984, Martin Stone, former Red Sox batting practice pitcher, invited the Spaceman to spring training. Marty Stone also understood his old friend was a colorful character and therefore remarked, "We're trying to build up the box office attraction of the team. This wouldn't hurt."

As for the major league team, the San Francisco Giants, they could have easily used a veteran southpaw like the Spaceman. The Giants would end up 66-96 in 1984 and their left-handed starting pitcher, Mark Davis would finish 5-17, 5.36. In other words, he sucked. The fact that the Giants drew 1,001,545 at Candlestick Park that summer (11th out of 12 teams) certainly was indicative that having a true character, especially one who had grown up in Marin County, was not exactly bad for business.

Bill Lee was roughed up in his first appearance for the Phoenix Giants in 1984. Then the Spaceman went out and threw a total of ten scoreless innings in his following three appearances, after which Jim Lefebvre, who along with Tom Haller had zero intention of providing the veteran southpaw with a real chance to make the ball club, visited Lee in the clubhouse and essentially told him to get lost.

Bill had also heard from his former manager in both Boston and Montreal, Hall of Famer Dick Williams, who told Bill that if he showed up at San Diego's spring training base in Yuma, Arizona, that he would give him an opportunity to make his ball club since he knew what Bill could do. However, upon his arrival at the ballpark, both Ballard Smith, the owner of the Padres, and Jack McKean, the venerable general manager, stopped the Spaceman from entering the playing field. Both men told Bill Lee that his presence was not welcome. Lee explained that manager Dick Williams had invited him to try out for the ball club, but they insisted that Lee's presence was not appreciated.

Bill Lee and his wife Pam, who had accompanied her husband on the trip, were not going to just abandon the purpose of the visit. Eventually, Bill snuck his way into the clubhouse where he was greeted by his friendly and great manager, Dick Williams, who sadly told Bill the truth, something that very few in major league baseball had the intestinal fortitude to admit. Dick Williams informed his former star pitcher, "Bill, my hands are tied." Bill "Spaceman" Lee, who had dedicated his entire life to playing the game he loved, had been handed an unofficial lifetime ban. Like "Shoeless Joe" Jackson, Bill Lee would never be permitted to wear another major league uniform.

Martin Stone told his old friend, Bill Lee, that there was nothing he could do. The San Francisco Giants ultimately made all personnel decisions and had full autonomy.

Somewhat incredibly, Bill later found out that he had also been blackballed from playing ball in Japan. The tentacles of major league baseball are far-reaching, but at least he now was learning the true identities of the scumbags, whose names he had been aware of for quite some time.

CHAPTER ONE HUNDRED FIVE

The King and His Court

"A celebrity is a person who works hard all of their life to become well known, and then wears dark glasses to avoid being recognized."
—Fred Allen

Steve Dalkowski never made it to the major leagues but is nearly invariably recognized as the hardest thrower in history. He wasn't. As great as Satchel Paige, Sandy Koufax, and Walter Johnson were, no one threw harder than a man who was born Myrle Vernon King, but came to be known as Eddie Feigner.

Myrle King, or Eddie Feigner, was clocked anywhere between 104 to 114 mph and his curve ball dropped 18 inches. Feigner was not a large man, either and his sport was fast-pitch softball. Perhaps even more incredibly, Feigner barnstormed for 55 years and his records will never be broken by another human being.

Eddie Feigner enlisted in the Marine Corps and upon leaving the service he began his remarkable career as the most dominant pitcher in the annals of American sport as an underhanded fast-pitch softball pitcher. Never heard of Eddie Feigner? Well, if you are a baseball fan, I'm sure you've heard of Willie Mays, Willie McCovey, Brooks Robinson, Roberto Clemente, Maury Wills, and Harmon Killebrew. During one occasion in a game televised on *The Wide World of Sports*, Feigner struck out all six legends back to back! Eddie Feigner was unhittable.

The earthling known as William Francis Lee, III, also faced Eddie Feigner. Improbably, a friend of the author, a gentleman named Ted Carpenter, himself a legendary fast-pitch softball pitcher, also squared off versus Feigner, with much the same results as nearly all of "The King's" opponents achieved, that being ignominious loss.

Consider the following: Eddie Feigner pitched in 10,000 games, won 9,743 of them, hurled 930 no-hitters including 238 perfect games, struck out 8,698 hitters while blindfolded, pitched behind his back and between his legs and often from second base! Perhaps even more unlikely, at least one major league team, reportedly the Los Angeles Dodgers, offered

Feigner a major league contract to become a starting pitcher and throw underhanded!

Eddie Feigner rejected the Dodgers offer, and the reason behind his decision is perhaps even more bizarre. You see, at the time of the offer, Eddie Feigner was making considerably more money than any major league baseball player! By touring worldwide, Feigner was earning $100,000 a month and traveling worldwide.

How dominant was Eddie Feigner? Consider the following: Feigner took the field with only three other teammates! He, of course, had a catcher, a first baseman, and a shortstop. Of course, since rarely did the hitters on opposing teams make contact against Feigner's offerings, fielders were a negligible entity. In fact, many of his opponents complained that, since Feigner's batting order comprised of four men, his great hitters would generally bat each inning, an enormous advantage.

I had mentioned my friend, a 6′ 5″ gentleman named Edward "Ted" Carpenter. Each and every time Peg and I would stop in to "briefly" visit Ted upon our excursions to south coastal Maine, after discussing baseball with "Carp," he would motion for Peg to sit down and exclaim, "Relax, this may take a while. Your husband requires an education about the game of baseball." And truthfully, I indeed did.

It was on one of these visits that I learned about Ted's fast-pitch softball career. Ted was an overpowering left-handed hurler, one so proficient at his craft that he hurled several no-hitters and during a four-year period had only lost a total of six games... ALL of them to Eddie Feigner, and this despite the fact that Ted was some twenty years his junior!

Ted would often regale us with tales of being defeated by Feigner. Hey, who wouldn't be proud of losing to perhaps the most dominant pitcher in the annals of softball or baseball? However, it was the story Ted told regarding his initial meeting with Eddie Feigner that was the most amazing. Having never faced Feigner before, being considerably younger and larger than the diminutive Feigner, Ted, also an overpowering pitcher, was not lacking confidence.

Each of the two men overpowered the opposing batters through the first three innings, but in a scoreless game in the fourth inning, Carpenter came to bat against the King. Feigner donned a blindfold and walked out to second base to face the towering Carpenter. Ball one. Ball two. Ball three. Ted Carpenter backed out of the box and addressed Feigner's catcher, former major league Houston Astros slugger John Bateman. Carp asked, "I thought he was better than that?"

Bateman, a character in his own right, responded, "Don't believe everything you see on television." ...Ball four. Ted Carpenter, now full of himself, trotted to first base while thinking to himself, "I can beat this guy!"

It should be noted that in fast-pitch softball, a baserunner is not permitted to take a lead off a base until the ball leaves the pitcher's hand. Feigner returned to the mound and removed his blindfold and prepared to face the next batsman. Feigner went into his windup and threw the next pitch behind his back, except it wasn't to home plate, but to his first baseman who immediately tagged Carpenter, who had been standing no more than a foot off the base. Out! Eddie Feigner then pranced off the hill and pointed to his humiliated opposing pitcher and directed a shout, "That's the first and last time you'll ever reach base against me!" And it was. He had intentionally walked Ted Carpenter to pick him off and completely demoralize him. This was common practice for Feigner.

Upon my recalling this instance to Bill Lee, the Spaceman interrupted me by telling me he had done the very same thing to him. Following that initial time, Lee would warn his teammates to not get pissed off when Feigner embarrassed them. Bill stated that his job was to prevent anyone from charging the mound. The Spaceman recalled touring with Eddie Feigner as follows:

"I toured with 'The King and his Court' through New Brunswick and Ontario one summer. Feigner was certainly no youngster, but he was still great. Feigner had a great catcher named Estrada from Washington State, just north of Portland, the brother of actor Erik Estrada of 'Chips.' We played about three five-inning games in Woodstock (Ontario), Grand Falls (New Brunswick) and Edmonston (New Brunswick). By the time we reached Edmonston it was raining pretty hard and the game was rained out. I had gone out to get Feigner a pint of vodka, something I would do between each game. By the time we got off the bus and he got out of his van, Feigner was hammered. Since the game had been rained out and there was a crowd there to see Feigner, he felt compelled to talk to his fans. He took the microphone and told the gathering he was going to give a "talk." He gives this twenty-minute speech and he appeared stone-cold sober! He gave the greatest semiconscious presentation to this large group of fans and they gave him a standing ovation. Then we all drove back to Moncton,

New Brunswick. The man was amazing."

As for my old friend, Ted Carpenter, we lost him to esophageal cancer several years ago. Upon passing his home in Moody, Maine each summer and fall, we are saddened upon driving by the house where he would provide me with a wonderful education about the game of baseball. Ted's nephew was not too shabby of a hurler, either. Chris Carpenter, an equally imposing 6′ 6″ presence on the hill, won a Cy Young Award while pitching for the St. Louis Cardinals, a team he presently works for as an executive in their front office.

As stated, Eddie Feigner's name at birth was "Myrle King." However, he was put up for adoption at birth by his mother, who had Myrle at an all too young age. Myrle was almost immediately adopted by the Feigner family, who also lived in Walla Walla, Washington. Therefore, Myrle King became Eddie Feigner. Many years later, as a teenager, Eddie Feigner contracted the job of cutting a young woman's lawn in Walla Walla. Neither the woman nor Feigner realized at the time that she was Feigner's biological mother!

> Note: "Eddie Feigner and I played on the reservation where Anna Mae Aquash was born!" —*Bill "Spaceman" Lee*
>
> "It would behoove all those reading this book to research the incredible life of the late, great Anna Mae Aquash, a life cut short by unspeakable injustice." —*Bill "Spaceman" Lee*

CHAPTER ONE HUNDRED SIX

Hallowed Hall of Assholes

"It is my sincere desire that my research and hard work will help create a world where we will all learn to walk this Earth, safe, enlightened and free from the perils of cruelty, ignorance, and all of the other dark and sinister forces, which make assholes." —*Alexei Maxim Russell in* Alexei Maxim Russell's Field Guide to Assholes.

"Explain to me how you having a problem with me is my problem?" —*Dan Pearce*

In the initial 105 chapters of this monument to literary greatness, we have made mention of countless dishonorable scoundrels and miscreants. These unworthy ne'er do-wells have in one way or another adversely affected either the physical or mental well-being of the earthling known as William Francis Lee, III, an act which in some foreign nations would be punishable by no less than death.

In order to sufficiently reprimand these wretched disreputable disturbers of the peace (after all, the Spaceman is descended from Mary, Queen of Scots), since the lot of this ignominious group's deeds have already been documented in the prior chapters of this book, we will now rank them according to their level of incorrigibility. And to be entirely effective, we will have a countdown until we reach the very bottom of what it is to have zero redeemable value.

In most instances, these rankings will not be further explained, unless we feel that some confusion may exist.

10. Bill "Spaceman" Lee—the subject of this book insisted that he be included on this list of disreputable individuals, and upon further review (actually there was no review, it wasn't necessary), he has legitimately earned this distinction. Just read the book and if you disagree with the Spaceman's inclusion on this list of reprobates, well, it is likely that you are an asshole, too.

9. Haywood (Hayride) Sullivan & Bill Crowley—It's a tie. These two fine upstanding individuals have both committed numerous ill-advised (just exactly WTF does "ill-advised" mean anyhow? Does someone really advise such foolishness?) acts, including Crowley's feeble attempt to banish George Kimball from the Fenway Park press box.

8. Keith Hernandez—a great-fielding villain whose memory regarding his "drug partners" is suspect at best and highly questionable. He does receive a few brownie-points, however, for his disdain for Mr. Met. Listening to Hernandez broadcasting during Mets games, I get the impression he would rather be elsewhere... most likely because he would rather be elsewhere.

7. Congressman Albert "Dapper" O'Neil & Al Campanis—two latter day segregationists.

6. Bowie Kuhn—for more reasons than imaginable.

5. Hal Lanier—A man with no sense of history who should have paid heed to his father, Max.

4. Billy Martin—as the Spaceman so aptly described him, "a no-good dirty rat."

3. Tom Haller & Jim Lefebvre—once more, we have a tie. These two devious and discreditable bootlickers conspired to help those treacherous bastards in barring Bill Lee away from the game he so loves(d).

2. Walter O'malley—this designation particularly pains the author of this tome. O'malley is the contemptible lowlife that not only ripped the hearts out of tens of thousands of Brooklyn Dodgers fans, but also attempted to trade Jackie Robinson. As Billy Hamill, the late father of the great columnist and author Pete Hamill so eloquently stated, "My goal in life is to locate Walter O'malley's grave and urinate on it." I share that endeavor. O'malley will forever remain #1 reprehensible asshole to yours truly.

1. & 1A. John McHale & Jim Fanning—We have a winner! Or perhaps winners, in this instance... it is virtually impossible to choose a larger asshole between these two nefarious weasels. As documented throughout this tale, these two ignoble cretins have somehow reached the very pinnacle of despicability. #1 & 1A are interchangeable, dependent on the memory and moment.

Note: as for the author himself, either Scott Russell or Kilgore Trout, you can rest assured that this scurrilous depraved imbecile is most definitely an asshole of epic proportion. However, he is far too modest and handsome to sing his own praises. And he is fucking proud of it!

CHAPTER ONE HUNDRED SEVEN

Honorable Mention Assholes

One can only imagine his disappointment on not attaining Bill "Spaceman" Lee's "Hallowed Hall of Assholes" registry. After all, despite the designation being subjective, simply being selected to this roster of noteworthy scoundrels provides a validation that can only be achieved by truly despicable acts, or one would certainly think so. Therefore, we have created an "honorable mention" category.

To be clear, being labeled an asshole does not preclude an individual from perhaps also being a person worthy of respect and in some rare instance, admiration. It is merely an earmark, indicating a proficiency in the art form. Conversely, a good person can also be stamped as an asshole. The stigma is real. Get over it. Move on with your life.*

> * Note: For those no longer among the living, well, we have not quite figured that out yet. The Spaceman did remark just this morning (that's a while ago for those reading this book) that both he and the author are more than likely "on the back nine, and since we're on the seventeenth hole, who gives a fuck?"

There will be no countdown for the "Honorable Mention Register of Assholes," however. I am not even going to take the time to alphabetize it or rank it. If you want that much friggin' research, seek out Ken Burns, Jane Leavy, or John Thorn. The Spaceman and yours truly are on our last legs; let us die in peace, thereby pissing off as many people as we possibly can.

So, in the name of bipartisanship, here is a list of honorable mention assholes. If you are angry at your exclusion, well, you might be an asshole:

- Dr. Harry Edwards—As the Spaceman stated, "Edwards' heart is in the right place, but his head is up his ass."
- Jeff Dowd (The Big Lebowski)—"at least the bastard is funny."
- Bernie Carbo—"I love Bernie, but he can be an asshole."
- Dave Kingman—"No explanation necessary to anyone who's met him."

- Carlton Fisk—"Carlton Fisk is the only man who will be on his deathbed for three years."
- Jerry Remy—"Middle infielder. It's synonymous."
- Rick Burleson—See Remy.
- Ralph Chambers—"Kicked me off the Moncton Mets. They have this plaque of Chambers on the wall to commemorate his 'contributions.' I used to pee on it, but the bastards moved it higher on the wall, and at my age I can no longer piss that high."
- John Stearns
- Vern Rapp
- George W. Bush—"Not a bad dude, though. Just a bit slow."
- Tom Yawkey—"At least he's done some good things, too."
- Ballard Smith & Jack McKean
- Henry Aaron—"Yes, he's an American hero, but he pissed me off. Not only that, but if he had retired a half-year earlier, I would've given up his final home run, but he decided to play some more."
- Carl Yastrzemski—At least he attempted to convince Zim to start me, but who the hell is going to listen to the son of a Polish potato farmer? Ask Luis Aparicio if Yaz is an asshole."
- Dick Young
- Eddie Feigner—"Double designation. He was also an admirable asshole."
- John Kennedy—"Middle infielder."

CHAPTER ONE HUNDRED EIGHT

Mostly Honorable and Virtuous List

Well, at least not entirely defiled

Note: an asterisk indicates that the person was on occasion, also an asshole.

"Chuck" Diana's noble dog, Mike & Deirdre Mulkern, Ozzie Virgil, Jr., Dick Gregory—"A Saint!", Tony Perez, John Milner, Ferguson Jenkins, Jim Willoughby, Ed McNally, Randy White, Gordy Grayburn aka "Dr. Zoom," Ben Benson, Rod Dedeaux, George Kimball—lovingly, Carl Yastrzemski,*Woody Harrelson—"The best dope smoking actor of all time." Frank Mahovlich, Bobby Hull,*Jimmy Piersall,*Dick Williams,*Tommy Lasorda, Dan Shaughnessy,*Peter Gammons, Marvin Miller, Marty Stone, Alex Karras —"Precious!", Bill Campbell, Rogelio Moret, Rodney Scott, Louis Ledoux, Rick Wise, Luis Tiant, Dennis Eckersley, Jim Kaat, George Scott, Phil Shinnick, David Silber, Jack & Mikki Scott.

Speaking of Saints...
The Spaceman Meets the Protopopovs and Vice Versa

For many years, the author and his wife were benefactors of "An Evening with Champions," a figure skating exhibition benefitting the Dana Farber Children's Cancer Institute. Of course, we invited the earthling known as William Francis Lee, III to the event. It was at one of these events that two of the most eccentric athletes of our times were introduced to each other.

Oleg Alekseyevich Protopopov was one of the most dominant athletes of the twentieth century. As a pairs figure skater representing the Soviet Union, Oleg and his partner, the beautiful Ludmila Belousova, ruled the world of ice skating to the tune of winning 13 gold medals. These championships included being the first Olympic pairs gold medal ever attained by the Soviets. This breakthrough occurred in 1964. Then they repeated their triumph in 1965 by winning the gold at both the World and European Championships and thus becoming the first Russians to ever win those. Oleg and lovely Ludmila were renowned for their grace and humility on and off the ice.

They were married in December 1957, although Ludmila retained her maiden name of Belousova although they became known as Oleg and Ludmila Protopopov. The elegant pair invented what was referred to by the media as "The Death Spiral," an amazing and thrilling maneuver never seen before. However, Oleg refused to call it by its seemingly dour name and routinely called it "The Life Spiral" or "The Love Spiral."

During a competition in September 1979, Oleg and his beautiful bride applied for asylum and from then on would make their winter home in Switzerland and their summer home in Lake Placid, New York. I can state unequivocally that I have never met more gracious, humble, or genuinely compassionate human beings in my life. Each year Oleg and Ludmila would greet us as if we were long-lost family members. There was no false pretense, they just exuded kindness.

Oleg Protopopov was, as I stated, eccentric. In fact, he was extremely eccentric, but always delightful. Consider that one of Oleg's good friends was a Dr. Volkov who lived in St. Petersburg, Russia. Oleg claimed that Dr. Volkov had solved the mystery of aging by replacing the hydrogen in our bodies. By replacing hydrogen, this would negate the gravitational pull and prevent us from getting older. Oleg told me that major pharmaceutical companies had placed a "hit" on his life and that Dr. Volkov had gone into hiding. Oleg also informed Peg and me that he routinely underwent daily enemas, thus cleansing any poisonous buildup within his body. Strange? Perhaps, but consider that in his late eighties Oleg Protopopov still skates elegantly on the ice.

Sadly, we lost Ludmila on September 26, 2017 at the age of eighty-one. Ludmila Yevgenyevna Belousova was one of the most sweet-natured, kindhearted, and gentle women who ever walked on planet Earth.

It was at Harvard University that I introduced the Spaceman to the Protopopovs, neither of them knowing anything about each other or the sports they competed at. I then walked away to allow nature to take its course. As Bill Lee and Oleg began what appeared to be a deep philosophical discussion, I was approached by the brilliant young co-chair of the event, a Harvard Senior named Kris Mendez. Kris smiled and said, "God, would I love to be able to hear whatever Oleg and Bill Lee were discussing." The conversation went on for a considerable amount of time. I know in my heart that if it were videoed, it would have made a great documentary on PBS.

CHAPTER ONE HUNDRED NINE

Addendum to the Hallowed Hall of Assholes

> "A guy who walks and straddles the rails goes nowhere. The man whose legs leave the rail crushes his nuts." *—Bill "Spaceman" Lee*

The earthling known as William Francis Lee, III, really enjoyed playing for Rod Dedeaux and Dick Williams, two winners. The recently departed Eddie Kasko, not so much. Kasko, another middle infielder as Lee reminds us, is just another in a long line of second basemen and shortstops who have been the bane of his existence. For the record, Kasko managed Bill Lee from 1970-73.

Eddie Kasko, who passed on June 27, 2020 at the age of eighty-eight, was not considered a genius by the Spaceman. As Bill remarked upon learning of Kasko's passing, "Kasko was a towel eating, washrag shitting, bespectacled, little slick-fielding motherfucker." How is that for an intriguing resume? Eddie Kasko could often be seen seated in the Red Sox dugout chewing on a towel.

Politics have no place in sports, but unfortunately, the self-appointed "bastions of integrity" run the show. The vast majority of Red Sox fans can rattle off the most disappointing years of the storied franchise, seasons such as 1975, 1978, and 1986, but as "Spaceman" Lee points out, the 1972 campaign was a bitter pill to swallow. The season began or did not begin in this instance, because of the "lockout" that delayed the season's openers until mid-April. The delay also resulted in an uneven schedule, one in which teams were forced to play a different amount of games than one another. It was truly bizarre, and it resulted with the Red Sox visiting Detroit in a three-game season-ending series, albeit one that had the Tigers playing one more game than the Red Sox! The winner of that series would go on to the postseason.

Because of the lockout, the players had to agree to a new collective bargaining agreement before they would be allowed to play. The Red Sox opened the '72 season at Tiger Stadium in Detroit on Saturday, April 15. The starting pitchers were Detroit's outstanding rotund left-hander, Mickey Lolich, and Marty Pattin toed the rubber for the Sox. In the top of the first inning, the Red Sox were poised to take a formidable lead. They loaded the bases with one out and Sox slugger Rico Petrocelli stepped to the plate. Rico promptly smashed a base hit to left field which scored Tommy Harper. Luis Aparicio, the runner at second base, came tearing around third base with what would have been the second run, but Luis fell down.

Luis Aparicio, Hall of Fame shortstop, a renowned great base-stealer and baserunner simply fell to the ground. Yes, the field conditions were slick after some precipitation, perhaps a harbinger of things to come. Carl Yastrzemski, another Hall of Famer, but a player renowned for running with his head down, never noticed Aparicio had gone down. Therefore, upon Yaz arriving at third base, he was surprised to see it occupied by Aparicio. Yastrzemski, of course, was tagged out. End of rally. The Tigers won the game 3-2. It portended this was not to be a good year for the Red Sox.

Fast forward to Monday, October 2, 1972, the beginning of the aforementioned three game series that would decide who plays in the postseason and who goes home, both literally and figuratively. Home plate was an elusive destination for Luis Aparicio in 1972, at least in Detroit.

Incredibly, just as he had been on opening day, Mickey Lolich was the Detroit starting pitcher. With the Tigers ahead 1-0 in the third inning, the Red Sox seemed to be mounting a significant rally. With one out and the speedy duo of Tommy Harper at second and Luis Aparicio at first, Red Sox superstar Carl Yastrzemski stepped to the plate. Sound familiar? Yaz blasted a Lolich pitch deep into the right-centerfield gap, way over the head of the Tigers centerfielder Mickey Stanley. For those that recall Tigers Stadium, the fence was 440 feet away!

Obviously, Tommy Harper scored standing up and Luis Aparicio, and you cannot make this shit up, stumbled as he approached third base. Just as the field in Detroit was slick on April 15, guess what? It had rained once more. Not only did Aparicio, stumble, but as he regained his feet, he tripped over third base! Aparicio, who had all friggin' day to score since the ball was deep in the outfield, rather than attempting to complete his trek to home plate, decided to return to third base! Remember who hit the ball? Yup, it was Yastrzemski who was wont for running with his fucking head down.

As Yaz pulled up at third base with an easy triple, he was once more surprised, and not pleasantly, at seeing Luis Aparicio standing on the already occupied base. Captain Carl had no option other than attempt to return to second base, but that did not turn out too well, either, as Aurelio Rodriguez, who as the Spaceman pointed out, was the only player with all the vowels in his name (seriously, who thinks of that kind of stuff?), tagged him out. End of rally. The Tigers and Lolich would go on to win 4-1, which pretty much signified the end of the season.

Please recall now that the Spaceman was not too enamored with manager and recent addition to the "Hallowed Halls of Assholes," Eddie Kasko, and here is why:

Not only did Kasko create an unlikely set of circumstances leading to what certainly was bad karma, but not giving Lee an opportunity to start ballgames in 1972, Bill felt, led to the demise of the team. Farfetched? Well, hear him out:

"Why was John Curtis pitching and not me? By having Curtis pitch that game against Lolich, we had already lost. And I was drunk on a pool table in Birmingham and that's documented. I was 9-2, 2.74 in 1971 and the SOB wouldn't start me? What the fuck was he thinking? Well, here's what happened: During the off-season, I had been taking college courses to graduate from USC, Spanish 3 and a communications course at the university in Lakeland, a college whose architect was Buckminster Fuller. On the way home I stopped in a 'head-shop' and picked up a Rolling Stones 'tongue' T-shirt that read, 'Lick Dick in '72.' Kasko saw me in the clubhouse wearing the shirt and I never got a start. That cost us a pennant."

The Spaceman continued:

"If Kasko had given me the ball two weeks earlier and halfway through the season, things would've been much different. Speaking of assholes, when we were at the Lindell AC in Detroit, those two radio pricks Cliff Keane and Larry Claflin said we didn't deserve to win because of the strike! What the fuck?! Aparicio falls down on opening day, Yaz runs with his head down and in the final series the same exact thing happens at the same fucking ballpark with the same pitcher on the mound! 1972 sucked as much as 1975, 1978, and 1986."

CHAPTER ONE HUNDRED TEN

Ellie Rodriguez, Graig Nettles, and Mary Lou: Three Sluggers

"The secret behind a happy marriage remains a secret."
—*Henny Youngman*

"Marriage is a great institution, but who wants to live in an institution?" —*Groucho Marx*

Upon my asking the identity of the three greatest hitters he ever faced, the earthling known as William Francis Lee, III did not hesitate in responding, and he ranked them in countdown order:

3. Graig Nettles—"Although Nettles had a terrific right hand, he was aided by the fact that when he clobbered me, my left shoulder had already been severely injured and I couldn't bring my left arm up to defend myself. However, all things being equal, that was a good shot."

2. Ellie Rodriguez—"Ellie got me good with a one-punch right hand outside of the Caguas ballpark. It was payback for hitting him after Willie Montanez decided to do the cha-cha-cha after hitting a home run off me and dancing around the bases like Dennis Rodman on Valentine's Day. I was pissed and I took it out on Ellie. Ellie charged the mound and I knocked him down with a left hook before everyone else jumped in and stopped the fight."

1. "We have a winner! The former Mary Lou Helfrich, my first wife, hit me with the best fucking right hand I've ever been clobbered with. I was unconscious for a good five minutes. It was in 1978 and I blame *Sports Illustrated* and another Mike Lupica type crepe-souled Gucci shoe wearing little prick named Curry Kirkpatrick!"*

> * The author believes that this type of designation is not necessarily intended with malice. As with Dr. Hunter S. Thompson, when he referred to someone as "a mutant pig-fucker" and threatened to "rip his lungs out," it normally meant that he actually admired you... at least somewhat.

As best as I can, I will now attempt to describe the animosity between the Spaceman and Ellie Rodriguez. As Lee stated above, he did not take kindly to Willie Montanez, a colorful and flashy ballplayer, emulating Mikhail Baryshnikov after blasting a home run off Lee. Lee is old school, but then again, so is Ellie Rodriguez. Therefore, when Lee not only drilled Rodriguez in the ribs with a fastball but preceded the act by yelling at him from the mound, Senor Rodriguez did what any self-respecting former Golden Gloves winning boxer would do and charged the mound. In truth, the Spaceman did not direct his anger wisely, Rodriguez, a fine gentleman incidentally, one who hailed from Fajardo, Puerto Rico, but was raised in the Bronx, was not the kind of individual Bill Lee should have provoked.

After Rodriguez's short excursion to confront Lee, Bill stepped aside to deftly block Rodriguez's right hand and got lucky by landing a solid left hook which decked the charging off-balanced catcher. As in most baseball "fights," the two men were separated before any additional fisticuffs could ensue, very likely a good thing for the Spaceman, because, well, he was not a Golden Gloves winning fighter. In fact, Bill was not a fighter.

The events following the Lee-Rodriguez "conflict" remain somewhat contentious to this day, dependent on whom you speak with. What is known, however, is that on November 20, 1970, Eliseo Rodriguez waited outside the ballpark in Caguas, and the first person he saw getting off the Mayaguez team bus was none other than the Spaceman. Again, being an actual fighter was a great advantage for Rodriguez. One quick right hand and the "fight" ended before it began. Unfortunately for Bill Lee, his trip to the ground was interrupted by a handrail. Dental repair was required.

It should be noted that Eliseo Rodriguez was a darned good defensive catcher who played for the Yankees, Kansas City, Milwaukee, and the Dodgers. It should also be noted that Ellie and I share a friend, a gentleman named David Diaz, also a former Bronx native, who is an encyclopedia of baseball knowledge. Ellie's son, Ellie, Jr. is a golf pro at the Dorado Beach Country Club and is a graduate of Fordham University in the Bronx, and

Lee, an avid golfer, will hopefully reunite with his old "boxing" partner over a few rounds of golf.

As the Spaceman and the author have discussed ad infinitum, life is often astrologically connected in weird ways. In his youth, Ellie Rodriguez lived in the Bronx at 174th Street and Boston Road… as did the author. In fact, I lived at 1428 Crotona Park East just around the corner and up a steep hill from Boston Road. And then I moved to 1683 Boston Road! Ellie and I were neighbors!

It gets even more cosmic: Ellie Rodriguez attended P.S. 61 in the Bronx, as did I. Ellie then attended J.H.S. 98 (Herman Ritter Junior High School) as did I. But as good of a right-hand as Ellie Rodriguez had, Bill's former Miss Alaska, Miss Universe contestant wife, Mary Lou, possessed a right-hand that Joe Louis would be envious of.

I had mentioned the Spaceman not being particularly fond of either *Sports Illustrated* or its writer, Curry Kirkpatrick, both of whom contributed to the former Mary Lou Helfrich landing a perfect right hand to the temple of Bill "Spaceman" Lee, placing the southpaw in a comatose state for five minutes. Hang on, folks, this is a good one.

In 1978, the earthling known as William Francis Lee, III, had already been taken to task by the conservative Red Sox management by the time he was featured in a *Sports Illustrated* article in August of 1978. Fined and reprimanded for staging a one-day walkout after his teammate and friend Bernardo Carbo had been traded, a transaction which began the demise of the '78 team, in a piece written by *Sports Illustrated* staff writer Curry Kirkpatrick, the Spaceman's future in Boston became even more dubious.

It was in August of 1978 that Don Zimmer, in his infinite wisdom, decided that his bothersome left-hander could "no longer get major league hitters out," a debatable opinion since an established pitcher with a 3.46 ERA is generally viewed by most baseball aficionados as a desirable commodity. But this is Don Zimmer we are discussing, and we have certainly pointed out Zim's less than cogent logic. Then came Curry Kirkpatrick's article on Lee, a fine article, truthfully. Except that the essay also contained photographs. Wives read magazines, too. Lots of them, in fact.

In Kirkpatrick's feature article on the Spaceman, there was a wonderful photo of Bill and Mary Lou's three children, Michael, Andy, and Kate climbing a rope and cavorting on it and beneath a tree outside of their home in Belmont, Massachusetts. Domestic tranquility. The piece was titled, "In an Orbit All his Own," and it accurately described Mary Lou as Bill's "blonde frizz-curled jewel of a wife"... and the next panel included a photograph of the Spaceman seated on a barstool at Daisy Buchanan's surrounded on both sides by two rather attractive young women. In front of the two women, on the bar, were two Molson Goldens. As Lee attempted to explain to his enraged wife, "It looked like I had bought the beers for the girls, but I had just purchased them and I was in the process of carrying them back to where Curry Kirkpatrick was conducting his interview. The *Sports Illustrated* photographer took a photograph at that very moment and the two young women just happened to see an opportunity for a photo op. Mary Lou was livid, of course."

On another occasion, without getting into specific details, Mary Lou, an enormously patient and brilliant young woman, and one not entirely devoid of "flakiness" herself, became even more incensed as she and the Spaceman were seated in a car outside their home at the Knollsbrook Condominiums in Stoughton. A brief discussion ensued regarding a myriad of issues. What resulted was a much more powerful clout than Muhammad Ali floored Sonny Liston with at Lewiston, Maine. As Lee recalled:

"I was out for a good five minutes. Mary Lou came from a military family. Her grandfather was the commander of the Allied fleet in the Pacific before Admiral Halsey. The Dutch, of course, controlled the Pacific. She had a hell of a right."

In the fine article by Kirkpatrick, incidentally, he wrote:

"More often than not, Lee's act has been punctuated by his blurting out a lyric or two from a rock song with which nobody in his right mind would be familiar with unless he has an FM receiver firmly embedded in his gizzard."

As for the Red Sox front office, Kirkpatrick noted:

"In Lee, team officials saw a flaming radical, junk-balling journeyman left-hander with no fastball, no loyalty and no moral values. Yet they also saw a media hero who visited all the sick children, kept the sports talk shows in clover and drew crowds at Fenway Park."

"Spaceman" Lee, of course, was far better than a "journeyman pitcher."

Those that read the article were not surprised to learn that during the middle of a tight game at USC, Lee called a conference on the mound, and as coach Rod Dedeaux, Lee's catcher, and several infielders converged on the mound, the Spaceman informed them that his lips were chapped. The loquacious Rod Dedeaux, arguably the greatest baseball coach in NCAA history was never at a loss for words. As the Spaceman told the author, Rod peered at his eccentric left-hander and responded, "I'm not out here to kiss you, Bill."

Lee was quoted, and accurately so, that the Red Sox had "the whitest team in baseball," and added, "Just look at the hierarchy of the ball club. We could have a winning team made up of the black and Latin American guys who've been traded away."

Upon the author relocating from New York to Boston during the tumultuous 1970s, I befriended a beautiful young Armenian American woman named Linda Kalaydjian. Linda hooked me up with a few communications majors at Emerson College who asked if I could possibly convince the Spaceman to possibly appear on their radio program on a Saturday morning. Upon arriving at the studio, a brilliant golden-throated young African American student named Steve Jackson, who hailed from Pasadena, asked Bill while on the air, "So, what does it take to be a Red Sox."

Bill, and there was no delay or pause button, immediately and truthfully responded, "Well, first of all, you've got to be white." It was a candid, truthful, and honest reply. At the time, Jim Rice was the only remaining African American on the ball club.

CHAPTER ONE HUNDRED ELEVEN

Seeing Double

"Get your facts first, then you can distort them as you please."
—Mark Twain

In March of 1977, the author found himself seated in the lounge at the Holiday Inn in Winter Haven, Florida. The occasion was spring training and it also happened to coincide with something called a "honeymoon" with my first wife. Imagine spending your honeymoon with the earthling known as William Francis Lee, III, our mutual friend, George Kimball, and the Boston Red Sox. The reason why we were indoors and not outside at Chain O' Lakes Park was because that afternoon's ballgame had been rained out. For those not aware, it fucking rains in Florida every day, it's just the amount of precipitation that varies.

What better way to pass the time away than to get sufficiently sloshed while watching a who's who of the planet stop by to pay their respects to the great George Kimball, who as I mentioned earlier holds the unfortunate distinction of having introduced me to my first wife? In and out they strode, the crème de la crème of society all the way down the scale to what some might perceive as the dregs of society, but all friends of Kimball, who seemingly was well-known to every living creature on planet Earth. The great Doris Kearns Goodwin, her equally erudite *New York Times* husband author, Richard Kearns Goodwin, journalists, ballplayers, performers, perhaps a trapeze artist or two, and most definitely a few women of questionable repute. Just where I fit in is still up for debate.

After a libation or eight, I noticed that Jim Willoughby, one of the Spaceman's teammates and good friends, was standing somewhat forlornly near the front entrance of the dimly lit establishment. "Willow" was, of course, one of the esteemed members of the bane of manager Don Zimmer's existence, the renowned counter-culture group of Red Sox known as the Buffalo Head Gang. Kimball excused himself, arose from the table, and approached Willow, who had beckoned him. Willow appeared "ashen-faced."

Upon returning to our table, George Kimball sat back down and said softly:

"Willow's in huge trouble. His wife just arrived unexpectedly from California with their two kids."

I surmised what I had suspected and therefore asked Kimball, "Well, can't he get rid of the woman he's with?"

George, himself a man who often found himself "over the line," responded:

"It's not that easy, Scotty. You see, the woman in his room is his other wife, and neither woman is aware of the other's existence."

Now, you may ask how a man can get himself in such a predicament, but this was Jim Willoughby we were talking about, and no, Willow is not a dumb guy, but as Kimball explained:

"Amazingly, Willow has families on both coasts. He plays winter ball and has somehow kept both families unaware of the other." A bit later I asked the Spaceman to even offer conjecture as to how Willow, a bright guy, ever managed to get himself into a situation which most Hollywood producers would not even accept as a script. Lee then offered:

"Firewater has always adversely affected the thought processes of Native Americans."

For the record, Jim Willoughby is a great guy, but of course, as a member of the allegedly infamous Buffalo Head Gang, quite a character in his own right. And yes, Willow is a Pottawatomi Indian. Willow's great aunt was apparently Mamie Echo Hawk, who served as the tribe's chief lobbyist in Washington, D.C. Upon ending his playing career, Willow was named coach of the Suffolk University baseball club in Massachusetts in December 1980, but that employment ended abruptly after four months, following a "bat-throwing incident." There was no mention if "firewater" may have been involved. Several years later, Willow joined the Winter Haven Red Sox in the Senior Professional Baseball League, joining his former Buffalo Head brethren "Spaceman" Lee, Bernie Carbo, Rick Wise, and Fergie Jenkins, who served as coach.

Willow eventually became a construction contractor and built houses on the west slope of the Sierra Nevadas. Willoughby has been married three times, although the author does not know if the three women are aware of each other's existence.

Recently, the Spaceman told the author of still another magnificent and equally improbable tale involving another former teammate. Hold on to your hats for this one. As the Spaceman explained:

"In 1977, we had a right-hander on our club named Tom Murphy, a tall kid (6' 3" tall) from Ohio University, a really good guy. Murphy was quiet and a real hard worker. Not too many people knew, but Murphy had an identical twin. We were in Anaheim to play the Angels, and Zimmer walked over to where Murphy was shagging flies in the outfield during batting practice. At least Zimmer thought it was Tom Murphy. It wasn't.

"Murphy's identical twin brother had gone into the Red Sox locker room before the game and put on Murphy's uniform. Zim goes over to Murphy and begins to speak with him about what his role would be that night as a reliever. Suddenly Murphy, the twin, looks at Zimmer and starts yelling at him:

"'Get out of my face, you fat ugly motherfucker! Who the fuck told you to bother me? Get your ass back in the dugout where you belong!' Don Zimmer was of course, shocked.

"Zimmer walked away shaking his head. Zim was irate but he had no idea what to do. He had never once had a problem with Tom Murphy."

As for Jim Willoughby, Lee recalls still another incident involving the eccentric relief pitcher. As Lee remembered:

"Willow got himself in another predicament. Willow, who was a paranoid guy to begin with, had gone into the locker room and swallowed an entire ball of hash during batting practice. Then Willow returned to the outfield, but he was glassy-eyed and Bernie (Carbo) and I could see he was completely wrecked. He staggered over to where we were standing and began to weave back and forth. Just before Willow was about to go down, Bernie and I held him up. Our pitching coach, Al Jackson, saw that Willoughby was in distress and asked, 'What the fuck is wrong with Willow?'"

Well, the Spaceman and Bernie filled their pitching coach in regarding what had occurred. Jackson wisely advised, "Jesus, don't let Zim see him like this!" As Lee continued:

"Bernie and I practically carried Willow into the bullpen and propped him up underneath some blankets. He was completely stoned on the hash. He fell asleep in a sitting position. Eventually he began to awake, but I think he was hallucinating. He didn't even move an inch until Zimmer called down to the bullpen in the late innings. Zim wanted Willow to warm up. Willow got up, staggered to the pitching rubber, threw a few pitches and the next thing you know, Zimmer waved him into the game. Willow goes out to the mound, although I don't think his feet ever touched the ground, throws one pitch, and gets a groundball out. It was the most amazing fucking pitching performance I've ever seen. From a coma to a one-pitch out!"

CHAPTER ONE HUNDRED TWELVE

Fields of Dreams

> "Ninety percent I'll spend on good times, women and Irish Whiskey. The other ten percent I'll probably waste." —*Tug McGraw upon being asked what he planned to do with his substantial World Series share in 1980.*

Frank Edwin "Tug" McGraw was one of the most beloved and eccentric players in major league history. Tug was also a good friend of the earthling known as William Francis Lee, III. As was Bill Lee, of course, Tug was left-handed.

Tug McGraw loved to have fun. He was also a terrific relief pitcher, a closer who saved 180 games during his 19-year major league career. Somewhat improbably, Tug toiled for only two ball clubs during those glorious 19 years, the New York Mets from 1965-1974 and the Philadelphia Phillies from 1975-1984. McGraw won two World Series championships, one with the Mets in 1969 and another in 1980 with the Phillies, and in fact, recorded the last out of that World Series versus the Kansas City Royals. That Phillies victory ended a 97-year Phillies World Series drought! However, Tug is perhaps best remembered for his battle cry for the 1973 pennant winning Mets, "Ya gotta believe!"

Tug liked to party, and perhaps appropriately was the last active major league player to have played for Casey Stengel! McGraw's nickname "Tug," derived from hilarity. As an infant, McGraw's mom, Mabel named him "Tug" because of how aggressive he was while breast feeding. As the Spaceman stated, "Tug was always a breast man."

McGraw pulled off a rare double, as he was beloved by both Mets and Phillies fans, not a common occurrence. The Spaceman and Tug were truly kindred spirits and on occasion travelled together. As Lee recalled:

"Once we were in Seoul, Korea and we got absolutely hammered. Both of us could hardly stand up. We decided to walk it off, but we were so hung over neither of us could think straight. We saw this palace up on a hill and Tug suggested we walk up to it and 'find God.' It was hotter than hell and these guards stopped us and shouted, 'You can't go any further!'

They wound up detaining us. After they finally let us go, we walked over to the U.S. embassy. Tug is pissed, he wanted to see God. Tug walked over to a Marine guard (Tug was a Marine, too) and Tug introduces himself. Word gets out that they have a 'distinguished visitor,' and the next thing you know, the U.S. ambassador to Korea takes us out to lunch."

The Spaceman also recalled seeing McGraw "passed out in a fireplace in Pennsylvania. He just collapsed there. His wine glass was over backwards."

Bill Lee and Tug McGraw were two of a kind. Lee recalls what occurred when both men attempted to return to the hotel they were staying at, but as the Spaceman remembered:

"Tug and I were hungover. The sun was coming up and it was time to return to our wives. However, we were pounding on the door and yelling, but they wouldn't let us in. So, we went outside and looked up trying to figure out why they wouldn't let us in. Two pregnant women were standing on the deck and looking down at us as if we were two idiots, which, of course, we were. We were on the wrong fucking floor! Tug looked at me and said, 'Billy, don't let anyone know that we weren't 'high' enough.' So, we were banging on the wrong door, but what's new. We've been banging on the wrong doors all our lives."

"On that trip to Okinawa," said Lee, "McGraw and I got to fly on F-16 flight simulators, and we got to shoot at Migs. The AFB general was from Cody, Wyoming, and he said, 'Anytime you're in Cody, come look me up. I live up in the hills.'"

On that trip to Korea, the Spaceman was with a group including Tug McGraw and Gaylord Perry. How's that for a threesome?! While on that trip, the group stopped to play a game at Camp Hansen AFB in Kin on the Island of Okinawa. Yeah, that Okinawa. As Lee recalled:

"We were visiting military bases to promote M.C.I., which was a brand-new telephone company in those days. I came up to bat in the last inning with two men on base. I got ahold of a pitch and I blasted it for a home run, but at the exact moment the ball was clearing the fence, a cannon went off! They play taps at the end of the day, and the cannon signified it was time to play taps. Everyone stands up and is saluting, and I'm running around the bases! It looked like the scene from *The Natural* when Robert Redford hits the home run that shatters the lights at Buffalo's War Memorial Stadium, and everything seems to be frozen in time. Except I really hit this home run, but with less pyrotechnics. I slowed down as I trotted around the bases to savor the moment. It was surreal. I had thought of my dad who had fought at Okinawa. It was apropos."

As the Spaceman recounted, his departure from Okinawa was perhaps a bit too thrilling:

"We took off in an L10-11 Japanese Airline in the middle of a hurricane. There were 85 mph sustained winds. Our pilot told us that they line up their planes, so they fly directly into the paths of hurricanes and typhoons. They got on that runway and fired up the engines. We went down that runway at probably 55 mph and there was no sensation. The plane went straight up as if we were in an elevator, and there seemed to be no forward motion. It was just a vertical rise like we were in a helicopter. It was smooth, there was absolutely no turbulence, and we got up above the typhoon. I wanted to kiss the pilot."

Tug McGraw served in the United States Marine Corps Reserves from 1965-1971 and attained the rank of Corporal. Tug once joked that he served at Camp Lejeune where he became a "trained killer." Sadly, Tug McGraw developed a brain tumor, but founded "The Tug McGraw Foundation" in 2003, to enhance the quality of life of children and adults with brain tumors. In 2009, the foundation expanded to help those with PTSD (post-traumatic stress disorder,) as well as assist marines recovering from battlefield injuries.

Sadly, Tug McGraw, friend of the Spaceman, succumbed to brain cancer in 2004.

Many are not aware that Tug's son is legendary country and western singer, Tim McGraw.

CHAPTER ONE HUNDRED THIRTEEN

Crossfire

"I don't have to attend every argument I'm invited to." —*W.C. Fields*

"Everybody's got to believe in something. I believe I'll have another beer." —*W.C. Fields*

"Why are you all upset? You all got half the money and all the pussy." —*"Spaceman" Lee*

The earthling named William Francis Lee, III, spent a rather delicate Thanksgiving recently with several family members, including Diana, his current wife, and Mary Lou and Pam, his ex-wives. If you required any further proof of Bill Lee's courage, or perhaps insanity, well, you now have it.

I believe I heard the Spaceman mutter something about a "maelstrom to hell," but it is entirely possible I merely imagined it. It is also conceivable that Bill finally was the one who discovered the location of the "Bermuda Triangle." As Lee recalled:

"I was being discussed in depth and they were all talking while I was in the next room getting hammered. I may as well have been laying in an open coffin with a boutonniere on my lapel. I actually had a smile on my face, but alcohol may have been involved."

The author was soon made privy to an incident involving Mary Lou early on in their relationship. As the "Spaceman" recalled:

"I was teaching Mary Lou how to drive.* We were passing a semi-truck on a three-lane highway in Los Banos heading to the Sierra Nevadas in Oakdale, outside of Gilroy heading over to the Central Valley. That's when I realized what a shitty driver she was.** We were in a 1960 Ford station wagon, a car with sheepskin Mouton cushions. It was a beautiful car. It was my grandfather's last car; he gave it to me, so it had to be 1969. It was thick Mouton, a good winter car. Mary Lou is preparing to pass a semi, so she cuts out and sees another semi coming towards us from the other direction. She was hesitant, so I told her to ease off the gas and back up behind the truck, so she stands on the brakes. She's out in the middle." The Spaceman took a deep breath before continuing:

"I grabbed the wheel, she grabbed it back from me and we're doing a 360 between two semi-tractor trailers! She happened to do the rotation. They both passed her gently, but we wound up halfway in a ditch off the road, and then she starts crying. I'm checking all my body parts and can't believe I'm still alive! I told her, 'I'll take it over from here.' That was her first experience in passing a truck on the highway, which of course, is dangerous, an awe-inspiring thing for the first time, because you're accelerating at a speed you're not comfortable with. Just think; all of my kids would not have been born."

Lee also told of a time that they did another 360 back home in Massachusetts, but that had more to do with the fact that Mary Lou had landed a perfect right hand on the Spaceman's skull, which, of course, generally has a negative impact on driving.

| * this "fact" requires verification from Mary Lou.

| * again, this requires verification.

INTERLUDE #5

"If at first you don't succeed, try, try again. Then quit. There's no point in being a damned fool about it." —*W.C. Fields*

"Ah, the patter of little feet around the house. That's nothing like having a midget for a butler." —*W.C. Fields*

Because of his eccentricity, his worldview, and his oft perceived counter-culture persona, the one factor that many may overlook is that the earthling known as William Francis Lee, III was a damned good pitcher. Three consecutive 17 game seasons, two World Series starts in which he left with late-inning leads, both of which were relinquished by his bullpen, coming back from a devastating injury to become the N.L. left-handed pitcher of the year in 1979, and on and on. And then, of course, being blackballed from baseball at a time the Spaceman was physically and mentally prepared to add to his MLB resume.

Of the more meaningful criteria in measuring a pitcher's effectiveness is to study how he fares versus some of the most elite hitters in baseball history, and ALL of those included in this brief study comprise only those enshrined at the Hall of Fame, rendering this yardstick particularly compelling.

The fact is that Bill "Spaceman" Lee faced 21 Hall of Fame batsmen during his 14-year, albeit shortened major league career, and that in itself is an indication of just how few major leaguers are enshrined in the private institution in upstate New York. Only a handful of these legends, all household names to ardent baseball fans, experienced consistent success versus my zany left-handed friend. These are the facts in alphabetical order:

Henry Aaron	3-12, .250	1 home run, 2 RBIs
Luis Aparicio	1-2, .500	0 home runs, 1 RBI
Johnny Bench	4-12, .333	0 home runs, 0 RBIs
George Brett	5-20, .250	1 home run, 3 RBIs
Lou Brock	2-3, .667	0 home runs, 0 RBIs
Rod Carew	11-34, .324	1 home run, 3 RBIs

Reggie Jackson	20-55, .364	3 home runs, 9 RBIs
Al Kaline	9-33, .273	2 home runs, 8 RBIs
Harmon Killebrew	6-20, .300	2 home runs, 5 RBIs
Paul Molitor	2-14, .143	0 home runs, 1 RBI
Eddie Murray	5-12, .417	1 home run, 4 RBIs
Tony Perez	1-5, .200	1 home run, 3 RBIs
Brooks Robinson	8-31, .258	0 home runs, 3 RBIs
Frank Robinson	5-30, .167	0 home runs, 1 RBI
Ron Santo	4-13, .308	2 home runs, 3 RBIs
Mike Schmidt	4-23, .174	0 home runs, 2 RBIs
Ozzie Smith	2-13, .154	0 home runs, 1 RBI
Willie Stargell	0-4, .000	0 home runs, 0 RBIs
Billy Williams	1-9, .111	0 home runs, 0 RBIs
Dave Winfield	2-7, .286	0 home runs, 0 RBIs
Robin Yount	11-30, .367	0 home runs, 4 RBIs
Total	**106-382, .277**	**14 home runs, 53 RBIs**

Now for a closer examination: What we can easily see is that Reggie Jackson owned the Spaceman. What we can also plainly deduct is that collectively, the 21 Hall of Famers Bill Lee faced during his career amounted to nothing more than a fair to good hitter with little power.

Now consider how the Spaceman fared versus the other TWENTY Hall of Famers not named Reggie Jackson. That adds up to 86-327, .263 with 11 home runs and 44 RBIs, the equivalent of a fair at best middle infielder, that species being the bane of Lee's existence.

The Spaceman would also be pleased to know that his off-the-field nemesis, Ellie Rodriguez, may have 'hit" him outside the ballpark, but on the playing field, the Golden Gloves boxer was a paltry 4-20, .200 with 0 home runs and 2 RBIs versus Lee.

As for Bucky "Fucking" Dent, who should have faced Lee and not Torrez, off whom he hit that back-breaking home run, Russell Earl Dent was 9-38, .237, with 0 home runs and 8 RBIs. In other words, Don Zimmer fucked up, but you already knew that.

CHAPTER ONE HUNDRED FOURTEEN

An Unabridged Compendium

(Yes, that's contradictory)

Say What?

Non-Sequiturs on Steroids

"My luck is getting worse and worse. Last night, for instance, I was mugged by a Quaker." —*Woody Allen*

When one is "assigned" to do a biography of Bill "Spaceman" Lee, a "fallout" is the accumulation of perhaps pointless, illogical, inane, but hopefully innocuous, albeit mindless babblings. Make of them what you wish, although they most likely make more sense than the rest of this volume.

"No two snowflakes are alike." —*Bentley of Jericho, Vermont**

* Wilson Alwyn "Snowflake" Bentley, a hero of the Spaceman, was born on February 9, 1865 in Jericho, Vermont. He was affectionately called "Snowflake," because of his wonderful work with snow crystals. He became world renowned as the world's greatest authority on snowflakes. He was acclaimed throughout the world due to his pioneering work in photomicrography. On January 15, 1885, he became the first person to ever photograph a single snow crystal. Bentley photographed well over 5,000 snow crystals and never found two alike. On December 23, 1931, "Snowflake" Bentley died at the family farmhouse in Jericho. The mind boggles upon considering how Don Zimmer would have reacted in hearing the Spaceman wax ecstatic regarding "Snowflake" Bentley. I know how I reacted, though. I retired to bed with a severe migraine and briefly reconsidered writing this biography.

"I would watch the Hollywood Stars play baseball at Hollywood Park. The baseball players were gods to me. The other kids were getting autographs and I would hide. I was so shy." *—Bill Lee*

"Once in the Senior League I was just sunning myself in the bullpen. I wasn't playing that day. One of my teammates, Al Bumbry, hit a ball over the first base bag. Bobby Bonds was playing right field, but he had a bad arm. He fielded the ball and flipped it to me and shouted, 'Hey, Bill, throw it to second.' So I did. Too late, though, it was a clean double." *—Bill Lee*

"Billy Packer is a really good guy. One time at breakfast, he told me that when Bobby Knight threw the chair that the entire thing was staged. He said that Knight had a kid to scout that day and had to leave the arena, so he arranged to get tossed out. Packer also attempted to get me and Knight out on a boat on a lake in Montana. But he admitted that, 'One of you would never make it back to shore.'" *—Bill Lee*

"Billy Packer told me that Bobby Knight was late for practice one day because his dog ran away after a hunt. I told him that was one dog I wanted to meet." *—Bill Lee*

"Dr. Richard Alpert, a really cool guy, was Dr. Timothy Leary's companion. I spent the entire winter of '77 hanging out with him in Watertown, Massachusetts when I was all banged up. I was learning how to install speakers. He became 'Baba Ram Dass,' a spiritual leader. I put the speakers in his Volkswagen bus when he dropped out of society and went to the deserts of Arizona. Dass resurfaced in Maui and he planned to buy Charles Laquidera's house last year, but he had the unfortunate problem of dying, which precluded that possibility". *—Bill Lee*

"My roommate Sonny Siebert was the greatest athlete I ever saw. He was ambidextrous. He was 'Bill Bradley good' in basketball. The only thing wrong with him was he'd get up at four in the morning and stand in front of the mirror to practice his pitching motion. He'd be standing in front of a full-length mirror in his damned tighty-whities while going through his windup. Who the fuck wants to wake up to that?!" *—Bill Lee*

"Dick Radatz wouldn't visit me in Vermont until I put a satellite dish in so he could place his bets on the bowl games on New Year's Day. He had the same bookie as Pete Rose did out in Covington, Kentucky. I just had a new shower installed, and the big SOB stood on it and all the sheeting fell out. Radatz wrecked my shower. One time I was driving around Sugarbush with Radatz when the sheriff pulled us over outside of a bar. Radatz had a forty-eight-ounce diet coke and half a bottle of Captain Morgan's rum. He was bigger than life. He and Gary Bell were fucking crazy. Both with bad algorithms." *—Bill Lee*

"I was with Gary Bell in New York one time and this guy wanted to pay me one hundred dollars to throw oranges at his bare ass." *—Bill Lee*

"Do you know how foxes get rid of their fleas? They go down to a river or lake and grab a piece of wood. They get in the water up to their snout and all the fleas climb onto the wood. Then the fox lets go of the wood." *—Bill Lee*

"God, I loved that dog, Chuck. I wonder what he would have done when he was digging beneath the Siberian tiger cages at the Calgary Zoo, if those tigers had gotten out. My guess is he would've just followed 'em." *—Bill Lee*

"Billy North, who one time had his fill of Reggie Jackson's shit, got him wedged in a locker and pounded the hell out of him, took me out to a field where we were smoking a joint. He showed me a patch where he was growing marijuana in a raised bed with a fence around it. I looked down and I saw it was surrounded by a moat with rattlesnakes guarding it. No one was going to steal his fucking stash!" *—Bill Lee*

"Once in Hawaii, Tom House and I were dating these identical twins, the Elkins Sisters. Two left-handers with identical twins. We were parked on the side of the road. We thought those were the four most perfect breasts we'd ever seen." —*Bill Lee*

"In 1984 I'm playing for the La Guaira Tiburones (the Sharks) down in Venezuela. I'm on the beach and the sun has not come up yet. I hike up to a canyon and I get up on the ridge overlooking Caracas and peer out into the Caribbean, and waiting for the sun to rise and I'm awaiting the end of the Earth while thinking about George Orwell, but it's the most beautiful morning I've ever seen, so I walk back down and say, 'And so it goes.'" —*Bill Lee*

INTERLUDE #6

"I still miss my ex, but guess what? My aim is getting better."
—W.C. Fields

ONE ACT PLAY

After spending nine years at a sanitarium in Ogden, Utah named "The Home for Deranged Middle Infielders and Unwed Parakeets," Don Zimmer is finally released upon being declared sufficiently recovered. Upon returning home he is told that a former unnamed Red Sox pitcher is delivering a dissertation about "Heisenberg's Uncertainty Principle" and how it relates to former Red Sox catcher, Moe Berg.

Since Zim thinks the lecture is about baseball, he decides to attend. However, when he sees that the earthling known as William Francis Lee, III is introduced as the keynote speaker, he flies into an uncontrollable rage and is led off in a straitjacket. Seated in the audience is Fergie Jenkins who shakes his head sympathetically.

CHAPTER ONE HUNDRED FIFTEEN

Paul

"No two snowflakes are alike." —*Bentley of Jericho*

"My brother Paul was probably a better ballplayer than I was," said the earthling known as William Francis Lee, III, "but genes can be tricky."

As you are reading this, please keep in mind that if the Spaceman is a direct descendent of Jesus Christ, well then, so is his brother Paul. Ponder that for a moment. Before continuing I would suggest several sips of Makers Mark.

The following is a brief assessment of Paul Lee by his brother, Bill:

"Paul was a great athlete at Terra Linda High School. He was a compact version of Mike Schmidt and had a great future in baseball if he hadn't decided to play football. He ran a 9.8 100 and still holds the rushing record at Terra Linda.

"On his very first play at Cal State Santa Barbara, he was signaling for a fair catch when a kid from UCLA clobbered him and broke his collarbone. His clavicle was destroyed and that was the end of his great throwing arm. He had a cannon for an arm, too. During his second game, he made a cut against West Texas State and a kid hit him on the back of his ankle and tore his Achilles.

"Paul could really hit, though. In 1972 he led the Intercounty Canadian League in hitting. He played for the Branford Red Sox in Ontario. He was smooth. He played on the same Little League team with Tim Foli, coached by my father.

"Paul earned a master's degree from Farleigh Dickinson University and became an executive at AT&T, just like my dad. He had a long line of sports cars from a Triumph to a BMW to an XK. When he opened his garage door, he would drive to exactly the spot where an orange Super Bowl hung from a string and he would always stop when he reached an exact point that the orange Super Bowler reached that precise point on his windshield. You can't possibly be more anal retentive than that!

"One day he drove to that spot and he began going nuts. He thought he had a scratch on his car, but it turned out to be a spider web. Paul and I are complete polar opposites. I'm the kind of guy who hits my car with a ballpeen hammer before I even get into the fucking thing. I've got a BMW that's been in my garage for twenty years and I've got tires on top of the car and I put my garbage inside of them.

"Paul sits in a fucking chair with two Siamese cats on his lap and smokes a big cigar just like my dad. He drinks Makers Mark. He's always been anal retentive. In '08 I saved his life twice, once when he had a bicycle accident. I got him to an ambulance and rode with him to the hospital. Paul is 'there,' but he's never really there. He's like Calvin Coolidge, 'Silent Cal.' Paul and his wife wore matching 'AT&T' pajamas."

Now that fact contains some disturbing imagery.

CHAPTER ONE HUNDRED SIXTEEN

The Time Don Zimmer Did Something Right!

> "If you reveal your secrets to the wind, you should not blame the wind for revealing them to the trees." *—Khalil Gibran*

> "If I screw up, I'm gonna say, 'You know what? I really screwed up.' That's all you can do. Some people gonna forgive you, some people not gonna forgive you. That's just the way it works."
> *—Sir Charles Barkley*

> "When I die, if the word 'thong' appears in the first or second sentence of my obituary, I've screwed up." *—Albert Brooks*

It is apparent upon reading *Zim: A Baseball Life* with Bill Madden, that very little was actually the fault of Don Zimmer and that the "gerbil" was often a victim of circumstance. Fergie Jenkins? Well, he couldn't pitch at Fenway Park, although the facts prove otherwise. The earthling known as William Francis Lee, III? Well, at 10-10, 3.46, he was no longer capable of winning games. Bernie Carbo? Well, he was no longer the same player, and on and on.

The final game of a crucial series against the Yankees, before which Hall of Fame captain Carl Yastrzemski begged Zimmer to start the Spaceman, a Yankee killer? No, he called me a gerbil! Why didn't the ball get past Lou Piniella in right field? Pure luck, of course. Why did Zimmer start Bobby Sprowl over Bill Lee or anyone else? Well, Johnny Podres told him Sprowl was ready to go deep into the game. Why did the Red Sox fade in 1979? Well, Dennis Eckersley had a poor second half, Jerry Remy got hurt, Butch Hobson had a bad shoulder (when exactly did Butch Hobson have a good shoulder? Elbow, truthfully) and on and on, ad infinitum. Hell, when Zimmer played for the Dodgers, he preferred Chuck Dressen as his manager because he went to the racetrack with him. Now there is a great endorsement for a manager. Meanwhile, Don Zimmer apparently was merely a casualty of circumstance, a mere scapegoat, a martyr, as it were. However, if it was not for Don Zimmer, my beloved Brooklyn Dodgers would have never won their first World Series!

"Wait until next year," was the annual cry at Ebbets Field in Brooklyn, but next year never seemed to come. It never came, that is, until fate, in the name of Don Zimmer, intervened! In actuality though, Don Zimmer did not barge in, but by kindly vacating his position in the seventh game of the 1955 World Series, Zimmer's noble gesture enabled the Brooklyn Dodgers to finally win a World Series.... To be entirely forthcoming, Don Zimmer did not "kindly vacate" his position in the batting order, but was removed from it by manager Walter Alston, a move that literally resulted in "next year" finally arriving.

As the singularly handsome and world renowned author Scott Russell described in his magnificent 2017 novel *Prophet's End*, the epic Dodgers-Yankees 1955 World Series had come down to a winner-take-all seventh game at Yankee Stadium in the Bronx. As Russell wrote in his masterpiece:

"Meanwhile, Johnny Podres was indeed pitching shutout ball, just as he had done in the dream. When Gil Hodges drove 'Pee Wee' Reese home with a sacrifice fly in the top of the sixth inning, Billy cheered while also recalling the details of his dream. Billy thought to himself as Reese crossed home plate with the second run, that the probability of having Sandy Amoros making a game-saving catch was nil. After all, Amoros was not even in the game! However, when Dodger outfielder George 'Shotgun' Shuba entered the game as a pinch-hitter for second baseman Don Zimmer shortly after Hodges' sacrifice fly, Billy's wheels began turning.

"The move by Dodger manager Walter Alston would necessitate changes on defense. Therefore, when the Dodgers took the field in the bottom of the sixth inning, Dodger left-fielder Jim Gilliam switched to second base and Sandy Amoros entered the game as a defensive replacement in left field!"

Well, I won't go into details, but the rest is history, and by all means, buy Scott Russell's book, but Sandy Amoros, who would not have been in the game save for Don Zimmer's removal, made perhaps the second most memorable game-saving catch in World Series history. And all because Don Zimmer was removed from the equation. As Casey Stengel would say, "You can look it up."

If only Don Zimmer had been removed from the 1978 Boston Red Sox during their 14 game collapse, one of which Don Zimmer proudly proclaimed he had managed the Boston Red Sox to one of its most exciting seasons, his legacy may have not looked upon with ridicule to members of Red Sox Nation.

CHAPTER ONE HUNDRED SEVENTEEN

The Sham That Is Cooperstown

"Gil Hodges is a Hall of Famer. He belongs in Cooperstown."
—*Willie Mays*

"That feller's (Hodges) the best first baseman I've seen since Lou Gehrig." —*Casey Stengel*

"No one has had more impact on my career than Gil Hodges."
—*Tom Seaver*

"I believe Gil to have been one of the finest men I met, in sports or out of it." —*Pulitzer prize-winning* NY Times *sports columnist, Arthur Daley*

"They broker backdoor deals at the Hall of Fame."
—Boston Globe*'s award-winning columnist Dan Shaughnessy**

> * It should be noted that Dan Shaughnessy is enshrined at the Hall of Fame, having been awarded the J.G. Taylor Spink Award! Now that's integrity.

As an old Brooklyn Dodgers fan, the author is a huge fan of the immortal Gil Hodges, a GREAT ballplayer, a great human being, a great manager, and a decorated war hero. Other than that, Gil had nothing going for him. However, my experience with the "Baseball Hall of Fame" in Cooperstown, New York, was not a pleasant one. I will explain. I wrote this in 2017. Nothing has changed:

Gil Hodges Not in the Hall of Fame... an Ongoing Travesty.

My experience with the alleged "Hall of Fame," the exclusive private institution that is situated in the charming little village of Cooperstown, New York, the place where baseball was not even invented, soured me forever in regard to its credibility. I wrote the following in 2017:

HALL OF FAME MEMBERSHIP RENEWAL

Well, my membership renewal form to the "National Baseball Hall of Fame and Museum" in Cooperstown has arrived in the mail. My membership privileges will expire on June 18, 2017 and we generally sign up for five years. In the renewal application that arrived, I was encouraged to "renew your membership and continue to receive great benefits, including *Memories and Dreams* magazine, a Hall of Fame yearbook, lapel pin, shopping discounts and a personalized member card featuring the team of your choice."

And all I would have to do is include my payment and return it in the postage paid envelope! Therefore, on behalf of all Gil Hodges fans, I am returning the order form with the following note:

Dear National Baseball Hall of Fame and Museum,

I have received your application for my renewal in the National Baseball Hall of Fame and Museum and am currently considering this wonderful opportunity. Therefore, I wish to include all of my family members, so if you would kindly forward ten individual applications to distribute among those voting in order to decide our future participation, I will see to it that these applications are distributed among them.

I look forward to your response.

Sincerely,
Scott D. Russell
Member since 2007

For those not familiar with our "experience" with the HOF, here is a brief explanation. For many, many years, a passionate group of Gil Hodges supporters, led by the likes of Lu Patterson Sisco, Ronald G. Liebman, Bob Williams, Russ White and Claire Elizabeth Hall, among others, lamented the fact that Gil Hodges, perhaps the greatest defensive first baseman in history, one of the greatest run producers, a great manager and a decorated war hero, was denied enshrinement into the Hall of Fame in Cooperstown, and many, in fact, believed that he had been denied entry by underhanded acts.

Therefore, I decided to do my small part and compiled the most definitive statistical study on the subject, one that proved conclusively Hodges' domination over other enshrined players.

My study, much like the wonderful research presented by the late, great Dick Bresciani, a report that literally catapulted a deserving Jim Rice into the HOF, was clear concise and definitive. I proved conclusively (actually, Hodges did so with his bat) that Hodges was one of the ELITE run producers in MLB history. Rather than "attack" by spewing mindless modern-day metrics, I resorted to factual data that could not be refuted. Gil Hodges simply had a greater runs scored/RBI percentage per at bat than over 80 percent of those batsmen enshrined and an even greater percentage than his peers (corner infielders during his career). You see, at the end of nine innings, they have this quaint tradition of adding up the runs scored. That decides the outcome of the game. Imagine that! There were NO pitchers in the study, only Gil Hodges' peers.

Upon contacting Cooperstown, I had communications with a gentleman named Craig Muder, the Director of Communications. Mr. Muder informed me that if I would forward our "argument" to his attention, that he would "distribute the booklets among the Veterans Committee" who, of course, were voting concerning Hodges' fate. I (we) were lied to. Upon finding out that the booklets were never distributed to any members of the Veterans Committee, I placed another call to Mr. Muder, who confirmed the fact they had not been distributed. When I asked why, he responded, as God is my judge, "Because they never requested them." I then asked Mr. Muder why they would request something they did not know existed and he truthfully answered, "I don't know, that's a good question."

Yes, as the great Dan Shaughnessy stated so eloquently, and keep in mind that Dan is enshrined in Cooperstown, "They broker backdoor deals at the HOF." That's integrity! They had no intention whatsoever of enshrining Gil Hodges, who was the preeminent defensive first baseman of his time, a man of impeccable character, a war hero, having been awarded medals for his brave and selfless actions at both Tinian and Okinawa, and a terrific manager. Gil won several pennants and two World Series with the Dodgers and another as manager of the Mets. They play political games up there in that tiny little charming village by the lake. But they deceive. No Gil Hodges? No Cecil Travis? No Tony Oliva? No Tommy John? No Jim Kaat. Oh, and the evening before the Veteran's Committee was to decide Dick Allen's fate, they replaced Bob Watson, a Dick Allen advocate, with Dave Dombrowski, an Allen opponent. Dick Allen was denied enshrinement... by that ONE vote. Dirty dealing.

Gil's son, Gil Hodges, Jr. wasn't even aware that his dad was a decorated war hero! Gil, as many members of "The Greatest Generation" had done, just placed his medals in a box and never mentioned them, much like Bill Lee's dad, William Francis Lee, Jr. had done. Gil Hodges, a heavy smoker, tragically passed two days short of his 49th birthday, one of the most beloved players and managers in major league history.

As I stated above, one of Gil Hodges' greatest advocates is a gentleman named Bob Williams, a friend of the author. Bob Williams has also been the spring training PA announcer for various major league teams during the spring training Cactus League season. Bob Williams who knows a great deal about the game of baseball is also the son of perhaps the most legendary comedian in television history. You see, Bob's dad was "The King of Comedy," the late, great Milton Berle. "Uncle Miltie," as was one of his sobriquets, rubbed elbows with the giants of the industry, and was also a huge Dodgers fan, one, in fact, who was a friend of perhaps the most dominant left-handed pitcher of the 20th Century, the great Sandy Koufax. Recently I spoke with Bob Williams regarding his thoughts on the "Spaceman." As Williams said:

"I never met Bill Lee, but I always admired the great characters of the game as they contributed to my love of the game. That's how my love for the game grew stronger and that begins with Gil Hodges, whose career was coming to a kid in New York City. I was left with one team when the Dodgers left for L.A. in 1958. I was seven years old and I was used to having three sets of baseball cards and suddenly the cards read "San Francisco" instead of "New York" and "Los Angeles" instead of "Brooklyn." That can be a little bit confusing.

I still have my favorites and guys like Bill Lee are so much part of the fabric of the game and the fabric of our society. Everything these days is so cookie-cutter and although we have some good actors and bad actors, there are still some memorable people in the game today, but not like they were when we were kids. Obviously, it's too bad we didn't have more

African American and Cuban players, too, but we were growing up during a time that was all changing.

For the most part, I felt that the great characters of the game got along with just about everybody. Many people thought that Bill Lee was "whacked," or was a bit off center, but I think that those players had more to offer in life. I admired Lee because once he got on the mound and toed the rubber, he was one of the finest lefthanders in the game and his record is conducive of that.

For Lee to have played on a team north of the border and to meet all the people he met and could tolerate and he was capable of smelling a phony from miles away. That's the impression I got and I've been accused of being a few French fries short of a happy meal myself. But I think that people like us have a lot to offer because we don't see it at 180, we see everything at 360. A lot of people have blinders on, and I have a great amount of respect for Bill Lee. I believe we would have gotten along personality wise, but you never know.

There were a few characters around who were similar to Bill, but I don't place Mark Fidrych in the same category as Bill Lee. Jimmy Piersall and Mickey McDermott, yes. I spent time with Mickey during the final years of his life and I pulled him out of a few bars on occasion, too. The game became a lot more fun to watch with the advent of Bill Lee and players of color."

That was quite a tribute from the son of Milton Berle, "The King of Comedy."

Now, you may ask what my "argument" for Gil Hodges is doing in a biography of Bill "Spaceman" Lee. You will find out shortly.

CHAPTER ONE HUNDRED EIGHTEEN

The De Facto Hall of Fame

> "God's been good to me. They didn't think Buck was good enough to be in the Hall of Fame. That's the way they thought about it and that's the way it is. So, we're going to live with that. Now, if I'm a Hall of Famer to you, that's all right with me. Just keep loving old Buck. Don't weep for Buck. No, man, be happy, be thankful."
> —*Buck O'Neil*

There is a misconception that John Jordan "Buck" O'Neil, Jr. has been enshrined at the Baseball Hall of Fame in Cooperstown, New York. He has not. What is true, however, is that the Hall of Fame posthumously dedicated a life-size bronze statue of O'Neil near the entrance of its museum. Ironically, O'Neil was posthumously awarded the "Presidential Medal of Freedom" on December 7, 2008, merely two months after Buck had passed. The honor was bestowed upon Buck O'Neil by former president George W. Bush, the Spaceman's fellow REMF. And so it goes.

There are numerous analogies to draw between Buck O'Neil and the earthling known as William Francis Lee, III, the two most notable being the fact that both were prevented from playing major league baseball, one man because of the color of his skin, and the other for a myriad of reasons including defending a teammate with that same skin color. Another analogy is that despite being prevented from playing their beloved sports in what is commonly referred to as "major league baseball," neither man was bitter in regard to his fate, although both men certainly had the right to be. Instead both men decided to honor the game they so cherished by becoming ambassadors to the greatest of sports.

Both Buck O'Neil and Bill "Spaceman" Lee were seemingly perpetual pied pipers, always promoting the game of baseball and especially teaching it to youngsters. The author has never known Bill Lee to say no. If there was a charity event, an exhibition, a youngster to meet or a game to play in, the Spaceman was there. Bill accepted invitations to Cuba, to Russia, to Mexico and to every corner of the earth where baseball could be both played and taught.

It is virtually impossible for a white person to fully understand what it is like to not only have been denied the privilege of competing at a sport, but to be judged based on the color of his or her skin. Then there are those actors and actresses who were victims of the McCarthy witch hunt and stripped of their careers, dignity, and in some instances, their lives. For many of the same political reasons, Bill "Spaceman" Lee was blackballed from playing and instructing or having anything officially to do with major league baseball, and all because he challenged the conservative establishment. Bill Lee's banishment was an "unofficial" proclamation, but anyone with a modicum of intelligence fully understands that all doors were and remain bolted shut to him to this moment.

This eviction is especially unjust when considering what the Spaceman had/has to offer and his undying love for the game that so loved and still loves, but never loved him back. Consider for a moment about Lee's teammates at USC, all fellow disciples of their legendary coach Rod Dedeaux. Men such as the great Tom Seaver, Jim Barr, Tom House, Brent Strom, and Ray Lamb, all of whom are or have been employed by major league baseball teams under numerous designations. Think about Bill's equally "flaky" teammate in Montreal, Ross "Scuz" Grimsley, who has been employed by several major league organizations.

Despite Bill Lee's cruel and unwarranted exclusion from the game he has so honored throughout the years, and I cannot reiterate this enough, the Spaceman is NOT bitter in the least. In fact, as he recently told me, "If I had been permitted to continue with my major league career, as most southpaws do, I would have most likely been a valuable commodity until my early forties. At that point I would have retired to become a self-sufficient farmer, although I still would have taught youngsters the love of the game. Therefore, I owe major league baseball a great debt for enabling me to continue to participate in it, and professionally for perhaps longer than any pitcher in professional history."

The facts certainly validate the Spaceman's assessment of his career. Bill Lee, who incidentally was the last Red Sox player to miss time during the regular season for his military obligation during the 1970 season, served in the U.S. Army Reserve for six years during the Vietnam War. Did you know that it was Lee's responsibility to notify the families of dead soldiers?

Consider the following, all indicative of how remarkably lengthy Bill Lee's pitching career was:

On September 2, 2018, Bill played professionally for the Ottawa Champions, a professional league, at the age of seventy-one. In September 2010, Bill Lee hurled 5 & 2/3 innings for the Brockton Rox, a team in the Canadian-American Association of Professional Baseball and earned the win, a victory making him the oldest pitcher to ever appear in or win a professional baseball game. On August 23, 2012, the Spaceman pitched a nine-inning complete game for the San Rafael Pacifics, defeating the Na Koa I Kaika Maui 9-4. Bill Lee's bat and uniform were donated to the Baseball Hall of Fame in Cooperstown as that game made him the oldest pitcher to make a starting appearance, pitch a complete game, and to earn a win in a professional game and drive in a run.

It is shameful that in the year 2020, Bill "Spaceman" Lee is still persona non grata in major league baseball.

Well, the author of this tome will now make an "OFFICIAL" announcement. Since the "Baseball Hall of Fame" in Cooperstown, New York, the place where baseball was not even invented, deceived yours truly upon receiving our Gil Hodges presentation, we are creating our own Baseball Hall of Fame, and hereby are immediately enshrining our initial four inductees, none of whom are presently preserved at their private institution. Oh, and if we build a castle, you are friggin' welcome to visit it.

Therefore, the charter members of our de facto Baseball Hall of Fame are in alphabetical order: Gil Hodges, "Shoeless Joe" Jackson, William Francis Lee, III, and Buck O'Neil. We have no admission or membership fees and if you desire to forward statistical arguments, as it were, for a player's induction qualifications, we will gladly distribute them to our "Veterans Committee."

CHAPTER ONE HUNDRED NINETEEN

The Final Verse of the Books of Bokonon

The Last Calypso

> "The hand that stocks the drug stores rules the world.
> Let us start our Republic with a chain of drug stores, a chain of gas chambers, and a national game. After that, we can write our Constitution." —*Bokonon, from Kurt Vonnegut's* Cat's Cradle.

The author awoke amidst the ruins of what once was the Otsego Hotel to a deafening silence. It was as if all the oxygen on planet Earth had been sucked out of it. Just yesterday I had arrived at the charming quaint village of Cooperstown, New York, the place where baseball was not invented. Upon my arrival, the town was bustling with people, vendors on the streets and in shops, hawking baseball memorabilia and other souvenirs. I was present to witness history, to see my friend, the earthling known as William Francis Lee, III, inducted into his rightful place at the Baseball Hall of Fame.

Imagine my surprise at seeing a solid frozen mass at the site where Bill "Spaceman" Lee's plaque was to be added to those such as Babe Ruth, Lou Gehrig, Willie Mays, Ted Williams, Sandy Koufax, Oscar Charleston, Satchel Paige, and Joe DiMaggio. In a complete daze, I wandered out to the banks of Lake Otsego, where I had recently taken a boat ride. The boat had cruised down Lake Otsego, but the lake was also gone and replaced by a solid mass of ice, and this in spite of the fact that it was mid-summer, the last week in July, in fact.

Only two days prior to what most certainly announced the end of civilization, I had viewed the Kingfisher Tower Castle from our tour boat. The tour guide had provided us with a history of the castle, which was a miniature castle designed in the style of the eleventh or twelfth century. With its approximate twenty-foot square base and its parapet and conical roof, it appeared majestic, but desolate. Edward Clark, the builder-owner, had that very lonesome look in mind. As the tour guide explained, "Please note that the castle is very private. No tours are available, and no one is permitted to view it from other than a boat."

Edward Clark, in fact, had been a member of another private and exclusive family, whose institution, the "Baseball Hall of Fame" on Main Street, is one owned and operated by the descendants of Edward Clark.

In a semi-state of shock, I walked down the banks of what was once Lake Otsego to the castle that rested on the eastern shore of Otsego Lake at Point Judith. It was there that I saw a black man sitting on a rock. In his hands was the Hall of Fame Induction Program, one with Bill "Spaceman" Lee on its cover. The man was clad only in a white bedspread with blue tufts.

As I turned my eyes towards the castle beyond the black man's shoulders, I noticed what appeared to be a man peering down from atop one of its stained-glass windows. It was then I noticed that the man was Bernie Carbo and that he was smiling as he raised his middle finger to the world down below. I averted my eyes back to where the black man was seated on the rock.

"Bokonon?" I asked.

Bokonon smiled and responded, "Yes."

At that very moment I peered down and saw a monstrous plaque embedded in the solid mass of what once was a beautiful lake. It was a plaque signifying that a man named Thomas A. Yawkey had been enshrined at the private institution known as "The Baseball Hall of Fame" in the year 1980. Yawkey had been the last baseball owner to allow blacks to play a sport called baseball. He had also owned a plantation in South Carolina in a country called the United States of America. He had owned a team for forty-four years, but never won the league's World Series. However, Yawkey had also contributed tens of thousands of dollars to the private institution.

It was then that I asked Bokonon what had occurred. Bokonon did not hesitate in providing the following answer:

"Fish got to swim
Bird got to fly
Spaceman got to pitch
Or he wither and die
Ice-nine come
Ice-nine stay
Saddest words of all
No game today."

POSTSCRIPT

The only surviving outpost on planet Earth in the year 2037 is located on the Pine Ridge Indian Reservation in South Dakota. It is there that the members of the tribe enjoy free visits to the "Anna Mae Aquash, Guy Waterman, and Spaceman Lee Heritage Museum."

There is a plaque at the entrance of the historical gallery signifying that Ms. Aquash had been a Mi'kmaq Indian who had been born in a place called Shubenacadie, Nova Scotia, which was a beautiful town which was reduced to stone and ice by a human's invention called "Ice-Nine."

At the entrance to the museum also rests a beautiful bronze exhibit, a statue of an earthling named William Francis Lee, III. The sculpture shows a smiling Lee with his arm around the shoulder of another bronze statuette depicting another much shorter man named Don Zimmer. However, Zimmer is not smiling. Atop Zimmer's head rests what appears to be a helmet with the interlocking letters "N" & "Y" emblazoned on it. Inscribed at the base of the statue are the words, "Keep your hands off me, you California faggot!" A few Native American historians believe that the statue of Zimmer was styled after a character named "Franz Liebkind" in an old Mel Brooks' motion picture, but that is merely conjecture.

Visitors to the museum often engage in lengthy debates regarding a series of other bronze sculptures, many of which appear to be busts of other earthlings, and Native American scholars have often referred to this collection as the "Get Over It" series.

An example of these artifacts includes the names of humans with rather intriguing, however confusing inscriptions adorning them. These bronze pieces include the following:

> "RALPH BRANCA—SO, I GAVE UP A FUCKING HOME RUN, GET OVER IT!"

> "BILL BUCKNER—SO, I MADE A FUCKING ERROR, GET OVER IT!"

> "BILL MAZEROSKI— SO, I HIT A FUCKING HOME RUN, GET OVER IT!"

"BUCKY DENT—SO, I HIT A FUCKING HOME RUN, GET OVER IT!"

"DON ZIMMER—SO, I'm FAT, UGLY, AND STUPID, GET OVER IT!"

The elders of the Native American tribe have concluded that apparently many ancients were not partial to whatever "hitting a home run" entailed.

As the women of the tribe offer frybread to those visitors to the reservation, nearby, in a meadow outside of the museum, Native American children can be seen running around in an open field with strange markings and what appear to be small pillows arranged in a diamond shape. These children apparently are playing in a game they call "Rounders," although the adults seemed confused as to their enthusiasm. The sun is shining brightly.

POSTSCRIPT # 2

"What if everything is an illusion and nothing exists? In that case, I definitely overpaid for my carpet." —*Woody Allen*

Seriously, who the fuck writes two postscripts anyhow? However, this is an actual authorized biography of Bill "Spaceman" Lee, which makes it different than any other.

While the author and the earthling known as William Francis Lee, III are aware that literally dozens of people will be offended by the contents of this book, please keep in mind that we warned ("warned" sounds a bit harsh, though) that much of this is foma, although it's good to live by the foma. Therapeutic, in fact.

It may interest you to know that somewhat incredibly, there are many subjects we failed to include in this lengthy tome. Time and time again, I proposed that we exclude some of the more outrageous events that the Spaceman experienced during his visit to planet Earth. I mean, how in hell could I possibly write a chapter about a beautiful Venezuelan girl offering Lee a blow job if she'd hit a particular superstar player "in the nuts with a fastball?" No, really. And since we both admire the intended victim, we have no intention of divulging the name of the "target," and no, Bill just laughed off the offer, but "damn," he said, "it was tempting. The girl was hot."

As for me, the author, either Scott Russell or Kilgore Trout, a few years ago I had begun to pen my autobiography but abandoned the idea because after reading the initial three chapters, I became incredulous. If I did not believe what the hell I had written, why would anyone else?

True story, though: I genuinely declined an opportunity to meet Dr. Hunter S. Thompson. As I recall, I received a telephone call from the great George Kimball at my apartment in Boston's Back Bay in 1973. George asked if I would join him for lunch at the "Plough and Stars" on Massachusetts Avenue in Cambridge. Now, I should note that "lunch" with George nearly invariably did not include food, but I was game. What the hell. I was willing, that is, until George offered, "Hey, meet me there at noon. I'll introduce you to Dr. Thompson."

I responded, "Are you referring to Dr. Hunter S. Thompson?"

I received an affirmative reply, to which I answered, "No thanks. I'll pass."

"Why?"

"Well, for one thing, he's a drug addled psychotic maniac."

George, never at a loss for words, countered, "Well, so am I."

"Yes, George, and I can hardly handle you. How the hell am I going to contend with two of you?"

In truth, the Spaceman and I bit our tongues in neglecting to include several outrageous tales in this book. I mean, seriously, how in hell could we write that Bill had to bail out Bernie and his buddy, Scipio Spinks after they were both arrested with a transvestite in Port St. Lucie? Whoops, we let that one slip, didn't we? There were a few incidents at the Fallon Ranch in Nevada, which is basically a brothel, that we chose not to get into either, both literally and figuratively. Some things are best left unsaid, and some folks are best left unidentified.

What if I told you that on occasion, the Spaceman would go to the trainer's quarters before the races and as Lee stated, "I would take a quarter of the Butazol they fed the horses and then go out and pitch."

Once in the mid '70s, I telephoned the Spaceman to inform him that our hero, Kurt Vonnegut was going to be a featured speaker at the Boston Globe Book Festival at the Hynes Auditorium on Boylston Street. "Count me in!" Bill exclaimed.

For approximately forty-five minutes, we sat enthralled as Vonnegut mesmerized us with his incredible wit and unlimited imagination. Upon the conclusion of Vonnegut's spellbinding speech, it was announced that Mr. Vonnegut would be meeting his fans and signing his new book out in the corridor.

"C'mon, Bill, let's go meet Vonnegut."

I was shocked when Bill responded, "No, I'll meet you out in the lobby afterwards."

I asked the Spaceman why he was going to pass up on an opportunity to meet his idol. Bill's response baffled yours truly:

"Scotty, I'd rather keep my idols at a distance."

It took me nearly forty-three years to understand why. I had written a novel called *Prophet's End*. My book was a tribute to first responders and to an otherworldly beautiful and inspirational young woman named Jennifer Bricker. The character, "Jennifer Swanson" was based directly on Jen. However, *Prophet's End* was dedicated to my idol, the incomparable columnist and author, Pete Hamill. Hamill was, in fact, a character in my book!

After writing the story, I attempted to somehow locate Mr. Hamill in the hope that I could present a copy of the book to honor him. However, both his representatives and publishers had placed a rather impenetrable cocoon around him. In time, I had learned that he had been seriously ill and in fact, had nearly died. At one point, Pete had received the last sacraments of the Catholic Church. Finally hope arrived from an unlikely source. I had seen an older video of Mr. Hamill speaking at NYU's "Glucksman Ireland House," which housed the Irish students. On a whim, I telephoned Glucksman and spoke with a lovely Irish lass named Miriam Nyhan-Grey, the Associate Director of Glucksman Ireland House. A few months had gone by as Ms. Grey had returned to Dublin to give birth to her first child.

One glorious day, Ms. Grey contacted yours truly, and with her lilting Irish brogue invited me to a "Pete Hamill Tribute" to take place on Monday, December 10, 2018. Would I be interested? Ya think?

I did not belong there, folks. Only three hundred invitations went out and the speakers included the likes of Dan Barry, James McBride, Joanna Molloy, Jim Dwyer, Sam Roberts, Peggy Noonan, Carl Hiaasen, and Charles Sennott. Judy Collins sang "Amazing Grace."

Peg and I invited our two dearest friends in the world, Dr. Vladimir Privman and his wife, the beautiful Dr. Violetta Thierbach. M. Hamill, of course, was the final speaker of the evening. It was the thrill of a lifetime. I had forwarded a copy of my book, *Prophet's End* to Ms. Grey weeks before and she assured me that she would personally deliver it to "Peter," as they were close.

At the end of the evening, a line formed to greet Mr. Hamill, and I then recalled what Bill Lee had told me decades earlier about not wanting to meet his idol, Kurt Vonnegut. There were approximately seventy-five people in line to pay their respects to Pete Hamill. Forty-three years later, I now knew why the Spaceman was so reluctant!

I told Peg and our guests, Vladimir and Violetta that it was time to return to Vlad's home in Brooklyn, but first I wanted to thank Ms. Miriam Nyhan-Grey who had so thoughtfully invited me. I approached her and thanked her profusely for getting to see my idol speak in person.

Ms. Grey smiled and queried, "And whom might you be, and why aren't you in line?"

"I'm Scott Russell," I replied, "and I do not wish to bother Mr. Hamill."

Upon hearing my name, Ms. Grey became animated and scolded, "Nonsense! You came all the way from Massachusetts to see your hero, and you will meet your hero!"

Miriam Nyhan-Grey, whose arm strength belied her small stature, grabbed me by my wrist and practically dragged me to the front of the line! I apologized profusely to those I was placed in front of, and ALL smiled, laughed, and informed me that it was all good.

Of course, my heart was in my mouth. I was first in line, thanks to Miriam Nyhan-Grey. There was no time to be nervous.

"Mr. Hamill," I heard my own voice say, "you've been my idol for so many years. My name is Scott Russell."

Immediately upon hearing my name, the incomparable Pete Hamill reached out and grasped my hand tightly. Holding firmly onto my hand, Pete Hamill looked deeply into my eyes and said, "Thank you. Thank you!"

Those who know me are aware that I am known to speak incessantly. We were halfway across the borough of Brooklyn, the birthplace of Pete Hamill and the home of Dr. Vladimir Privman and his wife, Dr. Violetta Thierbach, when Vlad broke the silence.

"So, Scott. Are you ever going to wash your hand again?"

The following day, my friend, Dr. Sandy Price, a professor at Arizona State University, asked, "Did you ask Pete Hamill if he read your book?"

"Of course, not," I replied. "That would be the equivalent of a Little League hitter inquiring of Ted Williams, 'Did you see me hit?'"

The Spaceman and I sincerely hope you enjoyed the story of his improbable but intriguing life, a life that is still evolving. Bill Lee belongs in both the Baseball Hall of Fame, as he is a truly great ambassador, and in public office, where he couldn't possibly do any worse than the current imbeciles "running" our once proud nation into the ground. Who knows? Perhaps we will write another book with just as much foma.

As for the toll of writing a book with the Spaceman, can anyone recommend a good analyst?

Scott Russell
or Kilgore Trout

"IF THINGS DON't IMPROVE BY MID-NOVEMBER, MY CANADIAN WIFE AND I WILL ROW ACROSS THE TIM O'BRIEN RAINY RIVER INTO THE OJIBWA FOG AND DISAPPEAR LIKE CARL HUBBELL's FADEAWAY.
—*WILLIAM FRANCIS LEE, III*

A LETTER FROM THE AUTHOR

This is the only book I have ever written that caught me by surprise, and in more ways than I thought imaginable. I had never even considered writing the biography of Bill Lee and to be entirely candid, I did not think I was worthy of the task. Make no mistake, I believed I was capable, but I also was not delusional to the extent that I felt there were not better and more qualified authors. It was the Spaceman himself who ordained yours truly as the chronicler of his time here on Earth and perhaps elsewhere.

Despite my knowing the subject matter and befriending him in 1973 upon my arrival in Boston, my relationship with William Francis Lee, III, although friendly, has been primarily from a distance throughout the years. Having the privilege of watching him participate in the sport he loves, listening to his outrageous wit, admiring his anti-establishment views and iconoclastic outlook, but most of all his vast intelligence and inherent decency, made me more appreciate his persona.

I first met Bill due to our mutual love of the game of baseball. In the process of getting acclimated to my new surroundings some forty-seven years ago, I gravitated towards Fenway Park, a historic landmark, a venue that by merely mentioning its name, conjures up thoughts of Babe Ruth, Ted Williams, and the game of baseball itself. As a "hobby" in which to busy myself, one that would provide an adrenaline rush to at partially replace my prior endeavors, I began compiling baseball statistics. Some claimed I developed a proficiency at it, but I don't know.

I had begun reading a sort of counter-culture weekly periodical called *The Boston Phoenix*, and in particular a column written by George Kimball, a truly brilliant journalist to his credit, but a man who would also be "discredited" for introducing me to my first wife, but that's another story entirely. Kimball, a man who would become a friend, wrote of the exploits of a young pitcher on the Red Sox, and one who was developing a reputation as one of the truly eccentric characters of the game. Through George, I would eventually meet "The Spaceman."

Bill Lee and I remained friends for all these decades, but time and distance prevented a "closer" relationship. However, Bill also seemed amazed at how I could recall seemingly remote details involving his career during those infrequent times we would either get together or communicate otherwise. Therefore, upon my wife, Peg and I reuniting with Bill at a celebrity golf tournament in Boothbay Harbor, Maine last fall, we regaled each other with tales of the distant past, some of which were actually true.... Then came our gathering in Ogunquit, Maine on New Year's. It was there that Bill "anointed" me with the distinct "opportunity" to possibly present the definitive description of his life on planet Earth, one that you are currently reading. Bill just felt that I was the one for the job.

I fully intended to tell this story by simply, and there has been nothing "simple" in Bill's life, reporting clever anecdotes, funny stories, and perhaps a few which were heretofore unknown.... Little did I know that my plan to write a biography that would hopefully be hilarious, poignant, perhaps powerful, but above all, truthful, would also wind up being explosive and shocking.

I must add that upon putting words to paper, that I had absolutely no agenda other than to describe the life of one of the most intriguing human beings I had ever met. I honestly believed I was merely having the Spaceman relive his life in random order, but I soon realized that despite deluding myself into thinking I had been privy to the majority of the events surrounding his existence, that I would soon be presented with an incredible amount of knowledge beyond my wildest expectations. I mean there is so much more to each of us than most of us would ever admit.

At the point I realized I was writing something truly extraordinary, I looked in the mirror. It was then I recalled some "facts" about myself. Of course, I thought, I am no different, either. I then considered one of the greatest statements ever uttered which was as follows:

> "Everyone has three lives: a public life, a private life and a secret life." —*Gabriel Garcia Marquez*

Be Well,
Scott D. Russell
North Attleboro, MA
2020

ABOUT THE AUTHOR

Scott Russell, or perhaps Kilgore Trout, the author of *The Spaceman Chronicles* is renowned as the only person credited with being capable of humming "The Battle Hymn of the Republic" in sixteen different languages. In fact, he is often called upon to perform this incredible feat and has never failed to produce, and this despite the fact that none of the sixteen languages can be identified.

The author was recently detained at O'Hare Airport in Chicago, after attempting to perform the "Heimlich Maneuver" on a voluptuous Swedish airline attendant. After questioning, he was released and promised to be "a good boy," although onlookers stated that the woman was not choking.

The author claims to be currently living in sin with fourteen Dominican nuns, three women of questionable repute, a Bulgarian midget, and a pet yak. Bill "Spaceman" Lee, the subject of this book was quoted as saying, "Scott Russell is an alchemist. Just as monks attempted to change urine into gold, an experiment that failed miserably, Scott has somehow succeeded in that endeavor... or was it he managed to turn gold into urine? I get so confused. Do you know what the monks got for their efforts? They got phosphorous. Yeah, they got phosphorous."

Bill "Spaceman" Lee, Scott Russell & Kilgore Trout have also written the following books:

THE WRONG STUFF BY BILL LEE & DICK LALLY

HAVE GLOVE WILL TRAVEL BY BILL LEE AND RICHARD LALLY

Note: It is impressive that after writing his first book with the Spaceman, Dick Lally was promoted to "Richard" Lally.

THE LITTLE RED (SOX) BOOK BY BILL LEE & JIM PRIME

BASEBALL ECCENTRICS BY BILL LEE & JIM PRIME

Personally, I am impressed that Jim Prime, the brilliant author from

Nova Scotia, has yet to change his name to Sir James Prime.

JOEY

PROPHET's END

THE SCOREKEEPER

VENUS ON THE HALF SHELL

PAN GALACTIC DESIGNATED HITTERS FROM OUTER SPACE

MY ONE NIGHT-STAND WITH ELKA, THE TOOTHLESS VENETIAN

COMING SOON!— *INSIDE THE MINDS OF THE GREATEST STRATEGISTS IN HISTORY—EXPLORING THE GENIUS OF DON ZIMMER, HORATIO NELSON, QIN SHI HUANG, JOHN PERSHING, GEORGE MARSHALL, SCIPIO AFRICANUS, MATTHEW RIDGWAY, CHARLEMAGNE & THE DUKE OF WELLINGTON*

Made in the USA
Middletown, DE
23 October 2023

41128157R00249